Film Review

1995-6

James Cameron-Wilson became a committed film buff when he moved to London at the age of seventeen. After a stint at the Webber Douglas Academy of Dramatic Art he joined *What's On in London*, and took over from F. Maurice Speed as cinema editor. Later, he edited the trade newspaper *Showbiz*, was commissioning editor for *Film Review*, was a presenter of *The Movie Show* on BSkyB and a frequent presenter of the Radio 2 *Arts Programme*. He is also the author of the books *Young Hollywood* and *The Cinema of Robert De Niro*. He currently writes for *Film Review, Flicks, The Times, The Sunday Times, Shivers* and *Midlands Now!*, and is syndicated in the *What's On* magazines.

F. Maurice Speed began his working life as an apprentice on the *Harrow Observer*. From early on, his work reflected an interest in the cinema, and he calculates that he has now spent well over seven years watching films. He has contributed to many newspapers, journals and magazines in both Britain and America, and his books include the pre-war *Movie Cavalcade* and the later *Western Film and TV Annual*. His position as the grand old man of British film criticism was confirmed when the London Film Critics' Circle presented him in 1991 with a special award in recognition of his lifetime achievement and the half-century for which he has now edited *Film Review*.

Film Review

1995-6

Including Video Releases

James Cameron-Wilson
and
F. Maurice Speed

Virgin

First published in Great Britain in 1995 by
VIRGIN BOOKS
an imprint of Virgin Publishing Ltd
332 Ladbroke Grove, London W10 5AH

Copyright © 1995 F. Maurice Speed and
James Cameron-Wilson

The right of F. Maurice Speed and James
Cameron-Wilson to be identified as the
authors of this work has been asserted by
them in accordance with the Copyright,
Designs and Patents Act 1988.

*A catalogue record for this book is available
from the British Library*

ISBN 0 86369 928 6

Designed and typeset by Fred Price

Printed in Great Britain by
Butler & Tanner Ltd

Contents

Introduction

James Cameron-Wilson

Welcome to the 51st edition of the longest-running film annual in the global history of the cinema. An affectionate, informative and lavishly illustrated companion to the year's cinema releases, *Film Review 1995-6* remains an essential guide for any cinemagoer worth his or her weight in movie tickets. At least, that is the aim. If, however, readers feel the annual is missing a vital ingredient, please address your comments (or complaints, admiration, what-have-you) on a postcard to me at Virgin Publishing, 332 Ladbroke Grove, London W10 5AH, United Kingdom.

And now that we've got that out of the way, let's concentrate on things at hand.

As usual the yearbook boasts its full complement of regular features, covering everything from gossip and reviews to box-office stars and awards. The knack, though, is knowing where to find it all. This year we've tried to arrange the contents in a somewhat more logical sequence, so that all the reviews – cinema releases, video and TV – follow one another, with books and soundtracks next to each other, and so on.

In a nutshell, I have contrived to build on the concept dreamed up by F. Maurice Speed all those years ago, adding bits here and there to flesh out the entire cinematic picture. Thus, if you want to know the five Oscar nominees for Best Supporting Actress, the distributor of the video *My Breast* or the name of the prostitute arrested with Hugh Grant, you can find it all under one cover.

While I have gone to enormous pains to make sure that the factual information is correct (keeping the hyphen in Daniel Day-Lewis and the 'h' out of Nicolas Cage), I have also attempted some levity in other departments. Much to my delight, the Movie Quotations of the Year chapter has proved to be extremely popular with readers, as has the Film World Diary, the latter incorporating a number of sins, from the box-office performance of films to who's divorcing who.

The reviews themselves have had to be kept to a manageable length (as the number of films released are forever on the increase), but I have attempted to allow as much room for an obscure Chinese feature as for a major Hollywood blockbuster. In fact, without the pecuniary demands of plumbing for the lowest common denominator, the cheaper film is frequently superior in content to its commercial counterpart. So while such famous titles as *Forrest Gump*, *Speed*, *True Lies* and *Bad Boys* prove to be instantly enthralling, it is less well-known films like *Bad Boy Bubby*, *Barcelona*, *Ermo*, *Fun* and *The Slingshot* that loiter in the memory.

With the video market in Britain now serving five times the number of people who watch movies in a cinema, it's good to know that such titles are not lost to perpetuity. So browse through the following pages, discover a few gems and head for the video shop. Or just sit back and recall the memories of the films you *have* seen.

Top Twenty Box-Office Hits

(for the period July 1994–June 1995)

1 Four Weddings and a Funeral
2 The Lion King
3 The Flintstones
4 The Mask
5 Forrest Gump
6 True Lies
7 Pulp Fiction
8 Speed
9 Interview With the Vampire
10 Stargate
11 Dumb and Dumber
12 Disclosure
13 Star Trek: Generations
14 Muriel's Wedding
15 Miracle on 34th Street
16 The Specialist
17 Maverick
18 Mary Shelley's Frankenstein
19 Clear and Present Danger
20 Reservoir Dogs

Andie MacDowell shines in the box-office hit of the year (and the biggest British triumph ever), Mike Newell's Four Weddings and a Funeral

Simba teams up with Pumbaa and Timon in Disney's colossal The Lion King

Elizabeth Perkins and John Goodman as Wilma and Fred Flintstone (with Pebbles) in The Flintstones

Jim Carrey gets destructive in The Mask

Robin Wright and Tom Hanks enjoy the sixties in Robert Zemeckis's Oscar-winning Forrest Gump

Top Ten Box-Office Stars

STAR OF THE YEAR
Jim Carrey

Just as Tom Hanks looked certain to snatch the box-office crown, along came the Canadian tornado Jim Carrey. While *Ace Ventura: Pet Detective* failed to make the UK top twenty last year, *Dumb and Dumber* charged in at number eleven, ousting such box-office colossi as *Disclosure*, *Star Trek: Generations* and *Maverick*. But this feat was nothing compared to what *The Mask* cooked up, the latter pulping *Forrest Gump*, *True Lies*, *Pulp Fiction* and *Speed*. And with *Batman Forever* shattering box-office records as I write, Carrey seems to be worth every dollar of the $20 million Columbia Pictures are paying him for *Cable Guy*. Sylvester Stallone, the only other superstar to be bestowed with $20m, fared less well in the British charts, with *The Specialist* limping into sixteenth place. Within the period covered, Hugh Grant had still to prove himself as a box-office icon, although his ability to sell newspapers is not in dispute. Runners up this year include Mel Gibson, Bruce Willis, Brad Pitt, Kurt Russell, Sharon Stone, Kenneth Branagh and Emma Thompson.

2 Arnold Schwarzenegger

3 Tom Hanks

4 Tom Cruise

5 Michael Douglas

6 Demi Moore

7 Sylvester Stallone

8 Harrison Ford

9 John Travolta

10 Keanu Reeves

Releases of the Year

In this section you will find details of all the films released in Great Britain from 1 July 1994 to the end of June 1995 – the period covered by all the reference features in the book.

The normal abbreviations operate as follows: Dir – for Director; Pro – for Producer; Assoc Pro – for Associate Producer; Ex Pro – for Executive Producer; Pro Ex – for Production Executive; Pro Sup – for Production Supervisor; Co-Pro – for Co-Producer; Pro Co-Ord – for Production Co-Ordinator; Ph – for Photographer; Ed – for Editor; Art – for Art Director; Pro Des – for Production Designer; M – for Music; and a few others which will be obvious.

Abbreviations for the names of film companies are also pretty obvious when used, such as Fox for 20th Century-Fox, Rank for Rank Film Distributors, and UIP for Universal International Pictures. Where known, the actual production company is given first, the releasing company last.

When it comes to nationality of the film, you will find that this is noted wherever possible – those films without any mention of country of origin can usually be taken as being American – but in these days of increasing international co-productions between two, three or even four countries it is sometimes difficult to sort out where the premier credit is due.

Unless otherwise specified (i.e. black and white), it can be taken that the film is made in Technicolor or a similar process.

Censorship certificates: U represents films suitable for persons of any age; PG (Parental Guidance) represents films which some parents might consider unsuitable for their children; 12 or 15 means no persons under that age will be admitted; and films certified with an 18 (approximately the old 'X' certificate) means that nobody under that age will be admitted to the cinema while that film is showing. 'No cert' means that no certificate has been issued by the initial showing of the film but this does not mean that one will not subsequently be issued.

All films reviewed by James Cameron-Wilson unless otherwise specified. Additional contributors: Charles Bacon, Ewen Brownrigg, Karen Krizanovich, Simon Rose and Mansel Stimpson.

Above the Rim

Too big for his Nikes, Kyle-Lee Watson is a high school basketball star with his eye on the NBA. However, unhealthy influences sway the good sense pumped into him by his mother and Kyle falls in with a double-dealing drug pedlar. With the number of basketball pictures around lately, this must rate as the worst, in which the sport is rendered lifeless and the plot is both hackneyed and predictable. Notwithstanding, the rap soundtrack sold well in the States.

Cast: Duane Martin (Kyle-Lee Watson), Leon (Shep), Tupac Shakur (Birdie), Bernie Mac (Flip Johnson), Tonya Pinkins (Mailika Williams), David Bailey (Mike Rollins), Marlon Wayans (Bugaloo), Byron Minns, Sherwin David Harris, Shawn Michael Howard, Iris Little Thomas, Eric Nies, Mill Raftery, Frank Martin.
   Dir: Jeff Pollack. Pro: Pollack and Benny Medina. Ex Pro: James D. Brubaker. Screenplay: Pollack and Barry Michael Cooper, from a story by Pollack and Medina. Ph: Tom Priestley Jr. Ed: Michael Ripps and James Mitchell. Pro Des: Ina Mayhew. M: Marcus Miller; numbers performed by 2Pac, Lord G, The Dogg Pound, SWV, H-Town, Snoop Doggy Dogg, O.F.T.B., 2nd II None, The Pharcyde, YZ, Naughty By Nature, The Beastie Boys, Nate Dogg & Warren G, etc. Costumes: Karen Perry. (New Line–First Independent.) Rel: 9 December 1994. 97 mins. Cert 15.

Abraham Valley - Vale Abraao

Based on a Portuguese variant of *Madame Bovary*, this very long feature by the veteran Manoel de Oliveira is certainly handsome. But it substitutes detailed intellectual analysis (often in voice-over) for any emotional heart, and the repetitive use of classical music is irksome. Nevertheless, just as those avant-garde films of Jean-Marie Straub that draw on literary texts have their admirers, so too does this demanding film. Its appeal, however, is of a strictly specialist nature. A Portuguese-French-Swiss co-production. [*Mansel Stimpson*]

Cast: Leonor Silveira (Ema), Luis Miguel Cintra (Carlos de Paiva), Cecile Sanz De Alba (young Ema), Rui De Carvalho (Paulino Cardeano), Luis Lima Barreto, Micheline Larpin, Diogo Doria.
   Dir and Screenplay: Manoel de Oliveira, from the book *Vale Abraao* by Agustina Bessa-Luis. Pro: Paulo Branco. Ph: Mario Barroso. Ed: de Oliveira and Valerie Loiseleux. Pro Des: Maria Jose Branco.

Drag race: Guy Pearce and Hugo Weaving lock wigs in Stephan Elliott's wildly entertaining The Adventures of Priscilla, Queen of the Desert *(from Rank)*

Costumes: Isabel Branco. (Madragoa Films/Gemini Films/Light Night Prods/Canal Plus–Artificial Eye.) Rel: 23 September 1994. 187 mins. Cert PG.

The Adventures of Priscilla, Queen of the Desert

Frankly, the idea of a movie about three drag queens travelling across the Australian outback sounds entirely resistible. However, as deftly handled by director Stephan Elliott, superbly photographed by Brian J. Breheny and acted with gusto by Guy Pearce, Hugo Weaving and, of all people, Terence Stamp (as a transsexual), this picturesque journey of self-discovery and sequins is a hoot. It would have been easy to blow the whole thing into some grotesque *Carry On Camping*, but the humour is pitched just right, with the lion's share of the laughs going to the disbelieving rustics in the backwater towns. Guy Pearce (TV's *Neighbours*) is a revelation as the raving queen Felicia, and so is Bill Hunter as a grizzled, overweight hippie with an eye for a pretty transvestite. Editing, music and frocks are all top-notch.

Cast: Terence Stamp (Bernadette), Hugo Weaving (Tick/Mitzi), Guy Pearce (Adam/Felicia), Bill Hunter (Bob), Sarah Chadwick (Marion), Mark Holmes (Benji), Julia Cortez (Cynthia), Ken Radley, Alan Dargin, Rebel Russell.
   Dir and Screenplay: Stephan Elliott. Pro: Al Clark and Michael Hamlyn. Ex Pro: Rebel Penfold-Russell. Ph: Brian J. Breheny. Ed: Sue Blainey. Pro Des: Owen Paterson. M: Guy Gross; numbers performed by Charlene, Village People, Abba, Paper Lace, Gloria Gaynor, Ella Fitzgerald, Vanessa Williams, etc. Costumes: Lizzy Gardiner and Tim Chappel. (PolyGram/Australian Film Finance Corp/Latent Image/Specific Films–Rank.) Rel: 14 October 1994. 104 mins. Cert 15.

A gun with no name: Martin Donovan and Damian Young in Hal Hartley's brilliant Amateur *(from Artificial Eye)*

Airheads

Loved *Heathers*, hated *Hudson Hawk*? Here director Michael Lehmann plays it safe with an ensemble flick about a garage rock group that just wants to be heard. Fraser, Buscemi and Sandler play heavy metal geeks who hold a radio station hostage to get airplay for their demo. A sympathetic DJ (Mantegna) and a slurry of others join in the fun. Soon the cops get involved and odd demands are met, like 67 copies of *Moby Dick* ('The book or the video?' 'There's a book?') and nude photos of Bea Arthur. A comedy of wholesome rock-ness, *Airheads* sweetly treads where we'd expect a B-movie to go. Just enough laughs and surprises to warrant a look-see. [*Karen Krizanovich*]

Cast: Brendan Fraser (Chazz), Steve Buscemi (Rex), Adam Sandler (Pip), Chris Farley (Wilson), Michael McKean (Milo), Judd Nelson (Jimmie Wing), Michael Richards (Doug Beech), Joe Mantegna (Ian), Ernie Hudson (O'Malley), Amy Locane (Kayla), Nina Siemaszko, Marshall Bell, Reginald E. Cathey, David Arquette, Michelle Hurst, Kurt Loder, Harold Ramis, Lemmy Von Motorhead.

Dir: Michael Lehmann. Pro: Robert Simonds and Mark Burg. Co-Pro: Ira Shuman. Ex Pro: Todd Baker. Screenplay: Rich Wilkes. Ph: John Schwartzman. Ed: Stephen Semel. Pro Des: David Nichols. M: Carter Burwell; numbers performed by Motorhead and Ice-T, DGeneration, Aerosmith, David Byrne, Stuttering John, 4 Non Blondes, House of Pain, Anthrax, Primal Scream, Dig, Ramones, etc. Costumes: Bridget Kelly. (Island World–Fox.) Rel: 18 November 1994. 92 mins. Cert 15.

Amateur

New York City; today. Isabelle is a former nun who's turned to writing pornography to make ends meet. Thomas is a bewildered amnesiac who cannot remember if he smokes or not. And Sofia is a Romanian porn actress with revenge on her mind. And they're all in danger of losing their lives ... Hal Hartley calls this, his fourth film, 'an action movie', but adds, 'It's a Hal Hartley action movie, and that probably means I've got it wrong somehow.' Actually, as long as Hal Hartley goes on making Hal Hartley movies he's got it right. And although the filmmaker employs the action-thriller genre to move *Amateur* from A to B, his film is essentially a black comedy in which the cast have no say. To see Isabelle Huppert (a great Hartley fan) utter the director's off-kilter dialogue with a completely straight face is a joy indeed.

Cast: Isabelle Huppert (Isabelle), Martin Donovan (Thomas), Elina Lowensohn (Sofia), Damian Young (Edward), Chuck Montgomery (Jan), David Simond (Kurt), Pamela Stewart (Officer Patsy Melville), Erica Gimpel, Jan Leslie Harding, Angel Caban, David Greenspan, Parker Posey, Dwight Ewell, Currie Graham, Patricia Scanlon.

Dir and Screenplay: Hal Hartley. Pro: Hartley and Ted Hope. Ex Pro: Jerome Brownstein, Lindsay Law, Scott Meek and Yves Marmion. Ph: Michael Spiller. Ed: Steven Hamilton. Pro Des: Steve Rosenzweig. M: Jeff Naylor and Ned Rifle. Costumes: Alexandra Welker. (UGC/Zenith/True Fiction Pictures/Channel Four/American Playhouse/La sept Cinema–Artificial Eye.) Rel: 6 January 1995. 105 mins. Cert 15.

Andre

Rockport, Maine; 1962. Straightforward, old-fashioned family yarn in which an animal-loving household adopts an orphaned baby seal. Displaying some remarkably human characteristics (blowing raspberries, playing basketball) Andre the harbour seal soon wins the heart of the local town while alienating the fishermen, who are upset by seals chewing through their nets. A showdown is inevitable, although Andre is not a mammal anyone can take for granted. Based on a true story, this is no *Free Willy*, but the title character's horseplay should keep younger children transfixed.

Cast: Keith Carradine (Harry Whitney), Tina Majorino (Toni Whitney), Keith Szarabajka (Billy Baker), Chelsea Field (Thalice Whitney), Shane Meier (Steve Whitney), Aidan Pendleton (Paula Whitney), Shirley Broderick (Mrs McCann), Joshua Jackson (Mark Baker), Andre (Tory), Annette O'Toole (adult voice of Toni), Andrea Libman, Jay Brazeau, Bill Dow, Joy Coghill, Duncan Fraser.

Dir: George Miller. Pro: Annette Handley and Adam Shapiro. Ex Pro: Peter Locke and Donald Kushner. Co-Ex Pro: Lawrence Mortorff. Co-Pro: Dana Baratta and Sue Baden-Powell. Screenplay: Baratta, based on the book *A Seal Called Andre* by Harry Goodridge and Lew Dietz. Ph: Thomas Burstyn. Ed: Harry Hitner and Patrick Kennedy. Pro Des: William Elliott. M: Bruce Rowland; numbers performed by Tyler Collins, The Coasters, The Drifters, The Flamingos, Shelley Fabares, Booker T & the MGs, Craig n Co, etc. Costumes: Maya Mani. (Turner Pictures–Rank.) Rel: 17 February 1995. 94 mins. Cert U.

Angels

When young Roger Bowman's father tells him that they'll be reunited as a family only when the California Angels baseball team wins the season, Roger knows that the odds are against it. For starters, the Angels are at the bottom of the league and are heading south. But, hark, when Roger prays for divine intervention, a host of winged baseball fanatics turn up to save the day. Set in a sanitised, politically correct edition of contemporary America, *Angels* is no *Field of Dreams*. Hell, with Christopher Lloyd as a bulging-eyed celestial host, we're meant to *believe* this piffle? Based on the 1951 film *Angels in the Outfield*.

Cast: Danny Glover (George Knox), Tony Danza (Mel Clark), Brenda Fricker (Maggie Nelson), Ben Johnson (Hank Murphy), Jay O. Sanders (Ranch Wilder), Christopher Lloyd (Al), Joseph Gordon-Levitt (Roger Bowman), Milton Davis Jr (JP), Taylor Negron, Tony Longo, Neal McDonough, Stoney Jackson, Tim Conlon, Matthew McConaughey, Dermot Mulroney, Jonathan Proby, Michael Halton, Devon Dear, Oliver Dear, Bill Dear.
 Dir: William Dear. Pro: Irby Smith, Joe Roth and Roger Birnbaum. Ex Pro: Gary Stutman. Screenplay: Dorothy Kingsley, George Wells and Holly Goldberg Sloan. Ph: Matthew F. Leonetti. Ed: Bruce Green. Pro Des: Dennis Washington. M: Randy Edelman; numbers performed by The Impressions and Swinging Blue Jeans. Costumes: Rosanna Norton. (Walt Disney–Buena Vista.) Rel: 26 May 1995. 104 mins. Cert U.

Angels in the Outfield
See *Angels*.

Arizona Dream
Johnny Depp, in yet another bizarre career move, plays a New York fish inspector who's kidnapped by a friend and driven to Arizona. There he's confronted by his uncle, a car salesman who dreams of building a stack of Cadillacs all the way to the moon. Other fantasy-blighted characters converge in a *son et lumière* of thwarted dreams, passion and surrealism in which an arrow-tooth halibut wins the day. The Sarajevo

Arizona apparition: Faye Dunaway dreams of Papua New Guinea in Emir Kusturica's hallucinogenic Arizona Dream *(from Electric)*

director Emir Kusturica, who won international acclaim for his last two films (*When Father Was Away on Business* and *Time of the Gypsies*), once again reveals a masterful control of his unique vision. This is cinema of another dimension: weird, funny, lyrical, hypnotic and totally true to itself. Love it or hate it.

Cast: Johnny Depp (Axel Blackmar), Jerry Lewis (Leo Sweetie), Faye Dunaway (Elaine Stalker), Lili Taylor (Grace Stalker), Vincent Gallo (Paul Legere), Paulina Porizkova (Millie), Tricia Leigh Fischer, Candyce Mason, Michael J. Pollard, Iggy Pop.
 Dir: Emir Kusturica. Pro: Claudie Ossard and Yves Marmion. Co-Pro: Richard Brick. Ex Pro: Paul R. Gurian. Screenplay: David Atkins. Ph: Vilko Filac. Ed: Andrija Zafranovic. Pro Des: Miljen Kljakovic. M: Goran Bregovic; numbers performed by Iggy Pop, Django Reinhardt, etc. Costumes: Jill M. Ohanneson. (Constellation/UGC/Hachette Premiere/Canal Plus–Electric.) Rel: 30 June 1995. 135 mins. Cert 15.

Attack of the 50 Foot Woman
Satirical, post-feminist update of the legendary(!) B-movie, with the leggy Daryl Hannah perfect casting as the poor little rich girl who cannot find love under six foot. Unfortunately, the

Seal of approval: The ubiquitous Tina Majorino with Tory in Andre *(from Rank)*

The legs have it: Daryl Hannah steps into the shoes of Allison Hayes in Christopher Guest's disappointing remake of Attack of the 50ft Woman *(from Entertainment)*

The demise of innocence: Alan Rickman and Georgina Cates introduce an ironic note to Peter Pan's clarion call – in Mike Newell's chilling An Awfully Big Adventure *(from Fox)*

Pictures/Warner Television/Bartleby Ltd–Entertainment.) Rel: 1 July 1994. 89 mins. Cert 12.

An Awfully Big Adventure

Deeply depressing, wonderfully crafted adaptation of Beryl Bainbridge's stark novel of the awful backstage machinations at a Liverpool repertory theatre. There, a number of terminally grotesque characters reveal the downside of adulthood and the theatre as Stella, a star-struck, inexperienced sixteen-year-old assistant stage manager, takes everything in. Besotted with the theatre's director – the cruel and occasionally charming Meredith Potter (Hugh Grant) – Stella learns some brutal life lessons as the past catches up with her, Meredith and the rep's consummate Captain Hook, P.L. O'Hara. Taking its ironic title from a line in *Peter Pan*, this is a chilling tale that takes no prisoners.

Cast: Alan Rickman (P.L. O'Hara), Hugh Grant (Meredith Potter), Georgina Cates (Stella), Alun Armstrong (Uncle Vernon), Peter Firth (Bunny), Prunella Scales (Rose), Rita Tushingham (Aunt Lily), Alan Cox (Geoffrey), Edward Petherbridge (Richard St Ives), Nicola Pagett (Dotty Blundell), Carol Drinkwater (Dawn Allenby), Clive Merrison (Desmond Fairchild), Gerard McSorley, Ruth McCabe, James Frain, Patti Love, Tom Hickey, Robbie Doolan.

Dir: Mike Newell. Pro: Hilary Heath and Philip Hinchcliffe. Ex Pro: John Kelleher, Mark Shivas and John Sivers. Screenplay: Charles Wood. Ph: Dick Pope. Ed: Jon Gregory. Pro Des: Mark Geraghty. M: Richard Hartley. Costumes: Joan Bergin. (Portman/British Screen/BBC/Wolfhound –Fox.) Rel: 7 April 1995. 112 mins. Cert 15.

Baby's Day Out

Three crooks – posing as baby photographers – kidnap the nine-month-old heir to a colossal family fortune. However, the bungling trio hadn't bargained on the baby's ingenuity – or speed crawling. Thus, Baby Bink (huh?) escapes into the Chicago traffic, to the shops, the zoo, the building site, and so on, while the three stooges – courtesy of John Hughes' underwhelming imagination – follow a few paces behind. *Very* contrived slapstick aimed at the *Home Alone / Three Men and a Baby* crowd, but proving too violent for younger kids (the scene in which Joe Mantegna's reproductive system

remake has no sense of pace and a lot of the jokes fall flat. In fact, if memory serves, the original was far funnier – albeit unintentionally. Director Christopher Guest fared much better with *The Big Picture*.

Cast: Daryl Hannah (Nancy Archer), Daniel Baldwin (Harry Archer), William Windom (Hamilton Cobb), Frances Fisher (Dr Cushing), Christi Conaway (Louise 'Honey'), Paul Benedict (Dr Loeb), O'Neal Compton (Sheriff Denby), Victoria Haas (Deputy Charlie Spooner), Lewis Arquette, Xander Berkeley, Hamilton Camp, Richard Edson.

Dir: Christopher Guest. Pro: Debra Hill. Ex Pro and Screenplay: Joseph Dougherty, from the screenplay by Mark Hanna. Co-Pro: Chuck Binder and Daryl Hannah. Ph: Russell Carpenter. Ed: Harry Keramidas. Pro Des: Joseph T. Garrity. M: Nicholas Pike. Costumes: Arianne Phillips. (HBO

There goes my baby: Identical twins Adam Robert Worton and Jacob Joseph Worton steal the acting honours as 'Baby Bink' in Patrick Read Johnson's contrived Baby's Day Out *(from Fox)*

catches fire is overlong and sadistic), and too moronic for the next generation up. Still, the blue screen effects are excellent.

Cast: Joe Mantegna (Eddie Mauser), Lara Flynn Boyle (Laraine Cotwell), Joe Pantoliano (Norby LeBlaw), Brian Haley (Veeko Riley), Cynthia Nixon (Gilbertine), Fred Dalton Thompson (FBI Agent Grissom), John Neville (Mr Andrews), Matthew Glave (Bennington Cotwell), Adam Robert Worton, Jacob Joseph Worton, Brigid Duffy, Guy Hadley, Eddie Bracken, Dan Frick, Robin Baber, Jennifer Say Gan, Anna Thomson, Neil Flynn, William Holmes, Mike Starr.

Dir: Patrick Read Johnson. Pro: John Hughes and Richard Vane. Ex Pro: William Ryan. Screenplay: Hughes. Ph: Thomas E. Beasley. Ed: David Rawlins. Pro Des: Doug Kraner. M: Bruce Broughton. Costumes: Lisa Jensen. Mechanical FX: Rick Baker. (Fox.) Rel: 12 August 1994. 98 mins. Cert PG.

Bad Boy Bubby

Incarcerated in a two-room cellar for 35 years, Bubby has known only his mother, her vocabulary, her brutality and her 'beauty'. For Mom, a fat, ugly misfit, Bubby is her secret, her joy, her sex slave. Told that the outside world is contaminated by toxic gases, Bubby cowers in his own limited space, free from preconceptions of behaviour, morality or beauty. He is a child. When, finally, he escapes, Bubby imitates the

world around him, like a child would; in particular the impatient abuse showered on his odd, unsophisticated demeanour. Taking this disturbing scenario as a microcosm for the detrimental effects of abused childhood (and therefore able to speed up the process for his dramatic ends), writer-director Rolf de Heer has created a mesmerising work of astonishing emotional scope. As the man-child walking a tenuous path between violence and tenderness, the unknown Nicholas Hope gives a performance of shocking commitment. A courageous, harrowing and brilliant piece of cinema.

Cast: Nicholas Hope (Bubby), Claire Benito (Mom), Ralph Cotterill (Pop), Carmel Johnson (Angel), Sid Brisbane, Norman Kaye, Paul Philpot, Peter Monaghan, Natalie Carr, Rachel Huddy, Bridget Walters, Lucia Mastrantone, James Ammitzboll, Celine O'Leary, Todd Telford, Paul Simpson, Mark Brouggy, Emma Went, Bruce Glebert, Betty Summer-Lovett, Nellie Egan, Pandy Tsimeculos, Maryla Sallis, Janet Kanda, Heather Slattery, Fille Dusselee, Stephanie Cooper, Graham Duckett.

Dir and Screenplay: Rolf de Heer. Pro: de Heer, Domenico Procacci and Giorgio Draskovic. Ph: Ian Jones. Ed: Suresh Ayyar. Pro Des: Mark Abbott. M: Graham Tardif. Costumes: Beverly Freeman. (Fandango/South Australia Film Corporation–Entertainment.) Rel: 30 September 1994. 113 mins. Cert 18.

Bad Boys

Smooth, affluent ladies' man Mike Lowrey and henpecked family man Marcus Burnett have been partners in

Cruel is as cruel does: Nicholas Hope and Claire Benito in Rolf de Heer's stunning Bad Boy Bubby *(from Entertainment)*

Riding shotgun: Martin Lawrence gets tough as Frank John Hughes gets going – in Michael Bay's Bad Boys *(from Columbia TriStar)*

the Miami police force for six years. And they still can't stop bickering. Even when they're faced with their toughest case yet: to track down $100m in uncut heroin stolen from police headquarters by a ruthless French mastermind ... After a hiatus of five years, the producing team of Don Simpson and Jerry Bruckheimer (*Top Gun*, *Beverly Hills Cop*, *Flashdance*) are back with their winning box-office formula of gags, guns and girls – and a villain to kill for. While 30-year-old commercials director Michael Bay makes his feature film debut, this is Simpson and Bruckheimer's show – and a dynamic showcase for the talents of Martin Lawrence and Will Smith as the squabbling cops. Expect sequels.

Cast: Martin Lawrence (Marcus Burnett), Will Smith (Mike Lowrey), Téa Leoni (Julie Mott), Tcheky Karyo (Fouchet), Theresa Randle (Theresa Burnett), Joe Pantoliano (Captain Howard), Anna Thomson (Francine), Marg Helgenberger (Alison Sinclair), Karen Alexander (Max Logan), Michael Taliferro, Emmanuel Xuereb, Nestor Serrano, Julio Oscar Mechoso, Michael Imperioli, Heather Davis, Saverio Guerra, Kevin Corrigan.

Dir: Michael Bay. Pro: Don Simpson and Jerry Bruckheimer. Ex Pro: Bruce S. Pustin and Lucas Foster. Screenplay: Michael Barrie, Jim Mulholland and Doug Richardson, from a story by George Gallo. Ph: Howard Atherton. Ed: Christian Wagner. Pro Des: John Vallone. M: Mark Mancina; numbers performed by Juster, MN8, Diana King, Inner Circle, XSCAPE, Ini Kamoze, Jon B and Babyface, 2PAC, Keith Martin, Dink, Warren G, 69 Boyz, etc. Costumes: Bobbie Read. (Columbia TriStar.) Rel: 16 June 1995. 104 mins. Cert 18.

Bad Girls

Texas; the late 1800s. Bland, witless, dumb Western in which four prostitutes decide to put their old ways behind them. However, their progress to a better life is impeded by the law, a vengeful widow and a sadistic bank robber. While Madeleine Stowe preserves her dignity as the quartet's driving force (and Drew Barrymore has some good moments), the film is a lost opportunity for some fine actresses. For the record, director Jonathan Kaplan, executive producer Lynda Obst and screenwriter Ken Friedman took over the production two weeks after it had started filming. Tamra Davis (*CB4*) was the original director.

Cast: Madeleine Stowe (Cody Zamora), Mary Stuart Masterson (Anita Crown), Drew Barrymore (Lilly Laronette), Andie MacDowell (Eileen Spenser), James Russo (Kid Jarrett), Robert Loggia (Frank Jarrett), Dermot Mulroney (Josh McCoy), James LeGros (William Tucker), Neil Summers (Ned), Jim Beaver, Nick Chinlund, Richard EJ Reyes, Will MacMillan, Harry Northup, Don Hood, Zoaunne LeRoy, Rodger Boyce, Nik Hagler, Cooper Huckabee, Beulah Quo, Mark Carlton.

Dir: Jonathan Kaplan. Pro: Albert S. Ruddy, Andre E. Morgan and Charles Finch. Ex Pro: Lynda Obst. Screenplay: Ken Friedman and Yolande Finch, from a story by Ruddy, Charles Finch and Gray

Chicks in chaps: Andie MacDowell, Mary Stuart Masterson, Madeleine Stowe and Drew Barrymore stick 'em up in Jonathan Kaplan's banal Bad Girls *(from Fox)*

Frederickson. Ph: Ralf Bode. Ed: Jane Kurson. Pro Des: Guy Barnes. M: Jerry Goldsmith. Costumes: Susie DeSanto. (Ruddy Morgan–Fox.) Rel: 1 July 1994. 100 mins. Cert 15.

Bandit Queen

Based on the dictated prison diaries of Phoolan Devi, this is the true story of a low caste child bride who after a catalogue of injustices took up arms and fought back. Nicknamed 'The Bandit Queen' and 'The Goddess of Flowers' by the media, Phoolan became a champion of the lower castes and a scourge to the authorities. An Anglo-Indian co-production, *Bandit Queen* was banned in India where, apparently, Phoolan herself entered the fray to prevent the film from being shown. As a curiosity item, the piece is fascinating: in a country where, until 1977, a kiss on screen was taboo, here we have Tarantino-esque profanity, full-frontal nudity and a spectacular gang rape. However, as narrative cinema, *Bandit Queen* is cumbersome, artless and too preoccupied with the need to shock.

Cast: Seema Biswas (Phoolan Devi), Nirmal Pandey (Vikram Mallah), Manjoj Bajpai (Man Singh), Govind Namdeo (Sriram), Saurabh Shukla (Kailash), Anirudh Agarwal (Babu Gujjar), Rajesh Vivek, Raghuvir Yadav, Mandakini Goswami, Sunita Bhatt.

Dir: Shekhar Kapur. Pro: Sundeep Singh Bedi. Screenplay: Mala Sen; dialogue: Ranjit Kapoor. Ph: Ashok Mehta. Ed: Renu Saluja. Pro Des: Eve Mavrakis. M: Nusrat Fateh Ali Khan. Costumes: Dolly Ahluwalia. (Kaleidoscope/Channel Four–Mainline.) Rel: 17 February 1995. 119 mins. Cert 18.

Barcelona

The last decade of the cold war in Barcelona. Ted, an American sales rep with 'a romantic illusion problem', is visited by his obnoxious cousin, Fred, an officer in the US navy. Drawn together by mutual animosity, Ted and Fred have little in common except blood and unique methods of entertaining the opposite sex. And so they get on each other's nerves famously as they strive to find their universal perspective – and the right woman. Four years after the critical success of *Metropolitan*, Whit Stillman delivers his second feature, cementing his standing as one of America's most distinctive and witty filmmakers. This time exhibiting a greater confidence in his direction while exercising the same wonderful control over his actors, the filmmaker has produced a truly original, very funny comedy distinguished by reams of priceless dialogue. Stillman still needs to learn

Chris Eigeman and Mira Sorvino puzzle over love and the art of shaving in Whit Stillman's exquisite Barcelona *(from Rank)*

about pace and narrative drive, but for now more of the same will do very nicely.

Cast: Taylor Nichols (Ted Boynton), Chris Eigeman (Fred Boynton), Tushka Bergen (Montserrat), Mira Sorvino (Marta), Pep Munne (Ramon), Hellena Schmied (Greta), Thomas Gibson (Dickie Taylor), Nuria Badia, Jack Gilpin, Pere Ponce, Laura Lopez, Paca Barrera, Stillman Finley.

Dir, Pro and Screenplay: Whit Stillman. Assoc Pro: Edmon Roch and Cecilia Roque. Ph: John Thomas. Ed: Christopher Tellefsen. Pro Des: Jose Maria Botines. M: Mark Suozzo; numbers performed by The Glenn Miller Band, Cinco Latinos, Silver Connection, Jeff Young, Lou Christie, Bobby Solo, etc. Costumes: Edi Giguere. (Castle Rock/Westerly Films–Rank.) Rel: 27 January 1995. 101 mins. Cert 12.

Before Sunrise

Travelling through Europe on a Europass, a 24-year-old American invites a French student to spend fourteen hours with him in Vienna. They both know that he has to catch the next morning flight to the US, so they resolve to be adult and rational about their

Brief encounter: Ethan Hawke and Julie Delpy survey their romantic predicament in Richard Linklater's Before Sunrise *(from Rank)*

growing attraction for each other and to make their night in Vienna a special, spontaneous occasion. Forsaking his trademark ensemble comedies, Richard Linklater, celluloid mouthpiece for disenchanted Texan youth, makes a dramatic U-turn here to produce a very personal work of bold intimacy and simplicity. Virtually a two-character piece, *Before Sunrise* staves off comparisons to *My Dinner With Andre* thanks to some picturesque location work and the knowledge that these two sweet people have to – somehow – terminate their platonic affair. Very wordy, to be sure, but you won't hear this searching, off-the-wall dialogue in any other film.

Cast: Ethan Hawke (Jesse), Julie Delpy (Céline), Erni Mangold (palm reader), Dominik Castell (street poet), Karl Bruckschwaiger, Tex Rubinowitz.
Dir: Richard Linklater. Pro: Anne Walker-McBay. Ex Pro: John Sloss. Co-Pro: Ellen Winn Wendl, Gernot Schaffler and Wolfgang Ramml. Screenplay: Linklater and Kim Krizan. Ph: Lee Daniel. Ed: Sandra Adair. Pro Des: Florian Reichmann. M: Purcell, Szekeley; numbers performed by Loud, Kath Bloom, Fetish 69, Lou Christie, Kathy McCarty, etc. (Castle Rock/Detour Film/FILMHAUS Wien–Rank.) Rel: 21 April 1995. 101 mins. Cert 15.

The Beverly Hillbillies

When a backwoods family makes the biggest domestic oil strike in history,

they decide to move to Beverly Hills and show those other millionaires what grotesque, ignorant and nose-pickin' people country folk really are. Of all the culturally backward TV series of the 1960s, this one looked the least likely to make it to the big screen. But here it is, in all its dated, infantile and witless glory. Shoot the turkey.

Cast: Diedrich Bader (Jethro/Jethrine Clampett), Dabney Coleman (Mr Drysdale), Erika Eleniak (Elly May Clampett), Cloris Leachman (Granny Clampett), Rob Schneider (Tyler), Lea Thompson (Laura), Lily Tomlin (Miss Hathaway), Jim Varney (Jed Clampett), Buddy Ebsen (Barnaby Jones), Kevin Connolly (Morgan Drysdale), Lyman Ward (Chief Gallo), Zsa Zsa Gabor, Dolly Parton, Linda Carlson, Penny Fuller, Leann Hunley, Ernie Lively, David L. Crowley, Robert Easton, James O'Sullivan, Annalee Spheeris.

Dir: Penelope Spheeris. Pro: Spheeris and Ian Bryce. Screenplay: Lawrence Konner, Mark Rosenthal, Jim Fisher and Jim Staahl. Ph: Robert Brinkmann. Ed: Ross Albert. Pro Des: Peter Jamison. M: Lalo Schifrin; numbers performed by Joe Diffie, Jim Varney, Ricky Skaggs, The Oak Ridge Boys, Freddy Fender, Joe Walsh and Steve Earle, Hank Williams, Dolly Parton, etc. Costumes: Jami Burrows. (Fox.) Rel: 15 July 1994. 93 mins. Cert PG.

Beyond Rangoon

When her husband and young son are murdered in a burglary, Sarah Bowman, an American physician, embarks on a guided tour of the East to deflect her grief. But as she stares at the stone Buddhas of Burma her heart feels nothing. Then, stranded in Rangoon when her passport is mislaid, she witnesses the massacre of 1988 and is plunged into an escalating nightmare ... With foreign journalists banned in Burma to this day, the plight of the former British colony (now officially known as Myanmar) has received little international attention. John Boorman's lush, fast-paced and accessible drama fills in the gaps with aplomb and stamina – although, as a piece of filmmaking, it is a major disappointment from the director of *Deliverance*, *The Emerald Forest* and *Hope and Glory*. Luckily, the

Country comes to clown: Lily Tomlin and Jim Varney in Penelope Spheeris's wry take on provincial crudeness – The Beverly Hillbillies *(from Fox)*

strength of the story papers over some spotty acting and dire back projection.

Cast: Patricia Arquette (Laura Bowman), Frances McDormand (Andy), Spalding Gray (Jeremy Watt), U Aung Ko (U Aung Ko), Adelle Lutz (Aung San Suu Kyi), Kuswadinath Bujang, Victor Slezak, Jit Murand, Tiara Jacquelina, Johnny Cheah, Anna Howard, Charley Boorman.
   Dir: John Boorman. Pro: Boorman, Barry Spikings and Eric Pleskow. Co-Pro and Screenplay: Alex Lasker and Bill Rubenstein. Ex Pro: Sean Ryerson. Ph: John Seale. Ed: Ron Davis. Pro Des: Anthony Pratt. M: Hans Zimmer. Costumes: Deborah La Gorce Kramer. (Castle Rock–Rank.) Rel: 30 June 1995. 100 mins. Cert 12.

Black Beauty

In 1871, Anna Sewell was told she had eighteen months to live. Five years later she was still working on her only novel, *Black Beauty*, but was to die before she could fully appreciate its success. The greatest of all 'animal autobiographies', the book has been filmed three times since the advent of sound, but never as successfully as now in this moving, gloriously photographed edition. Once one has got over Alan Cumming's voice-over as the steed (which is actually very good, but Cumming never struck me as a horse), the film settles down into a beautifully observed series of vignettes. Intelligently pieced together by Caroline Thompson (who previously adapted Frances Hodgson Burnett's *The Secret Garden* for the screen), the film is never unduly melodramatic and the equine actors are magic.

Cast: Sean Bean (Farmer Grey), David Thewlis (Jerry Baker), Jim Carter (John Manly), Peter Davison (Squire Gordon), Alun Armstrong (Reuben Smith), John McEnery (Mr York), Eleanor Bron (Lady Wexmire), Peter Cook (Lord Wexmire), Andrew Knott (Joe Green), Alan Cumming (voice of Black Beauty), Adrian Ross-Magenty, Lyndon Davies, Anthony Walters, Rosalind Ayres, David Ryall, Vic Armstrong, Matthew Scurfield, Emma Richler, Conrad Asquith, Dick Brannick, Dido Miles, Graham Valentine, Niall O'Brien.
   Dir and Screenplay: Caroline Thompson. Pro: Robert Shapiro and Peter MacGregor-Scott. Ph: Alex Thomson. Ed: Claire Simpson. Pro Des: John Box. M: Danny Elfman. Costumes: Jenny Beavan. (Warner.) Rel: 17 February 1995. 88 mins. Cert U.

Blank Check

See *Blank Cheque.*

Blank Cheque

This wish-fulfilment fantasy for acquisitive kids has eleven-year-old Preston Waters filling in a gangster's blank cheque with a round million dollars and indulging in a wild spending spree. Although some of the high-priced toys

U Aung Ko and Patricia Arquette struggle to survive against the odds in John Boorman's indignant Beyond Rangoon *(from Rank)*

A dark horse: Black Beauty shows his true colours to Andrew Knott in Caroline Thompson's Black Beauty *(from Warner)*

he buys are fun, the script is bargain-basement stuff, the lad lacks charisma and the tricky direction is irritating. Worst of all is the tacky stuff about the value of a big, happy, huggy family. Yuk! [*Simon Rose*]

Cast: Brian Bonsall (Preston Waters), Karen Duffy (Shay Stanley), Miguel Ferrer (Quigley), James Rebhorn (Fred Waters), Tone Loc (Juice), Jayne Atkinson (Sandra Waters), Michael Lerner (Biderman), Michael Faustino, Chris Demetral, Rick Ducommun, Alex Zuckerman, Debbie Allen, Michael Polk.
Dir: Rupert Wainwright. Pro: Craig Baumgarten and Gary Adelson. Ex Pro: Hilary Wayne and Blake Snyder. Screenplay: Snyder and Colby Carr. Ph: Bill Pope. Ed: Hubert De La Bouillerie. Pro Des: Nelson

Bombs away: Forest Whitaker (sitting) finds his headphones wired to blow, as Jeff Bridges and Lloyd Catlett attempt to diffuse the situation – in Stephen Hopkins' gripping Blown Away *(from UIP)*

Coates. M: Nicholas Pike; numbers performed by Zendetta, Taylor Dayne, Right Said Fred, L.A. Guns, MMC, Rymes With Orange, etc. Costumes: Deborah Everton. (Walt Disney–Buena Vista.) Rel: 5 August 1994. 94 mins. Cert PG.

Blown Away

Boston; 1994. Just as he's considering a career in teaching, newly-married bomb disposal expert Jimmy Dove finds his squad needs him more than ever as a crazy Irishman starts picking them off one by one. In spite of the Irish accents, narrative disorder and familiarity of plot devices, *Blown Away* is a creditable, intriguing thriller with a great deal of suspense. A degree in physics or science might help to appreciate the elaborate bomb conceits of Tommy Lee Jones (as the whistling, chuckling baddie), but his use of everything from children's toys to coffee filters is none the less enthralling.

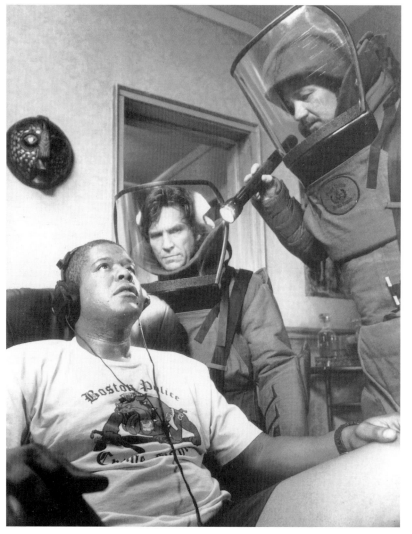

Cast: Jeff Bridges (Jimmy Dove/Liam), Tommy Lee Jones (Ryan Gaerity), Lloyd Bridges (Max O'Bannon), Forest Whitaker (Anthony Franklin), Suzy Amis (Kate), Stephi Lineburg, John Finn, Caitlin Clarke, Chris De Oni, Loyd Catlett, Ruben Santiago-Hudson, Lucinda Weist, Brendan Burns.
Dir: Stephen Hopkins. Pro: John Watson, Richard Lewis and Pen Densham. Ex Pro: Lloyd Segan. Screenplay: Joe Batteer and John Rice, from a story by Batteer, Rice and M. Jay Roach. Ph: Peter Levy. Ed: Timothy Wellburn. Pro Des: John Graysmark. M: Alan Silvestri; numbers performed by U2, The Pogues, The Wolfe Tones, The Sundays, Aretha Franklin, October Project, The Jayhawks, Big Head Todd and the Monsters, and Joe Cocker and Bekka Bramlett. Costumes: Joe I. Tompkins. (MGM/Trilogy Entertainment Group–VIP.) Rel: 2 September 1994. 120 mins. Cert 15.

Blue Sky

1962. Carly Marshall, explains her husband, is like water. One moment she can be a placid pond, the next pure steam, then a block of ice. Actually, Carly is heading for a meltdown, but her husband Hank – a high-ranking army scientist working on a top-secret nuclear project nicknamed Blue Sky – just soldiers on, turning a blind eye. So, she's crazy, he's blind and their daughter's just discovering the joys of sexual attraction. There may be blue skies over Alabama, but the heat is becoming oppressive. Yet only when matters of greater gravity intrude on the Marshall household do Hank and Carly pull together to face the world... A richly-veined story expertly realised by the late Tony Richardson (his last film), *Blue Sky* is an emotional, absorbing drama that skilfully pulls together a number of strands. And even as Jessica Lange holds centre stage as the volatile Carly, the supporting cast is uniformly excellent. Based on a true story.

Cast: Jessica Lange (Carly Marshall), Tommy Lee Jones (Hank Marshall), Powers Boothe (Vince Johnson), Carrie Snodgress (Vera Johnson), Amy Locane (Alex Marshall), Chris O'Donnell (Glenn Johnson), Anna Klemp (Becky Marshall), Mitchell Ryan, Dale Dye, Tim Scott, Annie Ross, Michael McClendon, Merlin Marston, Dion Anderson, Richard Jones, Gary Bullock, Angela Paton, Timothy Bottoms.
Dir: Tony Richardson. Pro: Robert H. Solo. Co-Pro: Lynn Arost. Screenplay:

Rama Laurie Stagner, Arlene Sarner and Jerry Leichtling. Ph: Steve Yaconelli. Ed: Robert K. Lambert. Pro Des: Timian Alsaker. M: Jack Nitzsche; numbers performed by Brook Benton and Dinah Washington, The Billy Lawson Band, Frankie Avalon, Etta James, etc. Costumes: Jane Robinson. (Orion Pictures–Columbia TriStar.) Rel: 7 April 1995. 105 mins. Cert 12.

Boys on the Side

Three women from spectacularly different backgrounds find themselves thrown together on a journey from the East Coast to LA. Along the way they discover that they can actually help and support each other, even though each one of them has a mighty big surprise in store ... At times resembling a help-yourself buffet of *Terms of Endearment*, *Thelma & Louise*, *Philadelphia* and any number of laminated, designer movies, *Boys on the Side* is a perceptively written, highly polished contrivance. And, thanks to a triumvirate of astonishing performances, it is frequently very funny and quite moving. Great soundtrack, too. From the writer of *Love Field* and *Single White Female*.

Wife in the fast lane: Jessica Lange, in her Oscar-winning performance, comes on to husband Tommy Lee Jones in Tony Richardson's Blue Sky *(from Columbia TriStar)*

Girls behind the wheel: Whoopi Goldberg, Mary-Louise Parker and Drew Barrymore act up in Herbert Ross's Boys on the Side *(from Warner)*

Cast: Whoopi Goldberg (Jane DeLuca), Mary-Louise Parker (Robin Nickerson), Drew Barrymore (Holly), Matthew McConaughey (Abe Lincoln), Anita Gillette (Elaine), James Remar (Alex), Billy Wirth (Nick), Dennis Boutsikaris (Massarelli), Estelle Parsons, Amy Aquino, Stan Egi, Stephen Gevedon, Indigo Girls, Jude Ciccolella, Gede Watanabe, Jonathan Seda, Aaron Lustig.

Dir: Herbert Ross. Pro: Ross, Arnon Milchan and Steven Reuther. Ex Pro: Don Roos and Patricia Karlan. Screenplay: Roos. Ph: Donald E. Thorin. Ed: Michael R. Miller. Pro Des: Ken Adam. M: David Newman; numbers performed by Whoopi Goldberg, Annie Lennox, Joan Armatrading, The Cranberries, Jonell Mosser, Sheryl Crow, Stevie Nicks, Sarah McLachlan, The Pretenders, Indigo Girls, Elvis Presley, Toni Childs, Bonnie Raitt, Melissa Etheridge, etc. Costumes: Gloria Gresham. (Le Studio Canal Plus/Regency Enterprises/Alcor Films/New Regency/ Hera–Warner.) Rel: 12 May 1995. 117 mins. Cert 15.

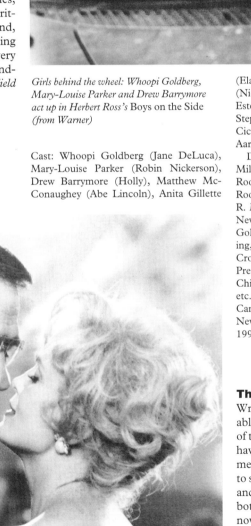

The Brady Bunch Movie

Wrenched smiling from their comfortable niche as the most inane TV family of the early seventies, the Brady Bunch have been given the big-screen treatment with a twist. While still dedicated to such utterances as 'groovy', 'far out' and 'it's a blast' – and sporting bell-bottoms and polyester – the Bradys are now at the mercy of the cruel, hard world of the nineties. And unlike the awful screen update of *The Beverly*

We've only just begun: Olivia Hack, Jennifer Elise Cox, Christine Taylor, Christopher Daniel Barnes, Paul Sutera and Jesse Lee lay on the saccharine in Betty Thomas's The Brady Bunch Movie *(from UIP)*

Hillbillies, this po-faced homage plays on its own innate naffness – and yet with unnerving verisimilitude to the original series. A blast.

Cast: Shelley Long (Carol Brady), Gary Cole (Mike Brady), Michael McKean (Mr Dittmeyer), Christopher Daniel Barnes (Greg Brady), Christine Taylor (Marcia Brady), Paul Sutera (Peter Brady), Jennifer Elise Cox (Jan Brady), Jesse Lee (Bobby Brady), Olivia Hack (Cindy Brady), Henriette Mantel (Alice), David Graf (Sam), Jean Smart (Mrs Dittmeyer), RuPaul (Mrs Cummings), Jack Noseworthy, Megan Ward, Moriah Snyder, Alanna Uback, Shane Conrad, Marissa Ribisi, R.D. Robb, Steven Gilborn, Alexander Pourtash, Keone Young, David Proval, Barry Williams, Patrick Thomas O'Brien, Ann B. Davis, Davy Jones, Micky Dolenz, Peter Tork, Tully Jensen, Christopher Knight.

A figment of his Imaginator: T. Ryder Smith as The Trickster in John Flynn's Brainscan *(from Guild)*

Dir: Betty Thomas. Pro: Sherwood Schwartz, Lloyd J. Schwartz and David Kirkpatrick. Ex Pro: Alan Ladd Jr. Screenplay: Laurice Elehwany, Rick Copp, Bonnie Turner and Terry Turner, based on characters created by Sherwood Schwartz. Ph: Mac Ahlberg. Ed: Peter Teschner. Pro Des: Steven Jordan. M: Guy Moon; numbers performed by Phlegm, Davy Jones, Zak, Lionel Cole, RuPaul, Mudd Pagoda, Suicidal Tendencies, Steve Tyrell, etc. Costumes: Rosanna Norton. (Paramount–UIP.) Rel: 9 June 1995. 98 mins. Cert 12.

Brainscan

Desensitised by a constant diet of horror films and magazines, school outsider Michael Brower is not impressed by the hype surrounding a new 'interactive' horror CD. But 'Brainscan' is more than just a game, mercilessly drawing on Michael's subconscious streak of cruelty and converting it into virtual reality. At last Michael has met his horror threshold, but what's that got to do with the grisly murders happening in his neighbourhood? With a concept like this, the opportunity for some spectacular special effects are sadly wasted, while the story itself fails to grip.

Cast: Edward Furlong (Michael Brower), Frank Langella (Det. Jack Hayden), T. Ryder Smith (The Trickster), Amy Hargreaves (Kimberly Keller), Jamie Marsh (Kyle Hillard), David Hemblen (Dr J. Fromberg), Victor Ertmanis, Vlasta Vrans, Dom Fiore.
  Dir: John Flynn. Pro: Michel Roy. Ex Pro: Esther Freifeld, Earl Berman, Andrew Martin and Bob Hayward. Screenplay: Andrew Kevin Walker, from a story by Brian Owens. Ph: Francois Protat. Ed: Jay Cassidy. Pro Des: Paola Ridolfi. M: George S. Clinton; numbers performed by Dandelion, Old, Alcohol Funnycar, White Zombie, Tad, The Butthole Surfers, Wade, etc. Costumes: Gaudeline Sauriol. Make-Up FX: Steve Johnson. (Triumph/Summit Entertainment–Guild.) Rel: 23 September 1994. 97 mins. Cert 18.

The Browning Version

With his valediction approaching, classics professor Andrew Crocker-Harris realises that, as a teacher of ancient literature, he has been a failure. Nobody is interested in Greek or Latin anymore, and next term not only will he be replaced but his subject too. But maybe one student, Taplow, could make all the difference . . . At one point, Crocker-Harris informs Taplow that 'the true art of learning is to conceal the learning'. This advice could well be taken on board by Albert Finney himself, who appears to be acting even when he's not doing anything. A more natural performer (like Anthony Hopkins) could have made Crocker-Harris as complex, sympathetic and credible as Terence Rattigan's play demands him to be. But even Hopkins could not have saved this picturesque remake of Rattigan's 1948 play from such forced updating as the unnecessarily foul language and awkward allusions to *perestroika* and computers. Furthermore, Mark Isham's intrusive music has the audacity to try and do the acting for the cast.

Cast: Albert Finney (Andrew Crocker-Harris), Greta Scacchi (Laura Crocker-Harris), Matthew Modine (Frank Hunter), Michael Gambon (Dr Frobisher), Julian Sands (Tom Gilbert), Ben Silverstone (Taplow), David Lever (David Fletcher), Oliver Milburn (Trubshaw), James Sturgess, Joe Beattie, Mark Bolton, Walter Micklethwait, Bruce Myers, Maryam d'Abo, Heathcote Williams, Jeff Nuttall, Dinah Stabb, Belinda Low, George Harris, Mark Long.
  Dir: Mike Figgis. Pro: Ridley Scott and Mimi Polk. Co-Pro: Garth Thomas. Assoc Pro: Olivia Stewart. Screenplay: Ronald Harwood. Ph: Jean Francois Robin. Ed: Herve Schneid. Pro Des: John Beard. M: Mark Isham. Costumes: Fotini Dimou. (Percy Main/Paramount–UIP.) Rel: 28 October 1994. 97 mins. Cert 15.

The Blue Version: Matthew Modine and Greta Scacchi inject some contemporary sex into Terence Rattigan's great play The Browning Version *(from UIP)*

Bulletproof Heart

See *Killer*.

Bullets Over Broadway

New York; the 1920s. Desperate to find financing for his 'serious' play, young playwright David Shayne succumbs to a gangster's condition that, in return for funding, he casts the latter's girlfriend

Guns, gags and greasepaint: Dianne Wiest in her Oscar-winning role as Helen Sinclair, with Woody Allen alter ego John Cusack, in Bullets Over Broadway *(from Buena Vista)*

An eye on the past: The sublime Jessica Tandy in Deepa Mehta's Camilla *(from Entertainment)*

in a 'key' role. However, not only is the floozy a lousy actress but her bodyguard – Cheech – is becoming a liability. Cheech thinks nothing of roughing David up or even demanding changes to the play. But then Cheech may just have some fine dramatic instincts ... I thought I'd never say this, but Woody Allen is becoming like McDonald's. That is, you always get what you expect. Here we have the familiar one-liners, the New York locations, the ensemble cast, the jazzy score and the artistic milieu. Except this time Woody sets his humour at a higher pitch, unleashing a comedy of farcical frenzy. Personally, I prefer the filmmaker when he's more subtle.

Cast: Jim Broadbent (Warner Purcell), John Cusack (David Shayne), Harvey Fierstein (Sid Loomis), Chazz Palminteri (Cheech), Mary-Louise Parker (Ellen), Rob Reiner (Sheldon Flender), Jennifer Tilly (Olive Neal), Tracey Ullman (Eden Brent), Joe Viterelli (Nick Valenti), Jack Warden (Julian Marx), Dianne Wiest (Helen Sinclair), Paul Herman, James Reno, Stacey Nelkin, Margaret Sophie Stein, Brian McConnachie, Edie Falco, Debi Mazar, Dayle Haddon, Howard Erskine.

Dir: Woody Allen. Pro: Robert Greenhut. Ex Pro: Jean Doumanian and J.E. Beaucaire. Co-Ex Pro: Jack Rollins, Charles H. Joffe and Letty Aronson. Co-Pro: Helen Robin. Screenplay: Allen and Douglas McGrath. Ph: Carlo Di Palma. Ed: Susan E. Morse. Pro Des: Santo Loquasto. M: numbers performed by Al Jolson, Eddie Cantor, The Three Deuces Musicians, Duke Ellington, Bix Beiderbecke, etc. Costumes: Jeffrey Kurland. (Miramax–Buena Vista.) Rel: 12 May 1995. 105 mins. Cert 15.

Bye Bye Love

California; 1995. Three divorced fathers find their lives irreparably altered in a 48-hour period. Mining the fertile lode of broken family life in America, *Bye Bye Love* is an adept dramatic comedy that juggles the inherent tragedy and humour of its subject with some skill. Weaving a number of characters and plot lines into a colourful tapestry, the film keeps up a steady pace yet never loses sight of its reality. Frequently very funny – thanks to some sharp and perceptive dialogue – it is at its funniest when dealing with the men's romantic aspirations. And Randy Quaid's dinner with the date from hell is a comic gem.

Cast: Matthew Modine (Dave), Randy Quaid (Vic), Paul Reiser (Donny), Janeane Garofalo (Lucille), Amy Brenneman (Susan), Eliza Dushku (Emma), Ed Flanders (Walter), Maria Pitillo (Kim), Lindsay Crouse (Grace), Ross Malinger (Ben), Johnny Whitworth (Max), Wendell Pierce (Hector), Jayne Brook (Claire), Dana Wheeler-Nicholson (Heidi), Amber Benson (Meg), Rob Reiner (Dr Townsend), Pamela Dillman (Sheila), Brad Hall (Phil), Cameron Boyd, Mae Whitman, Danny Masterson, James Arone, Marguerite Weisman, Daniel Weisman.

Dir: Sam Weisman. Pro: Weisman, Gary David Goldberg and Brad Hall. Co-Pro: Michael MacDonald. Screenplay: Goldberg and Hall. Ph: Kenneth Zunder. Ed: Roger Bondelli. Pro Des: Linda DeScenna. M: J.A.C. Redford; numbers performed by Jackson Browne, Phil Collins, Dean Martin, Spin Doctors, John Lennon and Paul McCartney, The Proclaimers, Linda Ronstadt, The Everly Brothers, The Beach Boys, Mary Chapin-Carpenter, Frankie Laine, Dave Edmunds, Crosby, Stills, Nash & Young, etc. Costumes: Linda Bass. (UBU–Fox.) Rel: 26 May 1995. 105 mins. Cert PG.

Camilla

Inspired by a true friendship, *Camilla* is the story of two women – separated by over 50 years of age – whose love of music drives their lives. For Freda Lopez, her marriage to a self-centred graphic artist has depleted her self-confidence as a songwriter. So a two-week break on the Georgia coast is arranged to shake her and her husband out of their stupor. There, she meets Camilla Cara, an eccentric and initially intimidating old bat who claims she was once a great violinist. Against the odds the two women strike up an extraordinary rapport that takes them both to a new place in their lives. A sweet story beautifully photographed, *Camilla* becomes so much more whenever Jessica Tandy is on screen, whose stamina, dignity and sense of fun sweeps the film before her. What an actress. A Canadian-British co-production.

Cast: Jessica Tandy, 84 (Camilla Cara), Bridget Fonda, 29 (Freda Lopez), Elias Koteas (Vincent Lopez), Maury Chaykin (Harold Cara), Graham Greene (Hunt Weller), Hume Cronyn (Ewald), Ranjit Chowdhry, George Harris, Atom Egoyan, Martha Cronyn, Sheilanne Lindsay, Don McKellar.

Dir: Deepa Mehta. Pro: Christina Jennings and Simon Relph. Ex Pro: Jonathan Barker. Screenplay: Paul Quarrington, from a story by Ali Jennings. Ph: Guy Dufaux. Ed: Barry Farrell. Pro Des: Sandra Kybartas. M: John Altman and Daniel Lanois. Sound:

Bruce Nyznik. (Shaftesbury/Skreba Prods/ Telefilm Canada/Ontario Film Development/British Screen–Entertainment.) Rel: 17 February 1995. 94 mins. Cert PG.

Captives

London; 1994. A prison dentist falls for a convict. The fundamental problem undermining this handsome, sincere film is the central premise. We are expected to believe that a beautiful, professional woman like Julia Ormond would risk her job (and safety) for a pathetic, incarcerated stranger like Tim Roth. Well, it won't wash. Had Ralph Fiennes been cast as the prisoner and somebody a little more ordinary been thrown under his spell, then the film would have had a credible edge. As it stands, *Captives* is an intriguing misfire.

Cast: Tim Roth (Philip Chaney), Julia Ormond (Rachel Clifford), Keith Allen (Lenny), Siobhan Redmond (Sue), Peter Capaldi (Simon), Colin Salmon (Towler), Richard Hawley, Jeff Nuttall, Kenneth Cope, Bill Moody, Nathan Dambuza, Annette Badland, Mark Strong, Sandra James-Young, Anthony Kernan, Tony Curran, Shaheen Khan.
  Dir: Angela Pope. Pro: David M. Thompson. Ex Pro: Anant Singh and Mark Shivas. Screenplay: Frank Deasy. Ph: Remi Adefarasin. Ed: Dave King. Pro Des: Stuart Walker. M: Colin Towns. Costumes: Odile Dicks-Mireaux. (BBC Films/Distant Horizon–Entertainment.) Rel: 29 April 1995. 99 mins. Cert 15.

Chasers

Misguided gender-switch on the Jack Nicholson black comedy *The Last Detail* (1973) in which two navy veterans chaperoned a petty thief to prison. Here, the felon is the gorgeous Erika Eleniak, charged with assault and going AWOL. Much unlikely tomfoolery ensues as the girl's escorts attempt to foil her attempts to escape. Too, too silly. [*Charles Bacon*]

Cast: Tom Berenger (Rock Reilly), Erika Eleniak (Toni Johnson), William McNamara (Eddie Devane), Crispin Glover (Howard Finster), Matthew Glave, Grand L. Bush, Dean Stockwell, Bitty Schram, Gary Busey, Seymour Cassel, Frederic Forrest, Marilu Henner, Dennis Hopper (Doggie).
  Dir: Dennis Hopper. Pro: James G. Robinson. Ex Pro: Gary Barber. Screenplay: Joe Batteer, John Rice and Dan Gilroy. Ph: Ueli Steiger. Ed: Christian A. Wagner. Pro

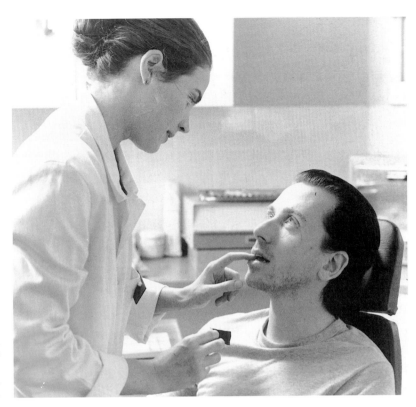

Des: Robert Pearson. M: Dwight Yoakam and Peter Anderson. Costumes: Michael Boyd. (Morgan Creek–Warner.) Rel: 16 December 1994. 101 mins. Cert 15.

Chasing the Deer

1745; Scotland. As Bonnie Prince Charlie masses Jacobitic troops to install his father on the Scottish throne, a pacifist father and son find themselves tragically divided by the civil war. It's hard to know how to review a film like this, a project obviously made with enormous love and commitment but missing its mark by a mile. Financed by the unique concept of inviting members of the public to buy shares and participate as extras in the film, *Chasing the Deer* displays a decidedly amateur feel. And while it looks good enough - with lingering shots of the Scottish Highlands - the direction, acting and editing leaves a lot to be desired.

Cast: Brian Blessed (Major Elliott), Iain Cuthbertson (Tullibardine), Jake D'Arcy (Tam), Mathew Zajac (Alistair Campbell), Jacqueline Pirie (Mary), Lewis Rae (Euan Campbell), Carolyn Konrad (Morag), Lynn Ferguson (Shonagh), Dominique Carrara (Charles Edward Stuart), Simon Kirk (Sgt Kirk), Fish (Angus Cameron), Jock Ferguson (Lord Murray), Michael Leighton, Charles Wilson, Terry Molloy,

Marathon woman: Julia Ormond tends to Tim Roth's heart and cavities – in Angela Pope's Captives *(from Entertainment)*

Kim Durham, Dominic Borrelli, Ross Dunsmore, Peter Ross.
  Dir: Graham Holloway. Pro: Bob Carruthers. Ex Pro: Gary Russell, Rob Whitehouse and David McWhinnie. Screenplay: Carruthers, Jerome Vincent and Steve Gillham, based on an idea by Michele Ayson. Ph: Alan Trow. Ed: Patrick Moore. No Production Designer. M: John Wetton, Runrig and Fish. Costumes: Lionel Digby. (Cromwell Prods/Lamancha Prods–Feature Film Co.) Rel: 16 December 1994. 97 mins. Cert PG.

Circle of Friends

Picturesque, touching adaptation of Maeve Binchy's novel of smalltown sexual repression in Ireland in 1957. On enrolling at the University of Dublin, three girlfriends find their lives transformed as they embark on the study of 'the sexual life of savages'. And into their protected, Catholic world is thrown the dashing Jack Foley, the star of the university rugby team with honourable intentions, surplus hormones and indecisive gaze. Delicately walking the line between mawkish blarney and twee nostalgia, *Circle of Friends* is beautifully judged, with a glowing performance from Minnie Driver as Benny.

Love hurts: Minnie Driver courted by Alan Cumming in Pat O'Connor's Circle of Friends *(from Rank)*

Idiot's delight: Jon Lovitz, Daniel Stern and Billy Crystal in search of a quick buck at the box-office disappoint themselves and their audience in Paul Weiland's unendurable City Slickers II: 'The Legend of Curly's Gold' *(from Columbia)*

Townsend, Ciaran Hinds, Seamus Forde, Tom Hickey, John Kavanagh, Ingrid Craigie, Ruth McCabe, Marie Mullen, Pauline Delaney, Brendan Conroy.

Dir: Pat O'Connor. Pro: Arlene Sellers, Alex Winitsky and Frank Price. Co-Pro: Ken Trodd. Ex Pro: Terence Clegg. Screenplay: Andrew Davies. Ph: Ken MacMillan. Ed: Jim Jympson. Pro Des: Jim Clay. M: Michael Kamen; numbers performed by Shane MacGowan and Maire Brennan, Long John Jump Band, Fats Domino, Little Richard and Kitty Kallan. Costumes: Anushia Nieradzik. (Savoy Pictures/Price Entertainment/Lantana–Rank.) Rel: 12 May 1995. 102 mins. Cert 15.

City Slickers II: 'The Legend of Curly's Gold'

After rediscovering himself 'out west', Mitch Robbins has got his life together: he is the new manager of a Manhattan radio station and is blissfully in love with his wife. Then he turns 40. Now he's starting to have nightmares about Curly, the trail boss he buried back in Utah, and is saddled with his younger brother, Glen, an incompetent whose sole speciality is the ability to instantly tally the number of letters in any given word. Then Mitch discovers a treasure map folded inside Curly's old stetson. Are all his troubles about to end - or are they just beginning? While the original *City Slickers* was blessed with a hilarious script and some well-drawn characters, it did tend to slip into buffoonery. Here, producer Billy Crystal and his co-scripters Lowell Ganz and Babaloo Mandel take the worst elements of the first film and magnify them, while providing far fewer good gags. Also, Crystal's sidekicks – Jon Lovitz as his brother and Daniel Stern as his loser of a friend – are two of the most irritating jerks to darken a screen this year.

Only Alan Cumming's Dickensian interpretation of her oily suitor seems misplaced.

Cast: Chris O'Donnell (Jack Foley), Colin Firth (Simon Westward), Minnie Driver (Benny Hogan), Geraldine O'Rawe (Eve), Saffron Burrows (Nan), Alan Cumming (Sean), Aidan Gillen (Aidan), Mick Lally (Dan Hogan), Tony Doyle (Dr Foley), Britta Smith (Mrs Hogan), Stanley

Cast: Billy Crystal (Mitch Robbins), Daniel Stern (Phil Berquist), Jon Lovitz (Glen Robbins), Jack Palance (Duke/Curly Washburn), Patricia Wettig (Barbara Robbins), Lindsay Crystal (Holly Robbins), Beth Grant (Lois), Noble Willingham (Clay Stone), David Paymer (Ira Shalowitz), Josh Mostel (Barry Shalowitz), Pruitt Taylor Vince, Bill McKinney, Jayne Meadows, Jennifer Crystal, Molly McClure, Bob Balaban.

Dir: Paul Weiland. Pro: Billy Crystal. Ex Pro: Peter Schindler. Screenplay: Crystal, Lowell Ganz and Babaloo Mandel. Ph: Adrian Biddle. Ed: William Anderson. Pro Des: Stephen J. Lineweaver. M: Marc Shaiman. (Castle Rock/Face Prods–

Pointing the finger: Harrison Ford gets to grips with Henry Czerny in Phillip Noyce's complex Clear and Present Danger *(from UIP)*

Columbia.) Rel: 23 September 1994. 115 mins. Cert 12.

Clean, Shaven

Hypnotic, low-budget drama in which a man suffering from schizophrenia goes in search of his young daughter who, for obvious reasons, is being kept from him. With no company but a rifle and a suspicious bundle in the boot, Peter Winter lives in his beat-up car as he cruises along Miscou Island, New Brunswick, battling with the voices inside his head. A few paces behind, detective Jack McNally is closing in . . . Three years in production, *Clean, Shaven* is not a pretty picture, but is a remarkable exercise in lean, atmospheric filmmaking. And with commendable economy it gouges its mark.

Cast: Peter Greene (Peter Winter), Robert Albert (Jack McNally), Jennifer MacDonald (Nicole), Megan Owen (Mrs Winter), Molly Castelloe (Melinda Payne), Rob Benevides, June Kelly, Grace Vibert, Marti Wilkerson.
 Dir, Pro and Screenplay: Lodge H. Kerrigan. Ex Pro: J. Dixon Byrne. Assoc Pro: Melissa Painter. Ph: Teodoro Maniaci. Ed: Jay Rabinowitz. Pro Des: Tania Ferrier. M: Hahn Rowe. (Miscou Island Prods–ICA.) Rel: 19 November 1994. 80 mins. No Cert.

Clear and Present Danger

Washington/Colombia; today. When CIA deputy director of Intelligence, Admiral James Greer, is struck down by pancreatic cancer, CIA analyst Jack Ryan steps in as acting deputy. It is in his new position as CIA bigwig that Ryan stumbles across some dodgy dealings in Colombia. Giving his word that there will be no military intervention in the Latin American republic, Ryan finds that some villains from the Oval Office are operating behind his back. Displaying the same complex plotting that made *All the President's Men* so compelling, this third adaptation of a Tom Clancy page-turner lacks both the immediacy of the truth and a human centre to make it as engrossing. Still, it is a masterfully constructed thriller that throws a searching spotlight on contemporary White House politics, and does boast some fascinating minutiae of the world of espionage.

Cast: Harrison Ford (Jack Ryan), Willem Dafoe (Mr Clark), Anne Archer (Cathy Ryan), James Earl Jones (Admiral James Greer), Joaquim De Almeida (Felix Cortez), Henry Czerny (Robert Ritter), Harris Yulin (James Cutter), Donald Moffat (Edward Bennett, US President), Miguel Sandoval (Ernesto Escobedo), Thora Birch (Sally Ryan), Ann Magnuson (Moira Wolfson), Tim Grimm (Murray), Belita Moreno (Fowler), Benjamin Bratt, Raymond Cruz, Dean Jones, Hope Lange, Tom Tammi, Jorge Luke, Jaime Gomez, Ellen Geer, Ted Raimi, Vondie Curtis-Hall, Rex Linn, Ken Howard, Reed Diamond, Aaron Lustig.
 Dir: Phillip Noyce. Pro: Mace Neufield and Robert Rehme. Screenplay: Donald Stewart, Steven Zaillian and John Milius. Co-Pro: Ralph Singleton. Ph: Donald M. McAlpine. Ed: Neil Travis. Pro Des: Terence Marsh. M: James Horner. Costumes: Bernie Pollack. Sound: Arthur Rochester. Special FX: Joe Lombardi and Paul Lombardi. (Paramount–UIP.) Rel: 16 September 1994. 141 mins. Cert 12.

Clerks

QuickStop Groceries, Leonardo, New Jersey; 1993. For Dante Hicks, working in a convenience store has become an emotional convenience. Until, that is, he's forced to work on his day off and is subjected to endless hassles and humiliation. A day in the life of a cash clerk, *Clerks* is fresh, funny and daring, swiftly overcoming the shortcomings of

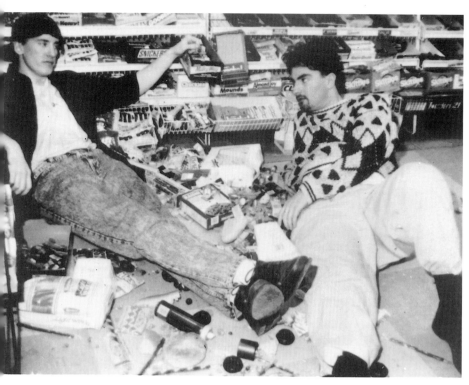

Speaking shop: Jeff Anderson and Brian O'Halloran in Kevin Smith's Clerks *(from Artificial Eye)*

its $27,575 budget and crude black and white photography. A ribald, witty script, deadpan performances and the occasionally inspired visual *non sequitur* (like the cat using the litter tray on the counter) add to the pleasure. FYI: Writer-director-co-producer Kevin Smith, 23, not only worked at the film's QuickStop for four years, but continued working there during production! Winner of the Filmmakers' Trophy Award at the 1994 Sundance festival.

Cast: Brian O'Halloran (Dante Hicks), Jeff Anderson (Randal), Marilyn Ghigliotti (Veronica), Lisa Spoonauer (Caitlin), Jason Mewes (Jay), Kevin Smith (Silent Bob), Scott Schiaffo (Chewlie's rep), Scott Mosier, Al Berkowitz, Walt Flanagan (the egg man), David Klein, Ken Clark, Donna Jeanne, Ernest O'Donnell, Kimberly Loughran, Joe Bagnole, John Henry Westhead, Leslie Hope, Lenin's Tomb (the cat).
    Dir and Screenplay: Kevin Smith. Pro: Smith and Scott Mosier. Ph: David Klein. Ed: Smith and Mosier. M: Scott Angley; numbers performed by Love Among Freaks, Girls Against Boys, Alice in Chains, Supernova, The Jesus Lizard, Bad Religion, Soul Asylum, etc. Opening credit animation: Walt Flanagan. (View Askew–Artificial Eye.) Rel: 5 May 1995. 90 mins. Cert 18.

The Client

Memphis/New Orleans; today. When an eleven-year-old boy witnesses a Mafia lawyer commit suicide, everybody wants him to talk: his mom, the cops, the Press, the FBI, the Mafia, and a shady character with a knife. Hell, some people even want him dead. What's a boy to do? Hire a lawyer, of course. But is reformed alcoholic and smoker Susan Sarandon up to the task? From the heart-stopping opening sequence, this is a thriller that not only moves but manages to be credible for most of the time. It helps that there are no star egos hogging the limelight, and non-professional Brad Renfro, in the central role, is well cast. But then everybody is good down the line, from Ms Sarandon as the tough-and-tender attorney to the smallest bit-part. Full marks to director Joel Schumacher, who crams the screen with vivid detail and never lets the pace lag. The best adaptation of a John Grisham novel yet.

Cast: Susan Sarandon (Reggie Love), Tommy Lee Jones (Roy Foltrigg), Mary-Louise Parker (Dianne Sway), Anthony LaPaglia (Barry Muldano), J.T. Walsh (McThune), Anthony Edwards (Clint Von Hooser), Ossie Davis (Harry Roosevelt), Brad Renfro (Mark Sway), Kim Coates (Paul Gronke), David Speck (Ricky Sway), Micole Mercurio (Mama Love), Walter Olkewicz (Jerome 'Romey' Clifford), Will Patton, Bradley Whitford, Anthony Heald, Kimberly Scott, William H. Macy, William Sanderson, Amy Hathaway, Jo Harvey Allen, Ron Dean, William Richert, Mark Cabus, John Diehl.

Law of the jungle: Brad Renfro, Mary-Louise Parker, Will Patton and Mark Cabus in a dramatic moment from Joel Schumacher's absorbing The Client *(from Warner)*

Running the gamut: Ruaidhri Conroy and Ian Hart don trainers in Vadim Jean's Clockwork Mice *(from Feature Film Co.)*

Dir: Joel Schumacher. Pro: Arnon Milchan and Steven Reuther. Co-Pro: Mary McLaglen. Screenplay: Akiva Goldsman and Robert Getchell. Ph: Tony Pierce-Roberts. Ed: Robert Brown. Pro Des: Bruno Rubeo. M: Howard Shore. Costumes: Ingrid Ferrin. (Regency Enterprises/Alcor Films–Warner.) Rel: 21 October 1994. 121 mins. Cert 15.

Clockwork Mice

Steve Drake, a new and idealistic young teacher at a school for emotionally disturbed children, is horrified by his pupils' rowdy behaviour. He is particularly frustrated by his inability to penetrate the defences of the fourteen-year-old son of an inveterate criminal. Then man and boy discover a mutual interest in running, a passion that unites the school and liberates old differences. While laying on the dramatics a little thick at times, the film is well written and blessed by some splendid performances, notably from John Alderton as a cheerfully tolerant headmaster.

Cast: Ian Hart (Steve Drake), Ruaidhri Conroy (Conrad James), Catherine Russell (Polly Pollard), Art Malik (Richard Laney), John Alderton (Swaney), Claire Skinner (Jane Fairy), James Bolam (Brian Wackey), Nigel Planer (Graham Parkey), Glen

Murphy, Frankie Bruno, Lilly Edwards, Robin Soans, Toyosi Ajikawao, Lee Barrett, Bobby Coombes, Ellam Lloyd Hull.

Dir: Vadim Jean. Pro: Paul Brooks. Ex Pro: Alan Martin and Gary Smith. Co-Ex Pro: Bruce Green and Alan Sharr. Line Pro: Simon Hardy and Simon Scotland. Screenplay: Rod Woodruff. Ph: Gordon Hickie. Ed: Liz Webber. Pro Des: David Munns. M: John Murphy and David Hughes. Costumes: John Krausa. (Metrodome–Feature Film Co.) Rel: 23 June 1995. 100 mins. Cert 15.

Le Colonel Chabert

France; 1808-17. Handsome and eloquent screen adaptation of Honoré de Balzac's 1832 novel, this is the story of a man who returns from the dead to stake his claim on his wife. Believed slain after his heroic charge at the Battle of

Paradise lost: Fabrice Luchini and Gérard Depardieu seek justice and revenge in Yves Angelo's masterly Le Colonel Chabert *(from Guild)*

Jane March, still sinning, in Richard Rush's appalling Color of Night *(from Guild)*

Color of Night

Overwrought, very silly thriller in which Bruce Willis plays a New York psychologist recovering from the suicide of one of his patients. In LA to recuperate with his old buddy and fellow shrink Scott Bakula, Bruce is further traumatised when his friend is stabbed 30 times by a patient. So Bruce does the honourable thing by taking on Bakula's loony clients, knowing that one of them is probably the killer. Pitched like a Gothic thriller, *Color of Night* is a rollercoaster ride of psychobabble and overacting, relieved only by Bruce Willis's reaction shots.

Cast: Bruce Willis (Dr Bill Capa), Jane March (Rose), Ruben Blades (Hector Martinez), Lesley Ann Warren (Sondra Dorio), Scott Bakula (Dr Bob Moore), Brad Dourif (Clark), Lance Henriksen (Buck), Kevin J. O'Connor (Casey), Andrew Lowery (Dale), Eriq La Salle, Jeff Corey, Kathleen Wilhoite, Shirley Knight.
 Dir: Richard Rush. Pro: Buzz Feitshans and David Matalon. Ex Pro: Andrew G. Vajna. Co-Pro: Carmine Zozzora and David Willis. Screenplay: Matthew Chapman and Billy Ray. Ph: Dietrich Lohmann. Ed: Jack B. Hofstra. M: Dominic Frontiere. Costumes: Jacqueline G. Arthur. (Hollywood Pictures/Cinergi–Guild.) Rel: 9 September 1994. 123 mins. Cert 18.

Jungle Fever: Laura Linney and Dylan Walsh (left) get into script problems with the natives in Frank Marshall's ludicrous Congo *(from UIP)*

Congo

Deep in the unexplored depths of the Congo rain forest lies a legend handed down from the days of Solomon. There, guarded by treacherous flora and fauna, lies the Lost City of Zinj, a vast treasure-trove of priceless diamonds. A motley expedition of Westerners, each with his own objective, fight and bribe their way into the Congo – overcoming such odds as unstable political governments, killer hippos and an erupting volcano. But, once there, the team discover that the region is overrun with an unidentified species of deadly, intelligent ape. Taking Michael Crichton's inspired and terrifying novel (written in 1980) and jettisoning the pertinent detail, the movie is reduced to yet another *Raiders of the Lost Ark* clone, complete with milk shake-accented rogues and flying polystyrene boulders. Cheesy special effects and electronically operated gorillas presumably account for the film's $60 million budget.

Cast: Dylan Walsh (Peter Elliot), Laura Linney (Karen Ross), Ernie Hudson (Monroe Kelly), Grant Heslov (Richard), Joe Don Baker (R.B. Travis), Tim Curry (Herkerner Homolka), Bruce Campbell (Charles Travis), Mary Ellen Trainor, Stuart Pankin, Carolyn Seymour, Romy Rosemont, James Karen, Robert Almodovar, Peter Jason, Jimmy Buffett, Joe Pantoliano. Vocal effects: Frank Welker.
 Dir: Frank Marshall. Pro: Kathleen Kennedy and Sam Mercer. Ex Pro: Frank Yablans. Screenplay: John Patrick Shanley.

Eylau, Chabert is condemned to history while his wife develops his fortune and marries a man with an eye on her wealth. But then nine years after Chabert's death, a scruffy man turns up at the door of an eminent Paris lawyer with an incredible story ... The directorial debut of the acclaimed French cinematographer Yves Angelo, *Colonel Chabert* looks magnificent, yet the film's physical stature never swamps its subtextual power. A prodigious achievement.

Cast: Gérard Depardieu (Chabert), Fanny Ardent (Countess Ferraud), Fabrice Luchini (Derville), André Dussollier (Count Ferraud), Daniel Prevost (Bou-card), Jacky Nercessian (Delbacq), Olivier Saladin, Maxime Leroux, Claude Rich, Jean Cosmos, Albert Delpy, Romane Bohringer, Julie Depardieu.
 Dir: Yves Angelo. Pro: Jean-Louis Livi. Ex Pro: Bernard Marescot. Screenplay: Angelo and Jean Cosmos. Ph: Bernard Lutic. Ed: Thierry Derocles. Set Design: Bernard Vezat. M: Beethoven, Mozart, Scarlatti, Schubert, Schumann and François Rauber. Costumes: Franca Squarciapino. (Film par film/Orly Films etc–Guild.) Rel: 21 April 1995. 111 mins. Cert PG.

Ph: Allen Daviau. Ed: Anne V. Coates. Pro Des: J. Michael Riva. M: Jerry Goldsmith; 'The Villager's Chant' by James Newton Howard and Lebo M. Costumes: Marilyn Matthews. Gorillas: Stan Winston. Martini illusion: Michael Weber and Ricky Jay. (Paramount/Kennedy/Marshall–UIP.) Rel: 30 June 1995. 108 mins. Cert 12.

Corrina, Corrina

1959; California. When her mother dies suddenly, seven-year-old Molly Singer loses the will to speak, resents her father's awkward attempts at camaraderie and refuses to kowtow to the nannies that her father introduces. Only when the clumsy, Afro-American Corrina joins the household does Molly blossom. Furthermore, she plots a romance between the older woman and her father ... One of the most remarkable things about *Corrina, Corrina* is that it marks the directing, producing and writing debut of stage actress Jessie Nelson, who based the screenplay on her own early years. An assured work directorially, the film displays the uncluttered clarity of a director long past the need to show off. If anything, it is the lack of chemistry between Goldberg and Liotta that lets the side down, good as both actors are. Credit, too, must go to Tina Majorino as Molly, a young performer of astonishing naturalism, range and credibility (previously seen in *When a Man Loves a Woman*). But all in all a moving experience.

Cast: Whoopi Goldberg (Corrina Washington), Ray Liotta (Manny Singer), Tina Majorino (Molly Singer), Wendy Crewson (Jenny Davis), Larry Miller (Sid), Erica Yohn (Grandma Eva), Jenifer Lewis (Jevina), Joan Cusack (Millie 'Jonesy' Jones), Don Ameche (Grandpa Harry), Harold Sylvester, Steven Williams, Patrika Darbo, Lucy Webb, Courtland Mead, Asher Metchik, June C. Ellis, Karen Leigh Hopkins, Lynette Walden.
Dir and Screenplay: Jessie Nelson. Pro: Nelson, Steve Tisch and Paula Mazur. Ex Pro: Ruth Vitale and Bernie Goldmann. Line Pro: Eric McLeod. Ph: Bruce Surtees. Ed: Lee Percy. Pro Des: Jeannine Claudia Oppewall. M: Rick Cox, with Thomas Newman; numbers performed by Louis Armstrong, Hank Ballard, John Beasley, Duke Ellington, Sarah Vaughan, Jackie Wilson, Big Joe Turner, Oscar Petersen, Billie Holiday, Oleta Adams, Brenda Russell, Ted Hawkins, Jevetta Steele, and Dinah Washington. Costumes: Francine Jamison-Tanchuck. (New Line Cinema–Guild.) Rel: 25 September 1994. 116 mins. Cert PG.

Cronos

Mexico City; 1536/1992. Part machine, part insect, the Cronos (Spanish translation: stopwatch) is a compact, intricate device created by an alchemist at the time of the Spanish Inquisition. Its purpose: to bestow eternal life. Four hundred years later a freak accident

A reason to live: Tina Majorino and Whoopi Goldberg find unexpected reserves of humanity in Jessie Nelson's Corrina, Corrina *(from Guild)*

Stopping the clock: Federico Luppi suffers immortality in Guillermo Del Toro's unsettling Cronos *(from Metro Tartan)*

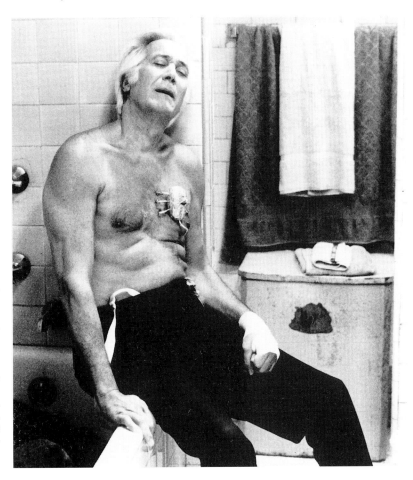

Everyday people: Zelda Harris and Delroy Lindo partake in Spike Lee's stoop culture in Crooklyn *(from Electric Avenue)*

ends the alchemist's life and the Cronos falls into the hands of an elderly antique dealer. At first the gentle, debonair shopkeeper is fascinated by his toy, but soon becomes dependent on it. And even as he sheds years overnight, his fixation with nose bleeds becomes a tad unsettling ... Winning countless international awards, *Cronos* marks the film debut of 29-year-old writer-director Guillermo Del Toro who, he swears, has been a fan of horror films since 'I was a very small child'. However, *Cronos* is less a blood-and-thunder splatterfest than a poetic tale of unease. A classic of its kind.

Cast: Federico Luppi (Jesus Gris), Ron Perlman (Angel De La Guardia), Claudio Brook (Dieter De La Guardia), Margarita Isabel (Mercedes), Tamara Shanath (Aurora), Daniel Gimenez Cacho (Tito), Jorge Martinez De Hoyos (narrator).
Dir and Screenplay: Guillermo Del Toro. Pro: Bertha Navarro and Arthur H. Gorson. Ph: Guillermo Navarro. Ed: Raul Davalos. Pro Des: Tolita Figueroa. M: Javier Alvarez; Franz Schubert. Make-Up: Necropia. (Prods Iguana–Metro Tartan.) Rel: 2 December 1994. 92 mins. Cert 18.

Crooklyn

Having exorcised much of his social anger and technical flash, Spike Lee zeros in on the family drama with surprising compassion and simplicity. Focusing on the Carmichael household in 1970s Brooklyn, Lee invites us into

a world divided between lyrical childhood and domestic discord. Admirable for its dogged refusal to kowtow to melodrama, *Crooklyn* is well served by a faultless cast, although Delroy Lindo's patriarch – a gentle, troubled giant – dominates the memory. Nevertheless, Lee's obsession with seventies memorabilia, driven home via countless TV clips (from *The Partridge Family* to *Soul Train*) and a ceaseless soundtrack of R&B hits, ultimately emasculates his film's sense of reality.

Cast: Alfre Woodard (Carolyn Carmichael), Delroy Lindo (Woody Carmichael), David Patrick Kelly (Tony Eyes), Zelda Harris (Troy Carmichael), Frances Foster (Aunt Song), Carlton Williams, Sharif Rashed, Tse-Mach Washington, Christopher Knowings, Jose Zuniga, Isaiah Washington, Ivelka Reyes, Spike Lee, N. Jeremi Duru, Norman Matlock, Patriece Nelson, Joie Susannah Lee, Vondie Curtis-Hall, Tiasha Reyes, Bokeem Woodbine, Mildred Clinton, Kewanna Bonaparte, Arthur French, Manny Perez, RuPaul.
Dir and Pro: Spike Lee. Co-Pro: Monty Ross. Ex Pro: Jon Kilik. Screenplay: Joie Susannah Lee, Cinque Lee and Spike Lee. Ph: Arthur Jafa. Ed: Barry Alexander Brown. Pro Des: Wynn Thomas. M: Terence Blanchard; numbers performed by The Stylistics, Stevie Wonder, Curtis Mayfield, Sly and the Family Stone, The Staple Singers, The Jimi Hendrix Experience, James Brown, Johnny Nash, Smokey Robinson and the Miracles, The Jackson 5, The Delfonics, The Chi-Lites, Aretha Franklin, Isaac Hayes, Bill Withers, The Spinners, The Crooklyn Dodgers, etc. Costumes: Ruth E. Carter. Sound: Skip Lievsey. (Universal/40 Acres/Mule Filmworks/Child Hoods Prods–Electric Avenue.) Rel: 31 March 1995. 114 mins. Cert 12.

Crumb

Six years in the making, this startlingly frank and revealing documentary explores the career and private life of the underground comic book artist Robert Crumb. Most famous for his creation of Fritz the Cat and the cult poster 'Keep On Truckin'', Crumb has many more layers to him – professionally, intellectually and privately. Terry Zwigoff, a close personal friend, manages to coerce an extraordinary cast of characters to speak their minds, drawing the viewer into a bizarre, disturbing and unmercifully funny universe. Crumb himself admits to once having a strong sexual attraction for Bugs Bunny, the female editor of *Jugs* magazine reveals that he has 'one of the biggest penises in the world', while Crumb's wife owns up to extra-marital sexual activity. A rare case of a filmmaker and his subject blending in perfect harmony.

Interviewees: Robert Crumb, Aline Kominsky, Charles Crumb, Max Crumb, Robert Hughes, Dana Crumb, Trina Robbins, Spain Rodriguez, Bill Griffith, Deirdre English, Beatrice Crumb, Dian Hanson, etc.
Dir: Terry Zwigoff. Pro: Zwigoff and Lynn O'Donnell. Ex Pro: Lawrence Wilkinson, Albert Berger and Lianne Halfon. Ph: Maryse Alberti. Ed: Victor Livingston. M: David Boeddinghaus; numbers performed by Boeddinghaus, Craig Ventresco, King Oliver, etc. Sound: Scott Breindel. (Superior Pictures/David Lynch–

Dark genius: A self-portrait of Robert Crumb, the subject of Artificial Eye's riveting documentary, Crumb

Artificial Eye.) Rel: 30 June 1995. 119 mins. Cert 18.

D2: The Mighty Ducks

By-the-numbers, heavily manipulative sequel to the surprise ice hockey hit of 1992. During the opening credits we see lawyer-turned-coach Gordon Bombay taking to professional hockey and then being brutally injured, so it's back to sharpening skates at old Jan's sports shop. Enter a slick, smooth-talking sports promoter who hires Bombay to re-group the old Ducks to compete in the Junior Goodwill Games in LA. But can the Ducks compete against the ruthless Icelandic team? And can Gordon regain his sense of fun that made the Ducks such good sports in the first place? And do we care? In spite of the painfully mediocre start and some awful reaction shots of wholesome tutor Kathryn Erbe, this unwelcome sequel does – eventually – hit its stride.

Cast: Emilio Estevez (Gordon Bombay), Michael Tucker (Mr Tibbles), Jan Rubes (Jan), Kathryn Erbe (Michele Mackay), Carsten Norgaard (Wolf Stansson), Maria Ellingsen (Marria), Joshua Jackson (Charlie), Shaun Weiss (Goldberg), Vincent A. Larusso (Adam Banks), Colombe Jacobsen (Julie Gaffney), Aaron Lohr (Dean Portman), Elden Ryan Ratliff, Matt Doherty, Brandon Adams, Garette Ratliff Henson, Marguerite Moreau, Ty O'Neal, Kenan Thompson, Mike Vitar, Justin Wong, Kareem Abdul-Jabbar, Cam Neely, Wayne Gretzky.
  Dir: Sam Weisman. Pro: Jordon Kerner and Jon Avnet. Ex Pro: Doug Claybourne. Screenplay: Steven Brill. Ph: Mark Irwin. Ed: Eric Sears and John F. Link. Pro Des: Gary Frutkoff. M: J.A.C. Redford; numbers performed by Peter Himmelman, Dwight Yoakam, Bone Club, Gary Glitter, Martha Wash, The B-52s, Suave, Tag Team, Queen, etc. Costumes: Grania Preston. (Walt Disney–Buena Vista.) Rel: 23 December 1994. 107 mins. Cert U.

Dallas Doll

Masquerading as a human panacea, Dallas Adair is an emotional predator disguised as a good Samaritan. Transplanted from the US to a quiet Sydney suburb to act as a consultant on a new golf course project, the American siren zeros in on a cosy middle-class family. Quite what her intentions are is not made clear (apart from satisfying her voracious sexual appetite), but soon she

has the Sommers clan eating out of her back pocket. At least, she manages to seduce Mr and Mrs Sommers and their eighteen-year-old son. Only the daughter and the vigilant family sheepdog, Argus, take a serious disliking to the seductive alien. A metaphor for the Australian fear of colonisation by the

D2: The Mighty Ducks: With a title like this, you know what to expect. Here, The Ducks face up to the greatest challenge of their lives and rediscover their desire to win (courtesy of the blurb from Buena Vista)

Shameful Sheila: Sandra Bernhard loosens up Victoria Longley in Ann Turner's Dallas Doll (from Metro Tartan)

Out of their minds: Milla Jovovich and Shawn Andrews in Richard Linklater's anarchic, hilarious and totally spaced out Dazed and Confused *(from Feature Film Co.)*

Americans and Japanese, *Dallas Doll* is quirky entertainment from the director of *Celia*. While never less than intriguing, and nurtured by a terrific turn from Sandra Bernhard as Dallas, the film lacks a certain pizzazz to carry it through its rougher patches.

Cast: Sandra Bernhard (Dallas Adair), Victoria Longley (Rosalind Sommers), Frank Gallacher (Stephen Sommers), Jake Blundell (Charlie Sommers), Rose Byrne (Lily 'Rastus' Sommers), Douglas Hedge (Major Terence Tonkin), Jonathon Leahy, Melissa Thomas, Elaine Lee, Alethea McGrath, Yumiko Iwanaga, Bobby (Argus).
Dir and Screenplay: Ann Turner. Pro: Ross Matthews. Co-Pro: Turner and Tatiana Kennedy. Line Pro: Barbara Gibbs. Assoc Pro: Sue Masters and Ray Brown. Ph: Paul Murphy. Ed: Michael Honey. Pro Des: Marcus North. M: David Hirschfelder; numbers performed by Doris Day, Paul Kelly, Sugo Wavo, Tiddas, etc. Costumes: Rosalea Hood. (Australian Broadcasting Corp/BBC Films–Metro Tartan.) Rel: 10 February 1995. 104 mins. Cert 18.

Days of Being Wild - Ahfei Zhenjuang

Incomprehensible Hong Kong drama in which six characters lounge around staring into space. Set almost entirely at night in a deserted Hong Kong of 1960, the film jumps from one sequence to the next in an accident of scenes that seem to collide haphazardly. Somewhere at the centre of the plot a man called Yuddi lives off his aunt, dreams of his unknown mother and treats his male and female friends like waste matter.

Cast: Leslie Cheung (Yuddi), Maggie Cheung (Su Lizhen), Andy Lau (Tide), Carina Lau (Mimi-Lulu), Rebecca Pan, Jacky Cheung, Tony Leung.
Dir and Screenplay: Wong Kar-wai. Pro: Rover Tang. Ex Pro: Alan Tang. Ph: Christopher Doyle. Ed: Kai Kit-wai. Pro Des: William Chang. M: Terry Chan. Costumes: Luk Ha-Fong. (In Gear Film Prods–Made in Hong Kong.) Rel: 25 November 1994. 94 mins. Cert 15.

Dazed and Confused

Middle America; 1976, summer. Uncannily accurate, wry and very funny satire on teenage rebellion set during the last day and night of high school before the summer break. Borrowing the anecdotal, ensemble format of *American Graffiti*, the film benefits from hilarious, spot-on dialogue and unerring performances from a young cast who inhabit their roles with sly conviction. Every jock, geek, pot-head and show pony gets his or her turn in the spotlight, bringing a well-rounded perspective to the joys and fears of high school and beyond. Doubtless to become a cult crowd-pleaser on the college circuit for years to come. A film truly in its own element.

Cast: Jason London (Randal 'Pink' Floyd), Shawn Andrews (Pickford), Rory Cochrane (Slater), Adam Goldberg (Mike), Anthony Rapp (Tony), Sasha Jensen (Don), Michelle Burke (Jodi), Christine Harnos (Kaye), Wiley Wiggins (Mitch), Esteban Powell (Carl), Ben Affleck (O'Bannion), Parker Posey (Darla), Matthew McConaughey (Wooderson), Joey Lauren Adams, Milla Jovovich, Marissa Ribisi, Deena Martin, Cole Hauser, Jeremy Fox, Jason O'Smith, Christin Hinojosa, Catherine Morris, Nicky Katt.
Dir and Screenplay: Richard Linklater. Pro: Linklater, James Jacks and Sean Daniel. Co-Pro: Anne Walker-McBay. Ph: Lee Daniel. Ed: Sandra Adair. Pro Des: John Frick. M: numbers performed by Aerosmith, Alice Cooper, War, Edgar Winter, Peter Frampton, Bob Dylan, Nazareth, Sweet, ZZ Top, Foghat, Deep Purple, Ted Nugent, Black Sabbath, Black Oak Arkansas, Dr John, Kiss, Steve Miller, Lynyrd Skynyrd, Thin Lizzy, etc. Costumes: Katherine (K.D.) Dover. (Universal/Gramercy/Alphaville/Detour–Feature Film Co.) Rel: 16 September 1994. 95 mins. Cert 18.

Dear Diary - Caro Diario

Winner of the Best Director award at the 1994 Cannes festival, *Dear Diary* is an original, beguiling film divided into three parts. The first is the most successful, in which the Italian filmmaker Nanni Moretti takes us on a personal trip round Rome on his Vespa. Here, he talks about architecture, bumps into Jennifer Beals and torments a film critic for his pretentious review of *Henry: Portrait of a Serial Killer*. Next, Moretti accompanies a friend on a tour of some Mediterranean islands in a pseudo-documentary episode that overstays its welcome. Then, in the chapter titled *Doctors*, the filmmaker gets rather morose, although still retaining his sense of humour. As a film diary, the movie is remarkable, jumping from comic incident to scholastic observation, while Moretti himself makes a wonderfully eccentric, po-faced subject.

Cast: Nanni Moretti (himself), Renato Carpentieri (Gerardo), Antonio Neiwiller (Mayor of Stromboli), Mario Schiano (Prince of Dermatologists), Jennifer Beals and Alexandre Rockwell (themselves), Carlo Mazzacurati, Raffaella Lebboroni, Marco Paolini.
 Dir and Screenplay: Nanni Moretti. Pro: Moretti, Angelo Barbagallo and Nella Banfi. Ph: Giuseppe Lanci. Ed: Mirco Garrone. Pro Des: Marta Maffucci. M: Nicola Piovani. Costumes: Maria Rita Barbera. (Sacher Film/Banfilm/La Sept Cinema/ Canal Plus/Rai Uno–Artificial Eye.) Rel: 25 November 1994. 100 mins. Cert 15.

Death and the Maiden
A country in South America; after the fall of the dictatorship. A victim of unspeakable torture and rape during the previous government's regime, Paulina Escobar is still racked with fear and hate fifteen years later. Then, one stormy night during a power cut, she believes she is finally face to face with her torturer. And so, with the unwilling assistance of her husband, Paulina submits her visitor to a brutal, impromptu trial. Casting somebody as physically imposing as Sigourney Weaver in the role of a woman provoked into enacting a terrible revenge seems a misconceived move. It automatically makes for a far more theatrical and hysterical performance which, in the hands of a more subtle, fragile actress – Jessica Lange, say – could have really pumped up the drama. Alas, Ms Weaver's wide-eyed, jaw-clenching turn rivets the film into its dramatic setting, forever denying the audience a sense of cinema.

Cast: Sigourney Weaver (Paulina Escobar), Ben Kingsley (Dr Roberto Miranda), Stuart Wilson (Gerardo Escobar).
 Dir: Roman Polanski. Pro: Thom Mount and Josh Kramer. Co-Pro: Bonnie Timmermann and Ariel Dorfman. Ex Pro: Sharon Harel and Jane Barclay. Screenplay: Rafael Yglesias and Ariel Dorfman, from the latter's play. Ph: Tonino delli Colli. Ed: Herve de Luze. Pro Des: Pierre Guffroy. M: Wojciech Kilar; Schubert. Costumes: Milena Canonero. Psychological research:

Elizabeth Lira. (Capitol Films/Channel Four/Flach Films/Canal Plus/TFI–Electric.) Rel: 21 April 1995. 104 mins. Cert 18.

Nanni Moretti (in motorcycle helmet) faces the music in his winning, idiosyncratic Dear Diary *(from Artificial Eye)*

Destiny Turns on the Radio
Pretension rules in this bizarre *film noir* comedy in which two small-time crooks find themselves up against a sleazily-dressed manito called Johnny Destiny.

Stage struck: Sigourney Weaver (right) taunts Ben Kingsley in Roman Polanski's heavy-handed Death and the Maiden *(from Electric)*

Office party: Demi Moore plots the unthinkable in Barry Levinson's stirring Disclosure *(from Warner)*

Destiny, described as 'a god with a small g', emerges naked from a yellow swimming pool, snatches Thoreau and Goddard's stolen loot and disappears into the night. Three years later Goddard breaks out of prison to get his money back, only to find that he's lost his girlfriend to a local mobster (a groin-scratching James Belushi) and that his nemesis isn't human. Quite where this film thinks it's headed is anybody's business, but with stock characters and slim jokes the trip is a vacuous one.

Cast: Dylan McDermott (Julian Goddard), Nancy Travis (Lucille), Quentin Tarantino (Johnny Destiny), James LeGros (Harry Thoreau), James Belushi (Tuerto), David Cross (Ralph Dellaposa), Sarah Trigger (Francine), Tracey Walter (Pappy), Allen Garfield (Vinnie Vidivici), Janet Carroll, Richard Edson, Bobcat Goldthwait, Barry 'Shabaka' Henley, Lisa Jane Persky, Ralph Brannen, Robert Sparks.

Dir: Jack Baran. Pro: Gloria Zimmerman. Co-Pro and Screenplay: Robert Ramsay and Matthew Stone. Ex Pro: Keith Samples and Peter Martin Nelson. Line Pro: Michael D. Pariser. Ph: James Carter. Ed: Raul Davalos. Pro Des: Jean-Philippe Carp. M: Steve Soles; numbers performed by Ned Albright, James Belushi, Booker T and the MGs, Louis Prima, etc. Costumes: Beverly Klein. (Savoy Pictures–Entertainment.) Rel: 23 June 1995. 110 mins. Cert 15.

Depp charge: Will the real Johnny Depp stand up? Don Juan De Marco *(from Entertainment)*

Disclosure

After being haunted by Glenn Close in *Fatal Attraction* and baited by Sharon Stone in *Basic Instinct*, Michael Douglas, Hollywood's favourite vulnerable Everyman, is now on the receiving end of Demi Moore's manipulative scalpel. Tom Sanders, husband, father of two and computer executive, is expecting a major promotion when he's passed over by Meredith Johnson, a former girlfriend. Invited to her office to discuss an imminent merger, Sanders finds himself on the receiving end of an aggressive seduction. Charging his new boss with sexual harrassment, Sanders suddenly realises that his self-respect, his marriage and even his job are under threat. Based on Michael Crichton's scorching bestseller, *Disclosure* is a genuine page-turner of a movie. Exploring the complex issue of contemporary sexual politics, the film works as both a provocative human drama and as a suspenseful techno-thriller. Ferociously entertaining.

Cast: Michael Douglas (Tom Sanders), Demi Moore (Meredith Johnson), Donald Sutherland (Bob Garvin), Caroline Goodall (Susan Hendler), Roma Maffia (Catherine Alvarez), Dylan Baker (Philip Blackburn), Rosemary Forsyth (Stephanie Kaplan), Dennis Miller (Marc Lewyn), Suzie Plakson, Nicholas Sadler, Jacqueline Kim, Joe Urla, Michael Chieffo, Joe Attanasio, Faryn Einhorn, Allan Rich.

Dir: Barry Levinson. Pro: Levinson and Michael Crichton. Ex Pro: Peter Giuliano. Screenplay: Paul Attanasio. Ph: Tony Pierce-Roberts. Ed: Stu Linder. Pro Des: Neil Spisak. M: Ennio Morricone. Costumes: Gloria Gresham. (Baltimore Pictures/Constant–Warner.) Rel: 10 March 1995. 128 mins. Cert 18.

Don Juan De Marco

The Nijinsky of lovers and the Shakespeare of pillow talk, a young man from Queens, New York, thinks that he is the legendary Don Juan. Of course, nobody believes him for an instant – except, maybe, for the 1,503 women left panting in his wake. So it's up to renowned psychiatrist Dr Jack Mickler to convince the lad that he's just another bum – while Jack's own sex life benefits wildly from his consultations. Thanks to the charisma of its stars – and a neat premise borrowed from *Miracle on 34th Street* – *Don Juan De Marco* is an enjoyable piece of whimsy that only runs out of breath when it juggles its options once too often.

Cast: Marlon Brando (Dr Jack Mickler), Johnny Depp (Don Juan De Marco), Faye Dunaway (Marilyn Mickler), Rachel Ticotin (Dona Inez), Bob Dishy (Dr Paul Showalter), Geraldine Pailhas (Dona Ana), Talisa Soto (Dona Julia), Marita Geraghty, Richard Sarafian, Tresa Hughes, Stephen Singer, Franc Luz, Carmen Argenziano, Jo Champa, Esther Scott, Nada Despotovich, Gilbert Lewis, 'Tiny' Lister Jr, Tom Mardirosian, Al Corley, Sanjay.

Dir and Screenplay: Jeremy Leven. Pro: Francis Ford Coppola, Fred Fuchs and Patrick Palmer. Ex Pro: Ruth Vitale and Michael De Luca. Co-Ex Pro: Robert Newmyer, Brian Reilly and Jeffrey Silver. Ph: Ralf Bode. Ed: Tony Gibbs. Pro Des: Sharon Seymour. M: Michael Kamen;

numbers performed by Selena and David Byrne. Costumes: Kirsten Everberg. (New Line/American Zoetrope–Entertainment.) Rel: 19 May 1995. 97 mins. Cert 15.

Dream Lover

Shamefully simple-minded drama about a rich young architect who falls for a woman he knows little about. Normally, the trick would be to get us to believe in the characters. Not so here. Still, Larry Miller is a hoot in a supporting role. Not to be confused with the 1986 Alan J. Pakula thriller of the same name.

Cast: James Spader (Ray Reardon), Madchen Amick (Lena Mathers), Bess Armstrong (Elaine), Fredrick Lehne (Larry), Larry Miller (Norman), Kathleen York (Martha), Scott Coffey (Billy), Kate Williamson, Tom Lillard, William Shockley, Irwin Keyes, Alexander Folk, Janel Moloney, Shawne Rowe, Clyde Kusatsu, Lucy Butler, Harriet Leider, Paul Ben Victor.

Dir and Screenplay: Nicholas Kazan. Pro: Sigurjon Sighvatsson, Wallis Nicita and Lauren Lloyd. Ex Pro: Steve Golin and Edward R. Pressman. Ph: Jean Yves Escoffier. Ed: Susan Crutcher and Jill Savitt. Pro Des: Richard Hoover. M: Christopher Young; numbers performed by Kathy Fisher, Kevin Welch and JAH Messengers. Costumes: Barbara Tfank. (PolyGram/Propaganda Films–Rank.) Rel: 11 November 1994. 103 mins. Cert 18.

Drop Zone

Adrenaline-fuelled action movie in which Wesley Snipes plays a US marshall who adopts a parachute to uncover a ruthless gang of sky-diving killers. When his charge, a notorious computer hacker, disappears on a 747 flight,

The woman who isn't: James Spader confronts his wife (Madchen Amick) in Nicholas Kazan's humdrum Dream Lover *(from Rank)*

Snipes jumps into action – even though his badge and gun are confiscated. While the formula is pretty familiar, the sky-diving stunts are spectacular and director John Badham (*Stakeout*, *Blue Thunder*) keeps things moving at a cracking pace. Good turns, too, from Yancy Butler (*Hard Target*) as a gutsy heroine and Gary Busey as a despicable villain.

Cast: Wesley Snipes (Pete Nessip), Gary Busey (Ty Moncrief), Yancy Butler (Jessie Crossman), Michael Jeter (Earl Leedy), Corin Nemec (Selkirk), Kyle Secor (Swoop), Grace Zabriskie (Winona), Andy Romano (Tom McCracken), Luca Bercovici, Malcolm-Jamal Warner, Rex Linn, Robert LaSardo, Sam Hennings, Claire Stansfield, Mickey Jones, Melanie Mayron, Kimberly A. Scott.

Dir and Ex Pro: John Badham. Pro: D.J. Caruso, Wallis Nicita and Lauren Lloyd. Co-Pro: Doug Claybourne. Screenplay: Peter Barsocchini and John Bishop, from a story by Barsocchini, Tony Griffin and Guy Manos. Ph: Roy H. Wagner. Ed: Frank Morriss. Pro Des: Joe Alves. M: Hans Zimmer; numbers performed by Randelle Stainback, Boz Scaggs, INXS, etc. Costumes: Mary E. Vogt. (Paramount/Nicita/Lloyd–UIP.) Rel: 24 March 1995. 102 mins. Cert 15.

Dumb and Dumber

Very, very silly (and frequently derivative) comedy in which two morons fumble from Rhode Island to Aspen,

Idiots' delight: Jim Carrey and Jeff Daniels find the joke in Peter Farrelly's phenomenally successful Dumb and Dumber *(from First Independent)*

A taste of love: Sihung Lung (with spoon) dishes out the goods in Ang Lee's sublime Eat Drink Man Woman *(from Buena Vista)*

enough gags into the stew you're bound to hit a number of home runs) *Dumb and Dumber* does, occasionally, take one by surprise. There are also plenty of amusing touches not built around the film's stars, although Jim Carrey's facial athleticism carries the movie into a realm of its own.

Cast: Jim Carrey (Lloyd Christmas), Jeff Daniels (Harry Dunne), Lauren Holly (Mary Swanson), Karen Duffy (J.P. Shay), Victoria Rowell (Beth Jordan), Mike Starr (Joe Mentalino), Charles Rockett (Nicholas Andre), Teri Garr (Helen Swanson), Joe Baker, Hank Brandt, Brady Bluhm, Cam Neely, Felton Perry, Brad Lockerman, Connie Sawyer, Lin Shaye, Harland Williams, Fred Stoller.

Dir: Peter Farrelly. Pro: Charles B. Wessler, Brad Krevoy and Steve Stabler. Co-Pro: Bobby Farrelly, Tracie Graham-Rice and Bradley Thomas. Ex Pro: Gerald T. Olson and Aaron Meyerson. Assoc Pro: Bradley Jenkel, Chad Oman and Ellen Dumouchel. Screenplay: Peter Farrelly, Bennett Yellin and Bobby Farrelly. Ph: Mark Irwin. Ed: Christopher Greenbury. Pro Des: Sidney J. Bartholomew Jr. M: Todd Rundgren; numbers performed by Crash Test Dummies, Apache Indian, Nick Cave and the Bad Seeds, The Proclaimers, Ray Colcord, Tom Wolfe, Echobelly, Jim Carrey and Jeff Daniels ('Mockingbird'), Green Jelly, The Butthole Surfers, The Primitives, Gigolo Aunts, Deee-lite, Roy Orbison, Caleb Guillotte and Dead Eye Dick, Pete Droge, Todd Rundgren, etc. Costumes: Mary Zophres. (New Line Cinema/Motion Picture Corp–First Independent.) Rel: 7 April 1995. 102 mins. Cert 12.

Colorado, in order to return an attaché case to its rightful owner. Along the way they foil a gang of rednecks, a pair of unlikely assassins-for-hire and overcome other impossible odds. Relying on the formula of *Airplane!* and *The Naked Gun* (in which by throwing

Eat Drink Man Woman

Unable to articulate his feelings, Mr Chu, the greatest living chef of Taipei, Taiwan, lavishes all his love on the fabulous meals he prepares for his three grown-up daughters every Sunday. But fine cuisine, like so many traditions of the Orient, has almost become a thing of the past and Mr Chu's edible gifts of affection are looked on as something to be endured, a duty. Indeed, Chu's daughters are too wrapped up in their own careers and romantic aspirations to see their father for who he is ... Director and co-writer Ang Lee describes this as the last in his 'father knows best' trilogy (following *Pushing Hands* and *The Wedding Banquet*), noting that 'if it is sex which haunts the film, it is food which preoccupies it'. Truly, food has seldom played such an important role in a film and its preparation is a joy to behold. But even without the culinary metaphors, *Eat Drink Man Woman* is an exquisite comedy-drama, a veritable feast for the eyes, heart and stomach.

Cast: Sihung Lung (Mr Chu), Kuei-Mei Yang (Jia Jen), Chien-Lien Wu (Jia Chien), Yu-Wen Wang (Jia Ning), Winston Chao (Li Kai), Ah-Lea Gua (Mrs Liang), Sylvia Chang (Jin-Rong), Chao-Jung Chen, Lester Chen, Yu Chen, Chin-Cheng Lu, Man-Sheng Tu.
   Dir: Ang Lee. Pro: Li-Kong Hsu. Assoc Pro: Ted Hope and James Schamus. Screenplay: Lee, Schamus and Hui-Ling Wang. Ph: Jong Lin. Ed: Tim Squyres. Art: Fu-Hsiung Lee. M: Mader. (Central Motion Picture/ Good Machine–Buena Vista.) Rel: 13 January 1995. 123 mins. Cert PG.

Ed Wood

It's pathetic, really. A man totally devoid of talent or insight is so obsessed by movies that he turns his life upside-down to become a filmmaker. Freely acknowledged as the worst director of all time, Edward D. Wood Jr has become a posthumous cult figure thanks to such abominable works as *Glen or Glenda* and *Plan 9 From Outer Space*. Johnny Depp, in a one-note performance, plays the young Wood with a pasted-on grin, failing to come to grips with a man content to throw films together while wearing women's underwear. Tim Burton is a decidedly more skilful director than his subject, but no amount of artful lighting (in black and white) and sly in-jokes can elevate such dispiriting material. John Waters would have given it a far more irreverent, enjoyable spin. Besides, the theme of shoestring movie production has been done to death.

Cast: Johnny Depp (Edward D. Wood Jr), Martin Landau (Bela Lugosi), Sarah Jessica Parker (Dolores Fuller), Patricia Arquette (Kathy O'Hara), Jeffrey Jones (Criswell), Bill Murray (Bunny Breckinridge), G.D. Spradlin (Reverend Lemon), Vincent D'Onofrio (Orson Welles), Mike Starr (Georgie Weiss), Lisa Marie (Vampira), Max Casella, Brent Hinkley, Juliet Landau, Clive Rosengren, Norman Alden, Leonard Termo, Ned Bellamy, Danny Dayton, Bill Cusack, Biff Yeager, Stanley Desantis, Don Hood, Gregory Walcott, Rance Howard, Vasek C. Simek.
   Dir: Tim Burton. Pro: Burton and Denisze Di Novi. Ex Pro: Michael Lehmann. Co-Pro: Michael Flynn. Screenplay: Scott Alexander and Larry Karaszew-

ski. Ph: Stefan Czapsky. Ed: Chris Lebenzon. Pro Des: Tom Duffield. M: Howard Shore. Costumes: Colleen Atwood. (Touchstone Pictures–Buena Vista.) Rel: 26 May 1995. 127 mins. Cert 15.

8 Seconds

The film's title refers to the required amount of time a bull rider has to hang on to his steer in order to gain points. This is odd, as my sources reveal that the time is in fact *25* seconds. But then *8 Seconds* is a better title. However, nothing in this surprisingly neutered, straightforward look at the tough, bloody world of bull riding rings true. The 'real life' story of the legendary rodeo star Lane Frost – who died two years after becoming world champion – the film is at its most authentic when unreeling archive footage over the closing credits. [*Charles Bacon*]

Cast: Luke Perry (Lane Frost), Stephen Baldwin (Tuff Hedeman), Cynthia Geary (Kellie Frost), James Rebhorn (Clyde Frost), Carrie Snodgress (Elsie Frost), Red Mitchell (Cody Lambert), Ronnie Claire Edwards, Linden Ashby, Clyde Frost, Elsie Frost, Paul Alexander, George Michael, John Growney, Vince Gill.
   Dir: John G. Avildsen. Ex Pro: Michael Shamberg. Ex Pro: Cyd LeVin and Jeffrey Swab. Co-Pro: Tony Mark. Screenplay: Monte Merrick. Ph: Victor Hammer. Ed: J. Douglas Seelig. Pro Des: William J. Cassidy. M: Bill Conti; numbers performed by John Anderson, Pam Tillis, Vince Gill, Patty Smyth, Reba McEntire, Billy Dean, etc.

Dead wood: Martin Landau (left), *with Johnny Depp, in his Oscar-winning performance as Bela Lugosi, giving some distinction to Tim Burton's dreary* Ed Wood *(from Buena Vista)*

Costumes: Deena Appel. (New Line/ Jersey Films–First Independent.) Rel: 21 October 1994. 105 mins. Cert PG.

L'Enfer - Hell

South-west France; 1994. Paul cannot believe his luck when Nelly agrees to marry him. Beautiful, sexy, outgoing, caring, maternal and full of the joys of spring, Nelly is the perfect wife. Yet Paul cannot accept that she loves him as wholeheartedly as he loves her. How can she? Gradually, as the honeymoon years fade, Paul starts spying on his wife, inventing scenarios of adultery that are probably in his mind. Claude Chabrol, the French master of suspense, returns to the top of his form after the debacle of *Madame Bovary* three years ago. Here he activates exemplary performances from his two leads (Emmanuelle Beart has never been better) and skilfully establishes his emotional arena, demonstrating a frightening understanding of the bacteria that can eat away at even the most idealistic marriage. A deeply unsettling but always compelling drama, *L'Enfer* is almost too bitter a pill to swallow. P.S. The film was originally started in 1964 under the direction of Henri-Georges Clouzot

Sex, jealousy, obsession: ingredients that transform Chabrol into a master filmmaker. Francois Cluzet and Emmanuelle Beart play the game in L'Enfer *(from Mayfair Entertainment)*

(and was to star Romy Schneider and Serge Reggiani), but was abandoned when Clouzot suffered a heart attack.

Cast: Emmanuelle Beart (Nelly), Francois Cluzet (Paul), Andre Wilms (Dr Arnoux), Marc Lavoine (Martineau), Mario David (Duhamel), Sophie Artur (Clothilde), Nathalie Cardone, Christiane Minazzoli, Dora Doll, Jean-Pierre Cassel, Thomas Chabrol.
    Dir: Claude Chabrol. Pro: Marin Karmitz. Screenplay: Henri-Georges Clouzot. Ph: Bernard Zitzermann. Ed: Monique Fardoulis. Art: Emile Ghigo. M: Matthieu Chabrol. Costumes: Corinne Jory. (MKS Productions SA/CED Prods/Canal Plus–Mayfair Entertainment.) Rel: 21 October 1994. 100 mins. Cert 15.

Ermo

Northern China; 1994. Ermo is a proud, resolute Chinese peasant whose circumstances have forced her to take on the role of breadwinner. Besides needing to support her disabled husband and young son, Ermo's greatest ambition is to acquire the biggest TV set on sale in the nearest town. This would put her one social notch above her neighbour, the 'fat, slack-assed' piece of yellow trash who regularly hurls insults her way. So by working ungodly hours making noodles, weaving baskets and giving blood, Ermo slowly builds up her savings ... One of the most resonant, exquisitely realised and

enjoyable (and frequently very amusing) looks at contemporary Chinese life, Ermo is blessed by a wonderfully deadpan and spirited performance from Alia in the title role. From the day-to-day detail of ancient noodlemaking to the magnificent photography, *Ermo* is a sheer pleasure.

Cast: Alia (Ermo), Ge Zhijun ('Chief'), Liu Peigi (blind man), Zhang Haiyan (blind man's wife), Yan Zhenguo (Huzi, aka Tiger), Michael Nader (Dex Dexter).
    Dir: Zhou Xiaowen. Pro: Jimmy Tan and Chen Kunming. Screenplay: Lang Yun, from the novel by Xu Baoqi. Ph: Lu Gengxin. Ed: Zhong Furong. Pro Des: Zhang Daqian. M: Zhao Xiaowen. Sound: Hong Yi. (Ocean Film Co/Shanghai Film Studio–ICA Projects.) Rel: 23 June 1995. 98 mins. Cert 15.

Even Cowgirls Get the Blues

A southern lass born with outsize thumbs adapts her deformity to become the world's greatest hitchhiker. Occasionally stopping off in New York to pursue a successful modelling career, Sissy Hankshaw inadvertently becomes involved with a gang of feminist cowgirls who hijack a beauty ranch to enforce their cause ... Another splendid example of a film failing to be the book on which it is based. Indeed, Tom Robbins' cult, offbeat story has spent some twenty years scrambling to the screen, while the completed picture, after drastic re-editing, has taken another year to reach the cinemas. Unfortunately, this is one book you can't put down - but you can leave the cinema. P.S. Note the ominous cameo from William S. Burroughs, whose unfilmable *Naked Lunch* was brought spluttering to the screen in 1991.

Cast: Uma Thurman (Sissy Hankshaw), Lorraine Bracco (Dolores Del Ruby), Angie Dickinson (Miss Adrian), Noriyuki 'Pat' Morita (The Chink), Keanu Reeves (Julian Gitche), John Hurt (The Countess), Rain Phoenix (Bonanza Jellybean), Victoria Williams (Debbie), Sean Young, Crispin Glover, Ed Begley Jr, Carol Kane, Dee Fowler, Arlene Wewa, Heather Graham, Roseanne Arnold, Buck Henry, Alan Arnold, Ken Kesey, Grace Zabriskie, Udo Kier, William S. Burroughs, Edward James Olmos.
    Dir and Screenplay: Gus Van Sant Jr. Pro: Laurie Parker. Line Pro: Eric McLeod. Ph: John Campbell and Eric Alan Edwards. Ed: Curtiss Clayton. Pro Des: Missy Stewart. M: k.d. lang and Ben Mink; numbers performed

Sissy, spaced chick: Uma Thurman pulls her thumb out in Gus Van Sant Jr's disastrous Even Cowgirls Get the Blues *(from Rank)*

by k.d. lang, Victoria Williams, Herb Alpert and the Tijuana Brass, The Lovin' Spoonful, Nancy Sinatra and Lee Hazlewood, etc. Costumes: Beatrix Aruna Pasztor. (PolyGram/New Line Cinema/Fourth Vision–Rank.) Rel: 6 January 1995. 96 mins. Cert 15.

Eversmile New Jersey

Daniel Day-Lewis has a way with a phrase. In *The Unbearable Lightness of Being* he made a chant of, 'Take your clothes off, I'm a doctor.' In this oddity, a Yugoslav-Argentinian co-production about an Irishman from New Jersey, he repeatedly exclaims, 'But I am a dentist' or 'But you don't understand, I'm a dentist.' He plays Fergus O'Connell, a kind of wandering priest of dental hygiene, who travels through Patagonia spreading the word about bacteria. Such dental philosophy is set against endless, desolate landscapes and vast multi-coloured skies. Not a lot happens, but the film exudes a quirky charm that keeps one involved. Filmed in 1989.

Cast: Daniel Day-Lewis (Fergus O'Connell), Mirjana Jokovic (Estella), Gabriela Acher (Celeste), Julio De Grazia (Dr Ulises), Ignacio Quiros (the 'Boss'), Boy Olmi (radio announcer), Miguel Ligero, Alberto Benegas.
    Dir: Carlos Sorin. Pro: Oscar Kramer. Ex Pro: Julia Palau and Michael Ryan. Assoc Pro: Rolando Epstein. Screenplay: Sorin, Jorge Goldenberg and Roberto Sheuer. Ph: Esteban Courtalon. Ed: Bryan Oates. Art: Coca Oderigo and Maria Julia Bertotto.

M: Steve Levine. Costumes: Margarita Jusid. (J & M Entertainment/Los Films Del Camino–Columbia.) Rel: 8 July 1994. 91 mins. Cert PG.

Exotica

Toronto; 1994. Inspired by a visit from a government tax auditor in 1993, the Armenian Cairo-born Canadian-bred filmmaker Atom Egoyan (*Speaking Parts, The Adjuster*) embarked on his sixteenth screenplay. This, his most complex and fulfilling work to date, is constructed like a striptease, in which Egoyan seductively peels layer by layer off his narrative. At first everything is revealed as if under the cold, superficial gaze of a stranger. But gradually we are permitted to see beneath the skin of a handful of alienated characters whom, we learn, have very good reasons for doing the bizarre things that they do. Furthermore, the film's central venue, an up-market strip club called 'Exotica', underscores the film's message that first impressions are invariably misleading. FYI: Egoyan's wife, Arsinee Khanjian, who plays the club's pregnant manageress, gave birth to the couple's first child shortly after filming.

Cast: Bruce Greenwood (Francis Brown), Mia Kirshner (Christina), Don McKellar (Thomas), Arsinee Khanjian (Zoe), Elias Koteas (Eric), Sarah Polley (Tracey), Victor Garber (Harold), David Hemblen, Calvin Green, Peter Krantz, Damon d'Oliveira, Billy Merasty, Maury Chaykin.

Dir and Screenplay: Atom Egoyan. Pro: Egoyan and Camelia Frieberg. Ph: Paul Sarossy. Ed: Susan Shipton. Pro Des: Linda Del Rosario and Richard Paris. M: Mychael Danna; 'Everybody Knows' performed by Leonard Cohen. Costumes: Linda Muir. (Ego Film Arts/Alliance Communication/Telefilm Canada–Artificial Eye.) Rel: 28 April 1995. 104 mins. Cert 18.

Faraway, So Close - In Weiter Ferne, So Nah!

Berlin; 1993. Continuing his exploration of the image as represented by cinema, Wim Wenders has produced another original that starts out as a sequel to his 1987 triumph *Wings of Desire* and then bolts off into a number of directions. Cassiel, the angel of the first film who can see and love all, loses his wings when he impulsively interferes with humanity by saving the life of a young girl. Now reduced to mortality, Cassiel is overcome by the smells, light

Skin deep: Nothing is what it seems in Atom Egoyan's seductive look at contemporary alienation in Exotica *(from Artificial Eye)*

and touch of human experience, but soon falls victim to its pressures. Sleeping rough, taking to schnapps and eventually indulging in a spot of crime, Cassiel must redeem himself and draws on his vast experience of those around him to do so. Part thriller, part comedy and part parable, *Faraway, So Close* constantly surprises even when it seems utterly lost in its own back yard. Ultimately, it serves as a warning encapsulated by Cassiel's statement that human eyes 'can no longer give'. Wenders himself observes that looking 'should be an active process between the world and yourself'. A worthy sentiment, perhaps, but Wenders' vision is often too personal and undisciplined to be comprehended by mere mortals. *Faraway, So Close* is certainly not for all tastes, but does offer plenty of crumbs to savour.

Cast: Otto Sander (Cassiel), Peter Falk (Peter Falk), Horst Buchholz (Tony Baker), Nastassja Kinski (Raphaela), Heinz Ruhmann (Konrad), Bruno Ganz (Damiel), Solveig Dommartin (Marion), Rudiger

Another lost and hound story: Jesse Bradford struggles through the wilderness in Far From Home: The Adventures of Yellow Dog *(from Fox)*

Vogler (Phillip Winter), Willem Dafoe (Emit Flesti), Lou Reed (Lou Reed), Mikhail Gorbachev (Mikhail Gorbachev), Marijam Agischewa, Henri Alekan, Tom Farell, Hanns Zischler.

Dir and Pro: Wim Wenders. Ex Pro: Ulrich Felsberg. Line Pro: Michael Schwarz. Screenplay: Wenders and Richard Reitinger. Ph: Jurgen Jurges. Ed: Peter Przygodda. Pro Des: Albrech Konrad. M: Laurent Petitgand; numbers performed by Nick Cave, U2, Lou Reed, Johnny Cash, Jane Siberry, The House of Love, Laurie Anderson, etc. Costumes: Esther Walz. Sound: Gunther Kortwich. (Road Movies/Tobis Filmkunst–Columbia TriStar.) Rel: 1 July 1994. 144 mins. Cert 15.

Far From Home: The Adventures of Yellow Dog

While treading decidedly familiar territory, this family drama filmed in the rugged terrain of British Columbia is so mercifully free of sentimentality that one cannot help but applaud it. The excellent Jesse Bradford (*King of the Hill*) plays Angus McCormick, a resourceful fourteen year old who befriends a highly intelligent Golden Labrador. When boy and dog are lost at sea, old Yellow takes the initiative and leads the way ... Whereas the performances, direction and photography are all top-notch, John Scott's gushing score seems to be working against the grain. Also, the physical rapport between Angus and Yellow does seem surprisingly undernourished.

Cast: Mimi Rogers (Katherine McCormick), Bruce Davison (John McCormick), Jesse Bradford (Angus McCormick), Tom Bower (John Gale), Joel Palmer (Silas McCormick), Dakotah (Yellow Dog), Margot Finley (Sara), Josh Wannamaker, Matt Bennett.

Dir and Screenplay: Phillip Borsos. Pro: Peter O'Brian. Ph: James Gardner. Ed: Sidney Wolinsky. Pro Des: Mark S. Freeborn. M: John Scott. Costumes: Antonia Bardon. (Fox.) Rel: 7 April 1995. 80 mins. Cert U.

Faust

Jan Svankmajer's second feature is as ambitious and imaginative as the Czech filmmaker's earlier work would lead one to expect. Here he relocates elements of the Faust legend to contemporary Prague while injecting Kafkaesque tones. Unfortunately, the use of Andrew Sachs to speak the words in this English version disrupts the atmosphere and, in any case, the film becomes too complex for its own good. But at its best *Faust* confirms an extraordinary talent, with actors and puppet figures brought together with aplomb. Newcomers would do better with *Alice* or Svankmajer's shorts but, despite being very demanding, *Faust* is powerful. [*Mansel Stimpson*]

Cast: Petr Cepek (Faust).

Dir and Screenplay: Jan Svankmajer. Pro: Jaromir Kallista. Ex Pro: Karl Baumgartner,

The rappers from hell: Mark Christopher Lawrence, Rusty Cundieff and Larry B. Scott don headgear in Cundieff's rough and ready Fear of a Black Hat *(from Metro Tartan)*

Keith Griffiths, Michael Havas and Hengameh Panahi. BBC Ex Pro: Colin Rose. Ph: Svatopluk Maly. Ed: Marie Zemanova. Pro Des: Svankmajer and Eva Svankmajerova. M: Johann Sebastian Bach and Charles Gounod. Costumes: Ruzena Blahova. Animation: Bedrich Glaser. Choreography: Daria Vobornikova. (Heart of Europe/Lumen Films/Athenor/BBC Bristol/Koninck/Pandora Film–ICA.) Rel: 23 September 1994. 95 mins. Cert PG.

Fear of a Black Hat

Inspired by Rob Reiner's *This is Spinal Tap*, writer-director-star Rusty Cundieff has fashioned his own 'mockumentary' targeting the rap industry. Here, a female sociology student records the lifestyle and professional fluctuation of a group called NWH (Niggaz With Hats), a band that disguises misogyny as political statement. While small sections of the film are truly hilarious (Tone-Def's lyrically scatological video 'I'm Just A Human' is a classic), Cundieff's broad approach misses the whole point of Reiner's film. The reason *Spinal Tap* was so funny was because Reiner made it like a straight documentary. There is no mistaking that *Black Hat* is anything but farcical parody which, considering the excesses of the rap world, is all a bit much.

Cast: Larry B. Scott (Tasty-Taste), Mark Christopher Lawrence (Tone-Def), Kasi Lemmons (Nina Blackburn), Rusty Cundieff (Ice Cold), Howie Gold (Guy Friesch), Barry Heins (Marty Rabinow), Rosemarie Jackson (Cheryl C.), Kurt Loder (himself), Devin Kamienny (Vanilla Sherbet), Lamont Johnson (MC Slammer), Eric Laneuville (Jike Spingleton), Faizon, Deezer D, Moon Jones, G. Smokey Campbell, Bob Mardis, Doug Starks, Daryl Savid.
Dir and Screenplay: Rusty Cundieff. Pro: Darin Scott. Ex Pro: Wm Christopher Gorog. Ph: John Demps Jr. Ed: Karen Horn. Pro Des: Stuart Blatt. M: numbers performed by N.W.H. Costumes: Rita McGhee. (Oakwood Films/ITC Entertainment–Metro Tartan.) Rel: 28 October 1994. 88 mins. Cert 15.

A Feast at Midnight

Modestly budgeted, modestly engaging English comedy set in an all-boys boarding school in which the New Age school dinners (semi-skimmed feta cheese, tofu lasagna) drive the inmates crazy. Enter ten-year-old Magnus Gove, a burgeoning gourmet who forms the clandestine Scoffers Club to serve up illicit helpings of *mousses aux chocolat* and *crème brûlées*. A slim idea, fattened up with accomplished playing from a largely enthusiastic young cast. [*Ewen Brownrigg*]

Cast: Christopher Lee (Major Victor E. Longfellow aka VELociRaptor), Robert Hardy (headmaster), Freddie Findlay (Magnus Gove), Aled Roberts (Goof), Andrew Lusher (Tava), Samuel West (chef), Carol Macready (Miss Plunder), Lisa Faulkner (Miss Charlotte), Edward Fox (Mr Gove), Stuart Hawley, Julie Dreyfus, Brian Cant.
Dir: Justin Hardy. Pro: Yoshi Nishio. Ex Pro: Jonathan Green and Alok Oberoi. Line Pro: Jonathan Hercock. Screenplay: Hardy and Nishio. Ph: Tim Maurice-Jones. Ed: Michael Johns. Pro Des: Christiane Ewing. M: David A. Hughes and John Murphy. Costumes: Verity Hawkes. (Kwai River Entertainment.) Rel: 26 May 1995. 106 mins. Cert PG.

Final Combination

Los Angeles; 1992. Routine crime thriller with Michael Madsen as an asthmatic LA cop with women trouble. When a phone sex fanatic starts knocking off beautiful women all over the west coast, Madsen teams up with a comely reporter (Lisa Bonet) to pool information. Unfortunately, their combined efforts cannot match what we – the audience – had correctly guessed two reels back. Previously known as *Lights Out*.

Cast: Michael Madsen (Matt Dickson), Lisa Bonet (Catherine Briggs), Gary Stretch (Richard Welton), Tim Russ (Det. Chuck Rowland), Damian Chapa (Donato), Carmen Argenziano (Lt Stein), Clarence Landry (Ike 'Point Man' Pointer), Susan Byun, Alan Toy, Shawn Huff, Connie Blankenship, Jimmy Ortega, Parker Posey, Sushil Tyagi, Thunderwolf, 2 Die 4.
Dir: Nigel Dick. Pro: Joni Sighvatsson, Steve Golin and Gregg Fienberg. Ex Pro: Gary Milkis. Screenplay: Larry Golin, from a story by Jonathan Tydor. Ph: David Bridges. Ed: Henry Richardson and Jonathan Shaw. Pro Des: Jon Gary Steele. M: Rolfe Kent; numbers performed by 2 Die 4, The Transatlantic Rhythm Kings, etc. Costumes: Alexandra Welker. (PolyGram/Propaganda Films–Rank.) Rel: 18 November 1994. 93 mins. Cert 18.

Fiorile

This is a beautifully told but ultimately unwieldy film chronicling the curse afflicting an Italian family over two

Mr Blond: Michael Madsen as a good guy for once in Nigel Dick's pedestrian Final Combination *(from Rank)*

centuries. Starting promisingly, *Fiorile* deftly creates a sense of atmosphere as a car drives through the night. On the way to visit his father, Luigi Benedetti regales his young son and daughter with the family legend, and so the film glides into the past with the minimum of fuss. But, following the first chapter – in which a peasant girl falls in love with a Napoleonic soldier – the film loses its grip. Frankly, the Taviani brothers, who directed *Padre Padrone* and *The Night of San Lorenzo*, are at their best when sticking to a single time frame.

Cast: Claudio Bigagli (Corrado/Alessandro Benedetti), Galatea Ranzi (Elisabetta/ Elisa Benedetti), Michael Vartan (Jean/ Massimo Benedetti), Lino Capolicchio (Luigi Benedetti), Giovanni Guidelli (Elio), Chiara Caselli (Chiara), Renato Carpentieri (Massimo Benedetti as an old man), Constanze Engelbrecht, Athina Cenci, Norma Martelli, Pier Paolo Capponi, Carlo Luca de Ruggieri, Laurent Schilling, Fritz Mueller Scherz, Laura Scarimbolo, Elisa Giani, Ciro Esposito, Giovanni Cassinelli.
Dir: Paolo and Vittorio Taviani. Pro: Grazia Volpi. Ex Pro: Jean Claude Cecile, Luggi Waldleitner and Karl Spiehs. Screenplay: Sandro Petraglia and the Tavianis. Ph: Giuseppe Lanci. Ed: Roberto Perpignani. Art: Gianni Sbarra. M: Nicola Piovani. Costumes: Lina Nerli Taviani. (Filmtre-Gierre Film/Pentafilm/Florida Movies/La Sept/Cinema/Canal Plus/Roxy Film/K.S.–Film-Arrow.) Rel: 31 March 1995. 118 mins. Cert 12.

Facing the flesh: Meg Ryan takes control in Steve Kloves' atmospheric Flesh and Bone *(from UIP)*

Flesh and Bone

Deep in the heart of contemporary Texas a vending machine salesman holds a secret that distances him from the rest of the world. But when he inadvertently becomes the chauffeur of a young woman in the throes of divorce, he finds his secret filtering to the surface. A grim, slow-moving character

Yabba-yabba doomed: Halle Berry (as Miss Stone, replacing Sharon Stone) and John Goodman (as Fred Flintstone, replacing James Belushi) in Brian Levant's heavy-handed, plastic-age mammoth hit, The Flintstones *(from UIP)*

study, *Flesh and Bone* creates a fascinating evocation of West Texas today, and is fleshed out with some peerless performances. Only Dennis Quaid, in a dramatic change of gear from his recent comedic turns, is occasionally caught acting (unknot those brows Dennis!).

Cast: Dennis Quaid (Arlis Sweeney), Meg Ryan (Kay Davies), James Caan (Roy Sweeney), Gwyneth Paltrow (Ginnie), Scott Wilson (Elliot), Christopher Rydell (Reese Davies), Julia Mueller, Ron Kuhlman, Barbara Alyn Woods, Betsy Brantley.

Dir and Screenplay: Steve Kloves. Pro: Mark Rosenberg and Paula Weinstein. Ex Pro: Sydney Pollack. Co-Pro: G. Mac Brown. Ph: Philippe Rousselot. Ed: Mia Goldman. Pro Des: Jon Hutman. M: Thomas Newman. Costumes: Elizabeth McBride. (Paramount/Mirage/Spring

Creek–UIP.) Rel: 11 November 1994. 126 mins. Cert 15.

The Flintstones

Years in gestation and nourished by 32 different writers, Steven Spielberg's $45m live-action homage to the 1960 - 66 TV series – featuring America's favourite 'modern Stone Age family' – arrives with a thump. Backed by a $100m marketing campaign and distinguished by Industrial Light & Magic special effects and Jim Henson's Creature Shop dinosaurs, the film is a visual disappointment. Self-described as 'a comedy on steroids', the film's humour consists of a whirlwind of sight gags, limp puns and affectionate references to the original sitcom. Wit there is none. A case of too many chefs trying to prove themselves.

Cast: John Goodman (Fred Flintstone), Rick Moranis (Barney Rubble), Elizabeth Perkins (Wilma Flintstone), Rosie O'Donnell (Betty Rubble), Kyle MacLachlan (Cliff Vandercave), Halle Berry (Miss Sharon Stone), Elizabeth Taylor (Pearl Slaghoople), Dann Florek (Mr Slate), Harvey Korman (voice of Dictabird), Hlynur and Marino Sigurdsson (Bamm-Bamm), Kate Pierson, Fred Schneider and Keith Strickland (the BC-52s), Richard Moll, Irwin '88' Keyes, Jonathan Winters, Elaine and Melanie Silver, Sheryl Lee Ralph, Jack O'Halloran, Laraine Newman, Jay Leno, Alan Blumenfeld, Sam Raimi, Dean Cundey, Joe Barbera, Bill Hanna.

Dir: Brian Levant. Pro: Bruce Cohen. Ex Pro: William Hanna, Joseph Barbera, Kathleen Kennedy, David Kirschner, Gerald R. Molen and (uncredited) Steven Spielberg. Co-Pro: Colin Wilson. Screenplay: Tom S. Parker, Jim Jennewein, Steven E. de Souza and (uncredited) Michael Wilson (plus another 28 uncredited writers), based on the animated series by Hanna-Barbera Productions, Inc. Ph: Dean Cundey. Ed: Kent Beyda. Pro Des: William Sandell. M: David Newman; numbers performed by The B-52s, Big Audio Dynamite, Was Not Was, Shakespear's Sister, Us 3, Green Jelly, etc. Costumes: Rosanna Norton. (Hanna-Barbera/Amblin/Universal–UIP.) Rel: 22 July 1994. 92 mins. Cert U.

Forrest Gump

For a guy with an IQ of 75, Forrest Gump hasn't done too badly. He may be slow, but his combination of sincerity, tenacity and adherence to do what he's told has forged him into one of the most feted and successful Americans of

the latter part of the twentieth century. But all Gump really wants is the love of one woman ... Tom Hanks is Forrest Gump and therein lies the film's dilemma. Hanks, with such a well-known body of work behind him, will always be Tom Hanks giving a performance, however good. Yet the actor also has the capacity to make us cry and laugh – within minutes. Yet *Forrest Gump* tries too hard at times to stir our emotions, which its inherently episodic nature doesn't help. Still, the visual gags, historical references and special effects make this a unique, irresistible ride.

Cast: Tom Hanks (Forrest Gump), Robin Wright (Jenny Curran), Gary Sinise (Lt Dan Taylor), Mykelti Williamson (Benjamin 'Bubba' Buford Blue), Sally Field (Mrs Gump), Michael Conner Humphreys (young Forrest), Richard D'Alessandro (Abbie Hoffman), Hanna R. Hall, Rebecca Williams, Harold Herthum, Peter Dobson, Alexander Zemeckis, Elizabeth Hanks, Afemo Omilami, Michael Burgess, Bill Roberson, Geoffrey Blake, Dick Cavett, Jim Hanks.
  Dir: Robert Zemeckis. Pro: Wendy Finerman, Steve Tisch and Steve Starkey. Co-Pro: Charles Newirth. Screenplay: Eric Roth, from the novel by Winston Groom. Ph: Don Burgess. Ed: Arthur Schmidt. Pro

Des: Rick Carter. M: Alan Silvestri; numbers performed by Elvis Presley, Duane Eddy, Wilson Pickett, Joan Baez, Creedence Clearwater Revival, The Four Tops, Aretha Franklin, Bob Dylan, The Beach Boys, The Mamas and the Papas, The Doors, Simon & Garfunkel, Jefferson Airplane, Scott McKenzie, The Byrds, The Fifth Dimension, Harry Nilsson, Three Dog Night, The Supremes, BJ Thomas, Randy Newman, Lynyrd Skynyrd, The Doobie Brothers, Gladys Knight & the Pips, Willie Nelson, Bob Seger, etc. Costumes: Joanna Johnston. (Paramount–UIP.) Rel: 7 October 1994. 142 mins. Cert 12.

Fortress

Like the penal colony in *No Escape* the fortress of the title is a maximum security, privately-owned, state-of-the-art prison run for profit. And, like Ray Liotta in the former, Christopher Lambert plays an erstwhile soldier whose conscience has bucked the system. In fact, Lambert – aka John Brennick (a good genre name, that) – is allegedly the most highly-decorated captain in the entire history of the 'black beret' brigade. But when he and his wife (Heather Locklear lookalike Loryn Locklin) decide to have a second baby,

Life is like a box of chocolates: Rebecca Williams and Tom Hanks in Robert Zemeckis's phenomenally successful Forrest Gump *(from UIP)*

they are thrown into jail. Of course, nobody has ever escaped from the fortress, but Lambert – like Liotta – cannot take no for an answer. OK, so *Fortress* isn't exactly the most original movie of the year (although it was made before *No Escape*), but it does boast some novel forms of cruelty. Like the penance in which inmates are forced to stand for hours within a narrow cage composed of laser beams. Thus, should they sway one inch they could lose a shoulder. It's such invention that keeps the film interesting, and there's enough suspense and gore to keep action fans very happy indeed.

Cast: Christopher Lambert (John Brennick), Kurtwood Smith (Poe), Loryn Locklin (Karen Brennick), Lincoln Kilpatrick (Abraham), Clifton Gonzalez Gonzalez (Nino), Jeffrey Combs (D-Day), Tom Towles (Stiggs), Vernon Wells, Denni Gordon, Heidi Stein.
  Dir: Stuart Gordon. Pro: John Davis and John Flock. Ex Pro: Graham Burke and Greg

Coote. Line Pro: Irene Dobson. Screenplay: Steve Feinberg, Troy Neighbors and Terry Curtis Fox. Ph: David Eggby. Ed: Timothy Wellburn. Pro Des: David Copping. M: Frederic Talgron. Costumes: Terry Ryan. (Village Roadshow/Davis Entertainment–Columbia TriStar.) Rel: 8 July 1994. 100 mins. Cert 15.

Fresh

The victim of a broken home, 'Fresh' is a twelve-year-old drug courier who lives in a small Brooklyn apartment with his eleven cousins and sundry relatives. Not allowed to see his vagrant father (Samuel L. Jackson), he snatches clandestine meetings with him in Washington Square where they play speed chess together. It is here that the boy learns the rules of life: to sacrifice his precious pieces to snatch the opponent's king. Thus Fresh sets an elaborate plan into action, using his closest friend and junkie sister to trap the neighbourhood's top drug barons. Executed with enormous style by first-time director Boaz Yakin, *Fresh* never flaunts its filmmaking prowess, letting the unblinking stare of its young protagonist dictate our emotions. A poetic, sensitive and profoundly disturbing film. A Franco-American co-production.

Cast: Sean Nelson (Michael 'Fresh'), Giancarlo Esposito (Esteban), N'Bushe Wright (Nichole), Samuel L. Jackson (Sam), Ron Brice (Corky), Jean LaMarre (Jake), Luis Lantigua (Chuckie), Cheryl Freeman (Aunt Frances), Natima Bradley (Rosie), Joe Zuniga, Yul Vasquez, Anthony Thomas, Anthony Ruiz.
Dir and Screenplay: Boaz Yakin. Pro: Lawrence Bender and Randy Ostrow. Co-Pro: Chrisann Verges. Ex Pro: Lila Cazes. Ph: Adam Holender. Ed: Dorian Harris. Pro Des: Dan Leigh. M: Stewart Copeland; numbers performed by Johnny Gill. Costumes: Ellen Lutter. (Lumière–Entertainment.) Rel: 12 May 1995. 113 mins. Cert 18.

Friday

Another dip into Afro-American stoop culture (sitting in doorways and talking), *Friday* is a vanity project from the angry Ice Cube who not only stars but also co-wrote the thing (with DJ Pooh) and produced it. A 'comic' day in the life of LA folk, the film proves to be mildly engaging while effecting some social commentary, revealing that, in spite of the overkill of drugs, guns and corruption, there is a desire to 'increase the peace'. Not subtle. [*Ewen Brownrigg*]

Cast: Ice Cube (Craig Jones), Chris Tucker (Smokey), Nia Long (Debbie), Tiny 'Zeus' Lister Jr (Deebo), Anna Maria Horsford (Mrs Jones), Regina King (Dana), Bernie Mac (Pastor Cleaver), John Witherspoon (Mr Jones), Angela Means (Felicia), Paula Jai Parker, Faizon Love, DJ Pooh, Vickilyn Reynolds, Anthony Johnson, Reynaldo Rey.
Dir: F. Gary Gray. Pro: Patricia Charbonnet. Ex Pro: Ice Cube and Bryan Turner. Co-Ex Pro: Helena Echegoyen. Screenplay: Ice Cube and DJ Pooh. Ph: Gerry Lively. Ed: John Carter. Pro Des: Bruce Bellamy. M: Hidden Faces; numbers performed by The Isley Brothers, Curtis Mayfield, The Temptations, James Brown, 2 Live Crew, Cypress Hill, Gladys Knight and the Pips, Rose Royce, War, Dr Dre, Rick James, Ice Cube, etc. Costumes: Shawn Barton. (New Line/Priority Films–Enter-tainment.) Rel: 30 June 1995. 97 mins. Cert 15.

La Frontera

Considering that first-time director Ricardo Larrain's film is about political exile in Pinochet's Chile, it is a surprisingly upbeat diversion. A morose maths teacher is 'relocated' to a remote village in southern Chile where he is left to ponder his fate. Then, gradually, his interaction with the eccentric locals, in particular a comely refugee from the Spanish Civil War, opens his eyes to an alternative world – based, not in politics, but the natural environment. Funny, touching and magically photographed. Winner of the Silver Bear at the 1992 Berlin Film Festival. A Spanish-Chilean co-production. [*Ewen Brownrigg*]

Cast: Patricio Contreras (Ramiro Orellana), Gloria Laso (Maite), Hectir Noguera (Father Patricio), Alonso Venegas (Delegate), Aldo Bernales, Patricio Bunster, G.N. 'La Batucana', Elsa Poblete.
Dir: Ricardo Larrain. Pro: Eduardo Larrain. Ex Pro: Eduardo Larrain and Ricardo Larrain. Screenplay: Jorge Goldemberg and Ricardo Larrain. Ph: Hector Rios. Ed: Claudio Martinez. Pro Des: Juan Carlos Castillo. M: Jaime De Aguire. Costumes: Montserrat Catala. Sound: Miguel Hormazabal. (Cine XXI/Television Espanola S.A./Ion Prods–Metro Tartan.) Rel: 21 April 1995. 115 mins. Cert 15.

Fun

The product of broken homes and abused childhoods, Bonnie, fourteen, and Hilary, fifteen, discover a mutual sense of rebellion when they meet beside a motorway one exhilarating and fateful day. Over the next 24 hours the girls exchange their most intimate secrets, pester neighbours and commit the ultimate crime. Based on the stage play by James Bosley, Rafal Zielinski's fresh and provocative drama frames the action in a detention centre (filmed in grainy monochrome), where the girls recall their brief friendship to a counsellor and magazine reporter. Acted with startling zest and conviction by Alicia Witt and Renee Humphrey, the

Games that people play: Renee Humphrey and Alicia Witt in Rafal Zielinski's haunting Fun *(from Metro Tartan)*

film offers a chilling examination of contemporary malaise. The piercing dialogue, ingenious structure and restless camera work all add up to a compelling, frightening picture of social disorder. A Canadian-American co-production.

Cast: Renee Humphrey (Hilary), Alicia Witt (Bonnie), William R. Moses (John), Leslie Hope (Jane), Ania Suli (Mrs Farmer), Alan Shapiro, Jonathan Lightstone.
Dir and Pro: Rafal Zielinski. Ex Pro: Rana Joy Glickman and Jeff Kirshbaum. Screenplay: James Bosley. Ph: Jens Sturup. Ed: Monika Lightstone. Pro Des: Vally Mastroni. M: Marc Tschanz. Costumes: Renee Johnston. Sound: Andy Koyama. (Prerogative Prods/Lighthouse Entertainment/Neo-Modern Entertainment–Metro Tartan.) Rel: 16 June 1995. 105 mins. Cert 18.

Funny Man

When an arrogant record producer wins a stately home in a poker game, he discovers that the place is haunted by a homicidal jester. And what the spectral clown thinks is funny is no joke. What, in essence, is a novel concept (such British staples as Punch and Judy, Lewis Carroll and garden gnomes taking on evil dimensions) is wasted here in a sorry case of cheap splatter over suspense. [*Charles Bacon*]

Cast: Tim James (Funny Man), Christopher Lee (Callum Chance), Benny Young (Max Taylor), Matthew Devitt (Johnny Taylor), Pauline Black (psychic commando), Ingrid Lacey (Tina Taylor), Chris Walker (Hard Man), George Morton, Rhona Cameron, Harry Heard, Jamie Heard, Bob Sessions, Ed Bishop.
Dir and Screenplay: Simon Sprackling. Pro: Nigel Odell. Ex Pro: Gareth Wiley and Steve Parsons. Co-Pro: Tim James and David Redman. Ph: Tom Ingle Jr. Ed: Ryan L. Driscoll. Pro Des: David Endley. M: Parsons/Haines. Costumes: Alex Westover. SFX: Neill Gorton and Jim Francis. (Nomad Pictures–Feature Film Co.) Rel: 7 October 1994. 90 mins. Cert 18.

George Balanchine's The Nutcracker

Like Cliff Richard, Macaulay Culkin has become something of a staple of the Christmas season. Employed here to lend star power to the New York City Ballet's interpretation of Tchaikovsky's classic (with choreography by George Balanchine), Little Mac *dances* the title role. Sadly, in spite of his training at The American School of Ballet, the young multi-millionaire looks silly in the company of such skilled co-stars. None the less, the film is stunning to look at and retains all the magic of the famous ballet. P.S. Macaulay's father, Kit Culkin, danced the title role himself in the late fifties. [*Charles Bacon*]

Cast: Darci Kistler (Sugarplum Fairy), Damian Woetzel (Cavalier), Kyra Nichols (Dewdrop), Bart Robinson Cook (Drosselmeier), Macaulay Culkin (Nutcracker Prince), Jessica Lynn Cohen (Marie), Wendy Whelan (Coffee), Margaret Tracey (Marzipan), Gen Horiuchi (Tea), Tom Gold (Candy Cane), Kevin Kline (narrator).
Dir: Emile Ardolino, from the stage production by Peter Martins. Pro: Robert A. Krasnow and Robert Hurwitz. Ex Pro: Arnon Milchan. Line Pro: Catherine Tatge. Ph: Ralf Bode. Ed: Girish Bhargava. Pro Des and Scenery: Rouben Ter-Arutunian. M: Pyotr Ilyich Tchaikovsky. Costumes: Karinska. Choreography: George Balanchine. (Elektra Entertainment/Regency Enterprises–Warner.) Rel: 16 December 1994. 95 mins. Cert U.

Last of the Apaches: Wes Studi as the noble, charismatic Geronimo *(from Columbia Pictures)*

Geronimo

Arizona/New Mexico/Mexico; 1885-6. Another noble, picturesque epic chronicling the horrific injustice dealt out by the American government in its genocidal fight against the Indian people. The very last American native warrior to be subjugated, Chiricahua Apache leader Goyahkla (nicknamed Geronimo by the Mexicans) fought to remain free after seeing his wife and two daughters murdered by the white man. Eventually, it took 5,000 troops – a quarter of the entire army – to capture Geronimo and 34 Apache men, women and children. This is his story. While criticised for being slow and stodgy, the film's focus on detail, the photography, spectacular scenery and two outstanding performances (Robert Duvall as a grizzled scout and Wes Studi as a dignified, charismatic Geronimo) make

Sadist of the year: Michael Madsen with shot-gun wife Jennifer Tilly in Roger Donaldson's cruel, gripping The Getaway *(from Warner)*

this a superior history lesson. According to the noted Old West historian John Langellier, *Geronimo* is the most authentic film yet made about the American Indian. US title: *Geronimo – An American Legend*.

Cast: Jason Patric (Lt Charles Gatewood), Robert Duvall (Al Sieber), Gene Hackman (Brig. Gen. George Crook), Wes Studi (Goyahkla 'Geronimo'), Matt Damon (Lt Britton Davis), Rodney A. Grant (Mangas),

Straw puppy: Macaulay Culkin fools around in Howard Deutch's painfully pedestrian Getting Even With Dad *(from UIP)*

Kevin Tighe (Brig. Gen. Nelson Miles), Steve Reevis (Chato), Carlos Palomino, Victor Aaron, Stuart 'Proud Eagle' Grant, Stephen McHattie, Richard Martin Jr, M.C. Gainey, Scott Wilson.

Dir: Walter Hill. Pro: Hill and Neil Canton. Ex Pro: Michael S. Glick. Screenplay: John Milius and Larry Gross. Ph: Lloyd Ahern. Ed: Freeman Davis, Carmel Davies and Donn Aron. Pro Des: Joe Alves. M: Ry Cooder. Costumes: Dan Moore. (Columbia Pictures.) Rel: 14 October 1994. 115 mins. Cert 12.

The Getaway

After ace bank robber Doc McCoy is sprung from a Mexican jail by corrupt businessman Jack Benyon, he is put back to work: doing what he does best. But even Benyon's code of ethics takes some swallowing, and soon McCoy and his gorgeous wife are on the run – from Benyon's men, the cops and a kitten-loving sadist called Rudy. A remake of Sam Peckinpah's peerless action-thriller of 1972 of the same name, *The Getaway* stars real-life couple Alec Baldwin and Kim Basinger in the roles originated by real-life couple Steve McQueen and Ali MacGraw. Here, Baldwin fails to match McQueen's innate magnetism and seems to pout when he should be smouldering. Also, Basinger is given little to do but pout in unison, although she is never less than stunning to look at. For sheer presence, though, Michael Madsen calls the shots, even if his sadistic bad guy act often borders on the unwatchable. The

problem with the film is that everybody is so unlikeable that it's hard to care what happens to any of them. Nevertheless, the action sequences are extremely well executed and the stunts are at the top of their class. P.S. Ms Basinger, who last played a character called Karen McCoy in *The Real McCoy*, plays Carol McCoy here.

Cast: Alec Baldwin (Doc McCoy), Kim Basinger (Carol McCoy), Michael Madsen (Rudy Travis), Jennifer Tilly (Fran Carvey), Richard Farnsworth (Slim), James Woods (Jack Benyon), Burton Gilliam (Gollie), Philip Hoffman (Frank Hansen), David Morse (Jim Deer Jackson), James Stephens (Harold Carvey), Royce D. Applegate, Daniel Villareal, Scott McKenna, Alex Colon.

Dir: Roger Donaldson. Pro: David Foster, Lawrence Turman and John Alan Simon. Assoc Pro and Costumes: Marilyn Vance. Screenplay: Walter Hill and Amy Jones, based on the novel by Jim Thompson. Ph: Peter Menzies. Ed: Conrad Buff. Pro Des: Joseph Nemec III. M: Mark Isham; 'Now And Forever' performed by Richard Marx. (Largo Entertainment/JVC Ent–Warner.) Rel: 1 July 1994. 115 mins. Cert 18.

Getting Even With Dad

It's hard to be disappointed by such an obviously contrived piece of senti-mental manipulation as this. But it's possible. Sweet Macaulay Culkin is a motherless eleven year old (complete with omnipresent snapshot of Mom's grave) dumped on his father's doorstep. Ted Danson is the parent more inter-ested in stealing coins than showing interest in the son he never knew. Macaulay doesn't approve of his father's activities, so he hides the stash from Danson's last haul. Danson now has to choose between his son and the money. You'll never guess what hap-pens. Actually, *Getting Even With Dad* is worse than you may think. Not only is it numbingly predictable, but it's shoddily made. The camera work is slapdash, the score manipulative and the editing ponderous. And no end of overly-familiar hits on the soundtrack can perk it up. Moreover, the manda-tory, accident-prone goons – here played by Saul Rubinek and Gailard Sartain – add insult to indignity. No wonder Little Mac demanded $8 mil-lion for his part.

Cast: Macaulay Culkin (Timmy Gleason), Ted Danson (Ray Gleason), Glenne Headly (Theresa), Saul Rubinek (Bobby), Gailard

Sartain (Carl), Hector Elizondo (Lt Romayko), Sam McMurray, Kathleen Wilhoite, Sydney Walker, Ron Canada, Dann Florek.

Dir: Howard Deutch. Pro: Katie Jacobs and Pierce Gardner. Ex Pro: Richard Hashimoto. Screenplay: Tom S. Parker and Jim Jennewein. Ph: Tom Suhrstedt. Ed: Richard Halsey. Pro Des: Virginia L. Randolph. M: Miles Goodman; numbers performed by Barrett Strong, The Rolling Stones, Professor Longhair, A.J.Croce, Ringo Starr, Taj Mahal, etc. Costumes: Rudy Dillon. (MGM–UIP.) Rel: 5 August 1994. 109 mins. Cert PG.

Gettysburg

Pennsylvania; 30 June - 4 July 1863. On the plus side, *Gettysburg* is a handsome, creditably acted and authentic account of American history's bloodiest battle. On the other hand it is preachy, sanitary and weighed down with too much exposition and talk of strategy. A multimedia, two-part epic (also fine-tuned as a three-part mini series and as a five-and-a-half hour video), *Gettysburg* – the motion picture – seems too long in parts but still seems to be missing vital plot links. Initially, it's hard to work out who's who, who's fighting who, and why. Still, Confederate Tom Berenger,

in a somewhat wooden performance, sums up the futility of the war with a dry, 'We'd rather lose the war than admit to our mistake.' The facts, indeed, are fascinating. At the Battle of Gettysburg alone, 53,000 men perished, while there were more fatalities in the civil war than in all the other American conflicts (including Vietnam) put together – and most of the soldiers died while reloading their muskets. Other pluses include a dignified, moving performance from Martin Sheen as Robert E. Lee, some beautifully modulated dialogue, sterling photography, a rousing score and some exciting battle sequences. But, this being a TV movie, the sheer horror of war is all too often subjugated for the mechanics of the history lesson.

Cast: Tom Berenger (Lt General James Longstreet), Jeff Daniels (Col Joshua Lawrence Chamberlain), Martin Sheen (General Robert E. Lee), Maxwell Caulfield (Col Strong Vincent), Kevin Conway (Sgt 'Buster' Kilrain), C. Thomas Howell (Lt Thomas D. Chamberlain), Richard Jordan (Brigadier General Lewis A. Armistead), James Lancaster (Lt Col Arthur Freemantle), Stephen Lang (Major General George E. Pickett), Sam Elliott (Brigadier General John Buford), Brian Mallon (Major General Winfield Scott Hancock), Richard

Soldier blue and grey: A scene from the battle of Little Round Top in Ronald F. Maxwell's ambitious Gettysburg *(from Mayfair Entertainment)*

Anderson (Major General George G. Meade), Patrick Gorman (Major General John Bell Hood), Bo Brinkman (Major Walter H. Taylor), Buck Taylor, John Diehl, Josh Mauer, David Carpenter, Dwier Brown, Leonard Termo, Andrew Prine, Cooper Huckabee, Morgan Sheppard, Kieran Mulroney, MacIntyre Dixon, Tim Scott, George Lazenby, Alex Harvey, Ken Burns, Ted Turner.

Dir and Screenplay: Ronald F. Maxwell, from the novel *The Killer Angels* by Michael Shaara. Pro: Robert Katz, Moctesuma Esparza, Mace Neufeld and Robert Rehme. Ph: Kees Van Oostrum. Ed: Corky Ehlers. Pro Des: Cary White. M: Randy Edelman. Costumes: Michael T. Boyd. (Turner Pictures/New Line Cinema/TriStar Television–Mayfair Entertainment.) Rel: 23 September 1994. 259 mins. Cert PG.

Go Fish

Chicago; 1994. Max is cute, single and a lesbian. But can ugly, bespectacled Ely overcome her shyness to embark on a new relationship with Max? Meanwhile, Ely's flatmate Daria is sleeping

When Max Met Ely ... Guinevere Turner and V.S. Brodie in Rose Troche's ground-breaking Go Fish *(from Mainline)*

with every dyke in town. As a film about lesbianism, *Go Fish* is fresh, funny and provocatively personal. As a piece of filmmaking it's idiosyncratic, bargain-basement cheap and infuriatingly pretentious. If in future director-producer-writer-editor Rose Troche can restrain her camera flourishes, her ability with actors and dialogue should pay dividends.

Cast: V.S. Brodie (Ely), Guinevere Turner (Max), T. Wendy McMillan (Kia), Migdalia Melendez (Evy), Anastasia Sharp (Daria), Brooke Webster, Betty Jeannie Pejko,

JoAnne C. Willis, Tom Kalin (voice only).

Dir and Ed: Rose Troche. Pro and Screenplay: Troche and Guinevere Turner. Ex Pro: Christine Vachon and Tom Kalin. Assoc Pro: V.S. Brodie. Ph: Ann T. Rossetti. M: Brenden Dolan and Jennifer Sharpe. (Samuel Goldwyn/Islet/Can I Watch Pictures/KVPI–Mainline.) Rel: 8 July 1994. 83 mins. Cert 18.

A Good Man in Africa

The eponymous good man in Africa is not, sadly, Morgan Leafy. Not that Morgan Leafy is a bad man, it's just that he's privy to most human weaknesses and can't wait to get off the Dark Continent. A mid-level diplomat in an insignificant West African nation, Leafy has only the comfort of flesh and

alcohol to alleviate his boredom. But with the arrival of the British High Commissioner and an encounter with the good Dr Alex Murray, the diplomat's life lurches from bad to worse. Although lovers of William Boyd's celebrated novel sunk their talons into this adaptation (scripted by Boyd himself), there is still much to savour for those unfamiliar with the book. Friels, as the stiff upper twit coasting into a snowballing nightmare, never pushes the slapstick beyond its own elasticity, while Connery lends his characteristic charisma to good effect. Some picturesque locations and a nimble wit add to the enjoyment.

Cast: Colin Friels (Morgan Leafy), Joanne Whalley-Kilmer (Celia Adekunle), Sean Connery (Dr Alex Murray), John Lithgow (Arthur Fanshawe), Louis Gossett Jr (Sam Adekunle), Diana Rigg (Chloe Fanshawe), Sarah-Jane Fenton (Priscilla Fanshawe), Jeremy Crutchley (Dalmire), Jackie Mofokeng (Hazel), Maynard Eziashi (Friday), Russel Savadier, Themba Ndaba, Lillian Dube, Peter Thage.

Dir: Bruce Beresford. Pro: John Fielder and Mark Tarlov. Co-Pro: Beresford and William Boyd. Ex Pro: Joe Caracciolo Jr, Avi Lerner, Sharon Harel and Jane Barclay. Screenplay: Boyd. Ph: Adrezj Bartkowiak. Ed: Jim Clark. Pro Des: Herbert Pinter. M: John Du Prez; numbers performed by Eric Agyeman, Lionel Cole and The George Lee Band. Costumes: Rosemary Burrows. (Southern Sun/Polar Entertainment/Capitol Films–UIP.) Rel: 25 November 1994. 94 mins. Cert 15.

Guarding Tess

Special agent-in-charge Douglas Chesnic likes to live by the book and on the edge. Trained to kill and think on his feet, he is the stuff of heroes – should the occasion arise. Unfortunately, Doug Chesnic is saddled with babysitting Tess Carlisle, former First Lady and crotchety old bag. And he's had enough. Fixing snacks and fetching golf balls is not his job. But then Doug hadn't bargained on Tess's influence with the current President of the United States ... A gentle love-hate comedy, *Guarding Tess* is neither credible enough nor funny enough to work as character study or gut-clutching farce. Still, it's nice to see a Hollywood film that doesn't bulldoze all the emotional buttons.

Cast: Shirley MacLaine (Tess Carlisle), Nicolas Cage (Doug Chesnic), Austin

Pendelton (Earl), Edward Albert (Barry Carlisle), James Rebhorn (Howard Shaeffer), Richard Griffiths (Frederick), John Roselius, David Graf, Don Yesso, James Lally, Brant Von Hoffman, Harry J. Lennix, Susan Blommaert, Dale Dye, James Handy, Stephen S. Chen, Hugh Wilson.

Dir: Hugh Wilson. Pro: Ned Tanen and Nancy Graham Tanen. Screenplay: Wilson and Peter Torokvei. Ph: Brian J. Reynolds. Ed: Sidney Levin. Pro Des: Peter Larkin. M: Michael Convertino, Mozart; 'Shout' performed by The Isley Brothers. Costumes: Ann Roth and Sue Gandy. (Channel/Tri-Star–Columbia TriStar.) Rel: 23 June 1995. 95 mins. Cert 12.

Gypsy

Even if Bette Midler's brassy, larger-than-life persona is not one's cup of Earl Grey, it is still gratifying to witness a star matched to the perfect part. Originally a stage vehicle for Ethel Merman, nobody today could so adequately fill the shoes of Rose Hovick, the ultimate stage mother. This TV adaptation of the celebrated musical slavishly follows the format of the 1962 film version, but should bring much delight to a new generation and fond memories for an older one. While Midler dominates the film (superbly), Cynthia Gibb as Gypsy Rose Lee, the stripper who escapes her mother's apron strings to fulfil her own showbiz dream, is a real surprise. Songs comprise all the old favourites, including 'Let Me Entertain You', 'Some People', 'Mr Goldstone', 'I Love You', 'If Mamma Was Married', 'Everything's Coming Up Roses', 'Rose's Turn', etc.

Cast: Bette Midler (Rose Hovick), Peter Riegert (Herbie), Cynthia Gibb (Louise/Gypsy Rose Lee), Ed Asner (Pop), Tony Shalhoub (Uncle Jocko), Jeffrey Broadhurst (Tulsa), Mike Nussbaum (Weber), Michael Jeter (Mr Goldstone), Jennifer Beck (June), Andrea Martin (Miss Cratchitt), Christine Ebersole (Tessie Tura), Linda Hart (Mazeppa), Anna McNeely (Electra), Sean Sullivan, Lacey Chabert, Elisabeth Moss, Peter Lockyer, Michael Moore, Patrick Boyd, Rachel Sweet, John LaMotta.

Dir: Emile Ardolino. Pro: Ardolino and Cindy Gilmore. Ex Pro: Robert Halmi Sr, Craig Zadan, Neil Meron and Bonnie Bruckheimer. Ph: Ralf Bode. Ed: William Reynolds. Pro Des: Jackson Degovia. M: Jule Styne; lyrics: Stephen Sondheim. Choreography: Jerome Robbins. Costumes: Bob Mackie. (RHI Entertainment–Entertainment.) Rel: 15 July 1994. 142 mins. Cert U.

Heavenly Creatures

Christchurch, New Zealand; 1952-4. Forsaking his trademark splatter effects and bad taste, New Zealand wunderkind Peter Jackson here explores the emotional history that forms a murderer. Taking the true story of New Zealand schoolgirls Pauline Parker and

Fie the beloved country: Joanne Whalley-Kilmer and Colin Friels in Bruce Beresford's A Good Man in Africa *(from UIP)*

Tactical tiff: Shirley MacLaine and Nicolas Cage lock horns in Hugh Wilson's Guarding Tess *(from Columbia TriStar)*

Killing for joy: Melanie Lynskey and Kate Winslet in Peter Jackson's remarkable Heavenly Creatures *(from Buena Vista)*

Juliet Hulme, Jackson concentrates not on the violence of their act, but on the social path that turned these young teenagers into killers. Both bright, imaginative girls, Pauline and Juliet were kindred spirits trapped in a provincial world that was stifling them. Threatened with separation, they did what they had to do to preserve their unique universe. This sympathetic approach to the killers' psyches is not only refreshing but illuminating; however, what is truly remarkable about the film is the intensity of the young actresses' performances and the bravura style that Jackson brings to his subject. Add to this some superbly realised fantasy sequences – revealing the 'fourth world' that the girls inhabited – and you have a stirring, ferociously original drama that will both provoke debate and haunt the heart.

Cast: Melanie Lynskey (Pauline Yvonne Parker), Kate Winslet (Juliet Hulme), Sarah Peirse (Honora Parker), Diana Kent (Hilda Hulme), Clive Merrison (Henry Hulme), Simon O'Connor (Herbert Rieper), Jed Brophy (John/Nicholas), Darien Takle (Miss Stewart), Elizabeth Moody (Miss Waller), Moreen Eason (Mrs Stevens), Peter Elliott, Gilbert Goldie, Geoffrey Heath, Kirsti Ferry, Liz Mullane, Pearl Carpenter.

Dir and Co-Pro: Peter Jackson. Pro: Jim Booth. Ex Pro: Hanno Huth. Screenplay: Jackson and Frances Walsh. Ph: Alun Bollinger. Ed: Jamie Selkirk. Pro Des: Grant Major. M: Peter Dasent; numbers performed by Mario Lanza. Costumes: Ngila Dickson. Special FX: Richard Taylor. (Wignut Films/Fontana/New Zealand Film Commission–Buena Vista.) Rel: 10 February 1995. 99 mins. Cert 18.

Highlander III: The Sorcerer

Japan/Morocco/New York/France/Scotland. Any film with a villain called Kane bodes ill, and *Highlander III* doesn't let us down. Chronologically set before the last sequel, this flash, illogical rip-off sees the immortal French-accented Scotsman fall in love again and face a new immortal enemy, Kane, an ancient Egyptian sorcerer with demonic dentistry. Defying credibility even by the standards of second-rate sci-fi, the film looks like an extended music video. Even the sword fights are un-inspired. A Canadian-French-British co-production.

Cast: Christopher Lambert (Connor MacLeod/Russel Nash), Mario Van Peebles (Kane), Deborah Unger (Alex Johnson/Sarah), Mako (Nakano), Martin Neufeld (Stenn), Michael Jayston (Jack Donovan), Gabriel Kakon (John), Raoul Trujillo, Jean-Pierre Perusse, Frederick Y. Okimura, Daniel Do, Emidio Michetti, Andre Oumansky, Paul Hopkins, Chip Chuipka.

Dir: Andy Morahan. Pro: Claude Leger. Co-Pro: Jean Cazes, Eric Altmayer and James Daly. Screenplay: Paul Ohl, based on a story by William Panzer and Brad Mirman, from characters created by Gregory Widen. Ph: Steven Chivers. Ed: Yves Langlois. Pro Des: Gilles Aird and Ben Morahan. M: J. Peter Robinson; numbers performed by James and Brian Eno, Definition of Sound, The Cocteau Twins, etc. Costumes: Jackie Budin, Mario Davignon and Micheline Rouillard. (Transfilm Inc./Initial Groupe/Fallingcloud–Entertainment.) Rel: 25 November 1994. 98 mins. Cert 15.

Highway Patrolman - El Patrullero

Eight years after *Sid and Nancy*, and seven years since his last film (the disastrous Nicaraguan epic *Walker*),

Liverpudlian director Alex Cox returns to form with this quirky, funny and textured dramatic comedy. Drawn from genuine reports of police corruption in Mexico, the film features the 21-year-old Mexican actor Roberto Sosa as a vertically-challenged rookie highway patrolman. At first resisting the bribes that are brandished in his face, the little cop soon finds that the pressures of domestic life force his hand ... While utilising shocking realism (a pig being gutted, a bloodied leg lying in the road) and employing some picturesque, documentary-style cinematography, the film is essentially a human comedy with a heart of gold. Filmed in Spanish, *Highway Patrolman* is reportedly the most expensive Mexican film to date.

Cast: Roberto Sosa (Pedro Rojas), Bruno Bichir (Anibal Guerrero), Vanessa Bauche (Maribel), Zaide Silvia Gutierrez (Griselda Marcos), Pedro Armendaris Jr (Sgt Barreras), Malena Doria, Towi Islas, Ernesto Gomez Cruz, Mike Moroff, Jorge Russek, Eduardo Lopez Rojas, Maricruz Najera.

Dir: Alex Cox. Pro and Screenplay: Lorenzo O'Brien. Ex Pro: Sammy O. Masada and Kuniaki Negishi. Ph: Miguel Garzon. Ed: Carlos Puente. Pro Des: Cecilia Montiel. M: Zander Schloss. Costumes: Manuela Loaeza. (Together Brothers Prods/ Ultra Films/Cable Hogue/Marubeni Corp– Metro Tartan.) Rel: 19 August 1994. 104 mins. Cert 15.

The asphalt jungle: Roberto Sosa and Vanessa Bauche in Alex Cox's engaging Highway Patrolman *(from Metro Tartan)*

Holy Matrimony

On the run for stealing the takings of the Iowa State Fair, consumer princess Havana hides out in a Hutterite community in Alberta, Canada. But due to a kink in Hutterite law, Havana finds herself forced to marry her twelve-year-old brother-in-law. A genuinely intriguing premise is botched by playing it for laughs, while the cast are encouraged to behave like marionettes in a puppet show. It's hard to believe that Leonard Nimoy, who directed *The Good Mother*, was responsible for this amateur garbage. Incidentally, this is the third film in a row in which Patricia Arquette has been on the run (cf. *Trouble Bound, True Romance*).

Cast: Patricia Arquette (Havana), Joseph Gordon-Levitt (Zeke), Tate Donovan (Peter), Armin Mueller-Stahl (Uncle Wilhelm), John Schuck (Markowski), Lois Smith, Courtney B. Vance, Jeffrey Nordling, Richard Riehle, Mary Pat Gleason, Alan Blumenfeld.

Dir: Leonard Nimoy. Pro: William Stuart, David Madden and Diane Nabatoff. Ex Pro: Ted Field and Robert W. Cort. Screenplay: David Weisberg and Douglas S. Cook. Ph: Bobby Bukowski. Ed: Peter E. Berger. Pro Des: Edward Pisoni. M: Bruce Broughton. Costumes: Deena Appel. (PolyGram/ Interscope Communications/Aurora Prods –Rank.) Rel: 17 February 1995. 93 mins. Cert PG.

Hoop Dreams

Extraordinary documentary in which three filmmakers – Steve James, Fred Marx and Peter Gilbert–follow the lives of two Chicago teenage boys over a period of five years. Taking a strictly linear approach to its subject matter, the film traces the boys' dreams to become basketball stars as they grapple with the American educational system and the social inadequacies of their own environment. By tackling two protagonists

Strange bedfellows: Patricia Arquette and Joseph Gordon-Levitt camp it up in Leonard Nimoy's regrettable Holy Matrimony *(from Rank)*

Kitchen stink: The incomparable Carmen Maura contemplates How To Be a Woman and Not Die in the Attempt *(from Mayfair Entertainment)*

The puppeteer panics: Paul Newman as the conniving Sidney J. Mussburger, whose plans go terribly awry in the Coen brothers' blissful The Hudsucker Proxy *(from Rank)*

simultaneously the film is often confusing (more frequent captions would have helped) and far too long. Nevertheless, critics on both sides of the Atlantic embraced this behemoth, hailing it as the best film of 1994. They should take another look at Michael Apted's documentary *35 Up.*

With: William Gates, Arthur Agee, Emma Gates, Curtis Gates, Sheila Agee, Arthur 'Bo' Agee, Earl Smith, Gene Pingatore, Isiah Thomas, Patricia Wier, etc.
  Dir: Steve James. Pro: James, Fred Marx and Peter Gilbert. Ex Pro: Gordon Quinn and Catherine Allan. Ph: Gilbert. Ed: Marx, James and Bill Haugse. M: numbers performed by Tony M, Billy Sheila, Bob Malach, Ricky Peterson, Gary Glitter, Ice Cube, etc. (Fineline Features/Kartemquin Films/KTCA TV–Feature Film Company.) Rel: 31 March 1995. 175 mins. Cert 15.

How To Be a Woman and Not Die in the Attempt - Como Ser Mujer y No Morir en el Intento

Carmen is a successful Spanish journalist trying to survive the travails of modern city life with just a modicum of dignity and pleasure. Unfortunately, her third husband is a workaholic male chauvinist pig who expects his wife to be there to pick up his pieces. A battle-of-the-sexes comedy of some insight, *How To Be ...* is constantly entertaining while scouting some painfully recognisable territory. Directed by the Spanish actress-singer Ana Belen.

Cast: Carmen Maura (Carmen), Antonio Resines (Antonio), Tina Sainz (Emila), Juanjo Puigcorve, Carmen Conesa, Paca Casares, Victor Garcia, Olalla Aguirre, Juan Diego Botto, Asuncion Balaguer, Jua Gea, Jose Carlos Plaza.
  Dir: Ana Belen. Ex Pro: Andres Vicente Gomez. Screenplay: Carmen Rico-Goddy, from her novel. Ph: Juan Amoros. Ed: Carmen Frias. Art: Gerardo Vera. M: Antonio Garcia De Diego, Pancho Varona and Mariano Diaz. (Ibero-Americana Films–Mayfair Entertainment.) Rel: 8 July 1994. 89 mins. Cert 15.

The Hudsucker Proxy

New York; 1958-60. When Waring Hudsucker, founder of the phenomenally successful Hudsucker Industries, jumps 45 floors to his death, the company's majority of shares have 30 days before they go public. Yet because the stock is worth so much, HI's own shareholders cannot afford to buy a controlling interest. So they have one month to emasculate the value of the company, and they need a patsy for the job, a sort of Hudsucker Proxy. When greenhorn mailboy Norville Barnes proposes a seemingly idiotic idea to vice-chairman Sid Mussburger, the boy is signed up as the new president. But

maybe his idea isn't that silly after all … OK, so the premise of *The Hudsucker Proxy* is hardly unique, but it is executed with such flair, verve and style – not to mention humour – that it is an unalloyed joy from beginning to end. At a cost of $25 million, the film looks twice that expensive, with fantastic, Kafkaesque sets standing in for the impressive Hudsucker building (a resplendent diving-board for depressed executives). Music, photography, production design and a crackerjack screenplay all wrestle for top honours, while only Jennifer Jason Leigh – giving a Katharine Hepburn-tinted performance – seems out of place.

Cast: Tim Robbins (Norville Barnes), Jennifer Jason Leigh (Amy Archer), Paul Newman (Sidney J. Mussburger), Charles Durning (Waring Hudsucker), Jim True (Buzz), John Mahoney (Chief), Bruce Campbell (Smitty), Bill Cobbs (Moses), John Seitz, Joe Grifasi, Roy Brocksmith, J.M. Hobson, Steve Buscemi, Peter Gallagher, Noble Willingham, Thom Noble, Anna Nicole Smith, Jerome Dempsey, David Byrd, Robert Weil, Jon Polito, Mike Starr, Sam Raimi.

Dir: Joel Coen. Pro: Ethel Coen. Ex Pro: Tim Bevan and Eric Fellner. Screenplay: Coen, Coen and Sam Raimi. Ph: Roger Deakins. Ed: Thom Noble. Pro Des: Dennis Gassner. M: Carter Burwell. Costumes: Richard Hornung. Sound: Skip Lievsay. (PolyGram/Warner/Silver Pictures/Working Title–Rank.) Rel: 2 September 1994. 111 mins. Cert PG.

i.d.

Harrowing, profoundly disturbing examination of Britain's lager culture in which four policemen go undercover to expose the ringleaders of organised football violence. John, an ambitious, dedicated cop in his early twenties, is doing well. He's got a nice girlfriend, a nice house and a good circle of friends. But, when called on, he can also be very nasty. It goes with the job. And to effectively infiltrate the hardline supporters of Shadwell United, John and his three colleagues have got to do more than knock back a few pints. But only John can truly blend in with the villains. Frighteningly so … Directed by Philip Davis, an actor best known for his appearances in the films of Mike Leigh, *i.d.* is compelling, brutal and credible, even when it tips into melodrama and throws up the odd caricature. As John, Reece Dinsdale is particularly impressive. An Anglo-German co-production.

Terror on the terraces: Reece Dinsdale goes undercover with a vengeance – in Philip Davis's disturbing i.d. *(from PolyGram)*

Cast: Reece Dinsdale (John), Richard Graham (Trevor), Claire Skinner (Marie), Sean Pertwee (Martin), Saskia Reeves (Lynda), Warren Clarke (Bob), Perry Fenwick (Eddie), Philip Glenister (Charlie), Charles De'ath (Nik), Lee Ross (Gumbo), Terry Cole, Steve Sweeney, Nicholas Bailey, Alan Cooke, Peter Blythe, Ian Redford, Philip Davis, Cindi O'Callaghan, Michelle Winstanley, Jacqueline Leonard, Eric Allan.

Dir: Philip Davis. Pro: Sally Hibbin. Co-Pro: Christina Kallas and Luciano Gloor. Ex Pro: Mark Shivas. Screenplay: Vincent O'Connell, from a story by James Bannon. Ph: Thomas Mauch. Ed: Inge Behrens. Pro Des: Max Gottlieb. M: Will Gregory. Costumes: Mike O'Neill. (BBC/The Sales Company/Parallax/Metropolis/Hamburg Film Fund–PolyGram.) Rel: 5 April 1995. 107 mins. Cert 18.

I Like It Like That

Mixing comedy, drama, romance and music into a vibrant cocktail, first-time director Darnell Martin not only shows a dynamic grip of cinema, but goes down into the history books as the first

Street life: Desiree Casado, Lauren Velez, Jon Seda and Thomas Melly fight to stay together in Darnell Martin's exhilarating I Like It Like That *(from Columbia TriStar)*

Afro-American woman to direct a major studio picture. As lively and technically confident as any of Spike Lee's later films, *I Like It Like That* is the non-stop, action-packed story of Lisette, a young black woman, her husband Chino, a Latino, their three kids, and the struggle they face keeping their life and marriage together in the Bronx. A powerful, entertaining and hard-hitting comedy pulled kicking and screaming from real life.

Cast: Lauren Velez (Lisette Linares), Jon Seda (Chino Linares), Rita Moreno (Rosaria Linares), Griffin Dunne (Stephen Price), Tomas Melly (Li'l Chino Linares), Jesse Borrego (Alexis), Lisa Vidal (Magdalena Soto), Emilio Del Pozo (Mr Soto), Desiree Casado, Isaiah Garcia, Vincent Laresca, E.O. Nolasco, Sammy Melendez, Jose Soto, Gloria Irizarry, Donald Jackson, Tookie Smith, Luis A. Marrero, Fredy Correa, Jerry Rivera.
  Dir and Screenplay: Darnell Martin. Pro: Ann Carli and Lane Janger. Ex Pro: Wendy Finerman. Co-Pro: Diana Phillips. Ph: Alexander Gruszynski. Ed: Peter C. Frank. Pro Des: Scott Chambliss. M: Sergio George; numbers performed by Barrio Boyzz, The Blackout Allstars, Cypress Hill, Fat Joe, K7, C&C Music Factory, Shabbakan, Jerry Rivera, Marc Anthony, etc. Costumes: Sandra Hernandez. (Think Again–Columbia TriStar.) Rel: 3 February 1995. 106 mins. Cert 15.

I Love a Man in Uniform

Canadian writer-director David Wellington takes three facts of life – cops face death every day but, hey, they wear great clothes and have lots of power – and makes an interesting fetishistic drama out of one man's cop obsession. Henry Adler (Canadian theatrical star Tom McCamus) is a bank clerk/actor who has landed a temporary role as a cop on a TV police drama. When a Marilyn Monroe lookalike robs the bank where he works, he slowly changes into the character he plays on TV – a tough but moral flatfoot who loves a hooker with a heart of gold. A detached feel, memorable visuals and a smooth performance from McCamus turn *I Love a Man in Uniform* into something much more than its small budget would have it appear. [*Karen Krizanovich*]

Cast: Tom McCamus (Henry Adler), Brigitte Bako (Charlie Warner), Kevin Tighe (Frank), David Hemblen (father), Alex Karzis (Bruce), Graham McPherson (Mr Pearson), Daniel MacIvor, Wendy Hopkins, Matthew Ferguson, Henry Czerny, Van Flores.
  Dir and Screenplay: David Wellington. Pro: Paul Brown. Ex Pro: Alexandra Raffé. Ph: David Franco. Ed: Susan Shipton. Pro Des: John Dondertman. M: Ron Sures and The Tragically Hip. Costumes: Beth Pasternak. (Alliance Communications/Miracle Pictures/Telefilm Canada/Ontario Film Development Corporation–Metro Tartan.) Rel: 10 March 1995. 97 mins. Cert 18.

I Love Trouble

For Julia Roberts, her brief career has been a bright and dazzling fuse leading to this bomb. At the time of going to press the highest paid actress in the world (for this she was paid $7 million), Ms Roberts has finally returned to the arena of romatic comedy that launched her (with *Pretty Woman*). Here, she plays a cub reporter for the *Chicago Globe* who trumps the card of ace columnist Nick Nolte who, naturally, cannot stand the competition. So, together and apart they vie to expose the secret behind a spectacular and suspicious train wreck ... Attempting to emulate the romantic comedies of the thirties and forties, *I Love Trouble* fails to sparkle or amuse and after a leaden, unintelligible start settles down into contemptible familiarity and mediocrity.

Cast: Julia Roberts (Sabrina Peterson), Nick Nolte (Peter Brackett), Saul Rubinek (Sam Smotherman), Robert Loggia (Matt Greenfield), James Rebhorn (The Thin Man), Kelly Rutherford, Olympia Dukakis, Marsha Mason, Eugene Levy, Charles Martin Smith, Dan Butler, Paul Gleason, Jane Adams, Lisa Lu, Nora Dunn, Hallie Meyers-Shyer, Clark Gregg, Anna Holbrook, Keith Gordon, Sally Meyers Kovler, Jonathan Kovler, Joseph D'Onofrio, Barry Sobel, Stuart Pankin, Megan Cavanagh, Patrick St Esprit, Michael Edgar Myers, Annie Meyers-Shyer, Rebecca Cross, Robin Duke.
  Dir: Charles Shyer. Pro: Nancy Myers. Co-Pro: Bruce A. Block. Screenplay: Myers and Shyer. Ph: John Lindley. Ed: Paul Hirsch, Walter Murch and Adam Bernardi. Pro Des: Dean Tavoularis. M: David Newman; numbers performed by Lenny Kravitz, David Palmer, etc. Costumes: Susan Becker. (Touchstone Pictures/Caravan Pictures–Buena Vista.) Rel: 18 November 1994. 123 mins. Cert PG.

Immortal Beloved

Any story of genius is fascinating and Beethoven's life is no exception. Bernard Rose, director of *Paperhouse*, *Chicago Joe and the Showgirl* and *Candyman*, has long been enraptured by Beethoven and in particular the enigma surrounding the composer's will, in which he left all his music and the capital of his estate to his 'immortal beloved'. Rose offers his own theory here, thus exchanging the hackneyed biographical format for a romantic detective story. Nevertheless, *Immortal Beloved* cannot escape the problem that dogs any screen biography: that is, how to condense a great life into two hours and keep it structurally sound. Still, the music's the thing and Gary Oldman is simply magnetic as the wayward prodigy. Filmed in the Czech Republic.

Cast: Gary Oldman (Ludwig Van Beethoven), Jeroen Krabbe (Anton Schindler), Isabella Rossellini (Countess Anna Marie), Johanna Ter Steege (Joanna Van Beethoven), Valeria Golino (Julia Guicciardi), Marco Hofschneider (Karl Van Beethoven), Christopher Fulford (Casper Van Beethoven), Barry Humphries (Chancellor Metternich), Donal Gibson (Karl Holz), Miriam Margolyes, Gerard Horan, Claudia Solti, Alexandra Pigg, Michael Culkin, Bernard Rose.

Dir and Screenplay: Bernard Rose. Pro: Bruce Davey. Ex Pro: Steve McEveety. Ph: Peter Suschitzky. Ed: Dan Rae. Pro Des:Jiri Hlupy. M: Beethoven. Music Director: Georg Solti. Costumes: Maurizio Millenotti. (Majestic Films/Icon–Entertainment.) Rel: 17 March 1995. 120 mins. Cert 15.

Innocent Lies

1938. Implausible, illogical and predictable descent into silliness in which an English police inspector attends the funeral of his ex-boss and best friend at a beauty spot on a secluded Brittany island. There he becomes acquainted with a wealthy family of ex-pat misfits, falling for the thumb-sucking charms of

In the film's most moving moment, Gary Oldman, as Ludwig Van Beethoven, 'listens' to the vibrations of his Moonlight Sonata – in Bernard Rose's Immortal Beloved *(from Entertainment)*

a young Englishwoman. Soon he finds himself enmeshed in an unlikely scenario involving incest, betrayal and murder. A ham-fisted attempt to blend Agatha Christie with an erotic French thriller, *Innocent Lies* falls foul of a ludicrous script and hammy performances. Atrocious. An Anglo-French pudding. [*Ewen Brownrigg*]

Cast: Stephen Dorff (Jeremy Graves), Gabrielle Anwar (Celia Graves), Adrian Dunbar (Alan Cross), Sophie Aubry (Solange Montfort), Joanna Lumley (Lady Helena Graves), Melvil Poupaud, Bernard Haller, Marianne Denicourt, Florence Hoath.

Dir: Patrick DeWolf. Pro: Simon Perry and Philippe Guez. Assoc Pro: Philippe Carcassonne. Screenplay: DeWolf and Kerry Crabbe. Ph: Patrick Blossier. Ed:

Long in the tooth: An immortal Tom Cruise drools over lunch in Neil Jordan's stylish Interview With the Vampire *(from Warner)*

Chris Wimble and Joelle Hache. Pro Des: Bernd Lepel. M: Alexandre Desplat. Costumes: Tom Rand. (PolyGram.) Rel: 30 June 1995. 90 mins. Cert 18.

Interview With the Vampire

Whenever Tom Cruise is on screen, the long-awaited adaptation of Anne Rice's celebrated novel comes alive. This is ironic as Daniel Day-Lewis was the first choice for the role and as Ms Rice herself carped, 'Cruise is no more my vampire Lestat than Edward G. Robinson is Rhett Butler.' Of course,

A cross to bear: Sam Neill flips out in John Carpenter's heavy-handed In the Mouth of Madness (from Entertainment)

Lestat is the most colourful character in a lugubrious tale of lonely vampires condemned to roam the centuries with little 'stomach for immortality'. And there is much ghoulish fun to be had from watching Cruise dance with a corpse and proclaim, 'There's life in the old lady yet!' Otherwise the film is a picturesque, eloquent but ultimately turgid tale, with Brad Pitt saddled with the central role of Louis, a creature of the night who wishes he was dead. Unfortunately, the sentiment is mutual. Still, there are some incredible visuals, great special effects and a provocative score. Yet, while the film may be faithful to the book, that doesn't make it a great movie.

Cast: Tom Cruise (Lestat), Brad Pitt (Louis de Pointe du Lac), Antonio Banderas (Armand), Stephen Rea (Santiago), Christian Slater (Malloy), Kirsten Dunst (Claudia), Domiziana Giordano (Madeleine), Thandie Newton (Yvette), Sara Stockbridge (Estelle), Virginia McCollam, Bellina Logan, Lyla Hay Owen, Lee Emery, Indra Ove, Helen McCrory, Roger Lloyd Pack, Nicole Dubois, Laure Marsac. Dir: Neil Jordan. Pro: Stephen Woolley and David Geffen. Co-Pro: Redmond Morris. Screenplay: Anne Rice. Ph: Philippe Rousselot. Ed: Mick Audsley. Pro Des: Dante Ferretti. M: Elliot Goldenthal; 'Sympathy For The Devil' performed by Guns 'N' Roses. Costumes: Sandy Powell. Make Up FX: Stan Winston. (Geffen Pictures–Warner.) Rel: 20 January 1995. 122 mins. Cert 18.

In the Mouth of Madness

'Reality is not what it used to be,' explains the agent of Sutter Cane, the twentieth century's top-selling novelist. Indeed, such is the power of Cane's latest novel, *In the Mouth of Madness*, that everybody who reads it is driven insane. When Cane disappears into thin air, his publishers employ insurance investigator John Trent to find him. A cheerful cynic, Trent thinks the whole thing is a publicity stunt – but the more he becomes involved with Cane's literature, the closer his concept of reality is warped by the forces of evil ... While introducing a fascinating premise, John Carpenter's film loses its dramatic grip in a predictable welter of optical wizardry, hokey sound effects and grotesque latex creations. Inspired by the novels of H.P. Lovecraft.

Cast: Sam Neill (John Trent), Jurgen Prochnow (Sutter Cane), Julie Carmen (Linda Styles), David Warner (Dr Wrenn), John Glover (Saperstein), Charlton Heston (Jackson Harglow), Bernie Casey, Peter Jason, Frances Bay, Wilhelm Von Homburg, Conrad Bergschneider, Katherine Ashby, Louise Beaven. Dir: John Carpenter. Pro: Sandy King. Ex Pro and Screenplay: Michael De Luca. Ph: Gary B. Kibbe. Ed: Edward A. Warschilka. Pro Des: Jeff Steven Ginn. M: Carpenter and Jim Lang. Costumes: Robert Bush. Sound: Owen Langevin. Visual FX: Bruce Nicholson. (New Line International/Katja Motion Pictures–Entertainment.) Rel: 16 June 1995. 95 mins. Cert 15.

I.Q.

The early 1950s; Princeton, New Jersey. Eager-to-please romantic comedy in which Albert Einstein plays Cupid with his insecure, brainy niece and an affable down-to-earth car mechanic. Some wonderful actors behave as if they're in a much better movie, but the script is not strong enough to disguise the rot. And, try as Meg Ryan and Tim Robbins might to generate some screwball sparkle, they come up with flat Tizer. Even Walter Matthau seems wasted as the German brain with a heart of gold. P.S. Meg Ryan and Tim Robbins previously co-starred in *Top Gun*.

Cast: Meg Ryan (Catherine Boyd), Tim Robbins (Ed Walters), Walter Matthau (Albert Einstein), Charles Durning (Louis Bamberger), Stephen Fry (James Morland), Lou Jacobi (Kurt Godel), Gene Saks (Boris Podolsky), Joseph Maher (Nathan Liebknecht), Tony Shalhoub (Bob Watters), Frank Whaley (Frank), Keene Curtis (Dwight D. Eisenhower), Alice Playten, Danny Zorn, Helen Hanft, Jeff Brooks, Rex Robbins, Daniel Von Bargen, Le Clanche Du Rand. Dir: Fred Schepisi. Pro: Schepisi and Carol Baum. Ex Pro: Scott Rudin and Sandy Gallin. Screenplay: Andy Breckman and Michael Leeson. Ph: Ian Baker. Ed: Jill Bilcock. Pro Des: Stuart Wurtzel. M: Jerry Goldsmith; numbers performed by Spike Jones, Little Richard and The Crew Cuts.

Relativity speaking: Einstein (Walter Matthau) is taken for a ride by garage mechanic Tim Robbins – in Fred Schepisi's disappointing I.Q. (from UIP)

Costumes: Ruth Myers. (Paramount/Sandollar–UIP.) Rel: 17 March 1995. 96 mins. Cert U.

It Could Happen to You

Charlie Lang is a good cop, and when he can't make the tip for a cup of coffee, he promises the waitress he will return. Furthermore, he will give her the option of choosing the cash or half of whatever he might make from the lottery that evening. She opts for the latter, which just happens to be two million dollars. Now, that's great for the waitress but not so good for Charlie's wife ... A sweet, old-fashioned fairy-tale, *It Could Happen to You* is as hopelessly romantic as last year's *Sleepless in Seattle*, if not as funny. Nicolas Cage and Bridget Fonda are no Hanks or Ryan, but they're pleasant enough, and bounce along smoothly on Andrew Bergman's meringue-light direction. Inspired by a true story.

Cast: Nicolas Cage (Charlie Lang), Bridget Fonda (Yvonne Biasi), Rosie Perez (Muriel Lang), Wendell Pierce (Bo Williams), Isaac Hayes (Angel), Seymour Cassel (Jack Gross), Stanley Tucci (Eddie Biasi), Red Buttons (Walter Zakuto), Richard Jenkins (C. Vernon Hale), Ann Dowd (Carol), Victor Rojas, J.E. Freeman, Kay Tong Lim, Robert Dorfman, Charles Busch, Beatrice Winde, Merwin Goldsmith, Ranjit

It happened to them: Bridget Fonda, Nicolas Cage and Rosie Perez pose for the media in Andrew Bergman's cosy It Could Happen to You *(from Columbia TriStar)*

And baby makes two: A proud Richard E. Grant with Samantha Mathis (and infant) in Tim Sullivan's enchanting Jack and Sarah *(from PolyGram)*

Chowdhry, Kathleen McNenny, Candece V. Tarpley.

Dir: Andrew Bergman. Pro: Mike Lobell. Ex Pro: Gary Adelson, Craig Baumgarten and Joseph Hartwick. Screenplay: Jane Anderson. Ph: Caleb Deschanel. Ed: Barry Malkin. Pro Des: Bill Groom. M: Carter Burwell; numbers performed by Mary-Chapin Carpenter, The Impressions, The Supremes, Wynton Marsalis, Lyle Lovett, Cathy Dennis, Billie Holliday, Tony Bennett, Frank Sinatra, etc. Costumes: Julie Weiss. (TriStar–Columbia TriStar.) Rel: 11 November 1994. 101 mins. Cert PG.

Jack and Sarah

London; 1994. Jack is a harried, overworked lawyer who likes to think he's in control (he isn't). Sarah is his placid, long-suffering wife. They're about to have a baby – if Jack doesn't have a seizure first. Then, following a cruel twist of fate, Jack is left holding the infant. All by himself ... After a hilarious start (Jack shopping for nipple pads, Jack going into labour in maternity class), *Jack and Sarah* emerges into a touching, briskly-paced dramatic comedy replete with priceless comic moments. Richard E. Grant (in his first leading role since the execrable *Killing Dad* six years ago), juggles the demands of neurosis and vulnerability with beguiling credibility, while a choice supporting cast ices the cake.

Cast: Richard E. Grant (Jack), Samantha Mathis (Amy), Judi Dench (Margaret), Ian McKellen (William), Cherie Lunghi (Anna), Eileen Atkins (Phil), Imogen Stubbs (Sarah), David Swift (Michael), Laurent Grevill (Alain), Kate Hardie, Sophia Sullivan, Niven Boyd, Tracy Thorne, Deborah Findlay, Matylelok Gibbs, John Grillo, Richard Leaf.

Before 1776 and all that: Greta Scacchi sizes up the opposition (Thandie Newton) in James Ivory's laboured Jefferson in Paris *(from Buena Vista)*

Dir and Screenplay: Tim Sullivan. Pro: Pippa Cross, Simon Channing-Williams and Janette Day. Ph: Jean-Yves Escoffier. Ed: Lesley Walker. Pro Des: Christopher J. Bradshaw. M: Simon Boswell; numbers performed by Simply Red, East 17, Oleta Adams, Massive Attack, Aretha Franklin, Gabrielle, Annie Lennox, etc. Costumes: Dany Everett. (PolyGram/British Screen/Canal Plus/Granada Film/Mainstream SA–PolyGram.) Rel: 9 June 1995. 110 mins. Cert 15.

Jefferson in Paris

Paris; 1784-89. Bum-numbing, structurally static depiction of Thomas Jefferson's five-year tenure in Paris as American ambassador, chronicling the eruption of the French Revolution and the future president's romance with both his Negro slave and an Anglo-Italian noblewoman (played by the Anglo-Italian Greta Scacchi). Exquisitely designed and produced, *Jefferson in Paris* fails to recruit the emotions although Thandie Newton, as Jefferson's fifteen-year-old maid (by whom

he reportedly had six children), is most vibrant and touching. Ultimately, though, this is even more boring than *The Age of Innocence*.

Cast: Nick Nolte (Thomas Jefferson), Greta Scacchi (Maria Cosway), Jean-Pierre Aumont (D'Hancarville), Simon Callow (Richard Cosway), Seth Gilliam (James Hemings), James Earl Jones (Madison Hemings), Michael Lonsdale (Louis XVI), Nancy Marchand (The Abbesse), Thandie Newton (Sally Hemings), Gwyneth Paltrow (Patsy Jefferson), Charlotte De Turckheim (Marie Antoinette), Lambert Wilson (Marquis de Lafayette), Beatrice Winde (Mary Hemings), Steve Kalfa (Dr Guillotin), Daniel Mesguich (Friedrich Mesmer), Estelle Eonnet, Todd Boyce, Bob Sessions, Elsa Zylberstein, Christopher Thompson, Jean-Francois Perrier, Anthony Valentine, Damien Groelle, Vernon Dobtchev, Jessica Lloyd, Jean-Paul Fouchecourt, Ismail Merchant, Vincent Cassel, Tim Choate.

Dir: James Ivory. Pro: Ismail Merchant. Co-Pro: Humbert Balson. Ex Pro: Donald Rosenfeld and Paul Bradley. Screenplay: Ruth Prawer Jhabvala. Ph: Pierre Lhomme. Ed: Andrew Marcus and Isabel Lorente. Pro Des: Guy-Claude Francoise. M: Richard Robbins. Costumes: Jenny Beavan and John Bright. (Touchstone Pictures/Merchant Ivory–Buena Vista.) Rel: 16 June 1995. 140 mins. Cert 12.

The Jungle Book

See *Rudyard Kipling's The Jungle Book*.

Junior

Junior is the nickname of a test-tube containing the cryogenically-preserved egg of one accident-prone Dr Diana Reddin (Emma Thompson). Junior is also the alias of the foetus being miraculously nourished in a stomach cavity of one Dr Alexander Hesse (Arnold Schwarzenegger). Brushing aside all scientific rationale, *Junior* is a high-concept comedy that skips through its paces with pre-packaged ease. However, in spite of all the enticing ingredients (Arnie, Emma and Danny DeVito are an extraordinary compound), *Junior* is a one-joke film. Arnie with sore nipples, Arnie suffering from morning sickness, Arnie crying at soppy TV commercials: it's the same joke. However, Schwarzenegger plays his expectant hunk with admirable restraint - and does look a picture in pink. P.S. Billy Crystal played the first pregnant man in the 1978 *Rabbit Test*.

Cast: Arnold Schwarzenegger (Dr Alexander Hesse), Danny DeVito (Dr Larry Arbogast), Emma Thompson (Dr Diana Reddin), Frank Langella (Noah Banes), Pamela Reed (Angela Arbogast), Judy Collins (Naomi), James Eckhouse, Aida Turturro, Welker White, Megan Cavanagh, Merle Kennedy, Mindy Seeger, Cassandra Wilson, Judy Ovitz, Ira Newborn, Lawrence Tierney, Matt Mulhern.

Dir and Pro: Ivan Reitman. Ex Pro: Joe Medjuck, Daniel Goldberg and Beverly J. Camhe. Screenplay: Kevin Wade and Chris Conrad. Ph: Adam Greenberg. Ed: Sheldon Kahn and Wendy Greene Bricmont. Pro Des: Stephen Lineweaver. M: James Newton Howard; numbers performed by Cassandra Wilson, Frank Sinatra, Bono and Patty Smyth. Costumes: Albert Wolsky. (Northern Lights/Universal–UIP.) Rel: 9 December 1994. 110 mins. Cert PG.

Just Cause

An eminent Harvard law professor (Sean Connery) is persuaded by his wife to 'get his hands muddy' on a case that was tied up years ago. It transpires that she herself was involved in the conviction of a backwoods black man, now locked up on Death Row. Accused of the barbaric rape and murder of an eleven-year-old girl, Bobby Earl has always maintained his innocence – give or take his confession at gun point. So, with a deep breath, Connery enters the treacherous waters of smalltown Florida law. Frequently unpleasant and far-fetched, *Just Cause* delivers enough detailed know-how to suspend disbelief in the John Grisham tradition. And, aided by a terrifying performance from Ed Harris as a remorseless psychopath, the film keeps a firm grip on the jugular.

Cast: Sean Connery (Paul Armstrong), Laurence Fishburne (Tanny Brown), Kate Capshaw (Laurie Armstrong), Blair Underwood (Bobby Earl Ferguson), Ruby Dee (Evangeline Ferguson), Ed Harris (Blair Sullivan), Christopher Murray (J.T. Wilcox), Scarlett Johansson, Daniel J. Travanti, Ned Beatty, Liz Torres, Lynne Thigpen, Taral Hicks, Victor Slezak, Kevin McCarthy, Hope Lange, Chris Sarandon, George Plimpton, Brooke Alderson, Colleen Fitzpatrick.

Dir: Arne Glimcher. Pro: Glimcher, Lee Rich and Steve Perry. Ex Pro: Sean Connery. Screenplay: Jeb Stuart and Peter Stone, from the novel by John Katzenbach. Ph: Jajos Koltai. Ed: William Anderson. Pro Des: Patrizia Von Brandstein. M: James Newton Howard; numbers performed by Beto and The Fairlanes, The Orioles, The Oscar Peterson Trio, etc. Costumes: Ann Roth and Gary Jones. (Warner/Fountainbridge Films–Warner.) Rel: 31 March 1995. 102 mins. Cert 18.

Kika

Madrid; 1993. A seedy American writer, a lesbian housekeeper, a mysterious voyeur, a futuristic TV reporter, a narcissistic photographer and a porn star on the run from the police all conspire to give Kika an exceptionally bad hair day. Typically off-the-wall, raunchy Pedro Almodóvar offering (his tenth feature), mixing such familiar elements as sex, fashion, the media, death and talk, talk, talk. However, as enticing as these ingredients may be and as funny and shocking as *Kika* often is, the film fails to gel. But does Almodóvar care? This is, after all, another joyful and accomplished celebration of madness and cruelty.

Cast: Peter Coyote (Nicholas), Verónica Forqué (Kika), Victoria Abril (Andrea 'Scarface' Caracortada), Alex Casanovas (Ramón), Rossy De Palma (Juana), Santiago Lajusticia (Paul 'Pablo' Bazzo), Francisca Caballero (Dona Paquita), Anabel Alonso, Bibi Andersen, Jesús Bonilla, Karra Elejalde, Claudia Aros.

Dir and Screenplay: Pedro Almodóvar. Ex Pro: Agustin Almodóvar. Line Pro: Esther Garcia. Ph: Alfredo Mayo. Ed: José Salcedo. Set Des: Javier Fernandez and Alain Bainee. M: various. Costumes: José Maria Cossio, Gianni Versace and Jean Paul

Emma Thompson and Arnold Schwarzenegger make an unlikely comedy duo in Ivan Reitman's high-concept Junior *(from UIP)*

Gaultier. Sound: Jean Paul Mugel. (El Deseo/SA/Ciby 2000–Electric.) Rel: 1 July 1994. 115 mins. Cert 18.

Killer

New York; 1994. Hardened by years of murder, a 36-year-old hitman is persuaded by his boss to 'whack' a woman who already knows she is to be terminated. Taken aback by his victim's acceptance of her fate, the hitman finds his curiosity turning into something entirely more passionate as he and she delay the inevitable. A thin idea, and not an entirely new one, is stretched to narrative chewing gum as the actors strive to make the most of staring at each other all night. It would have made a good short, though. Aka *Bulletproof Heart*.

Cast: Anthony LaPaglia (Mick), Mimi Rogers (Fiona), Matt Craven (Archie), Peter Boyle (George), Monika Schnarre (Laura), Joseph Maher (Dr Alstricht), Mark Acheson (Hellbig), Justine Priestly.

Dir: Mark Malone. Pro: Robert Vince and William Vince. Ex Pro: Robert Sigman, Gary Delfiner and Michael Strange. Screenplay: Gordon Melbourne, from a story by Malone. Ph: Tobias Schliessler. Ed: Robin Russell. Pro Des: Lynne Stopkewich. M: Graeme Coleman. Costumes: Maxyne Baker. (Keystone Films/Worldvision Enterprises– First Independent.) Rel: 9 June 1995. 98 mins. Cert 18.

Killing Zoe

In France to help a childhood friend pull off a bank robbery, Zed, an American safe-cracker, is surprised by the Paris he finds. On his first night he's visited by a

In the mouth of madness: Jean-Hugues Anglade and Gary Kemp do some serious homicide in Roger Avary's heart-pounding Killing Zoe *(from Rank)*

Kiss of Death

New York; 1994. Gritty, hard-nosed drama in which a former petty crook is sucked into a whirlpool of deceit and murder. Steadfastly sticking to his own code of honour, Jimmy Kilmartin finds himself stranded between New York's criminal underworld and an unethical police force. If he is to survive, he is going to have to start making up his own rules ... Smartly updating Henry Hathaway's classic 1947 *film noir* of the same name, scenarist Richard Price (*Sea of Love, Night and the City*) adds his own inimitable spin to a cracking story, providing much earthy dialogue and some dynamic characters. Nicolas Cage, after his recent stint as a light leading man, turns in a priceless villain that provokes both laughter and revulsion.

Cast: David Caruso (Jimmy Kilmartin), Samuel L. Jackson (Calvin), Nicolas Cage (Little Junior), Helen Hunt (Bev), Kathryn Erbe (Rosie), Stanley Tucci (Frank Zioli), Michael Rapaport (Ronnie), Ving Rhames (Omar), Philip Baker Hall, Anthony Heald, Angel David, John Costelloe, Anne Meara, Kevin Corrigan, Hugh Palmer, Hope Davis, Richard Price, Edward McDonald, Alex Stevens, Mark Hammer, Frank Dileo.

Dir: Barbet Schroeder. Pro: Schroeder and Susan Hoffman. Ex Pro: Jack Baran. Co-Pro and Screenplay: Richard Price. Ph: Luciano Tovoli. Ed: Lee Percy. Pro Des: Mel Bourne. M: Trevor Jones; numbers performed by 9 Lazy 9, Lisa Lisa, House of Pain, Salsa Picante, Liquid City, Hardfloor,

Smooching with the big boys: Nicolas Cage and Ving Rhames (right) casting bad vibes in Barbet Schroeder's Kiss of Death *(from Fox)*

prostitute called Zoe and is then shanghaied on a nocturnal binge of drinking, jazz and lots and lots of drugs. The next day he and a gang of misfits storm their way into a reserve bank, where Zed finds Zoe working as a secretary. Obviously, a lot of people are going to die... Although the characters are stereotypes, the set-up overly familiar and the violence gratuitous, *Killing Zoe* is a heist film so well made that it transcends its material. Interestingly, first-time director Roger Avary only wrote a heist film (over the course of one week) because he had free access to a bank. 'Necessity,' he explains, 'is the mother of invention.' Well, it ain't *Reservoir Dogs*, but it's bloody compelling.

Cast: Jean-Hugues Anglade (Eric), Eric Stoltz (Zed), Julie Delpy (Zoe), Gary Kemp (Oliver), Tai Thai, Bruce Ramsey, Kario Salem, Salvator Xuereb, Martin Raymond, Eric Pascal Chaltiel, Cecilia Peck, Gian Carlo Scanduizzi.

Dir and Screenplay: Roger Avary. Pro: Samuel Hadida. Ex Pro: Rebecca Boss, Quentin Tarantino and Lawrence Bender. Co-Pro: Jeff Schechtman. Ph: Tony Richmond. Ed: Kathryn Himoff. Pro Des: David Wasco. M: tomandandy. Costumes: Mary Claire Hannan. (PolyGram/Davis Film Prods–Rank.) Rel: 13 January 1995. 96 mins. Cert 18.

etc. Costumes: Theadora Van Runkle. (Fox.) Rel: 9 June 1995. 101 mins. Cert 18.

Ladybird, Ladybird

Harrowing, provocative and superbly realised film based on the true story of Maggie, a spirited Liverpudlian singer living in London. A victim of her own willingness to 'find trouble and go to bed with it', Maggie is refused contact with her four children (by four different fathers), but finds hope for a kinder future in the form of a mild-mannered Paraguayan refugee. He too is escaping a horrific past and maybe, together, they can start a new life and family. But because of her record of violence and poverty (an abused childhood, brutal boyfriends), Maggie finds herself up against Social Services and their unyielding interference. Not only is Maggie's story too terrible to contemplate, it is hammered home with a documentary realism that makes it leap off the screen. Direction, performances and an uncomfortable naturalism conspire to make this an unforgettable, daunting piece of British filmmaking.

Cast: Crissy Rock (Maggie), Vladimir Vega (Jorge), Ray Winstone (Simon), Pamela Hunt (Mrs Higgs), Sandie Lavelle, Mauricio Venegas, Clare Perkins, Jason Stracey, Scottie Moore, Alan Gold, James Bannon, Christine Ellerbeck.
    Dir: Ken Loach. Pro: Sally Hibbin. Screenplay: Rona Munro. Ph: Barry Ackroyd. Ed: Jonathan Morris. Pro Des: Martin Johnson. M: George Fenton. (Parallax Pictures/Channel Four–UIP.) Rel: 30 September 1994. 102 mins. Cert 18.

The Last Seduction

When Bridget Gregory stubs out her cigarette in an uncut apple pie labelled 'Love, Grandma', you know she is unredeemable. She gets worse as she spins her toxic, seductive web around any stray male unlucky enough to get in her way as she homes in on her ultimate victim - her husband. *The Last Seduction* works as prime *film noir* black comedy because its lead protagonist is a ruthless original - a beautiful, sexy woman who knows what she wants and is cold-blooded enough to get it without the obstruction of morality. Linda Fiorentino (*After Hours*, *The Moderns*) as the self-confessed 'absolute bitch' makes the most of her role without resorting to

The Maggie syndrome: Crissy Rock with Luke Brown, India Bayes and Lily Farrell in Ken Loach's emotionally excoriating Ladybird, Ladybird *(from UIP)*

vampish ham, while Steve Barancik's lean, mean screenplay never misses a trick.

Cast: Linda Fiorentino (Bridget Gregory/ Wendy Kroy), Peter Berg (Mike Swale), Bill Pullman (Clay Gregory), J.T. Walsh (Frank Griffith), Bill Nunn (Harlan), Herb Mitchell, Brien Varady, Dean Norris, Donna Wilson, Mik Scriba, Michael Raysses, Serena.

Dir: John Dahl. Pro: Jonathan Shestack. Co-Pro: Nancy Rea Stone. Screenplay: Steve Barancik. Ph: Jeffrey Jur. Ed: Eric L. Beason. Pro Des: Linda Pearl. M: Joseph Vitarelli; numbers performed by The ElderGreens, C.A. Terrell, Blues Traveler, Sandy Rogers and The Smokin' Joe Kubek Band. Costumes: Terry Dresbach. (ITC Entertainment–Metro Tartan.) Rel: 5 August 1994. 110 mins. Cert 18.

Looking to defile some apple pie: Linda Fiorentino as the ultimate self-made bitch in John Dahl's wickedly entertaining The Last Seduction *(from Metro Tartan)*

Smouldering on: Brad Pitt and Julia Ormond feel the urge in Edward Zwick's leviathan Legends of the Fall *(from Columbia TriStar)*

Legends of the Fall

Set at the beginning of the twentieth century and embracing a myriad of story strands, *Legends of the Fall* is a sweeping family saga that bites off more than it can chew. While the narrative itself is fortified by overlapping waves of irony, the greatest irony of all is that this hyperactive tale of love, pride and courage was actually based on a short story in *Esquire* magazine. Yet in spite of its compact genesis, the film feels like a mini-series cut down to a movie. And notwithstanding some superlative act-ing and craftsmanship, too much incident is crammed in to beg credibility, hardly helped by James Horner's symphonic score that brazenly underlines the melodrama. Ultimately, *Legends of the Fall*, which was nominated for a Golden Globe as best film of 1994 and won an Oscar for its cinematography, feels more like an illustrated concert than a movie.

Cast: Brad Pitt (Tristan Ludlow), Anthony Hopkins (Col. William Ludlow), Aidan Quinn (Alfred Ludlow), Julia Ormond (Susannah), Henry Thomas (Samuel Ludlow), Karina Lombard (Isabel Two), Tantoo Cardinal (Pet), Gordon Tootoosis (One Stab), Paul Desmond (Decker), Christina Pickles (Isabel), Robert Wisden, John Novak, Kenneth Welsh, Bill Dow, Sam Sarkar, Nigel Bennett, David Kaye, Christine Harder, Bart the Bear.

Dir: Edward Zwick. Pro: Zwick, Bill Wittliff and Marshall Herskovitz. Co-Pro: Jane Bartelme and Sarah Caplan. Ex Pro: Patrick Crowley. Screenplay: Wittliff and Susan Shilliday, from the short story by Jim Harrison. Ph: John Toll. Ed: Steven Rosenblum. Pro Des: Lilly Kilvert. M: James Horner. Costumes: Deborah Scott. (TriStar/Bedford Falls/Pangaea–Columbia TriStar.) Rel: 28 April 1995. 132 mins. Cert 15.

Leon

In Luc Besson's *Nikita*, Jean Reno played an emotionless, ruthless hitman known as The Cleaner. Four years later he reappears as Leon, now working the streets of New York with the efficiency of a Schwarzenegger villain, but with an eccentricity that only the French can master. Leon drinks milk by the quart, adores Gene Kelly and his best friend is a pot plant called Eliot. A man of routine who keeps himself to himself, Leon is answerable to no one – not, that is, until a twelve-year-old girl begs for sanctuary in his apartment. Mathilda's family has been wiped out by a corrupt DEA department and she has nowhere to turn. For the first time Leon is forced to care for – and not to annihilate – a human life ... While employing stereotypical genre characters – the ruthless hitman, the corrupt cop – director Luc Besson (*Subway*, *Nikita*) adds a human twist by throwing an innocent, streetwise girl into the stew, superbly realised by newcomer Natalie Portman. Gary Oldman is also sensational as the malignant, Beethoven-obsessed cop, in one of the decade's most stylish and suspenseful thrillers. US title: *The Professional.*

Cast: Jean Reno (Leon), Gary Oldman (Stansfield), Natalie Portman (Mathilda), Danny Aiello (Tony), Peter Appel (Malky), Michael Badalucco, Ellen Greene, Elizabeth Regen, Carl J. Matusovich, Randolph Scott, Keith A. Glascoe, Frank Senger, Luc Bernard, George Martin.

Dir, Pro and Screenplay: Luc Besson. Ex Pro: Claude Besson. Line Pro: Bernard Grenet. Ph: Thierry Arbogast. Ed: Sylvie Landra. Pro Des: Dan Weil. M: Eric Serra; 'Shape Of My Heart' performed by Sting. Costumes: Magali Guidasci. (Gaumont/Les Films Du Dauphin–Buena Vista.) Rel: 3 February 1995. 110 mins. Cert 18.

Lightning Jack

Lightning Jack Kane may be one of the fastest guns in the west, but he has a severe ego problem. Ashamed of his

Lolita lives: Natalie Portman in Luc Besson's Leon *(from Buena Vista)*

poor eyesight and meagre public recognition, the bank robber and cold-blooded killer sets about brushing up his image – with the help of an inexperienced mute. While never less than engaging, *Lightning Jack* has a startling low quota of laughs. Indeed, it is arguably the unfunniest, most agreeable comedy of the year. Still, this Western goes down in the history books as the first motion picture entirely financed on the stock exchange. Filmed on location in Utah, Arizona, New Mexico and Colorado, and on sound stages in Queensland.

Cast: Paul Hogan (Lightning Jack Kane), Cuba Gooding Jr (Ben Doyle), Beverly D'Angelo (Lana), Kamala Dawson (Pilar), Pat Hingle (Marshall Kurtz), Roger Daltrey (John T. Coles), L.Q. Jones (Tom), Richard Riehle, Frank McRae, Max Cullen, Sandy Ward, Roy Brocksmith, Ed Adams, Jess Franks.

Dir: Simon Wincer. Pro: Wincer, Paul Hogan and Greg Coote. Ex Pro: Graham Burke and Anthony Stewart. Line Pro: Grant Hill. Screenplay: Hogan. Ph: David Eggby. Ed: O. Nicholas Brown. Pro Des: Bernard Hides. M: Bruce Rowland. Costumes: Bruce Finlayson. (Lightning Ridge/Village Roadshow–Buena Vista.) Rel: 1 July 1994. 97 mins. Cert PG.

The Lion King

The Disney studio's 32nd full-length animated feature, this is the story of a lion cub (Simba) facing up to his responsibilities as the king of the beasts. Chased from his own kingdom by his wicked Uncle Scar, Simba grows up in a far-off jungle under the tutelage of a wise-cracking meerkat and a wart hog. But for how long can the deposed prince be fulfilled as a leonine variation of Baloo? Arguably the most technically accomplished cartoon ever made, *The Lion King* is moving, funny and always stunning to look at. And, as with any Disney creation, there are the incomparable animal characters: most notably Rowan Atkinson's hilarious, accident-prone hornbill and Ernie Sabella's Pumbaa, a flatulent, slow-witted wart hog. Also, the music, dialogue and photographic effects are all top-notch. P.S. *The Lion King* is the first Disney cartoon not inspired by previously published material (although it does prompt comparisons with everything from *Hamlet* to *Bambi*).

Voices: Jonathan Taylor Thomas (young Simba), Matthew Broderick (adult Simba), James Earl Jones (Mufasa), Jeremy Irons (Scar), Moira Kelly (adult Nala), Niketa

A roaring success and the pride of Disney: Simba and Uncle Scar in The Lion King

Calame (young Nala), Ernie Sabella (Pumbaa), Nathan Lane (Timon), Robert Guillaume (Rafiki), Rowan Atkinson (Zazu), Madge Sinclair (Sarabi), Whoopi Goldberg (Shenzi), Cheech Marin (Banzai), Jim Cummings (Ed).

Dir: Roger Allers and Rob Minkoff. Pro: Don Hahn. Ex Pro: Thomas Schumacher and Sarah McArthur. Assoc Pro: Alice Dewey. Screenplay: Irene Mecchi, Jonathan Roberts and Linda Woolverton. Ed: Tom Finan and John Carnochan. Pro Des: Chris Sanders. M: Hans Zimmer; songs by Tim Rice and Elton John; 'Can You Feel The Love Tonight' performed by Elton John. (Walt Disney–Buena Vista.) Rel: 7 October 1994. 87 mins. Cert U.

Little Big League

An eleven-year-old baseball fanatic's wildest dreams come true when he inherits the major league team The Minnesota Twins. The downside is that the team is on a losing streak, but then maybe all the players need is someone to restore their passion in the game ... The trouble with *Little Big League* is that

Into his league: Luke Edwards (left) *faces up to the big guns – in this case, O'Neil Compton – in Andrew Scheinman's* Little Big League *(from Rank)*

the premise is too predictable – yet any diversion from the anticipated path would sabotage the concept. Still, in spite of its length and yawning similarities to *Rookie of the Year*, the film is not as cloying as it could have been and does discharge the odd goose pimple. Good, natural performances, too, from Luke Edwards, Ashley Crowe (as Luke's mom) and Timothy Busfield. Directed by Castle Rock executive Andrew Scheinman.

Cast: Luke Edwards (Billy Heywood), Timothy Busfield (Lou Collins), John Ashton (Mac Macnally), Ashley Crowe (Jenny Heywood), Kevin Dunn (Arthur Goslin), Jason Robards (Thomas Heywood), Billy L. Sullivan (Chuck Lobert), Miles Feulner (Joey Smith), Bradley Jay Lesley (John 'Blackout' Gatling), Scott Patterson (Mike McGrevey), Jonathan Silverman, Dennis Farina, Wolfgang Bodison, Duane Davis, Leon 'Bull' Durham, Kevin Elster, Joseph Latimore, John Minch, Michael Papajohn, Troy Startoni, Antonio Lewis Todd, O'Neil Compton, Mark McGann, Ken Griffey Jr, Randy Johnson, Dean Palmer, Chris Berman.
 Dir: Andrew Scheinman. Pro: Mike Lobell. Ex Pro: Steve Nicolaides and Andrew Bergman. Screenplay: Gregory K. Pincus and Adam Scheinman. Ph: Donald E. Thorin. Ed: Michael Jablow. Pro Des: Jeffrey Howard. M: Stanley Clarke; numbers performed by Jeff Beck, Booker T & the MGs, The Band, John Fogerty, Dion, and Taj Mahal. Costumes: Erica Edell Phillips. (Castle Rock–Rank.) Rel: 7 April 1995. 120 mins. Cert PG.

Little Odessa

Set in New York's Russian community of Brighton Beach, James Gray's first feature is a commendable piece of atmospheric filmmaking. Eschewing florid camera moves and melodramatic cutting, Gray tells his grim story in unhurried, economic strokes. Tim Roth is Joshua Shapira, a Russian-American hitman banished from the streets of his childhood, but compelled to return on a professional assignment. But the memories are too strong and in spite of a facade of indifferent cool, Joshua is sucked back into a domestic maelstrom that can only result in ironic tragedy. Gray was drawn to realising a classic tragedy in a pocket of America seldom explored by the camera, and he has done just that. A powerful film, but a real downer.

Cast: Tim Roth (Joshua Shapira), Edward Furlong (Reuben Shapira), Moira Kelly (Alla Shustervich), Vanessa Redgrave (Irina Shapira), Maximilian Schell (Arkady Shapira), Paul Guilfoyle (Boris Volkoff), Natasha Andreichenko (Natasha), David Vadim (Sasha), Mina Bern (Grandma Tsilya), Boris McGiver, Mohammad Ghaffari, Michael Khumrov.
 Dir and Screenplay: James Gray. Pro: Paul Webster. Co-Pro: Kerry Orent. Ex Pro: Nich Wechsler, Claudia Lewis and Rolf Mittweg. Ph: Tom Richmond. Ed: Dorian Harris. Pro Des: Kevin Thompson. M: various. Costumes: Michael Clancy. (New Line–First Independent.) Rel: 5 April 1995. 98 mins. Cert 15.

High life, low comedy: Blake McIver Ewing and Brittany Ashton Holmes date in style in Penelope Spheeris's awful The Little Rascals *(from UIP)*

The Little Rascals

Update on the old Hal Roach shorts featuring the moppets from hell, in which Alfalfa (the one with the gravity-defying cowlick) violates the rules of The He-Man Womun Haters club by falling in love with – gulp – a girl! Thus, much speeded-up photography, lame pranks and the odd dash of political correctness ensue. Most of the cast can't act their way out of a wet paper nappy (the camera frequently picking up the kids' lack of concentration), all of which should make us appreciate the young stars we *do* have today. From the director of *The Beverly Hillbillies.*

Cast: Travis Tedford (Spanky), Bug Hall (Alfalfa), Brittany Ashton Holmes (Darla), Kevin Jamal Woods (Stymie), Zachary Mabry (Porky), Ross Elliot Bagley (Buckwheat), Blake McIver Ewing (Waldo), Jordan Warkol (Froggy), Courtland Mead (Uh-Huh), Sam Saletta, Blake Jeremy Collins, Juliette Brewer, Heather Karasek, Mel Brooks, Whoopi Goldberg, Daryl Hannah, Reba McEntire, Lea Thompson, Donald Trump, George Wendt.
Dir: Penelope Spheeris. Pro: Michael King and Bill Oakes. Ex Pro: Gerald R. Molen, Deborah Jelin Newmyer and Roger King. Screenplay: Spheeris, Paul Guay and Stephen Mazur, from a story by Spheeris, Guay, Mazur, Robert Wolterstorff and Mike Scott. Ph: Richard Bowen. Ed: Ross Albert. Pro Des: Larry Fulton. M: William Ross; numbers performed by Bug Hall, Randy Newman, Rosanne Cash, George Foster and Dr John. Costumes: Jami Burrows. (Universal/King World–UIP.) Rel: 14 April 1995. 82 mins. Cert U.

Little Women

The fourth screen incarnation of Louisa May Alcott's classic 1868 novel both enthralls and disappoints. Updated to a 1990s political sensibility, the film boasts some wonderful performances and a number of moving scenes, but cannot overcome the episodic nature and romantic excesses of the book. Winona Ryder is far too pretty as Jo, the plain, awkward and temperamental heroine, and the tamperings with the original are bound to infuriate the purists. Worse still, the whole tone of the film seems misplaced: the March children are on the verge of destitution, yet the film has a lush visual design (and a voluptuous score) that makes a mockery of their plight. A simpler style would

Sumptuous poverty: Winona Ryder, Trini Alvarado, Kirsten Dunst, Claire Danes and Susan Sarandon enjoy the poor life in Gillian Armstrong's Little Women *(from Columbia TriStar)*

have been far more effective. Still, there are welcome moments of good humour, and Christian Bale and Gabriel Byrne as Jo's suitors are excellent. Ultimately, however, one has to wonder at the wisdom of making yet another screen version of this old chestnut.

Cast: Winona Ryder (Jo March), Gabriel Byrne (Friedrich Bhaer), Trini Alvarado (Meg March), Samantha Mathis (older Amy March), Kirsten Dunst (younger Amy March), Claire Danes (Beth March), Christian Bale (Laurie), Eric Stoltz (John Brooke), Mary Wickes (Aunt March), Susan Sarandon (Mrs March), John Neville (Mr Laurence), Florence Paterson (Hannah), Corrie Clark, Rebecca Toolan, Matthew Walker.
Dir: Gillian Armstrong. Pro: Denise DiNovi. Co-Pro and Screenplay: Robin Swicord. Ph: Geoffrey Simpson. Ed: Nicholas Beauman. Pro Des: Jan Roelfs. M: Thomas Newman. Costumes: Colleen Atwood. (DiNovi Pictures–Columbia.) Rel: 17 March 1995. 118 mins. Cert U.

Talking dirty: Joanne Vannicola, Thomas Gibson and Ruth Marshall explore their sexuality in Denys Arcand's arresting Love and Human Remains *(from Rank)*

Love and Human Remains

Montreal; today. Candy is in the process of re-evaluating her sexuality; her gay flatmate, David, is finding himself inexplicably drawn to a heterosexual bus boy; Bernie is getting bored with the women he fucks and is looking for more dangerous stimulation; and Benita is a dominatrix who can see into the future . . . These and other troubled souls take a long hard look at sex, friendship and death in Denys Arcand's first English language film, a self-conscious comedy-drama adapted from Brad Fraser's play *Unidentified Human Remains and the True Nature of Love.* Because of the play's complex, almost cinematic structure, there are enough disparate elements to distract and entertain, and Arcand juggles them

Fatal distraction: Nadia Fares causes romantic chaos in Christopher Frank's intriguing Love in the Strangest Way *(from Gala)*

well. However, these characters cannot be believed and what they say – however witty and insightful – sits like rehearsed dialogue on their tongues. Ultimately, the film will be remembered for Thomas Gibson's star turn as David, a performance that at first feels uncomfortably stagy but grows in resonance and humour as we adjust to Arcand's mechanical realism.

Cast: Thomas Gibson (David), Ruth Marshall (Candy), Cameron Bancroft (Bernie), Mia Kirshner (Benita), Joanne Vannicola (Jerri), Matthew Ferguson (Kane), Rick Roberts (Robert), Aidan Devine, Robert Higden, Sylvain Morin, Alex Wylding.
Dir: Denys Arcand. Pro: Roger Frappier. Ex Pro: Frappier and Pierre Latour. Co-Pro: Peter Sussman. Screenplay: Brad Fraser. Ph: Paul Sarossy. Ed: Alain Baril. Pro Des: Francois Seguin. M: John McCarthy; numbers performed by Karen Young, T-99, Voivod, Snap and Universal Honey. Costumes: Denis Sperdouklis. (PolyGram/Max Films/Atlantis Films–Rank.) Rel: 22 July 1994. 100 mins. Cert 18.

Love, Cheat and Steal

On a personal level, Paul Harrington couldn't be happier. He's rich, successful and has just married a loving, beautiful woman many years his junior. There's trouble at the bank, but Harrington's looking into that and is on the verge of lancing the boil in his office. Then his new brother-in-law turns up out of the blue and things start to go terribly wrong . . . Unfortunately, first-time writer-director William B. Curran's stilted dialogue precludes the possibility of believing in any of his characters, try as the actors might to conceal the contrivance of the plot.

Cast: John Lithgow (Paul Harrington), Eric Roberts (Reno Adams), Madchen Amick (Lauren Harrington), Richard Edson (Billy Quayle), Dan O'Herlihy (Hamilton Fisk), Jason Workman (Whit Turner), David Ackroyd (Tom Kerry), Donald Moffat, Claude Earl Jones, Jack Axelrod, Bill McKinney, Mary Fanaro, Kathleen Beaton, Stuart McKinney.
Dir and Screenplay: William Curran. Pro: Brad Krevoy and Steve Stabler. Co-Pro: Chad Oman. Line Pro: Tracie Graham. Ph: Kent Wakeford and Janusz Kaminski. Ed: Carole Kravetz. Pro Des: Jane Ann Stewart. Costumes: Dorothy Amos. (Showtime Networks/Motion Picture Corp–ITC.) Rel: 6 January 1995. 96 mins. Cert 18.

Love in the Strangest Way - Elles N'Oublient Pas

Julien is happily married with a seven-year-old son, has a nice Paris apartment and is content in his work as a debt collector. Then, with his wife and son away on holiday, he notices a young beautiful woman sitting outside the cafe opposite his office. Whenever he passes the restaurant, or looks out of his office window, she is there. Soon, he asks her to dinner, an invitation that comes as a shock to the woman. Then, out of the blue, she calls his office and accepts the offer. They end up at his apartment, she takes her clothes off and, straddling his son's rocking horse, she smashes it. As it happens, this is just the first thing in Julien's life that the mysterious brunette destroys ... A truly accomplished Hitchcockian thriller (a term much abused) which, if it didn't resemble *Fatal Attraction* so much, would be ripe for a Hollywood remake. It's just a shame that the rapport between Julien and his wife is not made more credible. Still, it's compulsive viewing.

Cast: Thierry Lhermitte (Julien Bernier), Maruschka Detmers (Anne Bernier), Nadia Fares (Angela Galli), Umberto Orsini (Vienne), Marie-Christine Adam (Le Guennec), Johann Martel, Patrick Timsit, Bernard Freyd, Patrick Floersheim, Marina Rodriguez Tome.

Dir and Screenplay: Christopher Frank, from an idea by Jean-Marc Roberts. Pro: Michelle De Broca. Ex Pro: Jean Nachbaur. Ph: Bertrand Chatry. Ed: Catherine Dubeau. Pro Des: Dominique André. M: Jean-Marie Senia. Costumes: Yvette Frank. (Fildebroc/TF1 Films/Capac/Ice Film/Canal Plus–Gala.) Rel: 4 November 1994. 107 mins. Cert 15.

Mad Dogs and Englishmen

London/Kent; 1994. Ludicrous concoction about a spoilt upper-class bitch with a heroin habit and a long-haired, leather jacketed American messenger boy with an unconvincing laugh. Quite how the latter falls for the former is unexplained, even when he tells her that he's 'looking for the real Antonia – the Antonia that cares'. Throw in a parallel plot about a dotty drug enforcement officer (a manic Joss Ackland) who's been banging his own daughter, and you have the worst British film since *Beyond Bedlam*. Terrible dialogue, terrible performances, terribly misguided.

Cast: Elizabeth Hurley (Antonia Dyer), C. Thomas Howell (Mike Stone), Joss Ackland (Sam Stringer), Jeremy Brett (Tony Vernon-

The unruly royal: Nigel Hawthorne, Helen Mirren and Amanda Donohoe in Nicholas Hytner's The Madness of King George *(from Rank)*

Smith), Claire Bloom (Liz Stringer), Paula Hamilton (Charlotte), Frederick Treves (Sir Harry Dyer), Andrew Connolly (Clive Nathan), Chris Adamson (Max Quinlan), Louise Delamere (Sandy), David Harewood, Marcus Bentley, Nicola Duffett, Ian Henderson, Kate Howard, Russ Kane, Jason Lake, Patrick Lichfield, Hugh Sachs, Herbert Leslie Wright, Brett Forest and the voice of Alan 'Fluff' Freeman.

Dir: Henry Cole. Pro: Peter Watson-Wood and Nigel Thomas. Ex Pro: Ashley Levett. Screenplay: Tim Sewell, from a story by Cole. Ph: John Peters. Ed: Lionel Selwyn and Simon Hilton. Pro Des: Tony Stringer. M: Barrie Guard. Costumes: Lisa Johnson. (Movie Screen Entertainment/Moor Street Films–Entertainment.) Rel: 2 June 1995. 97 mins. Cert 18.

The Madness of King George

Nicholas Hytner's film, a visually sumptuous version of Alan Bennett's play *The Madness of George III*, is replete with admirable ingredients that seem in search of a recipe. Nigel Hawthorne as the genial, tragic monarch is a dynamic whirlwind of emotions and is well

Monster mash: Richard Briers and Robert De Niro in Kenneth Branagh's frenetic Mary Shelley's Frankenstein *(from Columbia TriStar)*

supported by Rupert Everett as his foppish son and Julian Wadham as a stony-faced William Pitt. The locations, music, photography and costumes are all exceptional too, but at the end of the day this is nothing more than a well-written page of English history. A story would've been nice. P.S. Arundel Castle doubles as Windsor Castle.

Cast: Nigel Hawthorne (George III), Helen Mirren (Queen Charlotte), Ian Holm (Willis), Amanda Donohoe (Lady Pembroke), Rupert Graves (Greville), Rupert Everett (The Prince of Wales), Anthony Calf (Fitzroy), John Wood (Thurlow), Julian Wadham (William Pitt), Jim Carter (Fox), Geoffrey Palmer (Warren), Charlotte Curley, Matthew Lloyd Davies, Nick Irons, Jeremy Child, Nicholas Selby, Barry Stanton, Struan Rodger, Janine Duvitski, Caroline Harker, Iain Mitchell, Roger Hammond, Cyril Shaps, Selina Cadell, Peter Woodthorpe, Roger Ashton-Griffiths, Robert Swann, Alan Bennett.
Dir: Nicholas Hytner. Pro: Stephen Evans and David Parfitt. Line Pro: Mark Cooper. Screenplay: Alan Bennett. Ph: Andrew Dunn. Ed: Tariq Anwar. Pro Des: Ken Adam. Set Decoration: Carolyn Scott. M: George Frederic Handel, adapted by George Fenton. Costumes: Mark Thomp-

son. (Samuel Goldwyn/Channel Four/Close Call–Rank.) Rel: 24 March 1995. 110 mins. Cert PG.

Major League II

The league's crummiest baseball players are reunited five years after the first film and have all changed for the worse. Most surprising of all is that Rick 'Wild Thing' Vaughn has become a respectable, upstanding citizen, and that Pedro Cerrano has traded in his voodoo for Buddhism. But change, dear viewer, is the last thing that the ill-fated Cleveland Indians need. A reasonably faithful photocopy of the first film, *Major League II* is, on the artistic menu of American cuisine, regurgitated bubble-gum.

Cast: Charlie Sheen (Rick 'Wild Thing' Vaughn), Tom Berenger (Jake Taylor), Corbin Bernsen (Roger Dorn), Dennis Haysbert (Pedro Cerrano), James Gammon (Lou Brown), Omar Epps (Willie Mays Hayes), Eric Bruskotter (Rube Baker), David Keith (Jack Parkman), Alison Doody (Flannery), Michelle Burke (Nikki Reese), Takaaki Ishibashi (Isuro Tanaka), Margaret Whitton (Rachel Phelps), Bob Uecker (Harry Doyle), Steve Yeager, Jay Leno, Jesse Ventura, Randy Quaid, Rene Russo.
Dir: David S. Ward. Pro: Ward and James G. Robinson. Ex Pro: Gary Barber. Screenplay: R.J. Stewart, from a story by Stewart, Tom S. Parker and Jim Jennewein. Ph: Victor Hammer. Ed: Paul Seydor and

Donn Cambern. Pro Des: Stephen Hendrickson. M: Michel Colombier and James Newton Howard; numbers performed by X, Little Feat, Maurice John Vaughn, Stevie Ray Vaughan and Double Trouble, Lyle Lovett and Jimmie Vaughan. Costumes: Bobbie Read. (Morgan Creek–Warner.) Rel: 28 October 1994. 105 mins. Cert PG.

The Mangler

In the town of Rikers Valley, Maine, the casualties and fatalities are mounting at the Victorian Blue Ribbon Laundry. For hard-bitten, stereotypical movie cop John Hunton the answer seems to be that too many people have missing bits in the Blue Ribbon's dramatic centre-piece: the five-ton, forty-foot industrial press (aka The Mangler). Furthermore, the spirit of The Mangler would appear to reside in a number of the local populace. A novel addendum to the well-splattered genre of demonic possession – from a short story by Stephen King – *The Mangler* is let down by a hackneyed script and stressed-out direction. The effects, however, are excellent. Next: *The Microwave Massacre.*

Cast: Robert Englund (Bill Gartley), Ted Levine (John Hunton), Daniel Matmore (Mark Jackson), Jeremy Crutchley (pictureman/mortician), Vanessa Pike (Sherry Ouelette), Demetre Phillips (George Stanner), Lisa Morris (Lin Sue), Vera Blacker, Ashley Hayden, Danny Keogh, Ted Leplat, Todd Jensen.
Dir: Tobe Hooper. Pro: Anant Singh. Ex Pro: Harry Alan Towers, Sudhir Pragjee, Sanjeev Singh and Helena Spring. Screenplay: Hooper, Stephen Brooks and Peter Welbeck. Ph: Amnon Salomon. Ed: David Heitner. Pro Des: David Barkham. M: Barrington Pheloung. Sound: Richard Sprawson. SFX: Brooks. Make-Up: Scott Wheeler. 'Mangler' created by: William Hooper. (Distant Horizon Filmex/Allied Film Prods–Guild.) Rel: 26 May 1995. 105 mins. Cert 18.

Man of the House

Seattle; 1994. When successful US attorney Jack Sturges moves in with single mom Sandra Archer, life looks like a bed of roses. But then Jack hadn't bargained on the psychological warfare declared by Sandra's eleven-year-old son, Ben. Ben sees Jack as a threat to his own relationship with mom – and it's up to Jack to solve the problem. Lightweight and sentimental, *Man of the House* is emotional popcorn – with the depth and charm of a TV sitcom. Actually, most sitcoms are usually more credible.

Cast: Chevy Chase (Jack Sturges), Farrah Fawcett (Sandra Archer), Jonathan Taylor Thomas (Ben Archer), George Wendt (Chet Bronski), David Shiner (Lloyd Small), Art LaFleur (Red Sweeney), Richard Portnow (Joey Renda), Richard Foronjy (Murray), Zachary Browne (Norm Bronski), Peter Appel, Chief Leonard George, George Greif, Ron Canada, Chris Miranda, Spencer Vrooman, Nicholas Garrett, Jimmy Baker, Sean Orr.

Dir: James Orr. Pro: Bonnie Bruchheimer and Marty Katz. Ex Pro: Margaret South. Screenplay: Orr and Jim Cruickshank, from a story by David Peckinpah and Richard Jefferies. Ph: Jamie Anderson. Ed: Harry Keramidas. Pro Des: Lawrence G. Paull. M: Mark Mancina; numbers performed by The Kingsmen, C&C Music Factory, The Children, Medicine Wheel, and Enigma. Costumes: Tom Bronson. Bee Consultant: Dr Norman E. Gary. (Walt Disney Pictures/All Girl Prods–Buena Vista.) Rel: 9 June 1995. 97 mins. Cert U.

Mary Shelley's Frankenstein

Without doubt, this is the most faithful screen translation yet of Mary Godwin's 1818 classic, including the

Cardiac arresting: Jim Carrey bringing the excesses of comic strip alive in Charles (Chuck) Russell's lunatic The Mask *(from Entertainment)*

prologue and epilogue in which we find the good baron being chased across the Arctic by his creation. However, by compressing the entire span of Victor Frankenstein's life into two hours, director Kenneth Branagh has bitten off more than he can chew, resulting in the creation of an operatic stew. It isn't until the belated arrival of The Creature himself (played with enormous pathos and strength by De Niro in grotesque make-up), that the film finally settles into its stride. Nevertheless, there is much to admire, not least the historical context into which the story is drawn, making even the fantastic seem convincing.

Cast: Robert De Niro (The Creature), Kenneth Branagh (Victor Frankenstein), Tom Hulce (Henry), Helena Bonham-Carter (Elizabeth), Aidan Quinn (Captain Walton), Ian Holm (Victor's father), John Cleese (Professor Waldman), Richard Briers (blind grandfather), Robert Hardy (Professor Krempe), Cherie Lunghi (Victor's mother), Trevyn McDowell (Justine), Celia Imrie, Gerard Horan, Mark Hadfield, Joanna Roth, Richard Clifford, Jimmy Yuill.

Dir: Kenneth Branagh. Pro: Francis Ford Coppola, Jim V. Hart and John Veitch. Ex Pro: Fred Fuchs. Co-Pro: Branagh and David Parfitt. Screenplay: Steph Lady and Frank Darabont. Ph: Roger Pratt. Ed: Andrew Marcus. Pro Des: Tim Harvey. M: Patrick Doyle. Costumes: James Acheson. Creature Make-Up: Daniel Parker. (Japan Satellite Broadcasting/IndiProd Co./American Zoetrope–Columbia Tri-Star.) Rel: 4 November 1994. 123 mins. Cert 15.

Ma Saison Préférée – My Favourite Season

Antoine, a distinguished neurologist and brain surgeon in Toulouse, and his older sister, Emilie, a successful public notary, have always had a volatile relationship. When their mother succumbs to the vagaries of old age, they find their relationship stretched and enlightened in a way neither had anticipated. Thanks to the performances of Daniel Auteuil and Catherine Deneuve as the sparring siblings, this heavy, self-indulgent film gains a strength and credibility that grips the attention even as it seems to be going nowhere.

Cast: Catherine Deneuve (Emilie), Daniel Auteuil (Antoine), Marthe Villalonga (Berthe), Jean-Pierre Bouvier (Bruno), Chiara Mastroianni (Anne), Carmen Chaplin (Khadija), Anthony Prada (Lucien), Michele Moretti, Ingrid Caven.

Dir: André Téchiné. Pro: Alain Sarde. Screenplay: Téchiné and Pascal Bonitzer. Ph: Thierry Arbogast. Ed: Martine Giordano. Pro Des: Carlos Conti. M: Philippe Sarde. Costumes: Claire Fraisse. (Films Alain Sarde/TF1 Films/DA Films/Canal Plus–Arrow.) Rel: 15 July 1994. 125 mins. Cert 15.

The Mask

Manipulated by women, humiliated by his boss and exploited by garage mechanics, Stanley Ipkiss is on a downward spiral. That is, until he discovers an ancient Norse mask that empowers all of his deepest desires. Instantly

Jodie Foster as the mother of con artists in Richard Donner's amblin', intensely likeable Maverick (from Warner)

transformed into a cross between the genie of the lamp and Kid Creole, Stanley Ipkiss has the town of Edge City at his feet. After a dismal opening, this bizarre blend of *Superman*, *Aladdin* and *Who Framed Roger Rabbit* takes off on all cylinders. *The Mask* – based on the *Dark Horse* comic series – proves to be a perfect vehicle for the unconventional personality of Jim Carrey, the zany ILM effects building on Carrey's persona rather than obscuring it. There are also good turns from Peter Riegert as a cynical, wise-cracking cop, and from Max as Stanley's game, tenacious Jack Russell. Enormous fun.

Cast: Jim Carrey (Stanley Ipkiss/The Mask), Peter Riegert (Lt Mitch Kellaway), Peter Greene (Dorian), Amy Yasbeck (Peggy Brandt), Richard Jeni (Charles Schumaker), Cameron Diaz (Tina Carlyle), Orestes Matacena (Niko), Jim Doughan (Doyle), Benjamin J. Stein (Dr Arthur Neuman), Tim Bagley, Nancy Fish, Johnny Williams, Reginald E. Cathey, Denis Forest, Max (Milo).
Dir: Charles Russell. Pro: Bob Engelman. Ex Pro: Russell, Mike Richardson and Michael De Luca. Assoc Pro: Carla Fry. Screenplay: Mike Werb, from a story by Michael Fallon and Mark Verheiden. Ph: John R. Leonetti. Ed: Arthur Coburn. Pro Des: Craig Stearns. M: Randy Edelman; numbers performed by Jim Carrey, Harry Connick Jr, Domino, Fishbone, Xscape, Vanessa Williams, Tony Toni Tone, K7, etc. Costumes: Ha Nguyen. Make-Up: Greg Cannom. (New Line/Dark Horse Entertainment–Entertainment.) Rel: 19 August 1994. 100 mins. Cert PG.

Maverick

Mel Gibson takes over the role of the gamblin', free-wheelin' Bret Maverick immortalised by James Garner in the 1957-62 TV series (and again in the 1981-2 *Bret Maverick*). With charm to spare, Gibson dominates the proceedings as Bret engages in a series of adventures in an attempt to make up the $25,000 he needs to enter James Coburn's exclusive poker championship. Along the way he encounters a wry lawman (Garner himself), a relentless con artist (Jodie Foster out of her depth) and a mischievous Indian warrior (Graham Greene enjoying himself). It's all terribly lightweight and ramblin', but is so likeable and well photographed that it's almost beyond criticism. P.S. Garner and Foster previously appeared together in the 1973 Disney comedy *One Little Indian*.

Cast: Mel Gibson (Bret Maverick), Jodie Foster (Annabelle Bransford), James Garner (Zane Cooper), Graham Greene (Joseph), James Coburn (Commodore), Alfred Molina (Angel), Max Perlich (Johnny Hardin), Dub Taylor, Geoffrey Lewis, Paul L. Smith, Dan Hedaya, Dennis Fimple, Denver Pyle, Clint Black, Art La Fleur, Jean De Baer, Paul Brinegar, Hal Ketchum, Corey Feldman, Frank Orsatti, Lauren Shuler-Donner, Gary Richard Frank, Steve Kahan, Vilmos Zsigmond, Waylon Jennings, Carlene Carter, Vince Gill, Janice Gill, William Smith, Doug McClure, Henry Darrow, Michael Paul Chan, Bert Remsen, Robert Fuller, Donal Gibson, William Marshall, Danny Glover, Margot Kidder.
Dir: Richard Donner. Pro: Donner and Bruce Davey. Co-Pro: Jim Van Wyck. Screenplay: William Goldman, based on the character created by Roy Huggins. Ph: Vilmos Zsigmond. Ed: Stuart Baird. Pro Des: Tom Sanders. M: Randy Newman; numbers performed by Clint Black, Randy Newman, Tracy Lawrence, Waylon Jennings and Mel Gibson. Costumes: April Ferry. (Icon–Warner.) Rel: 15 July 1994. 127 mins. Cert PG.

Miami Rhapsody

Marriage is like Miami: it's hot and stormy, but if it's that awful why is there so much traffic on the roads? There's plenty of marital congestion in this sprightly Woody Allenesque marriage-go-round, in which first-time director David Frankel skilfully jockeys a number of characters, liaisons, infidelities and break-ups. Speaking directly to camera, Sarah Jessica Parker meditates on her own upcoming nuptials with a zoologist, a relationship sorely tested by the connubial debris in her own family. While *Miami Rhapsody* may not be as funny as it thinks it is, many of the gags have insight and bite.

Cast: Sarah Jessica Parker (Gwyn Marcus), Mia Farrow (Nina Marcus), Antonio Banderas (Antonio), Gil Bellows (Matt), Carla Gugino (Leslie Marcus), Paul Mazursky (Vic Marcus), Kevin Pollak (Jordan Marcus), Barbara Garrick (Terri), Bo Eason (Jeff), Naomi Campbell (Kaia), Jeremy Piven (Mitchell), Kelly Bishop, Mark Blum, Norman Steinberg, Ben Stein, Donal Logue, Mary Chernoff, Elodia Riovega, Lisa Banes.
   Dir and Screenplay: David Frankel. Pro: Frankel and Barry Jossen. Ex Pro: Jon Avnet and Jordan Kerner. Ph: Jack Wallner. Ed: Steven Weisberg. Pro Des: J. Mark Harrington. M: Mark Isham; numbers performed by Louis Armstrong, Mark Isham, Insect Surfers, Ella Fitzgerald, etc. Costumes: Patricia Field. (Hollywood Pictures–Buena Vista.) Rel: 30 June 1995. 97 mins. Cert 15.

Milk Money

In spite of apparently unlimited access to pornography, three twelve-year-old boys from the comfortable suburbs of Middleton, Ohio, invest all their milk money in paying a grown woman to exhibit her physical assets. They settle on 'V', a Cincinnati prostitute with a heart of gold, who drives them home

Romantic congestion: Sarah Jessica Parker and Antonio Banderas weather the slip roads of love in David Frankel's amusing Miami Rhapsody *(from Buena Vista)*

when their bikes are stolen. There, in a Norman Rockwellian world of home-grown values, V finds she cannot leave and camps out in young Frank's tree house. Meanwhile, Frank engineers a liaison between the hooker and his widowed father ... What initially looks like a sex comedy for kids soon deteriorates into a grossly sentimental saga in which two opposites are improbably forced together to serve the film's 'high concept'. Melanie Griffith's lifeless one-note performance as V and some preposterous leaps in plot logic further sour the stew.

Cast: Melanie Griffith (V), Ed Harris (Dad), Michael Patrick Carter (Frank Wheeler), Malcolm McDowell (Waltzer), Anne Heche (Betty), Adam LaVorgna (Brad), Brian Christopher (Kevin), Jessica Wesson (Stacy), Casey Siemaszko, Philip Bosco, Kevin Scannell, Amanda Sharkey, Margaret Nagle, Kati Powell, Tom Coop.
   Dir: Richard Benjamin. Pro: Kathleen Kennedy and Frank Marshall. Ex Pro: Patrick Palmer and Michael Finnell. Screenplay: John Mattson. Ph: David Watkin. Ed: Jacqueline Cambas. Pro Des: Paul Sylbert. M: Michael Convertino. Costumes: Theoni V. Aldredge. (Paramount–UIP.) Rel: 5 April 1995. 109 mins. Cert 12.

Mina Tannenbaum

France; 1968-93. The story of the friendship between two French girls, from the uncertainty of childhood through to the ambivalence of adult identity. Both from Jewish back-

Portrait of the artist as a young woman: Romane Bohringer as Mina Tannenbaum *(from Mayfair Entertainment)*

grounds, Mina and Ethel are like chalk and cheddar, but share many familiar insecurities. And so, over the years, their relationship evolves, twists, recedes and grows. An absorbing, originally realised and heartfelt work, *Mina Tannenbaum* unfolds like a novel, artfully revealing the inner thoughts of its protagonists and accommodating marginal but telling detail. Romane Bohringer, in the title role, is particularly commanding, bringing to the film – in the words of her director – a 'singular grace and moving presence'.

Cast: Romane Bohringer (Mina Tannenbaum), Elsa Zylberstein (Ethel Benegui), Florence Thomassin (*la cousine*), Nils Tavernier (Francois), Stephane Slima (Didier), Eric Defosse (Serge), Jean-Philippe Ecoffey (Jacques Dana), Chantal Krief, Jany Gastaldi, Dimitri Furdui, Harry Cleven.
   Dir and Screenplay: Martine Dugowson. Pro: Georges Benayoun. Ex Pro: Benayoun, Paul Rozenberg, Anne-Dominique Toussaint and Pascal Jadecewicz. Ph: Dominique Chapuis. Ed: Martine Barraque and Dominique Gallieni. Pro Des: Philippe

Chiffre. M: Peter Chase. Costumes: Yan Tax. (IMA Films/Canal Plus–Mayfair Entertainment.) Rel: 7 October 1994. 128 mins. Cert 12.

Miracle on 34th Street

Serviceable remake of the 1947 classic in which a department store Santa is forced to defend his authenticity in court. Thanks to Richard Attenborough's innate passion and saintliness, his characterisation of Kriss Kringle lifts the film out of the mediocrity that threatens to engulf it. In fact, the message that we are doomed to a life of doubt if we cannot trust in something – even if it is a symbol – is more pertinent today than it ever was. While the charm is a little slick and the icing pretty deep, this *Miracle* at least purges the nasty taste left by the ghastly *Santa Claus: The Movie*.

Cast: Richard Attenborough (Kriss Kringle), Elizabeth Perkins (Dorey Walker), Dylan McDermott (Bryan Bedford), J.T.

A girl's best primate: Thora Birch and Dodger in Franco Amurri's winning Monkey Trouble *(from Entertainment)*

Walsh (Ed Collins), James Remar (Jack Duff), Mara Wilson (Susan Elizabeth Walker), Robert Prosky (Judge Harper), Jane Leeves (Alberta Leonard), Simon Jones (Shellhammer), William Windom (C.F. Cole), Joss Ackland (Victor Lamburgh), Jack McGee, Joe Pentangelo, Mark Damiano II, Jenny Morrison, Samantha Krieger, Lisa Sparrman, Kimberly Smith.

Dir: Les Mayfield. Pro and Screenplay: John Hughes, from the script by George Seaton, from a story by Valentine Davies. Ex Pro: William Ryan and William S. Beasley. Ph: Julio Macat. Ed: Raja Gosnell. Pro Des: Doug Kraner. M: Bruce Broughton; numbers performed by Natalie Cole, Aretha Franklin, Dionne Warwick, Sarah Mc-Lachlan, Elvis Presley, Kenny G and Ray Charles. Costumes: Kathy O'Rear. (Hughes Entertainment–Fox.) Rel: 2 December 1994. 110 mins. Cert U.

Monkey Trouble

Though no classic, *Monkey Trouble* is a family film that should enthral children and keep their parents/guardians amused. Inspired by his eight-year-old daughter's desire for a dog, the Italian filmmaker Franco Amurri set about concocting this story of a girl who clan-

destinely adopts a capuchin monkey. However, this monkey has been trained as a pickpocket, and its former owner, an uncouth gypsy (Harvey Keitel in his first U certificate role), will stop at nothing to get it back. Not only does the story work on both a credible and entertaining level, but there's a healthy message for the kids – and the monkey's miraculous. Formerly known as *Pet*.

Cast: Thora Birch (Eva Gregory), Mimi Rogers (Amy Gregory), Christopher McDonald (Tom Gregory), Harvey Keitel (Shorty Kohn), Kevin Scannell (Peter Boylan) Remy Ryan (Katie), Alison Elliott, Robert Miranda, Victor Argo, Adam Lavorgna, Jo Champa, John Lafayette, Aaron Lustig, Finster (Dodger).

Dir: Franco Amurri. Pro: Mimi Polk and Heide Rufus Isaacs. Ex Pro: Ridley Scott. Screenplay: Amurri and Stu Kreiger. Ph: Luciano Tovoli. Ed: Ray Lovejoy. Pro Des: Leslie Dilley. M: Mark Mancina. Costumes: Eileen Kennedy. Animal Trainer: Mark Harden. (New Line Cinema/Percy Main–Entertainment.) Rel: 14 October 1994. 96 mins. Cert U.

Mr Jones

Mental illness is a complex, disturbing subject, and although here it is given a slick Hollywood gloss (beautiful Swedish doctor; handsome, charismatic patient) it certainly touches a nerve. Richard Gere invests an irresistible energy into his role as Mr Jones, a child-man whose giddy flights of ecstasy are diagnosed as psychotic. So when the happy madman climbs on to the roof of a building and takes to the stage during a performance of Beethoven's 9th, he is consigned to the loony bin. Enter troubled doctor Elizabeth Bowen whose professional and emotional reasoning clashes as she begins to envy Mr Jones's joyful 'insanity'. Gere, in the role that should have been his *Forrest Gump*, uncorks a surprising vitality and charm, but fails to illuminate the reality of his character. Nevertheless, the film hits its buttons with some accuracy and creates an emotionally involving arena.

Cast: Richard Gere (Mr Jones), Lena Olin (Dr Elizabeth 'Libbie' Bowen), Anne Bancroft (Dr Catherine Holland), Tom Irwin (Patrick Shea), Delroy Lindo (Howard), Lauren Tom (Amanda Chang), Lisa Malkiewicz (Susan), Thomas Kopache (Mr Wilson), Bill Pullman (foreman), Bruce Altman, Peter Jurasik, Anna Maria Horsford, Killi Williams, Thomas Mikal Ford, Dana Lee, Irene Tsu, Annie Mc-

Enroe, Lucinda Jenney, Taylor Negron, Sheryl Lee (June).

Dir: Mike Figgis. Pro: Debra Greenfield and Alan Greisman. Ex Pro: Richard Gere and Jerry A. Baerwitz. Screenplay: Eric Roth and Michael Cristofer. Ph: Juan Ruiz Anchia. Ed: Tom Rolf. Pro Des: Waldemar Kalinowski. M: Maurice Jarre; 'I Got You (I Feel Good)' performed by James Brown. Costumes: Rita Ryack. (Rastar–Columbia TriStar.) Rel: 9 September 1994. 114 mins. Cert 15.

Mrs Parker and the Vicious Circle

Dorothy Parker, drama critic, book reviewer, poet, short story writer and scenarist, was the wittiest woman of her generation. She was also a hard-drinking, cynical, suicidal and bitter soul who lorded over the likes of James Thurber, Ogden Nash, George S. Kaufman and F. Scott Fitzgerald – and took many distinguished lovers. Alan Rudolph, director of *Welcome to LA*, *Choose Me* and *The Moderns*, has assembled a mouthwatering cast to portray the stars of the noto-rious Algonquin Round Table, and focuses on Parker's unconsummated affair with the writer Robert Benchley. But quite how Rudolph has managed to metamorphose the dramatic life and effervescent wit of Dorothy Parker into this dreary behemoth is a wonder of contemporary cinema. Jennifer Jason Leigh, normally a fine actress, doesn't help, swallowing most of Parker's *bons mots* in an impersonation that verges on verbal suction.

Cast: Jennifer Jason Leigh (Dorothy Parker), Campbell Scott (Robert Benchley), Matthew Broderick (Charles MacArthur), Andrew McCarthy (Eddie Parker), Tim McGowan (Alexander Woollcott), Nick Cassavetes (Robert Sherwood), David Thornton (George S. Kaufman), Rebecca Miller (Neysa McMein), Gwyneth Paltrow (Paula Hunt), Lili Taylor (Edna Ferber), Peter Gallagher (Alan Campbell), Malcolm Gets (F. Scott Fitzgerald), Keith Carradine (Will Rogers), Gary Basaraba, Jake Johannsen, Chip Zien, Matt Malloy, Sam Robards, Martha Plimpton, Jane Adams, Leni Parker, David Gow, James LeGros, Heather Graham, Jennifer Beals, Jean-Michel Henry, Wallace Shawn, Stephen

Love and emotional remains: Richard Gere whisks Lena Olin off her feet in Mike Figgis's compulsively diverting Mr Jones *(from Columbia TriStar)*

Baldwin, Peter Benchley, Stanley Tucci, Domini Blythe.

Dir: Alan Rudolph. Pro: Robert Altman. Ex Pro: Scott Bushnell and Ira Deutchman. Co-Pro: Allan Nicholls. Screenplay: Rudolph and Randy Sue Coburn. Ph: Jan Kiesser. Ed: Suzy Elmiger. Pro Des: Francois Sequin. M: Mark Isham. Costumes: John Hay and Renee April. (Miramax/Fine Line–Artificial Eye.) Rel: 10 February 1995. 123 mins. Cert 15.

Muriel's Wedding

Overweight, out of work and obsessed with bridal catalogues and Abba, Muriel Heslop has a self-image problem. When her girlfriends dump her (because 'you'll always be you'), Muriel decides to give herself an emotional and geographic make-over: even if it takes self-denial and daylight robbery. A standard ugly duckling comedy,

Nuptial miss: Toni Collette (with father Bill Hunter) makes the big day in P.J. Hogan's sublime Muriel's Wedding *(from Buena Vista)*

Muriel's Wedding succeeds as an entertainment because of a selfless, energised performance from Toni Collette as Muriel, a great script and a remorseless streak of cruelty. Tragically, while the film laughs at the dead-end lives of these hopeless, pathetic people, it's dealing with recognisable reality.

Cast: Toni Collette (Muriel Heslop), Bill Hunter (Bill Heslop), Rachel Griffiths (Rhonda), Jeanie Drynan (Betty Heslop), Gennie Nevinson (Deidre), Matt Day (Brice), Daniel Lapaine (David Van Arkle), Sophie Lee (Tania), Daniel Wyllie (Perry), Gabby Millgate (Joanie), Belinda Jarrett, Rosalind Hammond, Pippa Grandison, Chris Haywood, Nathan Kaye, Genevieve Picot, Barry Crocker, Robyn Pitt Owen, Annie Byron, Vincent Ball.
   Dir and Screenplay: P.J. Hogan. Pro: Lynda House and Jocelyn Moorhouse. Ph: Martin McGrath. Ed: Jill Bilcock. Pro Des: Patrick Reardon. M: Peter Best; numbers performed by Abba, Blondie, The Rubettes, Razorbrain, Peter Allen and A.A. Aardvaark. Costumes: Terry Ryan. (CIBY 2000/ Australian Film Finance Corporation–

Buena Vista.) Rel: 14 April 1995. 106 mins. Cert 15.

My Crazy Life – Mi Vida Loca

Slice of life, three-part drama set in Los Angeles' Hispanic neighbourhood of Echo Park. There, an assortment of young women love, fight and put on their make-up as they lament that their menfolk (the homeboys) will be in prison, disabled or dead by the time they're 21. Many real gang members play themselves, lending the film an extra edge of authenticity, although a stronger story would have helped to secure our interest. Sadly, this is no *Short Cuts*, which is particularly disappointing as writer-director Allison Anders promised great things with her last movie *Gas Food Lodging*.

Guns and pushchairs: Seidy Lopez and Angel Aviles reflect on their sorry lot – in Allison Anders' My Crazy Life *(from Metro Tartan)*

Cast: Angel Aviles (Sad Girl), Seidy Lopez (Mousie), Jacob Vargas (Ernesto), Marlo Marron (Giggles), Jessie Borrego (El Duran), Magali Alvarado (La Blue Eyes), Julian Reyes (Big Sleepy), Bertilla Damas (Rachel), Art Esquer, Christina Solis, Rick Salinas, Rosa Segura, Nelida Lopez, Monica Lutton, Devine.

Dir and Screenplay: Allison Anders. Pro: Daniel Hassid and Carl-Jan Colpaert. Ex Pro: Christoph Henkel and Colin Callender. Co-Pro: William Ewart and Francine Lefrak. Ph: Rodrigo Garcia. Ed: Richard Chew. Pro Des: Jane Stewart. M: John Taylor; numbers performed by The Crusados, Zapp, Tony, Toni, Toné, James Brown, Los Lobos, Brendon Wood, 4 Corners, Lighter Shade of Brown, War, etc. Costumes: Susan Bertram. (HBO Showcase/Film Four International/Cineville–Metro Tartan.) Rel: 24 March 1995. 92 mins. Cert 18.

My Girl 2

If the original *My Girl* wasn't bad enough, here comes the inevitable sequel, thanks to the first film grossing over $120m worldwide. It's now 1974 and the picture-perfect Anna Chlumsky is at that awkward age where she won't listen to the director about her enunciation problem. Still, if we can't

hear Chlumsky, there are plenty of familiar pop songs to punctuate the boredom. In fact, those tunes follow Chlumsky everywhere: in the car, down the street, and all the way to Los Angeles – where the thirteen year old goes in search of the memory of her late mom for a school project. Believe me, the yuk factor is *this* high.

Cast: Dan Aykroyd (Harry Sultenfuss), Jamie Lee Curtis (Shelly Sultenfuss), Anna Chlumsky (Vada Sultenfuss), Austin O'Brien (Nick Zsigmond), Richard Masur (Phil Sultenfuss), Christine Ebersole (Rose Zsigmond), John David Souther (Jeffrey Pommeroy), Angeline Ball (Maggie Muldovan), Aubrey Morris (Alfred Beidermeyer), Keone Young (Daryl Tanaka), Roland Thomson (Kevin), Gerrit Graham, Ben Stein, Anthony R. Jones, Jodie Markell, Richard Beymer, David Purdham, Kevin Sifuentes, Lauren Ashley, Charles Fleischer, Wendy Schaal.

Dir: Howard Zieff. Pro: Brian Grazer. Ex Pro: Zieff, Joseph M. Caracciolo and David T. Friendly. Screenplay: Janet Kovalcik. Ph: Paul Elliott. Ed: Wendy Greene Bricmont. Pro Des: Charles Rosen. M: Cliff Eidelman; numbers performed by Crosby, Stills, Nash & Young, The Supremes, Elton John, Rod Stewart, The Steve Miller Band, Jackson Browne, Edgar Winter Band, The Beach Boys, The Temptations, etc. Costumes:

Meeting people, going places: Mary-Louise Parker falls under the spell of Timothy Dalton – as boyfriend Eric Stoltz looks on – in Dan Algrant's very strange Naked in New York *(from Imagine/NFT)*

Shelley Komarov. (Imagine–Columbia Tri-Star.) Rel: 22 July 1994. 98 mins. Cert PG.

Naked in New York

After wooing Joanne with a giant rock (literally), Jake discovers Joanne is the perfect woman for him. For a start, they can't stop talking to each other. But when Jake moves to New York to see his play *Master of my Emotions* produced off-Broadway and Joanne's photographs are exhibited in Boston, they find their professional aspirations eroding their romantic future. For a while, first-time director-writer Dan Algrant's off-beat humour catches one off guard (Jake proclaiming that he 'always wanted to be a boat', and the introduction of a gruff-voiced chimpanzee), but soon feels contrived as it repeatedly obstructs the film's credibility. Still, Stoltz is perfect as the confused, idealistic playwright, and there are good turns from

The film they tried to ban: Woody Harrelson is interrogated by TV journalists Robert Downey Jr and Terrylene in Oliver Stone's controversial Natural Born Killers *(from Warner)*

Tony Curtis as a pragmatic producer and Kathleen Turner as a complete vamp.

Cast: Eric Stoltz (Jake Briggs), Mary-Louise Parker (Joanne White), Jill Clayburgh (Shirley Briggs), Ralph Macchio (Chris), Timothy Dalton (Elliot Price), Tony Curtis (Carl Fisher), Kathleen Turner (Dana Coles), Paul Guilfoyle (Roman Briggs), Whoopi Goldberg, Roscoe Lee Browne, Lynne Thigpen, Chris Noth, Arabella Field, Colleen Camp, Luis Guzman, Vasek C. Simmek, Eric Bogosian, Quentin Crisp, Ariel Dorfman, Griffin Dunne, Bruce Feirstein, Lady Miss Kier, Gael Love, Marsha Norman, Arthur Penn, Richard Price, William Styron.
Dir: Dan Algrant. Pro: Frederick Zollo. Ex Pro: Martin Scorsese. Screenplay: Algrant and John Warren. Ph: Joey Forsyte. Ed: Bill Pankow. Pro Des: Kalina Ivanov. M: Angelo Badalamenti. Costumes: Julie Weiss. (Imagine/NFT.) Rel: 2 September 1994. 93 mins. No Cert.

Natural Born Killers

Abused in childhood, young lovers Mickey and Mallory Knox embark on a killing spree that eventually elevates them to the stature of international icons. It is ironic that this satire of the media's obsession with violence allegedly prompted a string of copy-cat killings. Oliver Stone, emotionally drained from his Vietnam trilogy, embarked on this Quentin Tarantino-scripted assault course 'just for fun' (his words) – and transformed Tarantino's black comedy into a savage, no-holds-barred blood fest. And if Stone had fun, then it's the sort a sicko might have with a state-of-the-art computer graphics system. If a two-hour *mélange* of black and white, hand-held, slow-motion and wide-screen photography – plus video and animation – doesn't give you a headache, then I have the number of a good psychiatrist.

Cast: Woody Harrelson (Mickey Knox), Juliette Lewis (Mallory Knox), Robert Downey Jr (Wayne Gale), Tommy Lee Jones (Dwight McClusky), Tom Sizemore (Jack Scagnetti), Rodney Dangerfield (Mallory's dad), Edie McClurg (Mallory's mom), Sean Stone (Kevin), Russell Means (Indian), O-Lan Jones, Ed White, Richard Lineback, Lanny Flaherty, Corey Everson, Dale Dye, Terrylene, Jared Harris, Balthazar Getty, Jeremiah Bitsui, Lorraine Ferris, Glen Chin, Pruitt Taylor Vince, Everett Quinton, Steven Wright, Peter Crombie, Joe Grifasi, Marshall Bell, Louise Lombardi.

Dir: Oliver Stone. Pro: Jane Hamsher, Don Murphy and Clayton Townsend. Co-Pro: Rand Vossler. Ex Pro: Arnon Milchan and Thom Mount. Screenplay: Stone, David Veloz and Richard Rutowski, from a story by Quentin Tarantino. Ph: Robert Richardson. Ed: Hank Corwin and Brian Berdan. Pro Des: Victor Kempster. M:

Needlecraft: David Warner injects himself with illegal substances in H.P. Lovecraft's Necronomicon *(from ITC)*

tomandandy; numbers performed by Leonard Cohen, L7, The Shangri-Las, Duane Eddy, Patti Smith, The Cowboy Junkies, Bob Dylan, Patsy Cline, Peter Gabriel, Jane's Addiction, Nine Inch Nails, Russell Means, Barry Adamson, Juliette Lewis, Diamanda Galas, Dr Dre, The Ramsey Lewis Trio, Rage Against the Machine, Nusrat Fateh Ali Khan, etc. Costumes: Richard Hornung. (Regency Enterprises/Alcor Films/Ixtlan/New Regency/JD Prods–Warner.) Rel: 24 February 1995. 119 mins. Cert 18.

Necronomicon

Pretty abysmal trio of short horror stories from the pen of H.P. Lovecraft. Three directors inject their own sense of melodrama into the proceedings, each telling a tale as read by Lovecraft himself (genre favourite Jeffrey Combs) from the pages of a mystical book that holds the secrets of the universe. Well, the secret seems to be that dying is easy, but coming back from the dead is not a comfortable experience. The short story format is not one that can build much fear or suspense, although the icky special effects are fairly sickening.

The Library: Cast: Jeffrey Combs (H.P. Lovecraft), Tony Azito, Juan Fernandez. Dir: Brian Yuzna. Ph: Gerry Lively. Ed: Chris Roth. M: Joseph Lo Duca. Make-Up FX: Todd Masters.
The Drowned: Cast: Bruce Payne (Edward De La Poer), Richard Lynch (Jethro DeLaPore), Belinda Bauer (Nancy Gallmore), Maria Ford, Denice D. Lewis. Dir: Christophe Gans. Ph: Russ Brandt. Ed: Chris Roth. Make-Up FX: Tom Savini.
The Cold (based on H.P. Lovecraft's *Cool Air*): Cast: David Warner (Dr Madden), Bess Meyer (Emily Osterman), Millie Perkins (Lena), Gary Graham, Curt Lowens. Dir: Shu Kaneko. Ph: Gerry Liveley. Ed: Chris Roth. Make-Up FX: Screaming Mad George.
Whispers (based on *The Whisperer in the Darkness*): Cast: Signy Coleman (Sarah), Obba Babatunde (Paul), Don Calfa (Mr Benedict), Judith Drake (Mrs Benedict). Dir: Brian Yuzna. Ed: Keith Sauter. Make-Up FX: Todd Masters.
Pro: Samuel Hadida and Brian Yuzna. Co-Pro: Aki Komine. Ex Pro: Taka Ichise. Screenplay: Brent V. Friedman. Pro Des: Anthony Tremblay. Costumes: Ida Gearson. (Davis Film–ITC.) Rel: 29 July 1994. 90 mins. Cert 18.

Needful Things

Within the Gothic, smoky rooms of a shop called 'Needful Things', the denizens of the quiet seaside town of Castle Rock, Maine, find they can purchase the objects of their dreams. However, each item comes with a price. Handsome, proficiently acted and suitably tongue-in-cheek adaptation of Stephen King's 1991 bestseller, with Max Von Sydow enjoying himself enormously in the devil of a part.

Cast: Ed Harris (Sheriff Alan Pangborn), Max Von Sydow (Leland Gaunt), Bonnie Bedelia (Polly Chalmers), J.T. Walsh (Danforth Keeton III), Amanda Plummer (Nettie Cobb), Ray McKinnon (Deputy Norris Ridgewick), Duncan Fraser (Hugh Priest), Valri Bromfield (Wilma Jerzyk), Shane Meier, W. Morgan Sheppard, Don S. Davis, Campbell Lane, Eric Schneider, Frank C. Turner, Gillian Barber, Deborah Wakeham, Tamsin Kelsey, Lochlyn Munro, Robert Easton.
Dir: Fraser C. Heston. Pro: Jack Cummins. Ex Pro: Peter Yates. Screenplay: W.D. Richter. Ph: Tony Westman. Ed: Rob Kobrin. Pro Des: Douglas Higgins. M: Patrick Doyle; Schubert, Greig; numbers performed by Billy Ray Cyrus, Jerry Lee Lewis, Max Von Sydow, Rick Giles and Kitty Wells. Costumes: Monique Prudhomme. (Castle Rock/New Line–Rank.) Rel: 8 July 1994. 120 mins. Cert 15.

Nell

The Smoky Mountains, North Carolina; 1994. When a hermetic woodswoman is raped and bears a daughter, she keeps the child a secret from the rest of civilisation. But, with her face partially paralysed from a stroke, the woman can only convey so much of the English tongue to her

Speaking in tongues: Jodie Foster explores a brave new world in Michael Apted's riveting Nell (from PolyGram)

Jason James Richter stuck between a rock (right) and a hard face (left) in Peter Macdonald's The Neverending Story III *(from Warner)*

offspring. Thus, when the girl – Nell – is discovered by a doctor after the old woman's death, the 'wild child' appears to speak an unknown language. This prompts the interference of a local psychologist who views 'the woman of the woods' as a fascinating specimen. But Nell, who is in total communion with herself and her natural surroundings, has more to contribute to society than just 'scientific' insight. Set in the devastatingly beautiful scenery of the Appalachians, *Nell* casts a singular spell, accommodated by Jodie Foster's extraordinary performance in the title role. Developed by Foster's own production company, Egg Pictures, *Nell* is a most unusual picture that delivers a significant message with resonance and intelligence.

Cast: Jodie Foster (Nell), Liam Neeson (Jerome Lovell), Natasha Richardson (Paula Olsen), Richard Libertini (Alexander Paley), Nick Searcy (Todd Peterson), Robin Mullins (Mary Peterson), Jeremy Davies,

O'Neal Compton, Sean Bridgers, Joe Inscoe.

Dir: Michael Apted. Pro: Renée Missel and Jodie Foster. Co-Pro: Graham Place. Screenplay: William Nicholson and Mark Handley, based on the play *Idioglossia* by Handley. Ph: Dante Spinotti. Ed: Jim Clark. Pro Des: Jon Hutman. M: Mark Isham. Costumes: Susan Lyall. (PolyGram/Egg Pictures–PolyGram.) Rel: 10 February 1995. 114 mins. Cert 12.

The Neverending Story III

With the popular children's writer Michael Ende disowning the first two films, producer Dieter Geissler has been forced to change names and dream up new characters for this third and weakest entry in the neverending series. This time, Bastian Bux (now played by Jason James Richter, of *Free Willy* fame) stumbles on to the eponymous magical book in his new school library. With a quintet of overgrown bullies – 'The Nasties' – on his trail, Bastian ducks into the perpetual pages of his tome and is transported back to the world of Fantasia. However, thanks to a fearful cock-up, the boy is shot back to small-town America with five of his

otherworldly friends: a wise-cracking tree, a seven-foot stone baby, two tiresome gnomes and Falkor, the cowardly canine dragon. And The Nasties have the book which tells them what happens next ... Children should savour the lively combination of fantasy and reality, although adults will be hard put to appreciate the film's limited wit.

Cast: Jason James Richter (Bastian Balthazar Bux), Melody Kay (Nicole), Jack Black (Slip), Freddie Jones (Mr Coreander), Julie Cox (The Empress), Kevin McNulty (Barney), Tracey Ellis (Jane Bux), Tony Robinson, Moya Brady, Ryan Bollman, Carole Finn, Nicole Parker, P. Adrien Dorval, Frederick Warder, Mark Acheson, Jessica Walden, William Hootkins (voice only).

Dir: Peter Macdonald. Pro: Dieter Geissler and Tim Hampton. Screenplay: Jeff Lieberman, from a story by Karin Howard. Line Pro: Harry Nap and Harold Tichenor. Ph: Robin Vidgeon. Ed: Michael Bradsell. Pro Des: Rolf Zehetbauer. M: Peter Wolf; numbers performed by Meatloaf, Inner Circle, Yello, Roxette, Seal, Stoneman, Phillip Ingram and Siedah Garrett, Coda, Double Impact, Prince Ital Joe and Marky Mark, etc. Animatronic Creatures: Jim Henson's Creature Shop. (Cinevox Entertainment/Studio Bablesberg–Warner.) Rel: 16 December 1994. 95 mins. Cert U.

The Nightmare Before Christmas
See *Tim Burton's The Nightmare Before Christmas*.

Nobody's Fool
North Bath, upstate New York; 1994. Donald 'Sully' Sullivan is 60 and is cursed with no prospects, a bum leg and a dysfunctional family he barely knows. Things cannot get any worse. Or can they? Yet when Sully is introduced to his six-year-old grandson, he sees his past in a new perspective and the shock could just about change his life. Besides some awkward lapses in continuity and the occasional dull patch, *Nobody's Fool* is so well played by a top drawer cast – and so well written – that one cannot help but be drawn into its singular world of smalltown eccentricity. Above all, Paul Newman brings such an effortless polish to his role of the laid-back reprobate, that when he allows us the occasional glimpse into his tortured soul the effect is almost shattering.

Cast: Paul Newman (Donald 'Sully' Sullivan), Jessica Tandy (Miss Beryl), Melanie Griffith (Toby Roebuck), Bruce Willis (Carl Roebuck), Dylan Walsh (Peter Sullivan), Pruitt Taylor Vince (Rub Squeers), Philip Bosco (Judge Flatt), Elizabeth Wilson (Vera), Alex Goodwin (Will Sullivan), Margo Martindale (Birdy), Gene Saks (Wirf), Josef Sommer (Clive Peoples Jr), Philip Seymour Hoffman (Officer Raymer), Jay Patterson, Catherine Dent, Carl John Matusovich, Jerry Mayer,

Growing old disgracefully: Jessica Tandy and Paul Newman swap verbal barbs in Robert Benton's rewarding Nobody's Fool *(from Fox)*

Julia Louis-Dreyfus and Jason Alexander (both from TV's Seinfeld*) team up as the comatose parents of* North, *in Rob Reiner's titanic turkey (from Rank)*

Angela Pietropinto, Alice Drummond, Angela Torn, Richard Mawe, Kenneth Frawley, Marcus Powell, Page Johnson.

Dir and Screenplay: Robert Benton, from the novel by Richard Russo. Pro: Scott Rudin and Arlene Donovan. Ex Pro: Michael Hausman. Ph: John Bailey. Ed: John Bloom. Pro Des: David Gropman. M: Howard Shore; numbers performed by Patti Page, George Jones and Tammy Wynette, etc. Costumes: Joseph G. Aulisi. (Paramount/Capella/Cinehaus–Fox.) Rel: 24 March 1995. 110 mins. Cert 15.

North
Barry Levinson had his *Toys*, Robert Altman had his *Popeye*, Steven Spielberg had his *1941*. Now Rob Reiner has hung himself with the free rein provided by the success of such films as *When Harry Met Sally...*, *Misery* and *A Few Good Men*. An all-star comic farce set in New York, Texas, Hawaii, Alaska, China, Africa and France, *North* is a white elephant without tusks. Based on the novel by Alan Zweibel (who co-wrote the screenplay, co-produces and appears in the film), *North* is the story of an exemplary eleven year old whose brilliance goes unrecognised by his self-absorbed

parents. So North puts himself up for adoption in a highly publicised campaign engineered by a nefarious children's rebellion. But every doting couple he encounters has some fatal flaw (like his would-be African mother going topless), preventing him from meeting his allotted deadline and facing the prospect of life in an orphanage. From the obvious score (utilising such hackneyed comic prompts as 'Blue Hawaii' and the themes from *Dallas* and *Bonanza*), to the Mississippi-broad performances, to the inevitable conclusion, *North* is a major embarrassment.

Cast: Elijah Wood (North), Jon Lovitz (Arthur Belt), Jason Alexander (Dad), Alan Arkin (Judge Buckle), Dan Aykroyd (Pa

Future tense: Tcheky Karyo as Nostradamus *(from First Independent)*

Tex), Kathy Bates (Alaskan Mom), Faith Ford (Donna Nelson), Graham Greene (Alaskan Dad), Julia Louis-Dreyfus (Mom), Reba McEntire (Ma Tex), John Ritter (Ward Nelson), Abe Vigoda (Alaskan Grandpa), Bruce Willis (narrator), Jussie Smollet (Adam), Mathew McCurley (Winchell), Keone Young (Governor Ho), Robert Costanzo (Al), Marc Shaiman, Taylor Fry, Alana Austin, Alan Zweibel, Matthew Arkin, Alan Rachins, Helen Hanft, Lauren Tom, Richard Belzer, Alexander Godunov, Kelly McGillis, Rosalind Chao, Lucy Lin, Scarlett Johanssen, Jesse Zeigler, Dan Grimaldi, Wendel Josepher, Adam Zweibel.

Dir: Rob Reiner. Pro: Reiner and Alan Zweibel. Ex Pro: Jeffrey Stott and Andrew Scheinman. Screenplay: Zweibel and Scheinman. Ph: Adam Greenberg. Ed: Bob Leighton. Pro Des: J. Michael Riva. M: Marc Shaiman. Costumes: Gloria Gresham. (Castle Rock/New Line/Columbia–Rank.) Rel: 29 July 1994. 87 mins. Cert PG.

Nostradamus

Staring into the water of a stone font, Michel de Notredame (1503-66), doctor, astrologer and prophet, sees indescribable images of cruelty, destruction and annihilation taking place in the twentieth century. Can it be possible that one man – he thinks called 'Hisler' – would one day kill so many? Nostradamus is living in some pretty cruel times himself and has to cope with the Spanish Inquisition and losing his wife and children to the plague. This is an earnest, episodic and somewhat clunking look at the life of one of history's most amazing men, played with restrained intensity by Tcheky Karyo. In fact, it is the extraordinary details of the man's life that keeps the eyelids open and the mind begging for more. Directed by Roger Christian, who won an Oscar for set decoration on *Star Wars*.

Cast: Tcheky Karyo (Michel de Notredame), Amanda Plummer (Catherine de Medici), Julia Ormond (Marie), Assumpta Serna (Anne), Anthony Higgins (King Henry II), Diana Quick (Diane de Portier), Michael Gough (Jean de Remy), Maja Morgenstern (Helen), Rutger Hauer (The Mystic Monk), F. Murray Abraham (Julius Caesar Scaliger), Magdalena Ritter (Sophie), Bruce Myers, Leon Lissek, Michael Byrne, Bruce Alexander, Thomas Christian, David Gwillim, Amanda Walker, Amanda Boxer.

Dir: Roger Christian. Pro: Edward Simons and Harald Reichebner. Ex Pro: Peter McRae, Kent Walwin and David Mintz. Assoc Pro: Gerry Levy. Screenplay: Knut Boeser, based on a story by Christian and Piers Ashworth. Ph: Denis Crossan. Ed: Alan Strachan. Pro Des: Peter J. Hampton. M: Barrington Pheloung. Costumes: Ulla Gothe. (Allied Entertainments/Vereinigte Film Partners–First Independent.) Rel: 13 January 1995. 120 mins. Cert 15.

The Nutcracker

See *George Balanchine's The Nutcracker*.

Once Were Warriors

Hard-hitting, evocatively realised drama that lifts the lid off Maori life in a crumbling Auckland ghetto. There Beth and Jake and their five children struggle to find meaning in a life dominated by violence and poverty, a condition aggravated when Jake loses his job. However, it is Beth who has to carry the family's dignity, even when she's

Dignity in chaos: Rena Owen struggles to bring up a family in the Maori ghetto of Auckland – in Lee Tamahori's hard-hitting Once Were Warriors *(from Entertainment)*

advised to keep her mouth shut and her legs open. And when Jake, a bull elephant of a man, repeatedly beats her, Beth continues to love him. But for how long? Based on the controversial, best-selling novel by local author Alan Duff, *Once Were Warriors* marks a stunning directorial debut for Lee Tamahori, who elicits extraordinary performances from his cast and invests his film with a gritty, arresting visual style. An important milestone in New Zealand cinema.

Cast: Rena Owen (Beth Heke), Temuera Morrison (Jake Heke), Mamaengaroa 'Anita' Kerr-Bell (Grace Heke), Julian Arahanga (Nig Heke), Taungaroa Emile (Boogie Heke), Clifford Curtis (Uncle Bully), Shannon Williams (Toot), Rachael Morris Jr, Joseph Kairau, Pete Smith, George Henare, Mere Boynton, Calvin Tuteao.

Dir: Lee Tamahori. Pro: Robin Scholes. Screenplay: Riwia Brown, from a story by Alan Duff. Ph: Stuart Dryburgh. Ed: Michael Horton. Pro Des and Costumes: Michael Kane. M: Murray Grindlay and Murray McNabb; numbers performed by Mere Boynton, Rena Owen and Temuera Morrison, Survival, Gifted and Brown, Southside of Bombay, etc. (Communicado/ The New Zealand Film Commission/ Avalon Studios/New Zealand On Air– Entertainment.) Rel: 14 April 1995. 105 mins. Cert 18.

Only the Strong

Mechanical martial arts programmer introducing 'capoeira', a combination of dance, combat and thought control originating from Brazil. The vertically challenged Mark Dacascos, all gentle eyes and rippling muscles, plays Louis Stevens, a former green beret who returns to his old Miami high school to teach the kids self-respect, commitment and, yes, capoeira. However, he starts a local war when he inadvertently steps on the toes of a local hoodlum who happens to be an expert of – yes, you guessed it – capoeira. Dacascos, who has as much personality as a breeze block, caught the kicking bug from his

To Sir With Kung Fu: Mark Dacascos shows off in Sheldon Lettich's Only the Strong *(from Rank)*

parents: his father is in the Black Belt Hall of Fame and his mother was 'the number one female martial arts competitor in the US for five straight years.' Now you know.

Cast: Mark Dacascos (Louis Stevens), Stacey Travis (Dianna), Geoffrey Lewis (Mr Kerrigan), Paco Christian Prieto (Silverio), Todd Susman (Donald Cochran), Richard Coca (Orlando), Ryan Bollman (Donovan), Jeffrey Anderson Gunter, Roman Cardwell, Christian Klemash, John Fionte, Joselito 'Amen' Santo, Antoni Corone, Mellow Man Ace.
   Dir: Sheldon Lettich. Pro: Samuel Hadida, Stuart S. Shapiro and Steven G. Menkin. Ex Pro: Victor Hadida. Screenplay: Lettich and Luis Esteban. Ph: Edward Pei. Ed: Stephen Semel. Pro Des: J. Mark Harrington. M: Harvey M. Mason; numbers performed by Marcel 'ICB' Branch, Patrick 'Dizon' McCain and Donna Simon, Mellow Man Ace, Miami Boyz, Serapis Bey, etc. Costumes: Patricia Field (PolyGram/ August Entertainment/Firestone Pictures/ Davis Films–Rank.) Rel: 16 December 1994. 97 mins. Cert 15.

Only You

Pittsburgh/Italy; 1994. Incurably romantic film for anybody who can believe in a date with destiny. As an eleven year old, Faith Corvatch summoned up the name of her soulmate on a Ouija board:

Waiting for Mr Right: Marisa Tomei dreams of the ideal man in Norman Jewison's delightful Only You *(from Columbia TriStar)*

Damon Bradley. At a fairground, a fortune teller comes up with the same name. Fourteen years later Faith is engaged to Dwayne, a prosperous podiatrist (foot doctor) with a mild sense of humour. Then, ten days before the Big Day, Faith takes a call from a client of her fiancé: one Damon Bradley. As it happens, Damon is ringing from the airport on his way to Venice. Dropping everything, Faith boards the next plane to Italy with her best friend and sister-in-law, Kate, in tow ... While obviously designed to flutter the heartstrings, *Only You* is also very funny, charming and, thanks to Sven Nykvist's luxuriant photography, an eye-caressing experience. And, as contrived as it might be, the film is blessed with such engaging characters and is so seamlessly directed by Norman Jewison that the ride to an inevitable conclusion is a sheer delight. Previously known as *Just in Time* and *Him*.

Cast: Marisa Tomei (Faith Corvatch), Robert Downey Jr (Peter Wright), Bonnie Hunt (Kate), Joaquim De Almeida (Giovanni), Fisher Stevens (Larry), John Benjamin Hickey (Dwayne), Siobhan Fallon (Leslie), Billy Zane, Adam LeFevre, Antonia Rey, Phyllis Newman, Denise Du Maurier, Bob Tracey, Gianfranco Barra, Barbara Cupisti, Sergio Pierattini.
   Dir: Norman Jewison. Pro: Jewison, Cary Woods, Robert N. Fried and Charles Mulvehill. Assoc Pro: Michael Jewison. Screenplay: Diane Drake. Ph: Sven Nykvist. Ed: Stephen Rivkin. Pro Des: Luciana Arrighi. M: Rachel Portman; numbers per-

formed by Louis Armstrong, Michael Bolton, Ezio Pinza and Mary Martin, Quartetto Gelato, Agnes Balsta and Jose Carreras, etc. Costumes: Milena Canonero. (Yorktown Prods–Columbia TriStar.) Rel: 27 January 1995. 108 mins. Cert PG.

Outbreak

Even before the motaba virus mutates into a far nastier bug, its incubation period is 24 hours. In two to three days it can turn a carrier's organs into liquid. And its fatality rate is one hundred per cent. It's currently loose in northern California. Sam Daniels (Dustin Hoffman) is an expert on virulent diseases and is convinced there is an anti-serum to the motaba. But first he must locate and isolate the virus's host–before some military heavies obliterate him. As for the US army, their biological cock-up must remain secret – even at the cost of thousands of lives. Seldom (if ever) has a film illustrated the deadly efficiency of viral plague so efficiently, here deftly tracing the motaba's spread through French kissing, blood infection, coughing and, ultimately, contact through air. Lurching from techno-thriller to action adventure two thirds of the way in, *Outbreak* stretches credibility to the limit but never loses its momentum or dramatic impact.

Cast: Dustin Hoffman (Sam Daniels), Rene Russo (Robby Keough), Morgan Freeman (General Billy Ford), Cuba Gooding Jr (Major Salt), Patrick Dempsey (Jimbo Scott), Donald Sutherland (General Donald McClintlock), Kevin Spacey (Casey Schuler), Zakes Mokae, Malick Bowens, Susan Lee Hoffman, Benito Martinez, Dale Dye, Gina Menza, Michelle Joyner, Tim Ransom, Matthew Saks, Lance Kerwin, Brett Oliver, Jim Antonio, J.T. Walsh.
   Dir: Wolfgang Petersen. Pro: Petersen, Arnold Kopelson and Gail Katz. Ex Pro: Duncan Henderson and Anne Kopelson. Screenplay: Laurence Dworet and Robert Roy Pool. Ph: Michael Ballhaus. Ed: Neil Travis, Lynzee Klingman and William Hoy. Pro Des: William Sandell. M: James Newton Howard; numbers performed by Pete Droge, Michael Lang and Voxen. Costumes: Erica Edell Phillips. (Warner/ Punch Productions–Warner.) Rel: 21 April 1995. 127 mins. Cert 15.

The Pagemaster

A fourteen-year-old wimp who rationalises his fears through statistical logic finds himself stranded at a library during a ferocious storm. There, after banging his head, young Richard – like

Plague dog: Dustin Hoffman bringing a note of humanity to Wolfgang Petersen's techno-terrifying Outbreak *(from Warner)*

Dorothy – finds himself transported to another world: an animated universe of books. It is here that he befriends three volumes, Adventure, Fantasy and Horror, who help him outmanoeuvre the villains of literature – from the Hound of the Baskervilles to Dr Jekyll and Long John Silver. Through his adventures, Richard discovers un-tapped resources of heroism, even though it was all a dream. Or was it? While exihibiting noble sentiments, *The Pagemaster* is crude, charmless and ugly.

Cast: Macaulay Culkin (Richard Tyler), Christopher Lloyd (Mr Dewey/The Page-master), Ed Begley Jr (Alan Tyler), Mel Harris (Claire Tyler), Alexis Kirschner, Jessica Kirschner. Voices: Whoopi Goldberg (Fantasy), Patrick Stewart (Adventure), Frank Welker (Horror), Leonard Nimoy (Dr Jekyll and Mr Hyde), George Hearn (Captain Ahab), Dorian Harewood, Robert Piccardo, Phil Hartman.

Dir (animation): Maurice Hunt; (live action): Joe Johnston. Pro: David Kirschner and Paul Gertz. Pro (animation): David J. Steinberg and Barry Weiss. Screenplay: Kirschner, David Casci and Ernie Contreras. Ph: Alexander Gruszynski. Ed (animation): Jeffrey Patch. Ed (live action): Kaja Fehr. Pro Des (animation): Gay Lawrence and Valerio Ventura. Pro Des (live action): Roy Forge Smith. M: James Horner. Animation: Bruce Smith. (Turner Pictures–Fox.) Rel: 16 December 1994. 116 mins. Cert U.

Le Parfum d'Yvonne - The Scent of Yvonne

Lake Geneva; 1958. Continuing his theme of the inevitable fallout from romantic obsession (cf. *Monsieur Hire*, *The Hairdresser's Husband*), the French

Message in a bottle: Hippolyte Girardot and Sandra Majani in Patrice Leconte's redolent Le Parfum d'Yvonne *(from Artificial Eye)*

Last Tango in Paris, France: Peter Outerbridge and Leslie Hope on the cutting edge in Gérard Ciccoritti's Paris, France *(from Feature Film Co.)*

filmmaker Patrice Leconte spins a sensual tale lifted from Patrick Modiano's novella *Villa Triste*. And once again Leconte seduces the eye as he intrigues the mind with his luxurious images and disturbing narrative undercurrents. A young man, who may or may not be a Russian count, does little but 'age as slowly as possible', as he reads, observes and does mainly nothing in the lobby of the resort hotel The Hermitage. There, his blissful emptiness is rocked by the apparition of a beautiful woman called Yvonne, whose eccentric and wealthy male companion may or may not be a doctor. Combining forces, these three

irresponsible souls set the stage for irrevocable tragedy. Leconte once said that he wished his films were 'like small bottles of perfume, containing the essence of the story'. True to his word, *Le Parfum d'Yvonne* is a fragrant, visually arresting drama, whose story evaporates as fast as the scent Yvonne dabs behind her pretty ears.

Cast: Jean-Pierre Marielle (Rene Meinthe), Hippolyte Girardot (Victor Chmara), Sandra Majani (Yvonne), Richard Bohringer (Uncle Roland), Paul Guers (Daniel Hendrickx), Corinne Marchand, Philippe Magnan, Claude Dereppe, Marie Cosnay, Brigitte Petit.
   Dir and Screenplay: Patrice Leconte. Pro: Thierry de Ganay. Ex Pro: Monique Guerrier. Ph: Eduardo Serra. Ed: Joelle Hache. Pro Des: Ivan Maussion. M: Pascal Estève; numbers performed by Charles Aznavour ('Sa Jeuneuse') and Celia Cruz. Costumes: Annie Périer. (Lambart Prods/

Zoulou Films/Canal Plus–Artificial Eye.) Rel: 26 August 1994. 89 mins. Cert 18.

Paris, France

It was in Paris where the young writer Lucy Quick met the man of her sexual dreams and the inspiration for her second novel. But when he died suddenly, writer's block engulfed Lucy's literary future and she settled for a quiet life with her nondescript publisher husband in Toronto. However, the arrival of a volatile bisexual poet refuels her loins and intellect and she embarks on a vigorous sexual affair that has dramatic repercussions on all the men in her life. While filling the screen with more sex per inch than any Canadian film before it, and littering the dialogue with biographical reference (ranging from Godard and Sartre to Ed Gein and John Lennon), this bizarre black comedy looks like being an academic's wet dream. But soon pretension and claustrophobia (the whole thing is set in a few under-lit rooms) undermine any kick the filmmakers may have intended. A thoroughly depressing experience.

Cast: Leslie Hope (Lucy Quick), Peter Outerbridge (Sloan), Victor Ertmanis (Michael), Dan Lett (Willie), Raoul Trujillo (Minter).
   Dir: Gérard Coccoritti. Pro: Eric Norlen and Allan Levine. Ex Pro: Stéphane Reichel. Screenplay: Tom Walmsley, from his own novel. Ph: Barry Stone. Ed: Roushell Goldstein. Pro Des: Marian Wihack. M: John McCarthy. Costumes: Ann Tree Newson. (Alliance Communications Corp/ Lightshow/Telefilm Canada–Feature Film Company.) Rel: 29 July 1994. 112 mins. Cert 18.

Poetic Justice

Like his first film, *Boyz N the Hood*, John Singleton's *Poetic Justice* is based on real events and stems from South Central Los Angeles. The difference here is that the writer-director focuses on one woman and how she copes – or not – after the murder of her boyfriend. Working at a hair salon by day, Justice retreats into her shell at night, taking solace in the prolific poetry she writes. But, as the poet Maya Angelou stresses, 'Nobody can make it out here alone.' It takes a day trip to Oakland, California, for Justice to finally place her life in perspective. While filling the screen with vibrant street dialogue and

Naked fashion: Helena Christensen poses for Robert Altman's priceless Prêt-à-Porter *(from Buena Vista)*

Justice cause: Tupac Shakur and Janet Jackson confront their differences in John Singleton's Poetic Justice *(from Columbia TriStar)*

coaxing spontaneous performances from his cast, Singleton throws fresh light on Afro-American life – until, inexplicably, he succumbs to Hollywood cliché in the closing chapters. Still, Janet Jackson is surprisingly watchable and natural in her film debut, and put on pounds to look the part. Maya Angelou supplied the verse.

Cast: Janet Jackson (Justice), Tupac Shakur (Lucky), Regina King (Iesha), Joe Torry (Chicago), Tyra Ferrell (Jessie), Roger Guenveur Smith (Heywood), Tone Loc (J Bone), Khandi Alexander, Maya Angelou, Kimberly Brooks, John Cothran Jr, Dina D, Norma Donaldson, Rene Elizondo, Dedrick Gobert, Miki Howard, Baha Jackson, Jenifer Lewis, Lori Petty, Q-Tip, Michael Rapaport, Mikki Val, Keith Washington, Rose Weaver, Billy Zane.

Dir and Screenplay: John Singleton. Pro: Singleton and Steve Nicolaides. Ph: Peter Lyons Collister. Ed: Bruce Cannon. Pro Des: Keith Brian Burns. M: Stanley Clarke; numbers performed by The Isley Brothers, Pete Rock & C.L. Smooth, Usher Raymond, Coolio, Tony, Tone, Toné, Mista Grimm, Cultural Revolution, O'Jays, Naughty By Nature, Chaka Demus & Pliers, Babyface, Janet Jackson, Stevie Wonder, TLC, The Dogg Pound, Tammy Wynette, etc. Costumes: Darryle Johnson. (Columbia–Columbia TriStar.) Rel: 14 April 1995. 109 mins. Cert 15.

Prêt-à-Porter

Having focused his viewfinder on the country music scene in *Nashville* and, more recently, on the film industry in *The Player*, Robert Altman now zooms in on the unique universe of high

The sins of the father: Linus Roache – with Paul Barber and Robert Carlyle – in Antonia Bird's provocative, profoundly affecting Priest *(from Electric)*

fashion. Settling on Paris for his battle-ground, and spotlighting the 'prêt-à-porter' season – a week in which the world's most outrageous and celebrated designers and supermodels flaunt their spring collection – Altman introduces us to a dizzying array of eccentric personalities at loggerheads and in love with each other. Inter-weaving authentic icons from the world of *haute couture* with his fictitious char-acters, the filmmaker exhibits his dis-tinctive knack for effortlessly juggling a number of simultaneous plots, while losing none of his satirical bite. A fasci-nating, very funny and superbly crafted film. US title: *Ready-to-Wear*.

Cast: Sophia Loren (Isabella de la Fontaine), Marcello Mastroianni (Sergei), Julia Roberts (Anne Eisenhower), Tim Robbins (Joe Flynn), Kim Basinger (Kitty Potter), Stephen Rea (Milo O'Brannagan), Anouk Aimee (Simone Lowenthal), Lauren Bacall (Slim Chrysler), Lili Taylor (Fiona Ulrich), Sally Kellerman (Sissy Wanamaker), Tracey Ullman (Nina Scant), Linda Hunt (Regina Krumm), Rupert Everett (Jack Lowenthal), Forest Whitaker (Cy Bianco), Richard E. Grant (Cort Romney), Danny Aiello (Major Hamilton), Teri Garr (Louise Hamilton), Lyle Lovett (Clint Lammeraux), Jean Rochefort (Inspector Tantpis), Michel Blanc (Inspector Forget), Jean-Pierre Cassel (Olivier de la Fontaine), Ute Lemper (Albertine), Tara Leon (Kiki Simpson), Chiara Mastroianni (Sophie), Georgianna Robertson (Dane Simpson), Anne Canovas, Francois Cluzet, Rossy de Palma, Kasia Figura, Tom Novembre, Sam Robards, Harry Belafonte, Carla Bruni, Paolo Bulgari, Naomi Campbell, Cher, Helena Christen-sen, David Copperfield, Gianfranco Ferre, Elsa Klensch, Christian Lacroix, Jean Paul Gaultier, Claude Montana, Tatjana Patitz, Sonia Rykiel, Claudia Schiffer, Christy Turlington.

Dir and Pro: Robert Altman. Co-Pro: Scott Bushnell and Jon Kilik. Ex Pro: Bob Weinstein, Harvey Weinstein and Ian Jessel. Screenplay: Altman and Barbara Shulgasser. Ph: Pierre Mignot and Jean Lepine. Ed: Geraldine Peroni. Pro Des: Stephen Altman. M: Michel Legrand; numbers performed by Imi Kamoze, Janet Jackson, U2, Terence Trent D'Arby, Supercat, Ce Ce Peniston, M People, Salt 'N' Pepa, The Rolling Stones, The Cranberries, Deep Forest, Sam Phillips, The Brand New Heavies and The New Power Generation. Costumes: Catherine Leterrier. (Miramax–Buena Vista.) Rel: 3 March 1995. 133 mins. Cert 15.

Priest

Liverpool; 1994. A young Catholic priest with a passionate belief in his vocation is appointed to a run-down, inner-city diocese. Striving not to patro-nise his sorry flock, Father Greg finds the constraints of his position are begin-ning to suffocate him. Furthermore, his tentative affair with another man threat-ens to negate every positive stride he has made in the community. Should an act of love, albeit homosexual, wreck the good that a man has accomplished? Channelling potent issues into a dra-matic and entertaining framework – and boasting sharply etched characters rooted in reality – *Priest* is moving, shocking and thought provoking cine-ma. One of the most rewarding British films of the year. Scripted by Jimmy McGovern, writer of ITV's *Cracker*.

Cast: Linus Roach (Greg Pilkington), Tom Wilkinson (Matthew Thomas), Robert Carlyle (Graham), Cathy Tyson (Maria Kerrigan), James Ellis (Father Ellerton), Lesley Sharp (Mrs Unsworth), Robert Pugh (Mr Unsworth), Christine Tremarco (Lisa Unsworth), Paul Barber (Charlie), Rio Fanning, Bill Dean, Gilly Coleman, Fred Pearson, Jimmy Gallagher, Tony Booth, Adrian Luty, Bobby Martino, Mickey Poppins, Matyelok Gibbs, John Bennett.

Dir: Antonia Bird. Pro: George Faber and Josephine Ward. Ex Pro: Mark Shivas. Assoc Pro: Joanna Newbery. Screenplay: Jimmy McGovern. Ph: Fred Tammes. Ed: Susan Spivey. Pro Des: Raymond Langhorn. M: Andy Roberts. Costumes: Jill Taylor. (BBC/Electric/PolyGram–Electric.) Rel: 17 March 1995. 106 mins. Cert 15.

Princess Caraboo

Devon; 1817. Reconstructed from newspaper cuttings, this is the remarkable true story of a young woman who appeared out of nowhere to become a social icon within the circles of the English aristocracy. Arrested for vagrancy, 'Caraboo' is unable to defend herself in court due to her unfamiliarity with the English language. Rescued by a compassionate noblewoman, the girl is installed at a local manor where, gradually, it is construed that she is of Oriental extraction and of royal blood. There, she wins many hearts and admirers, although there are some who contest her authenticity. Lavished with all the care and attention to detail that one has come to expect from period British films, *Princess Caraboo* is a feast for the ears and eyes, and is blessed with some priceless performances (notably from Jim Broadbent and Kevin Kline). Yet, even as it beguiles, the film leaves one hungry for something a little more substantial.

Cast: Phoebe Cates (Caraboo), Jim Broadbent (Mr Worrall), Wendy Hughes (Mrs Worrall), Kevin Kline (Frixos), John Lithgow (Prof. Wilkinson), Stephen Rea (John M. Gutch), John Sessions (Prince Regent), John Wells (Rev. Hunt), Peter Eyre (Lord Apthorpe), Jacqueline Pearce (Lady Apthorpe), Roger Lloyd Pack (Magistrate Haythorne), John Lynch, Arkie Whiteley, Kate Ashfield, Anna Chancellor, Jerry Hall, Jamie Harris, Peter Howell, Barbara Keogh, Philip Lester, Steven MacIntosh, Tim McMullan, Murray Melvin, Jacqueline Tong, Edward Tudor-Pole.

Dir: Michael Austin. Pro: Andy Karsch and Simon Bosanquet. Ex Pro: Amyan Bernstein, Tom Rosenberg and Marc Abraham. Screenplay: Austin and John Wells. Ph: Freddie Francis. Ed: George Akers. Pro Des: Michael Howells. M: Richard Hartley. Costumes: Tom Rand. (Beacon Communications/TriStar/J&M Entertainment/Longfellow Pictures/Artisan Films–Entertainment.) Rel: 16 December 1994. 97 mins. Cert PG.

The Professional

See *Leon*.

Pulp Fiction

The joy of a Quentin Tarantino movie is that Tarantino not only writes great dialogue, joyfully stocks his films with pop-cultural references and invests his scenes with a unique vitality, but he is prepared to shatter the rules of conventional cinema. Here, with his second film as director, Tarantino constructs his narrative like a jigsaw puzzle – abandoning a piece there to follow a thread here, dispatching characters willy-nilly and introducing new stars without a moment's notice. Set in Los Angeles, *Pulp Fiction* revolves around the violent

Deception or misconception? Kevin Kline examines the evidence (real-life wife Phoebe Cates) in Michael Austin's enchanting Princess Caraboo *(from Entertainment)*

lives of a number of characters – all of them criminal – who discuss such things as coffee, hamburgers and foot massage before killing someone. Black, self-indulgent, sick, brilliant. N.B. Fans of John Travolta should think twice before

Look who's talking dirty: John Travolta is a new man in Quentin Tarantino's extraordinary Pulp Fiction *(from Buena Vista)*

seeing their hero in this, in which the actor displays an entirely new facet of his persona. Winner of the 1994 Palme d'Or at Cannes.

Cast: John Travolta (Vincent), Samuel L. Jackson (Jules), Uma Thurman (Mia), Harvey Keitel (The Wolf), Tim Roth (Pumpkin), Amanda Plummer (Honey Bunny), Maria de Madeiros (Fabian), Ving Rhames (Marsellus), Eric Stoltz (Lance), Rosanna Arquette (Jody), Christopher Walken (Captain Koons), Bruce Willis (Butch), Steve Buscemi (Buddy Holly), Quentin Tarantino (Jimmie), Laura Lovelace, Robert Ruth, Phil LaMarr, Burr Steers, Frank Whaley, Alexis Arquette, Paul Calderon, Bronagh Gallagher, Duane Whitaker, Peter Greene, Dick Miller, Julia Sweeney, Lawrence Bender.

Dir and Screenplay: Quentin Tarantino, from stories by Tarantino and Roger Avary. Pro: Lawrence Bender. Ex Pro: Dany DeVito, Michael Shamberg and Stacey Sher. Co-Ex Pro: Bob and Harvey Weinstein. Ph: Andrzej Sekula. Ed: Sally Menke. Pro Des: David Wasco. M: numbers performed by Dick Dale and His Del-Tones, Kool and the Gang, Al Green, The Tornadoes, Ricky Nelson, Dusty Springfield, The Centurians, Chuck Berry, Urge Overkill, Marie McKee, The Revels, The Statler Brothers and The Lively Ones. Costumes: Betsy Heimann.

A question of ethics: John Turturro stretches his memory in Robert Redford's mesmerising Quiz Show *(from Buena Vista)*

(Miramax/A Band Apart/Jersey Films–Buena Vista.) Rel: 21 October 1994. 153 mins. Cert 18.

The Punk and the Princess

Notting Hill, London; 1994. *Romeo and Juliet* revisited, with Juliet an American fringe actress star-crossed with a punk, while Friar Lawrence moonlights as a drug dealer. Undercooked satire on contemporary nineties youth based on the seventies novel by the late Gideon Sams (written when he was fourteen years old). Mixing styles and fashions with alarming abandon, writer-director Mike Sarne (whose last film, the disastrous *Myra Breckinridge*, died 24 years ago) fails to coax convincing performances from his young cast, driving the final nail into the coffin of his career. [*Charles Bacon*]

Cast: Charlie Creed-Miles (David), Vanessa Hadaway (Rachel), David Shawyer (David's father), Jess Conrad (Rachel's father), Jacqueline Skarvellis, Yolanda Mason, Alex Mollo, Peter Miles (Shakespeare), R.J. Bell, Martin Harvey, David Doyle, Matthew Salkeld, William Sarne, Helen Gill.

Dir and Screenplay: Mike Sarne. Pro: Sarne and Robin Mahoney. Ph: Alan M. Trow. Ed: Gwyn Jones and Matthew Salkeld. Art: Eleanor Baker. M: Claudia Sarne, Charlie Creed-Miles and Nigel Powell; numbers performed by Claudia Sarne, Martin Harvey, Charlie Creed-Miles,

Mike Sarne, Prima Shock, Videodrome, etc. (Videodrome/M2–Feature Film Co.) Rel: 9 December 1994. 92 mins. Cert 18.

Quiz Show

In 1957 television was sweeping America and few shows could challenge the popularity of NBC's *Twenty-One*. A tournament testing the general knowledge of two contestants closeted into separate booths, the programme saw its ratings soar when one Charles Van Doren became the reigning champion. Handsome, charismatic, supremely well educated and the son of the Pulitzer Prize-winning poet Mark Van Doren, Charley became a national icon. Of course, it helped that he knew the questions in advance ... A terrific true-detective comedy-drama, *Quiz Show* is an expertly crafted, superbly acted and brilliantly scripted entertainment that throws light on a fascinating *cause célèbre* in American TV history. Based on a chapter from Richard Goodwin's 1988 book *Remembering America*. P.S. Director Robert Redford was a quiz show contestant himself on Merv Griffin's *Play Your Hunch* in 1959.

Cast: John Turturro (Herbie Stempel), Rob Morrow (Dick Goodwin), Ralph Fiennes (Charles Van Doren), David Paymer (Dan Enright), Paul Scofield (Mark Van Doren), Hank Azaria (Albert Freedman), Christopher McDonald (Jack Barry), Johann Carlo (Toby Stempel), Elizabeth Wilson (Dorothy Van Doren), Allan Rich (Robert Kintner), Mira Sorvino (Sandra Goodwin), Barry Levinson (Dave Garroway), Grace Phillips (Vivian Nearing), George Martin, Paul Guilfoyle, Griffin Dunne, Michael Mantell, Byron Jennings, Timothy Busfield, Jack Gilpin, Bruce Altman, Martin Scorsese, Ernie Sabella, Debra Monk, Robert Caminiti, Le Clanche Du Rand, Carole Shelley, Jeffrey Nordling, Gina Rice, Adam Kilgour, Barry Snider, Chuck Adamson, Joseph Attanasio, Illeana Douglas, Stephen Pearlman, Douglas McGrath, Caryn Krooth, Katherine Turturro.

Dir: Robert Redford. Pro: Redford, Michael Jacobs, Julian Krainin and Michael Nozik and (uncredited) Barry Levinson and Mark Johnson. Co-Pro: Gail Mutrux, Jeff McCracken and Richard Goodwin. Ex Pro: Fred Zollo, Richard Dreyfuss and Judith James. Assoc Pro: Susan Moore. Screenplay: Paul Attanasio. Ph: Michael Ballhaus. Ed: Stu Linder. Pro Des: Jon Hutman. M: Mark Isham; numbers performed by Bobby Darin and Lyle Lovett. Costumes:

Kathy O'Rear. (Hollywood Pictures/ Wildwood Enterprises/Baltimore Pictures– Buena Vista.) Rel: 24 February 1995. 133 mins. Cert 15.

Rapa Nui

A recreation of what, supposedly, almost brought about the end of civilis- ation on Easter Island - 42 years before the Dutch arrived in 1722 - *Rapa Nui* is a visually provocative epic that lacks dramatic impetus. Mixing narrative strands of *Romeo and Juliet*, *Fitzcarraldo* and any number of tribal melodramas, the film takes forever to get started before gelling into an engrossing and ecologically-driven parable. Unfort- unately, the romantic principals – photogenic natives from opposing castes – engender little sympathy. It is the glorious photography and authen- tic Easter Island locations that give the film its distinction.

Cast: Jason Scott Lee (Noro), Esai Morales (Make), Sandrine Holt (Ramana), Eru Potaka-Dewes (Grandfather), George Hen- are (Tupa), Zac Wallace (Haoa), Tania Simon, Rena Owen.
Dir: Kevin Reynolds. Pro: Kevin Costner and Jim Wilson. Ex Pro: Barrie M. Osborne

Star-crossed lovers: Jason Scott Lee and Sandrine Holt fight for the right to romance each other in Kevin Reynolds' unwieldy Rapa Nui *(from Entertainment)*

and Guy East. Screenplay: Reynolds and Tim Rose Price. Ph: Stephen Windon. Ed: Peter Boyle. Pro Des: George Liddle. M: Stewart Copeland. Costumes: John Bloomfield. (Tig Productions/Majestic Films and Television International/RCS/

Newcomm–Entertainment.) Rel: 28 Oct- ober 1994. 106 mins. Cert 12.

Ready-to-Wear

See *Prêt-à-Porter*.

The Red Squirrel - La Ardilla Roja

As Jota is about to hurl himself from the top of a cliff, he is distracted by a motor- cyclist crashing on to the beach below. Running to the scene of the accident, Jota discovers that the leather-clad rider is a young woman. Furthermore, she cannot remember a thing – not even her name. So, step by step, Jota builds a new life for the girl, inventing a past that aids and abets the perfect affair. That is, an affair between a man without a future and a woman without a past. Julio Medem, who directed the 1991 *Vacas*, weaves a sensuous, pro- vocative romantic mystery, layering his film with a seemingly endless net- work of deceit, illusion and metaphor. Filmed in and around San Sebastian in 1993.

Cast: Emma Suarez (Lisa), Nancho Novo (Jota), Maria Barranco (Carmen), Carmelo Gomez (Felix), Karra Elejalde (Anton), Eneko Irizar (Alberto), Cristina Marcos, Monica Molina.
Dir and Screenplay: Julio Medem. Ex Pro: Fernando de Garcillan. Co-Pro: Lola Perez. Ph: Gonzalo Berridi. Ed: Maria Elena Saiz de Rozas. Art: Alvaro Machimbarrena. M: Alberto Inglesias; 'Let There Be Love' sung by Nat King Cole. (Sogetel–Metro Tartan.) Rel: 30 September 1994. 114 mins. Cert 18.

Amnesiacs anonymous: Emma Suarez as the girl without a past in Julio Medem's intrigu- ing The Red Squirrel *(from Metro Tartan)*

La Reine Margot

In spite of the title, this melodramatic, fired-up reading of Alexandre Dumas's historical novel is less about the randy French princess than the squabbling men in her life. With France on the brink of civil war, Margot, sister of the Catholic King Charles IX, is married off to the Protestant Henri of Navarre. However, this does little to stem the rising tide of bloodshed as the unbalanced king carries out the brutal orders of his mother, the cruel Catherine de' Medici - resulting in the St Bartholomew Day massacre of 1572. While there's plenty going on, including a fair amount of butchery and some steamy embraces, it's an uphill task to fathom out who's who and why they're so aggravated. Also, the royal household's predilection for dressing up like vagabonds only adds to the confusion. Still, it's fascinating Grand Guignol, while Virna Lisi, former sex symbol of the sixties, is an inspiration as Catherine and won the Best Actress Award at Cannes for her pains. A French-German-Italian co-production.

Cast: Isabelle Adjani (Margot), Daniel Auteuil (Henri of Navarre), Jean-Hugues Anglade (Charles IX), Vincent Perez (La Mole), Virna Lisi (Catherine de' Medici),

Royal muckraking: Jean-Hugues Anglade and Daniel Auteuil enjoy a brief fraternity in Patrice Chéreau's full-bloodied La Reine Margot *(from Guild)*

Dominique Blanc (Henriette of Nevers), Pascal Greggory (Anjou), Claudio Amendola (Coconnas), Miguel Bosè (Guise), Asia Argento (Charlotte of Sauve), Jean-Claude Brialy (Coligny), Julien Rassam, Thomas Kretschmann, Jean-Philippe Ecoffey, Barbet Schroeder, Tolsty, Bernard Verley, Jean-Michel Tavernier.

Dir: Patrice Chéreau. Ex Pro: Pierre Grunstein. Screenplay: Chéreau and Danièle Thompson. Ph: Philippe Rousselot. Ed: Francois Gédigier and Hélène Viard. Pro Des: Richard Peduzzi and Olivier Radot. M: Goran Bregovic. Costumes: Moidele Bickel. Sound: Guillaume Sciama and Dominique Hennequin. (Renn Prods/France 2 Cinéma/Canal Plus–Guild.) Rel: 13 January 1995. 145 mins. Cert 18.

Renaissance Man

Fired from his job as an advertising executive, Bill Rago cannot cope with the mounting bills of alimony, mortgage and good living. Desperate for a job – any job – he takes the first one offered: that of teacher to a class of army recruits. Rago knows as much about the army as his students do Shakespeare ('He's the guy in Central Park every summer' 'He must get mugged a lot'). It's an uphill struggle for all concerned, but this being a feelgood comedy from Penny Marshall (*Big*, *Awakenings*, *A League of Their Own*) you know exactly where it's headed. Having said that, the film is full of surprises, not least DeVito's moving recital of *Romeo and Juliet* (as Juliet), conjuring up fond memories of Mel Gibson's Shylock speech in *The Man Without a Face*. But better still is the cast of unknowns as the low-life students, each with a tragic story to tell. This may be pre-programmed entertainment (complete with popcorn-flavoured Shakespeare), but it skilfully pushes all the right buttons.

Cast: Danny DeVito (Bill Rago), Gregory Hines (Sgt Cass), Cliff Robertson (Col James), James Remar (Capt. Murdoch), Lillo Brancato Jr (Donnie Benitez), Stacey Dash (Miranda Myers), Kadeem Hardison (Jamaal Montgomery), Richard T. Jones (Jackson Leroy), Khalil Kain (Roosevelt Hobbs), Peter Simmons (Brian Davis), Greg Sporleder (Mel Melvin), Mark Wahlberg aka Marky Mark (Tommy Lee Haywood), Alanna Ubach (Emily Rago), Isabella Hofmann (Marie Leyton), Don Reilly (Henry V), Ben Wright, Ed Begley Jr, Ann Cusack, Jeb Brown, Paul Abbott, Jenifer Lewis, Matthew Keesler, Gary Dewitt Marshall, J.J. Nettles, Samaria Graham, Randy Hall.

Dir: Penny Marshall. Pro: Sara Colleton, Elliot Abbott and Robert Greenhut. Ex Pro: Marshall and Buzz Feitshans. Co-Pro: Timothy M. Bourne and Amy Lemisch. Screenplay: Jim Burnstein. Ph: Adam Greenberg. Ed: George Bowers and Battle Davis. Pro Des: Geoffrey Kirkland. M: Hans Zimmer; numbers performed by US3, Stevie Nicks, Mark Wahlberg (Marky Mark), John Cougar Mellencamp, etc. Costumes: Betsy Heimann. (Touchstone Pictures/Cinergi–Guild.) Rel: 15 July 1994. 129 mins. Cert 12.

Rice People – Les Gens de la Rizière

A remarkable first feature, *Rice People* uses a traditional filmmaking approach in portraying vividly the suffering of the poor country folk of Cambodia, whose lives, even in our own age, are dependent on the cultivation of rice. Rithy Panh's film is commendable in intention and artistry, and it is finely acted by a largely non-professional cast – including the two female leads. But *Rice People* does have a major weakness in that it offers two hours-plus of unrelieved misery. This makes it hard to take, yet the film could not be more heartfelt. [*Mansel Stimpson*]

Cast: Peng Phan (Yim Om, the mother), Mom Soth (Vong Poeuv, the father), Chhim Naline (Sokha, the oldest daughter), Va Simorn (Sokhoeun), Sophy Sodany (Sokhon), Muong Danyda (Sophon), Pen

Shakespeare versus the American language,
bro': Danny DeVito teaches the Bard to a
disbelieving class of army recruits – in Penny
Marshall's appealing Renaissance Man
(from Guild)

Sopheary (Sophoeun), Proum Mary (Sop-
hat), Sam Kourou (Sopheap).

   Dir: Rithy Panh. Pro: Jacques Bidou.
Screenplay: Panh and Eve Deboise, adapt-
ed from the novel by Shahnon Ahmad. Ph:
Jacques Bouquin. Ed: Andrée Davanture
and Marie-Christine Rougerie. Pro Des:
Nhean Chamnaul. M: Marc Marder. Cost-
umes: Vuong Kyry. Sound: Jean-Claude
Brisson. (JBA Prods/Thelma Films/La Sept
Cinema/Canal Plus/Channel Four–Gala
Films.) Rel: 16 June 1995. 125 mins. Cert
PG.

Richie Rich

Richie Rich is so rich that he's got the
legendary Reggie Jackson as his personal baseball trainer, Claudia Schiffer
as his aerobics instructor and his own
McDonald's down the hall. But, Richie
realises, money doesn't mean a hill of

Getting Even With Dough: Macaulay Culkin
plots revenge on Van Dough in Donald
Petrie's Richie Rich *(from Warner)*

According to Anthony Hopkins' Dr Kellogg, 'The tongue is the billboard of the bowels.' Matthew Broderick and Bridget Fonda defer to his wisdom in Alan Parker's outrageous The Road to Wellville *(from Rank)*

beans if you haven't got anybody to share it with. So when the dastardly Van Dough sets his sights on the Rich fortune, Richie is forced to round up some real kids to help him save the day. Compared to Macaulay Culkin's recent turkeys, *Richie Rich* isn't so bad, although Little Mac's listless performance (at a cost of $8 million) does nothing to distinguish this update of the Harvey Comics' strip. It is the adult actors – particularly Jonathan Hyde as Richie's unflappable valet – who carry the movie, aided by some quick-fire direction and editing.

Cast: Macaulay Culkin (Richie Rich), John Larroquette (Van Dough), Edward Herrmann (Mr Rich), Jonathan Hyde (Cadbury), Christine Ebersole (Mrs Rich), Michael McShane (Professor Keenbean), Mariangela Pino (Diane), Stephi Lineburg (Gloria), Chelcie Ross, Michael Maccarone, Joel Robinson, Jonathan Hilario, Reggie Jackson, Claudia Schiffer, Wanda Christine, Stacy Logan, Eddie Bo Smith Jr, Kent Logsdon, Dawn Maxey, Ben Stein, Sean A. Tate, Joel Ellegant, Justin Zaremby.
    Dir: Donald Petrie. Pro: Joel Silver and John Davis. Co-Pro: Jacqueline George and Jeffrey A. Montgomery. Ex Pro: Dan Kolsrud, Joe Bilella and Jon Shapiro.

Screenplay: Tom S. Parker and Jim Jennewein, from a story by Neil Tolkin. Ph: Don Burgess. Ed: Malcolm Campbell. Pro Des: James Spencer. M: Alan Silvestri. Costumes: Lisa Jensen. (Silver Pictures/Davis Entertainment–Warner.) Rel: 26 May 1995. 95 mins. Cert PG.

The River Wild

Striving to keep her marriage afloat, Gail arranges for her family to go on a rafting trip down Smith River in Montana. A former river guide herself, Gail ushers her reluctant husband and young son, Roarke, along for the ride and is thankful for the company of Wade, a charismatic water rat with a way with kids. Soon, young Roarke has happily attached himself to the stranger who, as it turns out, is even more unpredictable than the approaching rapids. With its combination of suspense, action, spectacular locations and human interest, *The River Wild* is a movie with something for everyone. Curtis Hanson, who honed his reputation as a director of toe-curling thrillers like *The Bedroom Window* and *The Hand That Rocks the Cradle*, here augments his position as a natural successor to Hitchcock.

Cast: Meryl Streep (Gail), Kevin Bacon (Wade), David Strathairn (Tom), Joseph Mazzello (Roarke), John C. Reilly (Terry),

Benjamin Bratt (Ranger Johnny), Stephanie Sawyer, Elizabeth Hoffman, Victor H. Galloway, William Lucking, Glenn Morshower.
    Dir: Curtis Hanson. Pro: David Foster and Lawrence Turman. Ex Pro: Ilona Herzberg and Ray Hartwick. Screenplay: Denis O'Neil. Ph: Robert Elswit. Ed: Joe Hutshing and David Brenner. Pro Des: Bill Kenney. M: Jerry Goldsmith; numbers performed by Gigolo Aunts, Screaming Trees, Ministry and The Cowboy Junkies. Costumes: Marlene Stewart. (Universal–UIP.) Rel: 24 February 1995. 112 mins. Cert 12.

The Road to Wellville

Like *La Grande Bouffe* 21 years before it, *The Road to Wellville* is an original that, with any luck, should provoke considerable debate and outrage. Exquisitely photographed and delightfully scored, the film focuses on the lower regions of the human anatomy as plumbed by Dr John Harvey Kellogg, inventor, writer, surgeon, vegetarian, celibate and bowel connoisseur. Holding court at the notorious Battle Creek Sanitarium in Michigan in 1907 – a grand amalgam of hotel, spa and hospital – Kellogg lectures on the evils of meat, mating and masturbation, while attracting such clientele as Henry Ford, Teddy Roosevelt and John D. Rockefeller. And while Anthony Hopkins dominates the film in an extraordinary performance, an all-star cast bustles around him weaving stories of their own. However, Alan Parker's brave, eloquent film isn't likely to appeal to many people, except for those with a scatological leaning and interest in the early days of medical quackery.

Cast: Anthony Hopkins (Dr John Harvey Kellogg), Bridget Fonda (Eleanor Lightbody), Matthew Broderick (Will Lightbody), John Cusack (Charles Ossining), Dana Carvey (George Kellogg), Michael Lerner (Goodloe Bender), Colm Meaney (Dr Lionel Badger), John Neville (Endymion Hart-Jones), Lara Flynn Boyle (Ida Muntz), Traci Lind (Nurse Irene Graves), Camryn Manheim (Virginia Cranehill), Norbert Weisser (Dr Spitzvogel), Roy Brocksmith, Monica Parker, Jacob Reynolds (young George Kellogg), Marshall Efron, Alexander Slanksnis, Carole Shelley, Gabriel Barre, Marianne Muellerleile.
    Dir and Screenplay: Alan Parker, from the novel by T. Coraghessan Boyle. Pro: Parker, Armyan Bernstein and Robert F. Colesberry. Ex Pro: Tom Rosenberg and Marc

Abraham. Ph: Peter Biziou. Ed: Gerry Hambling. Pro Des: Brian Morris. M: Rachel Portman. Costumes: Penny Rose. (Beacon/Dirty Hands–Entertainment.) Rel: 3 February 1995. 120 mins. Cert 18.

Rob Roy

The Scottish Highlands; 1713. When Robert 'Rob Roy' McGregor borrows a thousand Scottish pounds from the Marquis of Montrose to buy cattle, his money is stolen before he even sees it. Held to his debt by the Marquis, McGregor is forced into hiding – only to have his livestock slaughtered, his house burned to the ground and his wife raped. But how can one man fight the might of the redcoats with just a sword and his code of honour? A robust, lusty and surprisingly brutal romantic epic, *Rob Roy* is both gripping and moving and succeeds technically in all departments, from the splendid costumes and sound design to the giddy crane moves. However, it is the enthralling Highland scenery and Tim Roth's full-bloodied turn as a contemptible villain that audiences will remember – although Jessica Lange as Rob's iron-willed wife and Alan Sharp's elegant dialogue deserve the true merit.

Cast: Liam Neeson (Robert 'Rob Roy' McGregor), Jessica Lange (Mary McGregor), John Hurt (Marquis of Montrose), Tim Roth (Cunningham), Eric Stoltz (Alan McDonald), Brian Cox (Killearn), Andrew Keir (Duke of Argyll), Brian McCardie (Alasdair McGregor), Gilbert Martin (Will Guthrie), Vicki Masson (Betty), Gilly Gilchrist, Jason Flemyng, Ewan Stewart, David Hayman, David Palmer, Myra McFadyen, Karen Matheson.

Dir and Ex Pro: Michael Caton-Jones. Pro: Peter Broughan and Richard Jackson. Co-Pro: Larry DeWaay. Screenplay: Alan Sharp. Ph: Karl Walter Lindenlaub. Ed: Peter Honess. Pro Des: Assheton Gorton. M: Carter Burwell; numbers performed by Capercaillie and Karen Matheson and The Chieftains. Costumes: Sandy Powell. (United Artists/Talisman–UIP.) Rel: 19 May 1995. 139 mins. Cert 15.

Les Roseaux Sauvages – Wild Reed

In the summer of '62, the war between France and Algeria is coming to a head, casting a shadow over the emotional maturation of a group of adolescents swotting for their exams in the south-west of France. With the strains of Del Shannon and Chubby Checker ringing

Highland fling: Liam Neeson in the title role of Michael Caton-Jones's highly cinematic Rob Roy *(from UIP)*

in their ears, four students (three chaps, one *fille*) try to come to terms with themselves, their sexuality and the world. André Téchiné, director of *Rendez-vous* and *Ma Saison Préférée*, lavishes great care on the performances and *mise-en-scène*, but his film is desperately in need of a shot of humour and – let's be honest – credibility.

Cast: Frédéric Gorny (Henri Mariani), Gael Morel (Francois), Elodie Bouchez (Maite Alvarez), Stéphane Rideau (Serge Bartolo), Michèle Moretti (Mme Alvarez), Nathalie Vignes (Mariee), Jacques Nolot (Morelli), Laurent Groulout, Eric Kreikenmayer, Michel Ruhl, Fatia Maite.

Dir: André Téchiné. Pro: Alain Sarde and Georges Benayoun. Screenplay: Téchiné, Gilles Taurand and Olivier Massart. Ph: Jeanne Lapoire. Ed: Martine Giordano. Pro Des: Pierre Soula. M: Samuel Barber and Johann Strauss II; numbers performed by The Beach Boys, The Platters, Del Shannon and Chubby Checker. Costumes: Elisabeth Tavernier. (Ima Films/Canal Plus–Gala.) Rel: 3 March 1995. 113 mins. Cert 15.

The grin and bear: John Cleese and Baloo share a joke in Rudyard Kipling's The Jungle Book *(from Buena Vista)*

Rough Diamonds

Queensland; 1994. Stunningly old-fashioned yarn in which Jason Donovan plays a good ol' boy with cow trouble. Then, when he rams his cattle transporter into an innocent Mercedes, he finds himself in romantic trouble, as the haughty owner happens to be a young woman on the run from her unfaithful husband. And, before you can say 'G'day' a couple of times, Jason has his shirt off and is singing on the verandah. It's almost reassuring that they still make films like these. Almost. From the director of the critically-acclaimed *Caddie*, amazingly. [*Charles Bacon*]

Cast: Jason Donovan (Mike Tyrrell), Angie Milliken (Chrissie Bright), Peter Phelps (Dozer Brennan), Max Cullen (Magistrate Roy), Hayley Toomey (Sam), Jocelyn Gabriel (Lisa Bright), Kit Taylor (Les Finnigan), Lee James, Roger Ward, Maurice Hughes.
Dir: Donald Crombie. Pro: Damien Parer. Ex Pro: Parer and Jonathan Shteinman. Screenplay: Crombie and Christopher Lee. Ph: John Stokes. Ed: Wayne Le Clos. Pro Des: Georgina Greenhill. M: Peter Martin; numbers performed by Lee Kernaghan, Rick Carey, Terry Dean, Jason Donovan, Danni Ella Baha, Peter Phelps, etc. Costumes: Kim Sandeman and Chris Feld. (Forest Home/ Australian Film Finance Corporation/Film Queensland/Beyond Films/ Southern Star–ITC.) Rel: 20 January 1995. 100 mins. Cert PG.

Rudyard Kipling's The Jungle Book

Old-fashioned adventure more in the style of *Raiders of the Lost Ark* than Disney's previous animated version of 1967. Here, Mowgli (mispronounced as Moegly) has grown up into a strapping young man with spectacular pecs and a fatal crush on Kitty, the aristocratic daughter of an English officer. Thus the savage beast-lover is thrust into a world of ersatz civilisation, paving the way for an environment-friendly message the size of Nepal. The trouble is that the film looks like a 1950s romp complete with absurd stereotypes and cardboard villains. Also, all logic is sacrificed for effect, while countless scenes lack conviction or even cohesion. Still, the sound design is terrific.

Cast: Jason Scott Lee (Mowgli), Cary Elwes (Boone), Lena Headey (Kitty), Sam Neill (Brydon), John Cleese (Dr Plumford), Jason Flemyng (Wilkins), Stefan Kalipha (Buldeo), Ron Donachie (Harley), Liza Walker, Rachel Robertson, Natalie Morse, Casey (Baloo).
Dir: Stephen Sommers. Pro: Edward S. Feldman and Raju Patel. Ex Pro: Sharad Patel, Mark Damon and Lawrence Mortorff. Screenplay: Sommers, Ronald Yanover and Mark D. Geldman. Ph: Juan Ruiz-Anchia. Ed: Bob Ducsay. Pro Des: Allan Cameron. M: Basil Poledouris. Costumes: John Mollo. (Walt Disney–Buena Vista.) Rel: 17 February 1995. 112 mins. Cert PG.

The Saint of Fort Washington

It isn't much of a life, but it *is* life – with its petty comforts, moments of unexpected pleasure and heartache. Matthew is a twentysomething schizophrenic made homeless when his building is illegally demolished. Unaccustomed to survival by his wits, he teams up with Jerry, a black Vietnam vet with a gammy leg. Jerry gets by with a heap of optimism and by cleaning car windscreens, and guides Matthew on the ways of the street. Together, they forge a life built on dreams – although cold reality is never far away. A touching and occasionally heartbreaking look at the underbelly of New York, *The Saint of Fort Washington* neither sentimentalises nor patronises its subject, and is enlivened by some splendid performances. Nevertheless, the gentle camera moves and James Newton Howard's cosy music (not to mention Julia Fordham's gushing torch song 'Shame' played at the most inappropriate moment) do undermine the raw potency of the material. A matte finish would have been more fitting. N.B. This is the first film given permission to shoot at the homeless shelter of the title and at Potters Field on Hart's Island, a faceless cemetery for the down-and-out and unclaimed dead.

Cast: Danny Glover (Jerry), Matt Dillon (Matthew), Rick Aviles (Rosario), Nina Siemaszko (Tamsen), Ving Rhames (Little Leroy), Joe Seneca (Spits), Adam Trese (John), Harry Ellington, Ralph Hughes, Bahni Turpin, Robert Beatty Jr, Kevin Corrigan, Aida Turturro, Alison Mackie, Stephen Mendillo, Micheal Badalucco.

Dir: Tim Hunter. Pro: David V. Picker and Nessa Hyams. Ex Pro: Lyle Kessler and Carl Clifford. Screenplay: Kessler. Ph: Frederick Elmes. Ed: Howard Smith. Pro Des: Stuart Wurtzel. M: James Newton Howard; 'Shame' performed by Julia Fordham. Costumes: Claudia Brown. (J & M Entertainment/Carrie Prods–Fox.) Rel: 8 July 1994. 103 mins. Cert 15.

The Sandlot

See *The Sandlot Kids*.

The Sandlot Kids

Coming-of-age saga in which an eleven-year-old new boy in town befriends eight baseball fanatics in the suburbs of Salt Lake City during the summer of '62. Unable to catch a ball and unfamiliar with such basics of baseball as left field and Babe Ruth, Scotty Smalls earns his stripes by facing up to 'the beast' that lives beyond the fence next to the kids' playing field (the sandlot). A dramatic comedy aimed squarely at American children, *The Sandlot Kids* is a good-natured diversion, although the overacting of the pint-sized cast may drive some adults to distraction. US title: *The Sandlot*.

Hand to mouth: Danny Glover and Matt Dillon struggle for hope and shelter in Tim Hunter's moving The Saint of Fort Washington *(from Fox)*

Cast: Tom Guiry (Scotty Smalls), Mike Vitar (Benjamin Franklin Rodriguez), Patrick Renna (Hamilton 'Ham' Porter), Chauncey Leopardi (Michael 'Squints' Palledorous), Marty York (Alan 'Yeah-Yeah' McClennan), Brandon Adams (Kenny DeNunez), Denis Leary (Bill), Karen Allen (Mom), James Earl Jones (Mr Mertle), Art La Fleur ('The Babe'), Marlee Shelton (Wendy), Grant Gelt, Shane Obedzinski, Victor DiMattia, Arliss Howard. Narrator: David Mickey Evans.

Dir: David Mickey Evans. Pro: Dale de la Torre and William S. Gilmore. Ex Pro: Mark Burg, Chris Zarpas and Cathleen Summers. Screenplay: Evans and Robert Gunter. Ph: Anthony B. Richmond. Ed: Michael A. Stevenson. Pro Des: Chester Kaczenski. M: David Newman; numbers performed by Hank Ballard, The Drifters, The Tokens, Ray Charles, Booker T and the MGs, etc. Costumes: Grania Preston. (Island World–Fox.) Rel: 29 July 1994. 101 mins. Cert PG.

Would you let these kids play in your back yard? Patrick Renna, Brandon Adams, Mike Vitar, Shane Obedzinski (foreground), Marty York, Tom Guiry, Victor DiMattia (hidden behind Guiry), Grant Kelt and Chauncey Leopardi are The Sandlot Kids *(from Fox)*

Taking life by the horns: Christopher Cleary Miles and William Hurt in Chris Menges' affecting Second Best *(from Warner)*

Second Best

Llangunllo, Radnorshire, Wales; 1993. For Graham Holt, 'second best' is a way of life. As a child, he seemed to be an intrusion on his parents' marriage. As an adolescent, he couldn't bring himself to confront the opposite sex. And as a man he is cruising through life in an isolated vacuum. Then at 42, he decides to adopt a son. Being a single man, however, his choices are limited: he can foster a disturbed eleven-year-old boy with a fixation on his imprisoned father – or think again. A film daring to explore hitherto undeveloped areas in the cinema, *Second Best* is an intelligent, sensitive and visually arresting drama that draws from real life. And once one has got over the shock of seeing William Hurt brandishing a Welsh accent and spectacles, the rewards are numerous.

Cast: William Hurt (Graham Holt), Chris Cleary Miles (James), Jane Horrocks (Debbie), Alan Cumming (Bernard), Keith Allen (John), John Hurt (Uncle Turpin), Nathan Yapp (young Jimmy), Alfred Lynch (Edward Holt), Rachel Freeman (Elsie Holt), Mossie Smith (Lynn), Shaun Dingwall (Graham, aged 20), Jake Owen (Jimmy, aged 3), Adam Wills (Graham, aged 12), Prunella Scales, Paul Wilson, Sophie Dix, Jennifer Whitefoot, Doris Hare, Nerys Hughes, Anne Morrish, Peter Copley, Jodhi May.

Dir: Chris Menges. Pro: Sarah Radclyffe. Ex Pro: Arnon Milchan. Assoc Pro: Judy Freeman. Screenplay: David Cook, from his own novel. Ph: Ashley Rowe. Ed: George Akers. Pro Des: Michael Howells. M: Simon Boswell. Costumes: Nic Ede. (Regency Enterprises/Alcor Films/Fron Film–Warner.) Rel: 18 November 1994. 105 mins. Cert 12.

The Sexual Life of the Belgians – La Vie Sexuelle des Belges 1950-1978

Mildly diverting comedy (the first of a trilogy) in which an unattractive Belgian samples a wide variety of women over a 28-year period. Developing a passion for mamilla at his mother's breast (a two-year course), Jan Bucquoy grows into a common-or-garden bloke with all the vices a man can expect (with a dash of political activism thrown in). As an autobiographical look at one man's sexual conquests, *The Sexual Life of the Belgians* is astonishing in its unflattering honesty and, happily, never pushes a joke too far. A short film, but then Belgium is not a very big country.

Cast: Jean-Henri Compère (Jan Bucquoy), Noel Francq (Jan as a child), Isabelle Legros (Noella Bucquoy), Sophie Schneider (Therese), Pascale Binneri (Ariane Bucquoy), Michele Shor (Aunt Martha), Dorothee Capelluto (Mia), Jacques Druaux (father), Stefan Lernous (Eddy), Agatha Cornez (Daisy), Jan Bucquoy, Kristien Pottie, Anne-Marie Polster, Claudine Maton.

Dir, Pro and Screenplay: Jan Bucquoy. Ex Pro: Francoise Hoste. Ph: Michel Baudour. Ed: Matyas Veress. Pro Des: Nathalie Andre and Nicole Lenoir. M: Francis De Smet; numbers performed by Marc Aryan, Gene Vincent, The Dominoes, Country Blues Rock Bank of Flanders, etc. Costumes: Sabina Kumeling, Marriose Roose and Mariska Clerebaut. Sound: Jean-Gregoire Mekhitarian. (Transatlantic Films–Metro Tartan.) Rel: 26 May 1995. 80 mins. Cert 18.

SFW

'So Fucking What' (abbreviated to 'SFW' for T-shirt sales) is the motto of one Cliff Spab, a rebel without a cause who becomes a national hero when kidnapped by terrorists. With no apparent motive – other than to serve the plot of the film – a terrorist group calling themselves 'Split Image' take five hostages at a convenience store and video their declining health, aired on global TV like a nightly soap opera. Cliff, with his foul language and jaunty nihilism, becomes the star of the show and, when he foils the terrorists and rescues a co-captive, an international celebrity. On his release from hospital, Cliff finds himself in virtually every shop window, fronting everything from magazine covers to CDs and videos. A tiresome satire on fame and the media, the 'message' of *SFW* has already been done to death – and much, much better.

Cast: Stephen Dorff (Cliff Spab), Reese Witherspoon (Wendy Pfister), Jake Busey (Morrow Streeter), Joey Lauren Adams (Monica Dice), Pamela Gidley (Janet Streeter), John Roarke (Phil Donahue/Sam Donaldson/Alan Dershowitz/Ted Koppel/Larry King), David Barry Gray, Jack Noseworthy, Richard Portnow, Edward Wiley, Lela Ivey, Natasha Gregson Wagner, Annie McEnroe, Virgil Frye, Francesca P.

The Shadow *should know better: Penelope Ann Miller and Alec Baldwin in Russell Mulcahy's risible take on the radio hero (from UIP)*

Roberts, Soon Teck Oh, Blair Tefkin, Steven Antin, Melissa Lechner, Lenny Wolpe, Natalie Strauss, Amber Benson, Stephanie Friedman, Gary Coleman.

Dir: Jefery Levy. Pro: Dale Pollock. Ex Pro: Sigurjon Sighvatsson. Co-Pro: Mike Nelson. Assoc Pro: Gloria Lopez. Screenplay: Levy and Danny Rubin, from the novel by Andrew Wellman. Ph: Peter Deming. Ed: Lauren Zuckerman. Pro Des: Eve Cauley. M: Graeme Revell; numbers performed by Soundgarden, Pretty Mary Sunshine, Radiohead, Babes in Toyland, Therapy?, Paw, Hole, GWAR, Suicidal Tendencies, Stephen Dorff, Reese Witherspoon, etc. Costumes: Debra McGuire. (PolyGram/A&M Films/Propaganda–Rank.) Rel: 10 March 1995. 96 mins. Cert 18.

The Shadow

Just as The Shadow is settling into his role of millionaire playboy and mythical crime fighter (who can 'cloud men's minds' and appear invisible), along comes a beautiful socialite with telepathic powers and, worse still, the evil Shiwan Khan, last living descendant of Genghis Khan. What makes good radio or, indeed, a good comic strip, doesn't necessarily make good cinema. *The Shadow*, based on the 1930s' radio host who evolved into both comic and novel form, is a case in point. In spite of frenetic direction and a few good

Gunning for celebrity: Stephen Dorff as reluctant superstar – in Jefery Levy's dismal SFW *(from Rank)*

throwaway jokes, the film is an embarrassment. From Jerry Goldsmith's overwrought music to the clunky studio sets to the miscasting of Alec Baldwin in the title role, *The Shadow* fails miserably as cinema and as entertainment.

Cast: Alec Baldwin (Lamont Cranston/ The Shadow/Ying Ko 'The Butcher of Lhasa'), John Lone (Shiwan Khan), Penelope Ann Miller (Margo Lane), Peter Boyle (Moe Shrevnitz), Ian McKellen (Reinhardt Lane), Jonathan Winters (Barth), Tim Curry (Farley Claymore), Sab Shimono (Dr Tam), Andre Gregory, Brady Tsurutani, James Hong, Arsenio 'Sonny' Trinidad, Joseph Maher, John Kapelos, Max Wright, Aaron Lustig, Ethan Phillips, Sinoa, Larry Joshua, Alix Elias, Kate McGregor-Stewart.

Dir: Russell Mulcahy. Pro: Martin Bregman, Willi Baer and Michael S. Bregman. Ex Pro: Louis A. Stroller and Rolf Deyhle. Screenplay: David Koepp. Ph: Stephen H. Burum. Ed: Peter Honess. Pro Des: Joseph Nemec III. M: Jerry Goldsmith; 'Original Sin' performed by Taylor Dayne. Costumes: Bob Ringwood. (Universal–UIP.) Rel: 18 November 1994. 107 mins. Cert 12.

Gaelic Gothic: Ewan MacGregor, Kerry Fox and Christopher Eccleston raise their glasses to their new found wealth in Danny Boyle's sensational Shallow Grave *(from Rank)*

Breaking the trust: Sandrine Blancke and Alain Bashung as daughter and father in Aline Issermann's unblinking A Shadow of Doubt *(from Electric)*

A Shadow of Doubt - L'Ombre du Doute

In America and Europe only two out of fifty cases of child abuse are ever brought before the courts. Or so a caption reads at the end of this fine, well-intentioned film (although quite how anybody can accurately determine that figure is a moot point). This document – based on an amalgam of genuine cases – is a straightforward account of an eleven-year-old girl who dares to shop her father for touching her and forcing her to perform fellatio on him. While faithfully exploring the ghosts that haunt both daughter and parent, the film reveals few surprises – at least, from the moment that the girl's mother slaps her face for pointing the finger. It is a well-crafted polemic that successfully refrains from melodrama or sensationalism even if, at times, the father's anguish seems greater than his daughter's. Frankly, the 1984 American TV film, *Something About Amelia*, did it better.

Cast: Mireille Perrier (Marie), Alain Bashung (Jean), Sandrine Blancke (Alexandrine), Emmanuelle Riva, Michel Aumont, Luis Issermann, Roland Bertin, Dominique Lavanant, Thierry Lhermitte, Jean-Pierre Senti, Feodor Atkine, Simon De La Brosse, Josiane Balasko.
  Dir: Aline Issermann. Pro: CiBy 2000. Screenplay: Issermann, Martine Fadier-Nisse and Frederique Gruyer. Ph: Darius Khondji. Ed: Herve Schneid. Pro Des: Cyr Boitard. M: Reno Isaac. Costumes: Maritza Gligo. (CiBy 2000/TFI Films–Electric.) Rel: 26 August 1994. 105 mins. Cert 15.

Shallow Grave

From the opening speeded-up shots of Edinburgh to the establishing scenes of Juliet, David and Alex, this fresh, lean black comedy exudes a masterly flair. Juliet (a New Zealand doctor), David (a nerdy chartered accountant) and Alex (a wise-cracking cub reporter) share an apartment in Edinburgh and are letting out a room. The best of friends, the unlikely trio exhibit an unconventional sense of humour as they gleefully torment the gauche, uptight and geeky room applicants. Then they meet Hugo, a relaxed, confident novelist with cash to spare. He gets the room and in return gives his mischievous landlords more than they bargained for. In turn wickedly funny and brutally suspenseful, *Shallow Grave* excels in virtually every aspect of its creation – from the camera work to sound design. As a first film from TV director Danny Boyle, it is the closest thing to a miracle that the Scottish film industry has ever witnessed.

Cast: Kerry Fox (Juliet Miller), Christopher Eccleston (David Stephens), Ewan McGregor (Alex Law), Ken Stott (Det. Inspector McCall), Keith Allen (Hugo), Colin McCredie (Cameron), John Hodge (D.C. Mitchell), Jean Marie Coffey, Peter Mullan, Leonard O'Malley, Frances Low, Tony Curren, Billy Riddoch.

Dir: Danny Boyle. Pro: Andrew Mac-Donald. Screenplay: John Hodge. Ph: Brian Tufano. Ed: Masahiro Hirakubo. Pro Des: Kave Quinn. M: Simon Boswell and Leftfield; numbers performed by Andy Williams and Nina Simone. Costumes: Kate Carin. (Channel Four/Glasgow Film Fund/Figment Film–Rank.) Rel: 6 January 1995. 93 mins. Cert 18.

The Shawshank Redemption

Maine; 1946-67. Convicted of the murder of his wife and her lover, the vice-president of a large bank is condemned to serve two life sentences at Shawshank State Prison. There, Andy Dufresne is very much a fish out of water among the rapists, killers and other scum, but gradually carves himself a niche. His alliance with Red, the prison fixer, helps smooth the way and activates a friendship that rises above the confines of their insular world. Taking Stephen King's short story *Rita Hayworth and the Shawshank Redemption* as his skeleton, scenarist and first-time director Frank Darabont fleshes out a world of his own making, replete with rage, violence and dignity.

Paying their dues: Tim Robbins and Morgan Freeman contemplate the future in Frank Darabont's totally gripping The Shawshank Redemption *(from Rank)*

One of the greatest prison dramas ever made, *Shawshank* is blessed with some astonishing performances, an unerring score and peerless cinematography, while never losing sight of its humanity.

Cast: Tim Robbins (Andy Dufresne), Morgan Freeman (Ellis Boyd 'Red' Redding), Bob Gunton (Warden Norton), William Sadler (Heywood), Clancy Brown (Capt. Hadley), Gil Bellows (Tommy), James Whitmore (Brooks Hatlen), Mark Rolston (Bogs Diamond), Jeffrey DeMunn, Larry Brandenburg, Neil Giuntoli, Brian Libby, David Proval, Joseph Ragno, Jude Ciccolella, Paul McCrane, Frank Medrano, Ned Bellamy.

Dir and Screenplay: Frank Darabont. Pro: Niki Marvin. Ex Pro: Liz Glotzer and David Lester. Ph: Roger Deakins. Ed: Richard Francis-Bruce. Pro Des: Terence Marsh. M: Thomas Newman; numbers performed by The Ink Spots and Hank Williams. Costumes: Elizabeth McBride. (Castle Rock–Rank.) Rel: 17 February 1995. 143 mins. Cert 15.

Silences of the Palace – Les Silences du Palais

As the Tunisian monarchy enjoys its final days of sovereignty, a young ser-vant girl blossoms into a woman. But here, in the palace of the Beys, little Alia faces only silence in return for her searching questions about life, sex, morality and the identity of her father. Sumptuously photographed, superbly acted and intelligently paced, *Silences* marks an astonishing debut for the Tunisian film editor Moufida Tlatli. Here there are no fancy camera moves or gauche bouts of exposition, just an assured, leisurely style that pin-points the emotional inertia of the world in which Alia strives to escape from. Indeed, it is the scenes of domestic ritual – the housework, preparation of food, the cleaning of wool – that supplies the piece with its distinctive texture. A Franco-Tunisian co-production.

Cast: Ghalia Lacroix (Alia), Ahmel Hedhili (Khedija), Kamel Fazaa (Sidi Ali), Sami Bouajila, Hend Sabri, Najia Ouerghi, Hichem Rostom, Helane Catzaras.

Dir, Screenplay and Ed: Moufida Tlatli. Pro: Ahmed Baha, Eddine Attia and Richard

Magnien. Ph: Youssef Ben Youssef. Ed: Tlatli, Camille Cotte and Kerim Hammouda. Pro Des: Claude Bennys. M: Anouar Brahem. Costumes: Magdalena Garcia. (Mat Films/Channel Four–ICA.) Rel: 10 March 1995. 127 mins. No Cert.

Silent Fall

Two thousand years ago autists were worshipped as gods. Three hundred years ago they were burnt at the stake. Today they are pumped full of drugs and locked away. Thus expounds Dr Jake Rainer, a former child psychiatrist called on to help solve the murder of the parents of a nine-year-old autistic boy. The sole witness to the terrible slaughter, little Timmy Warden is unable to aid police because he cannot talk. It is Rainer's job to help bring the boy out of himself – before the trauma of his parents' death seals him off from reality forever … The son of two prominent child psychiatrists, first-time scenarist Akiva

Psycho-bauble: Ben Faulkner and Richard Dreyfuss merge sensibilities to uncover a murder in Bruce Beresford's Silent Fall *(from Warner)*

Goldsman knows of what he writes, but his knowledge of story structure leaves a lot to be desired. Consequently, *Silent Fall* plays like two different movies glued together. It's an intriguing double bill, but the sudden wrench from psychiatric drama to contrived thriller is an awkward one.

Cast: Richard Dreyfuss (Dr Jack Rainer), Linda Hamilton (Karen Rainer), John Lithgow (Dr Harlinger), J.T. Walsh (Sheriff Mitch Rivers), Ben Faulkner (Tim Warden), Liv Tyler (Sylvie Warden), Zahn Mc-Clarnon (Deputy Bear), John McGee Jr, Ron Tucker, Catherine Shaffner, Jane Beard, Helen Hedman.
   Dir: Bruce Beresford. Pro: James G. Robinson. Co-Pro: Penelope L. Foster, Jim Kouf and Lynn Bigelow. Ex Pro: Gary Barber. Screenplay: Akiva Goldsman. Ph: Peter James. Ed: Ian Crafford. Pro Des: John Stoddart. M: Stewart Copeland; Mozart. Costumes: Colleen Kelsall. (Morgan Creek –Warner.) Rel: 16 June 1995. 101 mins. Cert 15.

Silent Tongue

The concept of a Western starring Alan Bates and Richard Harris and directed by Sam Shepard does sound intriguing.

And the fact that it's about the ghost of a young Indian woman raises the eyebrows a notch higher. Throw in a deranged River Phoenix as a grieving cowpoke and the jaw begins to loll. Yes, *Silent Tongue* is a turkey. But it's a Sam Shepard turkey, which means it's contemplative and drenched in atmosphere and even, on occasion, quite absorbing. It's just a shame that the score is undistinguished, the camera work shoddy and that Alan Bates – as a perpetually inebriated Irishman – gives the worst performance of his career.

Cast: Alan Bates (Eamon McCree), Richard Harris (Prescott Roe), Dermot Mulroney (Reeves McCree), River Phoenix (Talbot Roe), Sheila Tousey (Awbonnie/ghost), Jeri Arredondo (Velada McCree), Tantoo Cardinal (Silent Tongue), Bill Irwin, David Shiner, Tim Scott.
   Dir and Screenplay: Sam Shepard. Pro: Carolyn Pfeiffer and Ludi Boeken. Ex Pro: Gene Rosow, Jacques Fansten, Bill Yahraus and Shep Gordon. Ph: Jack Conroy. Ed: Yahraus. Pro Des: Cary White. M: Patrick O'Hearn; The Red Clay Ramblers. Costumes: Van Broughton Ramsey and Jim Echerd. (Belbo Films/Alive Films/Canal Plus–Entertainment.) Rel: 27 January 1995. 101 mins. Cert 12.

Sin Compasion – No Mercy

Aggressively denouncing the glib ethics taught in philosophy class, an impoverished law student finds himself acting out his own code of justice – to tragic ends. Transposing *Crime and Punishment* to contemporary Peru, *Sin Compasion* is a sombre, deadly slow tract that deftly superimposes Dostoyevsky's controversial doctrines on contemporary Lima. Yet for all its contemplative and intellectual musings, the film fails to draw us into the real anguish of its protagonist, who comes off as a self-centred bore. Ultimately, one has to ask, 'Do we care?'

Cast: Diego Bertie (Ramón Romano), Adriana Davila (Sonia Martinez), Jorge Chiarella (Mayor Saul Portillo), Hernán Romero (Alejandro Velaochaga), Marcello Rivera (Julián Razuri), Mariella Trejos (Mme Aliaga), Ricardo Fernandez, Carlos Onetto.

Dir and Pro: Francisco J. Lombardi. Ex Pro: Gustavo Sanchez. Screenplay: Augusto Cabada. Ph: Pili Flores Guerra. Ed: Luis Barrios. Pro Des: Cecilia Montiel. M: Leopoldo La Rosa. Sound: Daniel Padilla. (INCA Films AMARANTA/CIBY 2000/ Fondation Hubert Bals–Gala.) Rel: 12 May 1995. 117 mins. Cert 15.

Sirens

The Blue Mountains, New South Wales; 1938. When the Revd Anthony Campion and his wife arrive in Australia from England, the bishop of Sydney requests that the young clergyman visits the famous artist Norman Lindsay. Lindsay's etching of a voluptuous naked women nailed to a crucifix has caused something of a local stir and the bishop believes that, as a foreigner, Campion might be able to persuade Lindsay to remove the offending picture from a new exhibition. But, far from thrusting the fear of God into the painter, Campion finds himself both intellectually and emotionally out of his depth as he and his wife come under the spell of Lindsay's world of sensual liberty. Although an enjoyable enough comedy with a fair quota of chuckles and plenty of eye-catching scenery (both pastoral and female), *Sirens* is never surprising, funny or even erotic enough to lift it above the level of a pleasant diversion.

Cast: Hugh Grant (Anthony Campion), Tara Fitzgerald (Estella Campion), Sam

No sex, please: English rose Tara Fitzgerald has her eyes opened in John Duigan's seductive Sirens *(from Buena Vista)*

Neill (Norman Lindsay), Elle Macpherson (Sheela), Portia De Rossi (Giddy), Kate Fischer (Pru), Pamela Rabe (Rose Lindsay), Mark Gerber (Devlin), John Duigan (earnest minister), Ben Mendelsohn, John Polson, Julia Stone, Vincent Ball, Scott Lowe, Lynne Emanuel, Peter Campbell.

Dir and Screenplay: John Duigan. Pro: Sue Milliken. Co-Pro: Sarah Radclyffe. Ex Pro: Justin Ackerman, Hans Brockmann and Robert Jones. Ph: Geoff Burton. Ed: Humphrey Dixon. Pro Des: Roger Ford. M: Rachel Portman. Costumes: Terry Ryan. (WMG/British Screen–Buena Vista.) Rel: 22 July 1994. 94 mins. Cert 15.

Six Degrees of Separation

All of us, Stockard Channing reveals, are removed from every other living person by no more than six associations – or are united by six degrees of separation. The trick is finding the right six people in that chain of introduction. However, Flanagan and Ouisa Kittredge, isolated in their luxurious Manhattan apartment, are cut off from humanity more than most. Then, one evening, the unexpected arrival of a wounded, charismatic black youth challenges their material complacency. A robust and visually witty adaptation of John Guare's award-winning play, this is both a thought-provoking and

Chef of hearts: Donald Sutherland, Ian McKellen and Stockard Channing witness the culinary skills of Will Smith (right) *in Fred Schepisi's invigorating* Six Degrees of Separation *(from Warner)*

hugely entertaining piece. And although Stockard Channing, recreating the role she played on Broadway and in London, was singled out for an Oscar nomination, the whole cast is on terrific form.

Cast: Stockard Channing (Ouisa Kittredge), Will Smith (Paul), Donald Sutherland (Flan Kittredge), Ian McKellen (Geoffrey), Mary Beth Hurt (Kitty), Bruce Davison (Larkin), Richard Masur (Dr Fine), Anthony Michael Hall (Trent), Heather Graham (Elizabeth), Eric Thal (Rick), Osgood Perkins (Woody Kittredge), Catherine Kellner (Tess Kittredge), Anthony Rapp, Jeffrey Abrams, Joe Pentangelo, Kelly Bishop, John Cunningham, Vasek Simek, Chuck Close, Daniel Von Bargen, Kitty Carlisle Hart, Madhur Jaffrey.

Dir: Fred Schepisi. Pro: Schepisi and Arnon Milchan. Ex Pro: Ric Kidney. Screen-

Three into six: Craig Sheffer, Meg Tilly and Eric Stoltz in Rory Keller's funny, quirky, insightful Sleep With Me *(from First Independent)*

play: John Guare. Ph: Ian Baker. Ed: Peter Honess. Pro Des: Patrizia von Brandenstein. M: Jerry Goldsmith; Dvorak, Debussy, Schubert, Tchaikovsky, Richard Wagner. Costumes: Judianna Makovsky. (MGM/ Maiden Movies/New Regency–Warner.) Rel: 9 June 1995. 111 mins. Cert 15.

Sleep With Me

Summing up the plight of the film's protagonists, Todd Field notes, 'Soon we'll be able to live for 200 years, but we won't be able to sit still for ten seconds.' Indeed, this seems to be the fate of Joseph, Sarah and Frank, three LA twentysomethings whose love and friendship come to the boil when Joseph proposes to Sarah. Deftly etched characters, sharp dialogue and some blissfully quirky moments illuminate this ensemble contemplation of sex and fraternity in the nineties. Yet in spite of the occasionally hilarious deviation (Thomas Gibson's wacky Cockney piss-take, for one), the humour is grounded in recognisable characters. And if the film's finale seems somewhat abrupt, *Sleep With Me* still leaves an exquisite aftertaste. You can do a lot worse than watch a cast of talented newcomers enjoying themselves. P.S. The film was scripted by six scenarists, each of whom wrote his own segment.

Cast: Craig Sheffer (Frank), Eric Stoltz (Joseph), Meg Tilly (Sarah), Todd Field (Duane), Dean Cameron (Leo), Thomas Gibson (Nigel), Tegan West (Rory), Parker Posey (Athena), Joey Lauren Adams (Lauren), Quentin Tarantino (Sid), Susan Traylor, Amaryllis Borrego, Vanessa Angel, June Lockhart, David Kriegel, Lewis Arquette.

Dir: Rory Kelly. Pro: Roger Hedden, Michael Steinberg and Eric Stoltz. Ex Pro: Joel Castelberg. Line Pro: Rana Joy Glickman. Screenplay: Kelly, Steinberg, Hedden, Neal Jimenez, Duane Dell'Amico and Joe Keenan. Ph: Andrzej Sekula. Ed: David Moritz. Pro Des: Randy Eriksen. M: David Lawrence. Costumes: Isis Mussenden. (August Entertainment/ Paribas Film Corp/Revolution Films–First Independent.) Rel: 11 November 1994. 94 mins. Cert 18.

The Slingshot - Kadisbellan

Described (accurately) as a cross between *My Life as a Dog* and *Au Revoir, Les Enfants*, Ake Sandgren's *The Slingshot* is the exquisitely crafted true story of a twelve-year-old boy struggling

Cries and whispers: Stellan Skarsgard and Jesper Salén strive for a life in an intolerant Sweden – in Ake Sandgren's poignant The Slingshot *(from Columbia TriStar)*

to grow up in one piece in 1920s Stockholm. The son of a Russian Jewish mother and a lame socialist father, Roland Schutt is a victim on every level. He is mentally tortured by his tyrannical father, is used for punching practise by his older brother (a nascent boxer), is picked on by the local kids and bullied by his small-minded teachers. But utilising every scrap of advice he can find, Roland builds up a world of his own making in which his bruised spirit can flourish. First-rate camera work, a lively score, some perfectly judged performances and above all a spirited sense of humour enrich this perfect gem of a movie. Filmed in Stockholm and Prague.

Cast: Jesper Salén (Roland Schutt), Stellan Skarsgard (Fritiof Schutt), Basia Frydman (Zipa Schutt), Niclas Olund (Bertil Schutt), Ernst-Hugo Jaregard (Lundin, Roland's teacher), Reine Brynolfsson, Jacob Legraf, Frida Hallgren, Axel Duberg, Ing-Marie Carlsson, Ernst Gunther.

Dir and Screenplay: Ake Sandgren, from

Sly and the familiar Stone: Stallone and Stone swap mouthwash in Luis Llosa's studied The Specialist *(from Warner)*

the novel by Roland Schutt. Pro: Waldemar Bergendahl. Ph: Goran Nilsson. Ed: Grete Moldrup. Pro Des: Lasse Westfelt. M: Bjorn Isfalt. Costumes: Inger Pehrsson. (AB Svensk Filmindustri/SVT Kanal 1 Drama/Nordisk Film A/S/Svenska Film Institute–Columbia TriStar.) Rel: 2 September 1994. 102 mins. Cert 12.

Smoking/No Smoking

Imagine a film almost five hours long divided into two sections with just two actors. Imagine that the entire thing is shot in a studio, and that the said actors (who are both French) act out a cast of nine English characters. Hardly the stuff of invigorating cinema. Alain Resnais, a master of celluloid artifice, takes on more than he can handle with this interminable translation of Alan Ayckbourn's eight-play series *Intimate Exchanges* (all of which have two different endings). Set in the bucolic idealism of a Yorkshire village, the film follows the interaction of nine characters over a period of five years. The gim-

mick is that a number of stories emerge from the same dramatic starting point: depending on what character chooses to say or do – or not. That is, the outcome of our lives are constantly at the mercy of any given remark or incident. Good theatre, maybe.

Cast: *Smoking*: Sabine Azema (Celia Teasdale/Sylvie Bell/Irene Pridworthy), Pierre Arditi (Toby Teasdale/Miles Coombes/Lionel Hepplewick/Joe Hepplewick). *No Smoking*: Sabine Azema (Celia Teasdale/Rowena Coombes/Sylvie Bell/Irene Pridworthy/Josephine Hamilton), Pierre Arditi (Toby Teasdale/Miles Coombes/Lionel Hepplewick). Narrator: Peter Hudson.

Dir: Alain Resnais. Pro: Bruno Persey and Michel Seydoux. Screenplay: Jean-Pierre Bacri and Agnes Jaoui, from Anne and Georges Dutter's translation. Ph: Renato Berta. Ed: Albert Jurgenson. Pro Des: Jacques Saulnier. M: John Pattison. Costumes: Jackie Budin. Drawings: Floc'h. (Arena Films/Camera One/France 2 Cinema/Canal Plus–Mainline.) Rel: 16 September 1994. *Smoking*: 140 mins; *No Smoking*: 145 mins. Cert PG.

Solitaire for 2

Slick, briskly paced romantic comedy in which an arrogant body language instructor stubbornly courts an attractive archaeologist with ESP. Directed, written and co-produced by Gary Sinyor, the 32-year-old co-director, co-writer and co-producer of *Leon the Pig Farmer*, *Solitaire for 2* lacks that Extra Special Pizzazz. Frankel, who was Sinyor's Leon, here makes an insufferable prat, while Amanda Pays as the psychic scientist is given little sympathetic charge. Add to that a series of contrived set pieces (a tryst in the Colonnade at Hampstead Heath, an engagement party in London's Natural History Museum, lunch in a Japanese garden) and you have a supermarket brand-name cola masquerading as Dom Perignon.

Cast: Mark Frankel (Daniel Becker), Amanda Pays (Katie), Roshan Seth (Sandip Tamar), Jason Isaacs (Harry), Maryam d'Abo (Caroline), Helen Lederer (female cop), Annette Crosbie (Mrs Dwyer), Neil Mullarkey (Parris), Liza Walker (Lucy), Right Said Fred, Alister Cameron, Michael Shaw, Michael Schneider, Joan Blackham, Norman Caro, Tony Banks MP, Catherine Russell, Otto Jarman, Stefan Schwartz.

Dir and Screenplay: Gary Sinyor. Pro: Sinyor and Richard Holmes. Ex Pro: Nigel Savage. Co-Ex Pro: Andrew Cohen, Stephen Alexander and Paul Brooks. Ph: Henry Braham. Ed: Ewa J. Lind. Pro Des: Carmel Collins. M: David Hughes and John Murphy; numbers performed by Roxy Music, Right Said Fred, Amanda Dillon and Thomas Lang. Costumes: Rodger Parker. (Entertainment.) Rel: 10 February 1995. 107 mins. Cert 15.

Somebody to Love

East Los Angeles; 1994. Alexandre Rockwell, who directed *In the Soup*, returns to the claustrophobic milieu of fringe filmmaking with this stillborn would-be poignant drama. Rosie Perez, in a part specially written for her, stars as Mercedes, a taxi dancer with dreams of becoming an actress who's in love with a self-centred married man and, in turn, is adored by a love-struck innocent from the desert. Although Ms Perez stretches her shrill persona a centimetre or so (after all, this is *her* film), *Somebody to Love* is nothing more than a work made up of isolated moments. At times it even resembles a picture stitched together by favours to the director (including cameos from Quentin Tarantino and Sam Fuller).

Cast: Rosie Perez (Mercedes), Harvey Keitel (Harry Harrelson), Anthony Quinn

(Emillio), Michael DeLorenzo (Ernesto), Steve Buscemi (Jackie), Sam Fuller (Sam Silverman), Stanley Tucci (George), Steve Randazzo, Gerardo, Paul Herman, Angel Aviles, Lorelei Leslie, Quentin Tarantino, Francesco Messina, Sully Boyer, Sam Rockwell, Lelia V. Goldini, Elizabeth Bracco.

Dir: Alexandre Rockwell. Pro: Lila Cazes. Assoc Pro: Sergei Bodrov. Ex Pro: Jean Cazes. Co-Ex Pro: Marie Cantin. Screenplay: Rockwell and Bodrov. Ph: Robert Yeoman. Ed: Elena Maganini. Pro Des: J. Rae Fox. M: Mader; numbers performed by Tito and Tarantula. Costumes: Alexandra Welker. (Lumiere Pictures/Initial Prods–Entertainment.) Rel: 2 June 1995. 100 mins. Cert 18.

Sparrow

Catania, Sicily; 1854. Cliché-loaded, haphazardly dubbed, appallingly written and generally very badly acted melodrama about a novice nun whose love for a handsome buck sends her off her hassock. As the Bambiesque sparrow, newcomer Angela Bettis is pretty enough, but is trapped in an expression of permanent amazement, while Franco Zeffirelli, whose name has been attached to some respectable projects, should have his wrist slapped and his zoom lens confiscated. It's so bad it's unbelievable.

Cast: Angela Bettis (Maria), Jonathon Schaech (Nino), Sinead Cusack (Mathilde), John Castle (Giuseppe), Valentina Cortese (Mother Superior), Vanessa Redgrave (Sister Agata), Mia Fothergill (Giuditta), Janet Maw, Gareth Thomas, Frank Finlay, Pat Heywood, Denis Quilley, Sara-Jane Alexander, Andrea Cassar, Annabel Ryan, Sheherazade Ventura.

Dir: Franco Zeffirelli. Pro: Mario and Vittorio Cecchi Gori. Screenplay: Zeffirelli and Allan Baker, from the novel by Giovanni Verga. Ph: Ennio Guarnieri. Ed: Richard Marden. Pro Des: Raimonda Gaetani. M: Claudio Capponi and Alessio Vlad. Costumes: Piero Jose. (Officina Cinematografica/Tiger Film/Nippon Film Development–Rank.) Rel: 14 October 1994. 107 mins. Cert 12.

The Specialist

Miami Beach, Florida; 1994. Sylvester Stallone is an artist. At least, he is an explosives specialist who 'shapes his charges and controls his explosions'.

He also flexes his pecs and abdominals beautifully, as Sharon Stone wanders around with very little on, begging Sly to eliminate her parents' killers. And that's just a telephone conversation. Will Stallone oblige Ms Stone? Is Ms Stone everything she says she is? And will James Woods steal the acting honours? After a very slow start in which well-toned people stare across smoky nightclubs and/or stare into their cocktails, this romantic thriller kicks into high gear and starts spilling the clichés. The explosions and bodies are very nice, but for the most part the humour is unintentional.

Cast: Sylvester Stallone (Ray Quick), Sharon Stone (May Munro), James Woods (Ned Trent), Rod Steiger (Joe Leon), Eric Roberts (Tomas Leon), Mario Ernesto Sanchez, LaGaylia Frazier, Tony Munafo, Cheito Quinonez, Marcela Cardona, Brent Sexton, Steve Raulerson, Jon Brent Curry.

Dir: Luis Llosa. Pro: Jerry Weintraub. Ex Pro: Steve Baron, Jeff Most and Chuck Binder. Assoc Pro: Tony Munafo and Susan Ekins. Screenplay: Alexandra Seros, 'suggested' by the novels of John Shirley. Ph: Jeffrey L. Kimball. Ed: Jack Hofstra. Pro Des: Walter P. Martishius. M: John Barry; numbers performed by LaGaylia Frazier, John Secada, Donna Allen, Gloria Estefan, Miami Sound Machine, etc. Costumes: Judianna Makovsky, Giorgio Armani and Donna Karan. (Warner.) Rel: 26 December 1994. 110 mins. Cert 15.

Speed is of the essence: Keanu Reeves becomes a bus boy in Jan De Bont's exhilarating action movie (from Fox)

Speed

A crowded bus headed for downtown LA is wired to explode if it slows to under 50mph. A great premise is pumped up with a number of additional twists, some neat throwaway humour and the best action sequences that money can buy. From the opening scene of an elevator plummeting down a skyscraper lift shaft to the climax on a subway, *Speed* is pure heroin for action junkies. Photography, music and above all John Wright's agile editing all add to the heat. A remarkable directing debut for Dutch cinematographer Jan De Bont, who previously lit such pictures as *Die Hard*, *Black Rain* and *Basic Instinct*.

Cast: Keanu Reeves (Jack Traven), Dennis Hopper (Howard Payne), Sandra Bullock (Annie), Joe Morton (Capt. McMahon), Jeff Daniels (Harry), Alan Ruck (Stephens), Glenn Plummer, Richard Lineback, Beth Grant, Hawthorne James, Carlos Carrasco, David Kriegel, Beau Starr, John Capodice, Sandy Martin, Neisha Folkes-LeMelle.

Dir: Jan De Bont. Pro: Mark Gordon. Ex Pro: Ian Bryce. Co-Pro: Allison Lyon. Screenplay: Graham Yost. Ph: Andrzej Bartkowiak. Ed: John Wright. Pro Des: Jackson De Govia. M: Mark Mancina. Costumes: Ellen Mirojnick. (Fox.) Rel: 30 September 1994. 115 mins. Cert 15.

Crossing the threshold of time: Kurt Russell and James Spader bring science and testosterone to an ancient civilisation – in Roland Emmerich's Stargate *(from Guild)*

Nerds in hell: Martin Clunes and Griff Rhys Jones in the former's directorial debut, Staggered *(from Entertainment)*

Staggered

While striving to inject a fresh comic sensibility into British cinema, *Staggered* trudges over old ground in hobnail boots. Martin Clunes stars as the English clod due to be married the following weekend, but – thanks to a malicious stag night prank – encounters the usual string of eccentric stereotypes while learning to put away nerdish things. Unfortunately, slack direction, flabby editing and shoddy camera work vandalise even the film's funniest moments. At times it even resembles a composite of previous British comedies, from *Local Hero* to *Clockwise* through to *Soft Top Hard Shoulder* and *Four Weddings and a Funeral*. Seen it, laughed at that, *pass*.

Cast: Martin Clunes (Neil), Michael Praed (Gary), Sarah Winman (Hilary), Sylvia Sims (Mother), Virginia McKenna (Flora), John Forgeham (Lubbock), Anna Chancellor (Carmen), Griff Rhys Jones (Graham), Steve Sweeney (nutter), Michele Winstanley, Kate Byers, David Kossoff, Helena McCarthy, Dermot Crowley, Michael Medwin, Julia Deakin, Annette Ekblom, Desmond McNamara, George Rossi, Neil Morrissey.

Dir: Martin Clunes. Pro: Philippa Braithwaite. Ex Pro: Christopher J. Parkinson and Clifford D. W. Davis. Line Pro: Helen Booth. Screenplay: Simon Braithwaite and Paul Alexander. Ph: Simon Kossoff. Ed: Peter Delfgou. Pro Des: Iain Andrews. M: Harry Fix. Costumes: Ralph Holes. (Big Deal–

Entertainment.) Rel: 8 July 1994. 95 mins. Cert 15.

Stargate

When renegade Egyptologist Daniel Jackson deciphers the hieroglyphic combination to an ancient stellar gateway, he volunteers to cross the unknown threshold. Thus, Daniel and military reconnaissance team are molecularly deconstructed and transported to another world – which may or may not hold the key to our own civilisation. After a terrific opening, *Stargate* holds up pretty well until about halfway through when it locks into automatic pilot and turns into a routine archaeological epic. Nevertheless, the effects are great, the action spectacular and Jaye Davidson – as an ersatz Egyptian deity – a unique villain.

Cast: Kurt Russell (Col Jonathan 'Jack' O'Neil), James Spader (Dr Daniel Jackson), Jaye Davidson (Ra), Viveca Lindfors (Catherine), Alexis Cruz (Skaara), Mili Avital (Sha'uri), John Diehl (Lt Kawalsky), Leon Rippy, Carlos Lauchu, Djimon, Erick Avari, French Stewart, Gianin Loffler, Christopher John Fields, Derek Webster, Jack Moore, Steve Giannelli, Cecil Hoffman (Sarah O'Neil), Frank Welker (voice of the Mastadge).

Dir: Roland Emmerich. Pro: Joel B. Michaels, Oliver Eberle and Dean Devlin. Ex Pro: Mario Kassar. Co-Pro: Ute Emmerich. Screenplay: Devlin and Emmerich. Ph: Karl Walter Lindenlaub. Ed: Michael J. Duthie and Derek Brechlin. Pro Des: Holger Gross. M: David Arnold. Costumes: Joseph Porro. (Le Studio Canal Plus/Centropolis/Carolco–Guild.) Rel: 6 January 1995. 119 mins. Cert PG.

Star Trek: Generations

The first big-screen spin-off of *Star Trek: The Next Generation* neatly ties up the old series with the new, with Captain T. Kirk bidding farewell to the Starship Enterprise. Enter Patrick Stewart as Jean-Luc Picard, captain of the new ship 78 years on, who, thanks to the miracles of space technology, gets to meet his legendary predecessor. But their encounter is far from a happy one as the humanoid alien Dr Soran (Malcolm

Ring out the old: Captain Jean-Luc Picard (Patrick Stewart) meets his idol, Captain Kirk (William Shatner), in David Carson's entertaining Star Trek: Generations *(from UIP)*

McDowell) prepares to eliminate an entire civilisation in his quest to return to Nexus, a contrived utopia. The special effects just get better and better and the imagination of the scriptwriters knows no bounds. Still, a workmanlike knowledge of the TV series would help.

Cast: Patrick Stewart (Captain Jean-Luc Picard), Jonathan Frakes (William T. Riker), Brent Spiner (Data), LeVar Burton (Geordi La Forge), Michael Dorn (Worf), Gates McFadden (Dr Beverly Crusher), Marina Sirtis (Deanna Troi), Malcolm McDowell (Dr Soran), James Doohan (Montgomery 'Scotty' Scott), Walter Koenig (Pavel Andreivich Chekov), William Shatner (Captain James Tiberius Kirk), Barbara March (Lursa), Gwynyth Walsh (B'Etor), Whoopi Goldberg (Guinan), Alan Ruck, Jacqueline Kim, Jenette Goldstein, Glenn Morshower, Tim Russ, Brian Thompson, Kim Braden.

Toffs in torment: Dinsdale Landen and Peter Bowles on the trail of the latter's kidnappers – in John Hay's agreeable The Steal *(from Warner)*

Dir: David Carson. Pro: Rick Berman. Ex Pro: Bernie Williams. Screenplay: Ronald D. Moore and Brannon Braga, from a story by Berman, Moore and Braga. Ph: John A. Alonzo. Ed: Peter E. Berger. Pro Des: Herman Zimmerman. M: Dennis McCarthy. Costumes: Robert Blackman. (Paramount–UIP.) Rel: 10 February 1995. 118 mins. Cert PG.

The Steal

Frisky little British comedy in which a gorgeous and amoral American computer expert, Kim (Helen Slater), is recruited to hack into a small London bank with nefarious ties. Trouble is, the bank is protected by its own self-contained computer, preventing Kim from accessing it externally. So elaborate steps have to be taken ... While an extended sub-plot involving the kidnap of an eminent aristocrat tilts the narrative into a diametric direction, *The Steal* boasts enough techno-jargon to keep the mind logged on. Crisp photography, a driving score and a nice array of underplayed cameos add to the enjoyment.

Cast: Alfred Molina (Cliff), Helen Slater (Kim), Peter Bowles (Lord Childwell), Dinsdale Landen (Sir Wilmot), Heathcote Williams (Jeremiah), Stephen Fry (Wimborne), Brian Pringle (Cecil), Patricia Hayes (Mrs Fawkes), Jack Dee, Ian Porter, Lindsay Holiday, Rob Freeman, Ann Bryson, Sara Crowe, Gabrielle Drake, Robin Driscoll, Bob Sessions.

Dir and Screenplay: John Hay. Pro: Gary Kurtz and Barbara Stone. Ex Pro: Frixos Constantine. Ph: Ronnie Taylor. Ed: David Martin. Pro Des: Phil Roberson. M: Barry Kirsch; numbers performed by Clae, God's Gift, Jamie Mac and Lena Fiagbe. Costumes: Ita Murray. (Poseidon–Warner.) Rel: 5 April 1995. 91 mins. Cert PG.

Strawberry and Chocolate – Fresa y Chocolate

Havana; 1993. Over ten years in development, *Strawberry and Chocolate* has evolved as an intelligent, warm-hearted comedy-drama that explores the tenuous attraction (both emotional and political) between an uptight communist student and an irreverent, gay artist. While shedding light on the contemporary lifestyle and intolerance of homosexuality in Cuba, the film uses the men's cultural courtship as a microcosm of the country's social unheaval. While Diego, the gay liberator (who actually champions Cuban culture) is portrayed as a mincing stereotype, his outward appearance actually serves as a filter for his interior complexity. He is, incidentally, superbly realised by Jorge Perugorria, in one of the year's best performances. Although obviously critical of the Castro regime, *Strawberry and Chocolate* has been enormously popular in Cuba, where it has won awards for best film, best director and best actor.

Cast: Jorge Perugorria (Diego), Vladmir Cruz (David), Mirta Ibarra (Nancy), Francisco Gatorno (Miguel), Jorge Angelino (German), Marilyn Solaya (Vivian).

Dir: Tomas Gutierrez Alea and Juan Carlos Tabio. Ex Pro: Camilo Vives, Frank Cabrera and Georgina Balzaretti. Screenplay: Senel Paz. Ph: Mario Garcia Joya. Ed: Miriam Talavera and Osvaldo Donatien. Pro Des: Fernando O'Reylly. M: Jose Maria Vitier. Costumes: Miriam Duenas. (Instituto Cubano del Arte Industria Cinematograficos–Metro Tartan.) Rel: 25 November 1994. 111 mins. Cert 18.

Street Fighter

Computer designed action-thriller in which a battalion of sub-plots and characters collide in a story involving a power-crazed warlord. Somewhere in south-east Asia the despot holds 63 people hostage and is demanding $20 billion for their release. Enter Jean-Claude Van Damme as a man called Guile ... Bearing in mind that this colossal, costly piece of junk was based on a video game, one cannot judge it too harshly. While defying logic at every turn, the film at least moves at the rate of knots and doesn't take itself seriously. And top marks to the five-man editing team who manage to sustain it all in fifth gear.

Cast: Jean-Claude Van Damme (Colonel William F. Guile, no less), Raul Julia (General M. Bison), Ming-Na Wen (Chun-Li Zang), Damian Chapa (Ken Masters), Kylie Minogue (Cammy), Simon Callow (A.N. Official), Byron Mann (Ryu Hoshi), Roshan Seth (Dhalsim), Wes Studi (Viktor Sagat), Grand L. Bush, Peter Tuiasosopo, Jay Tavare, Andrew Bryniarski, Gregg Rainwater, Miguel A. Nunez Jr, Robert Mammone, Kenya Sawada, Ed Pressman, Joe Bugner, David de Souza.

Dir and Screenplay: Steven E. de Souza, from the CAPCOM video game *Streetfighter II*. Pro: Edward R. Pressman and Kenzo Tsujimoto. Ex Pro: Tim Zinnemann, Jun Aida and Sasha Harari. Ph: William A. Fraker. Ed: Dov Hoenig. Pro Des: William Creber. M: Graeme Revell; numbers performed by Ice Cube, Public Enemy, New World Report, Paris, LL Cool J, Pharcyde, Hammer and Deion Sanders, etc. Costumes: Deborah La Gorce Kramer. 'Bison' costume: Marilyn Vance. (Capcom

Co.–Columbia TriStar.) Rel: 19 May 1995. 100 mins. Cert 12.

Sugar Hill

Two brothers from Harlem who, as children, watched their mother OD on heroin and saw their father gunned down by drug dealers, have taken over the drug market themselves. But Roemello is suffering a crisis of conscience and is planning to go straight. His brother, however, has other plans. After a promising opening, *Sugar Hill* stops dead in its tracks, periodically waiting for Wesley Snipes to appear out of the shadows and look moody. Unfortunately, in spite of some classy lensing and a moody score, the film is so lifeless and the dialogue so insipid that it's a hard slog to the inevitably violent climax. Previously known as *Skeezer* and *Harlem*.

Cast: Wesley Snipes (Roemello Skuggs), Michael Wright (Raynathan Skuggs), Theresa Randle (Melissa), Clarence Williams III (A.R. Skuggs), Abe Vigoda (Gus Molino), Ernie Hudson (Lolly Jones), Larry Joshua, Leslie Uggams, Joe D'Alessandro, Khandi Alexander, Devaughn Nixon, Marquise Wilson, O.L. Duke, Kimberly Russell, Raymond Serra, Nicki Corello, Sam Bottoms, Vondie Curtis-Hall.
   Dir: Leon Ichaso. Pro: Rudy Langlais and Gregory Brown. Ex Pro: Armyan Bernstein, Marc Abraham and Thomas B. Rosenberg. Screenplay: Barry Michael Cooper. Ph: Bojan Bazelli. Ed: Gary Karr. Pro Des: Michael Helmy. M: Terence Blanchard; numbers performed by Duke Ellington, Definition of Sound, Simple E, Otis Redding, Chaka Khan, etc. Costumes: Eduardo Castro. (Beacon Films/South Street Entertainment/Ghiznost Pictures–Entertainment.) Rel: 1 July 1994. 123 mins. Cert 18.

Suture

A provocative drama exploring the complex morality of human identity, *Suture* is an impressive debut from the writing-producing-directing duo of Scott McGehee and David Siegel. Having murdered his father – one of the wealthiest citizens of Phoenix – Vincent Towers meets his dirt-poor half-brother, Clay Arlington, at the funeral. Noting that their 'physical similarity is remarkable', Vincent invites Clay to stay with him at his baronial home. Then, with disarming ease, Vincent sets Clay up, dressing him in his own clothes, switching his ID and convincing Clay to drop him off at the airport – in his car, of course. On the return journey, Vincent's car, credit cards and Clay Arlington are blown sky high. Miraculously, Clay escapes with his life, but is amnesic and facially disfigured. In fact, he is in a perfect condition to have Vincent's identity grafted on to him: complete with wealth, position and a murder rap for his father's death. A first-rate script is brought slyly to life in anonymous widescreen black and white, while the whole conundrum of identity is enhanced by the 'identical' brothers being played by white and black actors. Yes, really.

Identity crisis: Half-brothers Dennis Haysbert and Michael Harris merge in David Siegel and Scott McGehee's intriguing Suture *(from ICA)*

Cast: Dennis Haysbert (Clay Arlington), Mel Harris (Dr Renee Descartes), Sab Shimono (Dr Max Shinoda), Michael Harris (Vincent Towers), Dina Merrill (Alice Jameson), David Graf (Lt Weismann), Fran Ryan (Mrs Lucerne), John Ingle, Sandy Gibbons, Mark Demichele, Capri Darling, Seth Siegel, Mark Siegel.
   Dir, Pro and Screenplay: Scott McGehee and David Siegel. Ex Pro: Steven

Moody blues: Wesley Snipes scowls his way through Leon Ichaso's frightfully depressing Sugar Hill *(from Entertainment)*

Soderbergh and Michele Halberstadt. Co-Pro: Alison Brantley, Buddy Enright and Laura Groppe. Assoc Pro: Eileen Jones. Ph: Greg Gardiner. Ed: Lauren Zuckerman. Pro Des: Kelly McGehee. M: Cary Berger; Richard Wagner, Brahms, Puccini, Haydn; numbers performed by Salsa Piccante, Johnny Cash, Tom Jones and Capri Darling. Costumes: Mette Hansen. Sound: Mark Mangini. (Kino-Korsakoff–ICA.) Rel: 27 January 1995. 96 mins. Cert 15.

Tales From the Crypt Presents Demon Knight

Big guns produced this feature film based on the *Tales From the Crypt* comic and TV show, with Richard Donner, Joel Silver, Walter Hill and Robert Zemeckis credited. Yet it is Billy Zane who steals the show as the devil's right-hand man who must get back a magical key protected by Christ's own blood. William Sadler co-stars as the 'demon knight' who guards the key until he can find a new custodian for it at his death. Although basically a good-versus-evil tale set in an eerie hotel, solid performances and able direction by Spike Lee's cinematographer Ernest Dickerson give it an added edge. Not very

Tank top: Lori Petty flexes her sinew in the title role of Rachel Talalay's abominable Tank Girl *(from UIP)*

scary, but some gruesome visual puns add spice. [*Karen Krizanovich*]

Cast: Billy Zane (the collector), William Sadler (Frank Brayker), Jada Pinkett (Jeryline), Brenda Bakke (Cordelia), CCH Pounder (Irene), Dick Miller (Uncle Willy), Thomas Haden Church (Roach), John Schuck (Sheriff Tupper), Gary Farmer (Deputy Bob Martel), John Kassir (voice of the crypt keeper), Charles Fleischer, Tim deZarn, Sherrie Rose, Ken Baldwin.

Dir: Ernest Dickerson. Pro: Gilbert Adler. Co-Pro: Scott Nimerfro, Wendy Wanderman and Alan Katz. Ex Pro: Richard Donner, David Giler, Walter Hill, Joel Silver and Robert Zemeckis. Assoc Pro: Alexander B. Collett and Dan Cracchiolo. Screenplay: Ethan Reiff, Cyrus Voris and Mark Bishop, from the comic originally published by William M. Gaines. Ph: Rick Bota. Ed: Stephen Lovejoy. Pro Des: Christian Wagener. M: Ed Shearmur. Main Theme: Danny Elfman. M Ex Pro: Michael Kamen; numbers performed by Filter, Rollins Band, Aretha Franklin, Wilson Pickett, Gravediggaz, Ministry, James Brown, Megadeth, etc. Costumes: Warden Neil. (Universal–UIP.) Rel: 2 June 1995. 93 mins. Cert 18.

Tank Girl

The year is 2033 and the world is suffering a post-apocalyptic drought. Water is now the currency of necessity and the evil Water and Power Company is soaking it all up. Enter Rebecca Buck – alias Tank Girl – a spirited, wise-cracking anti-heroine with vengeance on her mind … Really, this is a crude, shapeless and artless screen version of the cult comic strip, complete with lousy stunts, poorly choreographed action sequences and a witless script. Lori Petty, who replaced Emily Lloyd at the eleventh minute, is little help as the sexless, irritating superbitch.

Cast: Lori Petty (Rebecca Buck), Ice-T (T-Saint), Naomi Watts (Jet Girl), Malcolm McDowell (Kesslee), Don Harvey (Sergeant Small), Jeff Kober (Booga), Stacy Linn Ramsower (Sam), Reg E. Cathey, Scott Coffey, Ann Cusack, Brian Wimmer, Iggy Pop, Dawn Robinson, Billy L. Sullivan, James Hong, Charles Lucia.

Dir: Rachel Talalay. Pro: Richard B. Lewis, Pen Densham and John Watson. Co-Pro: Christian L. Rehr. Ex Pro: Aron Warner and Tom Astor. Screenplay: Tedi Sarafian, based on the comic strip by Alan Martin and Jamie Hewlett. Ph: Gale Tattersall. Ed: James R. Symons. Pro Des: Catherine Hardwicke; numbers performed by Bjork, Veruca Salt, Rachel Sweet, Ice-T, Richard Hell & the Voidoids, Bush, Hole, Devo, Joan Jett and Paul Westerberg, Stomp, Portishead, L7, Belly, Beowulf, Iggy Pop, etc. Costumes: Arianne Phillips. 'Ripper' Designs: Stan Winston. Assistant to Lori Petty: Lisa Petty. (United Artists/Trilogy Entertainment–UIP.) Rel: 23 June 1995. 104 mins. Cert 15.

Terminal Velocity

Good-time jock and sky-diving instructor Ditch Brodie doesn't know what's hit him when he takes on a beautiful new client. Neither do we, as the plot hurtles into a break-neck slipstream involving the FAA, the FBI and the KGB – or, as Brodie puts it, 'the KG-used-to-B'. From the suspenseful opening in a sandstorm in the Arizona desert to the climactic stunt of a lifetime, *Terminal Velocity* is a cracking, well-plotted thriller with adrenalin to spare. And even when events become too far-fetched to swallow, the action moves so fast you have no time to notice.

Cast: Charlie Sheen (Richard 'Ditch' Brodie), Nastassja Kinski (Chris Morrow), James Gandolfini (Ben Pinkwater), Christopher McDonald (Kerr), Gary Bullock, Hans R. Howes, Melvin Van Peebles, Suli McCullough, Cathryn de Prume, Richard Sarafian Jr, Sofia Shinas, Matthew Mazuroski, Cindi Shope, Chester Bennett, Mr Shutov, Sam Smiley, Rance Howard.

Dir: Dean Sarafian. Pro: Scott Kroopf and Tom Engelman. Ex Pro: David Twohy, Ted Field and Robert W. Cort. Co-Pro: Joan Bradshaw. Screenplay: Twohy. Ph: Oliver Wood. Ed: Frank J. Urioste and Peck Prior. Pro Des: David L. Snyder. M: Joel McNeely; numbers performed by Royal Jelly, Dan Markell, Jeff Harmon, etc. Costumes: Poppy Cannon-Reese. Visual FX: Christopher F. Woods. (Hollywood Pictures/Interscope/PolyGram–Buena Vista.) Rel: 7 April 1995. 102 mins. Cert 15.

Thin Ice
After a blazing altercation, a lesbian ice skater loses her partner for the Gay Games in New York. Desperate for a replacement, she homes in on Natalie, who is not only straight but has little faith in her skating ability. *Thin Ice* is a sentimental, desperately sincere low-budget drama that attempts to cast fresh light on the gay scene without recourse to preachiness or sensationalism. Unfortunately, the film is blighted by heavy-handed and self-conscious direction, bizarre camera angles, claustrophobic close-ups and a droning, meddlesome score. And no jokes about gay blades, please.

Cast: Charlotte Avery (Natalie Wilcox), Sabra Williams (Steffi Martin), James Dreyfus (Greg), Clare Higgins (Fiona), Ian McKellen (himself), Guy Williams (Charles), Barbara New (Felicity), Suzanne Bertish (Lotte), Gwyneth Strong, Martha Freud, Cathryn Harrison, Eamon Geoghegan, Jimmy Gardner, Laura Moore, Linda Carney, Jack Freud.
    Dir: Fiona Cunningham Reid. Pro: Cunningham Reid and Martien Coucke. Screenplay: Cunningham Reid and Geraldine Sherman. Ph: Belinda Parsons. Ed: Rodney Sims. Pro Des: Patricia Boulter. M: Claire Van Kampen, Richard Allen and Strauss. (Dangerous To Know–ICA Projects.) Rel: 28 April 1995. 88 mins. Cert 12.

Jump leads: Charlie Sheen and Nastassja Kinski hurl themselves into their art in Dean Sarafian's Terminal Velocity *(from Buena Vista)*

Three Colours Red - Trois Couleurs Rouge
The final chapter in Kieslowski's trilogy celebrating the three colours of the French flag, representing liberty, equality and fraternity. The most highly touted of the three at Cannes, this complex, sensual work certainly casts a spell, but its contrivances, in-jokes and majestic camera moves hardly endear one to its dramatic personae. Four characters' lives overlap, collide and are duplicated one spring in Geneva. There's Valentine, a model whose boy-friend is away on business in England. There's the retired judge, who eaves-drops on his neighbours in an effort to understand 'the truth' more clearly. There's Karin, who's recently set up a

weather service. And there's Auguste, Karin's boyfriend, a mirror image of the judge as a young man. When Valentine runs over the judge's dog, she completes the circuit of human intrigue, instigating a chain of romantic accident and grand design. Although ultimately, *Red* disappoints on an emotional level, its myriad narrative threads still tease the mind long after the closing credits – and court a second viewing.

Cast: Irene Jacob (Valentine), Jean-Louis Trintignant (The Judge), Frederique Feder (Karin), Jean-Pierre Lorit (Auguste), Samuel Lebihan, Juliette Binoche, Julie Delpy, Benoit Regent, Zbigneiw Zamachowski.

Dir: Krzysztof Kieslowski. Pro: Marin Karmitz. Ex Pro: Yvon Crenn. Screenplay: Kieslowski and Krzysztof Piesiewicz. Ph: Piotr Sobocinski. Ed: Jacques Witta. Pro Des: Claude Lenoir. M: Zbigniew Preisner. Sound: Jean-Claude Laureux. (MK2 Prods/France 3 Cinema/Cab Prods/TOR/Canal Plus–Artificial Eye.) Rel: 11 November 1994. 96 mins. Cert 15.

Threesome

Surprisingly frank sex comedy (that is, verbally frank for a mainstream Hollywood release) about two college guys and a girl eternally confused by their sexual disposition. Alex lusts after Eddy who lusts after Stuart who lusts after Alex, but all, apparently, love each other to distraction. While the film is never less than engaging, is exceptionally well written and generally well played (Stephen Baldwin is particular-

Circle of life in scarlet: Irene Jacob in Krzysztof Kieslowski's complex, sensual Three Colours Red *(from Artificial Eye)*

Two men and a babe: Josh Charles, Lara Flynn Boyle and Stephen Baldwin juggle love and carnality in Andrew Fleming's engaging Threesome *(from Columbia TriStar)*

ly effective as a lustful slob, although Lara Flynn Boyle is too old for the girl), *Threesome* lacks narrative thrust and purpose. Tighter editing would have helped.

Cast: Lara Flynn Boyle (Alex), Stephen Baldwin (Stuart), Josh Charles (Eddy), Alexis Arquette (Dick), Martha Gehman (Renay), Mark Arnold (Larry), Michele Matheson (Kristen).

Dir and Screenplay: Andrew Fleming. Pro: Brad Krevoy and Steve Stabler. Ex Pro: Cary Woods. Co-Pro: Brad Kenkel. Ph: Alexander Gruszynski. Ed: William C. Carruth. Pro Des: Ivo Cristante. M: Thomas Newman; numbers performed by Tears For Fears, Apache Indian, Duran Duran, U2, Bryan Ferry, Human Sexual Response, The The, General Public, Jah Wobble, New Order, Brad, Curve, Stephen Baldwin, etc. Costumes: Deborah Everton. (Motion Picture Corp/TriStar Pictures–Columbia TriStar.) Rel: 14 October 1994. 93 mins. Cert 18.

Thumbelina

Animation has advanced so far in the last few years that something as uninspired and bland as this can come as a huge disappointment. While the animation itself has its moments, there is nothing to write home about. Also, the dreary plot looks even more unwieldy blown up on the big screen: a diminutive beauty yearns for the companionship of a like-sized mate, and when she finds him – prince of the fairies, no less – she is kidnapped by an interfering toad and is then subjected to a string of bestial suitors. Barry Manilow wrote six mediocre songs for the occasion.

Voices: Jodi Benson (Thumbelina), Gino Conforti (Jacquimo), Barbara Cook (Mother), Will Ryan (Hero/Reverend Rat), June Foray (Tabetha), Kenneth Mars (King Colbert), Gary Imhoff (Prince Cornelius), Joe Lynch (Grundel), Charo (Mrs Delores Toad), Loren Michaels (Gringo), Gilbert Gottfried (Mr Beetle), Carol Channing (Mrs Fieldmouse), John Hurt (Mr Mole).

Dir: Don Bluth and Gary Goldman. Pro: Bluth, Goldman and John Pomeroy. Screenplay: Bluth, from the Hans Christian Andersen story. Ed: Thomas V. Moss. Pro Des: Rowland Wilson. M: William Ross and Barry Manilow; songs: Manilow, Jack Feldman and Bruce Sussman. (Warner.) Rel: 29 July 1994. 86 mins. Cert U.

Tim Burton's The Nightmare Before Christmas

After a twelve-year gestation, Tim Burton's extraordinary stop motion

Taking the Christ out of Christmas: Jack Skellington poses as Santa Claus in the imaginative, stop-motion Tim Burton's The Nightmare Before Christmas (from Buena Vista)

animated musical fantasy makes it to the screen – with knobs on. A perverse twist on the classic American children's poem 'The Night Before Christmas' (by Clement Clarke Moore), Tim Burton's *Nightmare* gleefully explores the wayward world of Halloweentown. There, a variety of grotesque figures – headed by Jack Skellington, the Pumpkin King – conspire to think up new ways to make All Hallows Eve more interesting and scary. Then, one night, Jack stumbles on to Christmas-town and plots to transform the Yuletide festival into a twisted carnival of his own making – to disastrous results. Utilising state-of-the-art animation and special effects, Disney builds on Burton's original concept to create a unique entertainment for older child-ren that should equally enthral adults. Danny Elfman's ten original songs add to the devilish fun.

Voices: Danny Elfman (Jack Skellington, singing/Barrel), Chris Sarandon (Jack

hotchpotch of shifting moods, contrived humour and iffy acting. Every supporting character seems intent on stealing the limelight, while the central protagonists act like they're auditioning for drama school. Worse still is the overwhelming music that drowns any shred of credibility that the audience may have been able to salvage from the wreckage.

Cast: Thomas Arklie (Simon Downs), Ian Williams (Mark), Tony Slattery (Terry), Dilly Keane (Siobhan), Jean Boht (Mrs Monica Downs), John Altman (Dogger), Caroline Munro, Gordon Milne, Nicholas Harrison, Lloyd Williams, Ian McKellen (voice only).
Dir: Peter MacKenzie Litten. Pro: Gary Fitzpatrick. Ex Pro: Stephen Garbutta. Screenplay: Johnny Byrne. Ph: John Ward. Ed: Jeffrey Arsenault. Art: Geoff Sharpe. M: Roger Bolton; numbers performed by Ruth Wallis, Echobelly, Erasure, Sinitta, MBD, Sheep on Drugs, etc. (TDF/London Lighthouse/British Screen–Metro Tartan.) Rel: 2 December 1994. 101 mins. Cert 15.

Dangerous moves: Jean-Claude Van Damme (right) puts his best gastrocnemius forward in Peter Hyams' rip-roaring Timecop *(from UIP)*

rules, you could find your own birth date up for auction. Daft, but fun. And the special effects are groovy. What more can you expect from a Jean-Claude Van Damme movie?

Cast: Jean-Claude Van Damme (Max Walker), Ron Silver (Senator Aaron McComb), Mia Sara (Melissa Walker), Bruce McGill (Matuzak), Gloria Reuben (Sarah Fielding), Scott Bellis, Jason Schombing, Scott Lawrence, Kenneth Welsh, Brent Woolsey, Brad Loree, Richard Farachi, Steve Lambert, Kevin McNulty, Nick Hyams, Laura Murdoch.
Dir and Ph: Peter Hyams. Pro: Moshe Diamant, Sam Raimi and Robert Tapert. Ex Pro: Mike Richardson. Screenplay: Mark Verheiden, from a story by Verheiden and Richardson, based on their comic series. Ed: Steven Kemper. Pro Des: Philip Harrison. M: Mark Isham. Costumes: Dan Lester. (Largo International/JVC Entertainment/ Signature/Renaissance/Dark Horse–UIP.) Rel: 6 January 1995. 98 mins. Cert 18.

Skellington, speaking), Catherine O'Hara (Sally/Shock), William Hickey (evil scientist), Glenn Shadix (Mayor), Paul Reubens (Lock), Ken Page (Oogie Boogie), Ed Ivory (Santa).
Dir: Henry Selick. Pro: Tim Burton and Denise Di Novi. Co-Pro: Kathleen Gavin. Screenplay: Caroline Thompson, from a story and characters by Burton. Ph: Pete Kozachik. Ed: Stan Webb. Art: Deane Taylor. M/Lyrics and Assoc Pro: Danny Elfman. Animation Supervisor: Eric Leighton. (Touchstone Pictures–Buena Vista.) Rel: 25 November 1994. 76 mins. Cert PG.

Timecop
The year is 2004 and time travel has become a reality. But as with all advances in technology, there is the crime that goes with it. For some, time travel is a very easy way to make a lot of money, particularly if you know your stock exchange or the result of the World Series. Max Walker is a top agent for the Time Enforcement Commission, and it is his job to stop any old Tom, Dick or Harry abusing the system. But when you've got a master criminal like Aaron McComb breaking the

To Die For
When his partner dies from AIDS, a promiscuous homosexual decides that 'life must go on' and refuses to let mourning screw up his life. But the ghost of his lover is more entrenched than he would have dared think. A gay slant on *Ghost* and *Truly, Madly, Deeply*, this is a painfully well-meaning, but ultimately embarrassingly sentimental

To Live - Huozhe
A recurring motif in Zhang Yimou's sixth feature film is a Chinese children's fable about a chicken that grows into a goose that grows into a sheep that grows into an ox. Posing this as an ironic metaphor for the false hopes generated by the turbulent social history of China from the 1940s to the 1970s, the film simmers with genuine optimism while never losing sight of the intrinsic ironies of its subject. Zhang has even injected a welcome dose of humour into his epic look at the tragedy and transition that buffets a small nuclear family at the mercy of historical change. Tracing the effects of the civil war of the 1940s, the formation of the People's Republic and the eruption of the Cultural Revolution have on a simple couple and their two children, Zhang mirrors all the pain, struggle and absurdity that his people have faced – and still face – in twentieth-century China.

Cast: Ge You (Fugui), Gong Li (Jiazhen), Niu Ben (Mr Nin, town chief), Guo Tao (Chunsheng), Jiang Wu (Erxi), Ni Da Hong (Long'er), Liu Tian Chi (adult Fengxia), Zhang Lu (teen Fengxia), Dong Fei (Youqing), Li Lianyi (Lao Quan), Xiao Cong, Huang Zhongle, Liu Yanjing, Zhao Yuxiu.
Dir: Zhang Yimou. Pro: Chiu Fusheng. Ex Pro: Kow Fuhong and Christophe Tseng. Assoc Pro: Barbara Robinson. Screenplay:

Turbulent times: Gong Li and offspring in Zhang Yimou's evocative To Live *(from Artificial Eye)*

Yu Hua and Lu Wei, from the novel by Yu. Ph: Lu Yue. Ed: Du Yuan. Pro Des: Cao Jiuping. M: Zhao Jiping. Costumes: Dong Huamiao. (ERA International/Shanghai Film Studios/Century Communications Ltd–Electric.) Rel: 14 October 1994. 125 mins. Cert 12.

Trapped in Paradise

Three moronic brothers rob the bank of smalltown Paradise, Pennsylvania, but then cannot get out – thanks to the fiercest blizzard of the century. Meanwhile, the townsfolk of Paradise welcome the outsiders with open arms as the FBI, state troopers, local police and two ruthless crooks go in hot pursuit. A stupendously unfunny, heavy-handed farce which milks every 'joke' before curdling it into cheese. Even Dana Carvey's protracted impersonation of Mickey Rourke soon becomes nauseating.

Cast: Nicolas Cage (Bill Firpo), Jon Lovitz (Dave Firbo), Dana Carvey (Alvin Firpo), John Ashton (Ed Dawson), Madchen Amick (Sarah Collins), Donald Moffat (Clifford Anderson), Richard Jenkins (Shaddus Peyser), Florence Stanley (Ma Firpo), Paul Lazar (Deputy Timmy Burnell), Sean McCann (Chief Burnell), Angela Paton, Richard B. Shull, Jack Heller, Andrew Miller, Vivian Reis, Frank Pesce, George Gallo Snr, Jonathan Allore, Sean O'Bryan.

Dir and Screenplay: George Gallo. Pro: Gallo and Jon Davison. Ex Pro: David Permut. Co-Pro: Ellen Erwin and David Coatsworth. Ph: Jack N. Green. Ed: Terry Rawlings. Pro Des: Bob Ziembicki. M: Robert Folk; numbers performed by Bing Crosby, Eddy Arnold and Dean Martin. Costumes: Mary E. McLeod. (Fox.) Rel: 3 February 1995. 110 mins. Cert PG.

Trial by Jury

New York; 1994. Extraordinarily ill-conceived 'thriller' about an upstanding single mother who is pressurised to hang a jury in the trial of a notorious mobster. Faced with the death of her

Who would have thought that one day William Hurt would support Joanne Whalley-Kilmer in a glossy pile of cliché like Trial by Jury? *(from Warner)*

For better, for worse: Arnold Schwarzenegger and Jamie Lee Curtis as Mr and Mrs Tasker in James Cameron's sublimely entertaining True Lies *(from UIP)*

beloved young son, Valerie Alston has no choice but to compromise her principles. Not only is the story poorly constructed, but the characters speak lines they shouldn't (entering the courtroom, Valerie observes, 'This must be the big murder case I've been reading about'). Joanne Whalley-Kilmer as the vulnerable New York mother and William Hurt as a scruffy employee of the mob are particularly implausible.

Cast: Joanne Whalley-Kilmer (Valerie Alston), Armand Assante (Rusty Pirone), Gabriel Byrne (Daniel Graham), William Hurt (Tommy Vesey), Kathleen Quinlan (Wanda), Richard Portnow (Leo Greco), William R. Moses (Paul Baker), Robert Breuler (Judge Feld), Margaret Whitton, Ed Lauter, Lisa Arrindell Anderson, Jack Gwaltney, Graham Jarvis, Joe Santos, Beau Starr, Bryan Shilowich, Stuart Whitman, Kevin Ramsey, Fiona Gallagher, Kay Hawtrey, Ardon Bess, Karina Arroyave, Andrew Sabiston, William Duell, John Capodice, Diego Fuentes, Mike Starr, David Cronenberg, Fleure Presner.

Dir: Heywood Gould. Pro: James G. Robinson, Chris Meledandri and Mark Gordon. Ex Pro: Gary Barber. Line Pro: Michael MacDonald. Screenplay: Gould and Jordan Katz. Ph: Frederick Elmes. Ed: Joel Goodman. Pro Des: David Chapman. M: Terence Blanchard. Costumes: Mary Malin. (Morgan Creek–Warner.) Rel: 2 December 1994. 105 mins. Cert 15.

True Lies

From the opening shot of Arnold Schwarzenegger emerging from a frozen lake to the logic-defying climax, *True Lies* entertains in spades. Arnie is Harry Tasker, an international spy working for Omega Sector, a top-secret government agency formed to combat nuclear terrorism. A human killing machine fluent in six languages, Tasker is at home in any situation – except at home. Unable to tell his wife of his true vocation, Harry poses as a sales rep for a computer company and is too preoccupied to realise he has a perfect marriage. Meanwhile, Mrs Tasker (Jamie Lee Curtis on splendid form) leads a humdrum existence and yearns for a life of excitement. At a reputed cost of $120 million, *True Lies* puts its

money where its camera is, and thanks to James Cameron's slick direction (and screenplay) keeps the action moving in spite of its hefty length. Effects, jokes and stunts are all out of this world. Amazingly, this epic spoof of James Bond was actually based on the French film *La Totale*.

Cast: Arnold Schwarzenegger (Harry Tasker), Jamie Lee Curtis (Helen Tasker), Tom Arnold (Gib), Bill Paxton (Simon), Tia Carrere (Juno), Art Malik (Aziz), Eliza Dushku (Dana Tasker), Charlton Heston (Spencer Trilby), Grant Heslov, Marshall Manesh, Jane Morris, Katsy Chappell, Mike Cameron, Tom Isbell.

Dir and Screenplay: James Cameron, from a screenplay by Claude Zidi, Simon Michael and Didier Kaminka. Pro: Cameron and Stephanie Austin. Ex Pro: Robert Shriver, Rae Sanchini and Lawrence Kasanoff. Ph: Russell Carpenter. Ed: Conrad Buff, Mark Goldblatt and Richard A. Harris. Pro Des: Peter Lamont. M: Brad Fiedel; numbers performed by Sade, John Hiatt, Living Color, Screaming Trees, The Bee Gees, Mother Tongue and The Tango Project. Costumes: Marlene Stewart. Digital Domain FX Supervisor: John Bruno. (Fox/Lightstorm Entertainment/ Universal–UIP.) Rel: 12 August 1994. 140 mins. Cert 15.

Carrying a big stick: John Coffey and his classmates fight it out on Murphy's Dunes in John Roberts' beguiling War of the Buttons *(from Warner)*

Vanya on 42nd Street

In a new translation by David Mamet, *Uncle Vanya* is presented in rehearsal in New York under the direction of Andre Gregory. Following the example of Carlos Saura's flamenco ballet feature *Blood Wedding*, Louis Malle uses the camera close-up and the simplicity of a run-through – without props or sets – to capture the emotional core of Chekhov's tragi-comedy. He succeeds brilliantly in the finale of Act II, but elsewhere modern America obtrudes to Brechtian effect. Despite the film being uneven, those familiar with the original will be fascinated. The acting is distinguished. [*Mansel Stimpson*]

Cast: Wallace Shawn (Vanya), Julianne Moore (Yelena), Andre Gregory (himself), Brooke Smith (Sonya), Larry Pine (Dr Astrov), George Gaynes (Serebryakov), Lynn Cohen (Maman), Phoebe Brand (Marina), Jerry Mayer (Waffles), Madhur Jaffrey (Mrs Chao).

Dir: Louis Malle. Pro: Fred Berner. Assoc Pro: Alysse Bezahler. Ph: Declan Quinn. Ed: Nancy Baker. Pro Des: Eugene Lee. M: Joshua Redman. Costumes: Gary Jones. (Mayfair Entertainment/Channel Four–Artificial Eye.) Rel: 30 December 1994. 119 mins. Cert U.

Wagons East

Unable to cope with the rigours of the Wild West, a gaggle of losers hire an overweight drunkard to guide them back to St Louis. However, the sight of an expanding wagon train heading east is bad news for the US government, which is desperate to encourage investment in the western states. While there is nothing wrong with the basic concept of *Wagons East*, the execution is so broad, the stereotyping so offensive and the script so devoid of invention, that the ride is unendurable. Furthermore, as the 43rd and last film in John Candy's career, it is a sorry testament to a comic actor who was just coming into his own.

Cast: John Candy (James Harlow), Richard Lewis (Phil Taylor), John C. McGinley (Julian), Ellen Greene (Belle), Robert Picardo (Ben Wheeler), Ed Lauter (John Slade), William Sanderson (Zeke), Rodney A. Grant (Little Feather), Melinda Culea (Constance Taylor), Robin McKee, Abe Benrubi, Thomas F. Duffy, David Dunard, Marvin McIntyre, Joel McKinnon Miller, Lochlyn Munro, Russell Means, Don Lake, Charles Rocket.

Dir: Peter Markle. Pro: Gary Goodman, Barry Rosen, Robert Newmyer and Jeffrey Silver. Ex Pro: Lynwood Spinks. Screenplay: Matthew Carlson, from a story by Jerry Abrahamson. Ph: Frank Tidy. Ed: Scott Conrad. Pro Des: Vince J. Cresciman. M: Michael Small. Costumes: Adolfo 'Fito' Ramirez. (Carolco/Outlaw Prods–Guild.) Rel: 10 March 1995. 107 mins. Cert PG.

War of the Buttons

In the sleepy villages of Ballydowse and Carrickdowse, nestled either side of a stretch of tidal water in south-west Ireland, troops are preparing for battle. Arms include sticks and catapults and the anticipated trophy of victory the buttons and laces of the opposing army. Adapted from the classic French novel *La Guerre des Boutons* by Louis Pergaud (previously filmed by Yves Robert in 1962), this is a most engaging dramatic comedy that should appeal to both adults and children. Indeed, the ensemble performance of the young, non-professional cast is remarkable,

courage to be different in order to be themselves'. Refusing to acknowledge that her daughter Charlotte is 'different' Leonor attacks the neighbours' garden gnomes with a pickaxe, burns copies of *Gulliver's Travels*, *Snow White* and *Tom Thumb*, and then embarks on an intensive cultural education for the girl, turning her into something of a child prodigy. Indeed, Charlotte becomes a thing of beauty and is befriended by a handsome, enigmatic and wealthy gentleman. But is she herself? Although a brave and provocative work of cinema, the film is somewhat neutered by a wishy-washy style which, rather than casting a magic spell, distances the viewer from the action. From the acclaimed Argentine director of *Camila* and *Miss Mary*. An Argentine-Italian co-production.

Cast: Marcello Mastroianni (D'Andrea), Luisina Brando (Leonor), Alejandra Podesta (Charlotte), Betiana Blum (Madama), Roberto Carnaghi (Padre Aurelio), Alberto Segado (Dr Blanes), Jorge Luz, Monica Villa, Juan Manuel Tenuta, Tina Serrano.

Dir: Maria Luisa Bemberg. Pro: Oscar Kramer. Co-Pro: Roberto Cicutto and Vincenzo De Leo. Screenplay: Bemberg and Jorge Goldenberg, from a short story by Julio Llinas. Ph: Felix Monti. Ed: Juan Carlos Macias. Art: Jorge Sarudiansky. M: Nicola Piovani. Costumes: Graciela Galan. (Aura Films–Artificial Eye.) Rel: 5 August 1994. 102 mins. Cert PG.

Marcello Mastroianni contemplates the unthinkable in Maria Luisa Bemberg's provocative We Don't Want to Talk About It *(from Artificial Eye)*

particularly as guided by first-time director John Roberts. Merit, too, must go to Colin Welland's adaptation, which elicits charm instead of sentimentality, and uncannily infiltrates the world of these County Cork schoolchildren.

Cast: Gregg Fitzgerald (Fergus), Gerard Kearney (Big Con), Anthony Michael Cunningham (Little Con), Thomas Kavanagh (Riley), Eveanna Ryan (Marie) Stuart Dannel Foran (Tich), John Coffey (Geronimo), Paul Batt (Gorilla), Liam Cunningham (the master), Colm Meaney (Geronimo's dad), Daragh Naughton, Brendan McNamara, Kevin O'Malley, John Cleere, John Crowley, Karl Byrne, Johnny

Murphy, Bairbre Dowling, Alan Devlin, Ger Ryan, Jim Bartley, Declan Mulholland.

Dir: John Roberts. Pro: David Puttnam. Ex Pro: Xavier Gelin, Stephane Marsil and David Nichols. Screenplay: Colin Welland. Ph: Bruno de Keyser. Ed: Jim Clark. Pro Des: Jim Clay. M: Rachel Portman; 'Life Shrinks' performed by Elvis Costello. Costumes: Louise Frogley. (Enigma Films/Productions de la Guéville–Warner.) Rel: 14 October 1994. 94 mins. Cert PG.

We Don't Want to Talk About It - De Eso No Se Habla

Somewhere in South America in the small town of San Jose de los Altares, the wealthy widow Leonor 'could no longer deny the evidence of her eyes that her pride and joy' – her two-year-old only daughter – 'was a dwarf'. Thus relates the dreamy voice-over on this extraordinary romantic fiction that is dedicated 'to all people who have the

Weekend at Bernie's II

New York/St Thomas/Virgin Islands; 1993. A lot better than it might have been, this unexpected sequel continues the adventures of loveable goons Andrew McCarthy and Jonathan Silverman and of Bernie, the corpse that won't go away (played with admirable sang-froid by Terry Kiser). This time, McCarthy and Silverman are after the stiff's stash of $2 million, as is everybody else. But now, thanks to a bungled voodoo spell, Bernie is periodically revived whenever he hears music. Many of the gags actually work quite well, and the picturesque scenes of the West Indies are mouthwatering. [*Charles Bacon*]

Cast: Andrew McCarthy (Larry), Jonathan Silverman (Richard), Terry Kiser (Bernie), Tom Wright (Charles), Steve James (Henry), Troy Beyer (Claudia), Barry Bostwick (Hummel).

Dir and Screenplay: Robert Klane. Pro: Victor Drai and Joseph Perez. Ex Pro: Angiolo Stella. Ph: Edward Morry III. Ed: Peck Prior. Pro Des: Michael Bolton. M: Peter Wolf. Costumes: Fionn. (Artimm–Warner.) Rel: 23 September 1994. 90 mins. Cert PG.

Welcome II the Terrordome

Sometime in the future in a ghetto somewhere in England the ozone layer has given out, pollution is rampant and drugs and racism are rife. Against this bleak backdrop tragedy unfolds in melodramatic slow motion. An angry, politically daring but seriously ill conceived call-to-arms for black emancipation in Britain, this is the sort of film that scares people away from the cinema. Furthermore, dud acting, unbelievable dialogue and muddy photography conspire to make the thing virtually unwatchable.

Cast: Suzette Llewellyn (Angela McBride), Saffron Burrows (Jodie), Valentine Nonyela (Spike), Brian Bovell (Officer Bovell), Felix Joseph, Ben Wynter, Sian Martin, Jason Traynor, Cynthia Powell, Natasha Romulus, Marcia Myrie.

Dir and Screenplay: Ngozi Onwurah. Pro: Simon Onwurah. Co-Pro: Valentine Nonyela, Dingi Ntuli and Gillian Hazel. Ph: Alwin H. Kuchler. Ed: Liz Webber. Pro Des: Lindi Pankiv and Miraphora Mina. M: John Murphy, David A. Hughes and Black Radical MKLL; numbers performed by Valentine Nonyela, Moves in Motion, Sense of Sound, The Ibo 1, Sian Martin, etc. Costumes: Claire Ditchburn, Sarah Wiltshire and Fennella Magnus. (Non-Aligned Communications/Channel Four–Metro Tartan.) Rel: 20 January 1995. 94 mins. Cert 18.

Wes Craven's New Nightmare

Since the cancellation of the *Nightmare on Elm Street* films, Freddy Krueger, the series' demonic star, has been released into the real world. Craven, who dreamed up Krueger and directed the first film back in 1984, is now writing a new screenplay and hopes to lure back Heather Langenkamp to play Nancy a third time. However, now that she is a mother and wife, Ms Langenkamp no longer wants to be involved in horror films, particularly as her association with *A Nightmare on Elm Street* still haunts her. But maybe only

Ms Langenkamp can stop Freddy Krueger's assault on the real world ... The most audacious excuse for a sequel ever invented, *Wes Craven's New Nightmare* features not only original cast members of the first film, but Craven himself and chairman of New Line Cinema Robert Shaye! A must for Freddy Krueger diehards, this film manages to be as scary as it is funny. Only Wes Craven himself could have pulled this off.

Cast: Robert Englund (himself/Freddy Krueger), Heather Langenkamp (herself), Miko Hughes (Dylan), David Newsom (Chase Porter), John Saxon (himself), Tracy Middendorf (Julie), Wes Craven (himself), Marianne Maddalena (herself), Sam Rubin (himself), Sara Risher (herself), Robert Shaye (himself), Nick Corri (himself), Tuesday Knight (herself), Matt Winston, Rob LaBelle, Cully Fredricksen, Fran Bennett, Lin Shaye, Jessica Craven.

Dir and Screenplay: Wes Craven. Pro:

Missed him? Freddy Krueger is back (seen here with Miko Hughes) in the audacious Wes Craven's New Nightmare *(from Rank)*

Marianne Maddalena. Co-Pro: Jay Roewe. Ex Pro: Craven and Robert Shaye. Co-Ex Pro: Sara Risher. Ph: Mark Irwin. Ed: Patrick Lussier. Pro Des: Cynthia Charette. M: J. Peter Robinson and Charles Bernstein. Costumes: Mary Jane Fort. (New Line–Rank.) Rel: 6 January 1995. 112 mins. Cert 15.

When a Man Loves a Woman

San Francisco; today. Michael Green, a pilot, and his wife, Alice, a high school counsellor, are desperately in love. But Alice has a problem and she's too ashamed to share it with her husband. Yet, as an imperceptible chasm grows

Days of vodka and roses: Mae Whitman, Andy Garcia, Meg Ryan and the excellent Tina Majorino in Luis Mandoki's unbearably honest When a Man Loves a Woman *(from Buena Vista)*

Killer elite: Jean Rochefort as the po-faced assassin in Pierre Salvadori's side-splitting Wild Target *(from Gala)*

between her and Michael, the signs are becoming obvious. Alice is an alcoholic. Michael wants to help, but Alice needs to confront her own demons alone, even if it costs her her marriage. Originally intended as a darkly comedic vehicle for Tom Hanks and Michelle Pfeiffer, the film has matured into a romantic drama that gives Andy Garcia and Meg Ryan the best roles of their careers. In the splashier part of the unsympathetic lush, Meg Ryan goes for the jugular with a performance that hurts in its honesty. But Andy Garcia, too, in the less showy part, reveals his wounds as a man whose self-centred attempts to save the one he loves tragically backfires. Seldom have both protagonists in a marital conflict been so well delineated, with both their strengths and weaknesses so accurately established. Tears are guaranteed.

Cast: Andy Garcia (Michael Green), Meg Ryan (Alice Green), Lauren Tom (Amy), Ellen Burstyn (Emily), Tina Majorino (Jess Green), Mae Whitman (Casey Green), Philip Seymour Hoffman (Gary), Eugene Roche, Gail Strickland, Susanna Thompson, LaTanya Richardson, Barik K. Willerford, Ellen Geer, Ronald Bass, Richard Bradford.
  Dir: Luis Mandoki. Pro: Jordan Kerner and Jon Avnet. Ex Pro: Simon Maslow, Ronald Bass and Al Franken. Screenplay: Bass and Franken. Ph: Lajos Koltai. Ed: Garth Craven. Pro Des: Stuart Wurtzel. M: Zbigniew Preisner; numbers performed by Percy Sledge, Brian Kennedy, Robert Cray, Los Lobos, Rickie Lee Jones and REM. Costumes: Linda Bass. (Touchstone Pictures–Buena Vista.) Rel: 2 September 1994. 126 mins. Cert 15.

Who's the Man?

Abysmal hip-hop comedy-thriller in which two inept Harlem barbers, emotionally blackmailed into police academy, stumble on to the trail of a murder. Designed as a vehicle for MTV rap stars Dr Dre and Ed Lover, the film attempts to probe some social issues but its hackneyed situations and exhausted plot contrivances bury the ship.

Cast: Ed Lover (Ed Lover), Doctor Dre (Doctor Dre), Badja Djola (Lionel Douglas), Cheryl 'Salt' James (Teesha Braxton), Jim Moody (Nick Crawford), Ice-T (Nighttrain/Chauncey), Denis Leary (Sgt Cooper), Richard Bright (Demetrius), Andre B. Blake, Rozwill Young, Colin Quinn, Todd I, Bowlegged Lou, Bernie Mac, Bill Bellamy, T-Money, Kim Chan, Joe Lisi, Fab 5 Freddy, Apache, Smooth B, KRS-One, Stretch, Karen T. Duffy, Garfield!, Kriss Kross, Naughty by Nature, Flavor Flav, B-Real, Grand Master Melle Mel, Run DMC and Jay, Yolanda Whitaker, Pepa, Humpty Hump, Heavy D, Queen Latifah, B-Fine, Paul A. George, Nikki D, No Face.

Dir: Ted Demme. Pro: Charlie Stettler and Maynell Thomas. Line Pro: Grace Blake. Screenplay: Seth Greenland, from a story by Greenland, Doctor Dre and Ed Lover. Ph: Adam Kimmel. Ed: Jeffrey Wolf. Pro Des: Ruth Ammon. M: Michael Wolff

and Nic. tenBroek; numbers performed by Bowlegged Lou, Naughty By Nature, Heavy D and Buju Banton, House of Pain, etc. Costumes: Karen Perry. (New Line/Tin Pan Apple/Thomas Entertainment–Metro Tartan.) Rel: 30 June 1995. 85 mins. Cert 15.

Wild Target - Cible Émouvante

Victor Meynard is urbane, cultured and lethal. The best paid, most efficient and least recognised assassin in Paris, he gleans tips from his mother but avoids all other human contact. When, however, he is caught in the act of murder by Antoine, a messenger boy, he takes the lad on as an accomplice, offering him a three-zone Paris travelcard as an incentive. However, when their first target – a beautiful, elusive con-artist – proves indestructible, Meynard suspects that Antoine is a jinx. But he hadn't bargained on the mettle of the con-artist. Jean Rochefort, France's greatest national comic treasure, underplays his role as the debonair assassin to superb effect, and is well matched by Marie Trintignant as the enchantress who changes his life. High praise, too, to director-writer Pierre Salvadori, who imbues every scene with distinction and never pushes a laugh too

Wolfman Jack: Nicholson imprisoned in a lycanthropic reality, in Mike Nichols' meditative Wolf *(from Columbia TriStar)*

far. If there can be such a thing, *Wild Target* is a sweet, romantic black comedy with unexpected depths of tenderness and bloodletting.

Cast: Jean Rochefort (Victor Meynard), Marie Trintignant (Renee Daudrieux), Guillaume Depardieu (Antoine), Patachou (Madame Meynard), Charlie Nelson (Hector Dremyan), Wladimir Yordanoff, Serge Riaboukine, Philippe Girard, Daniel Laloux, Philippe Harel.

Dir and Screenplay: Pierre Salvadori. Pro: Philippe Martin. Co-Pro: Gerard Louvin. Ph: Gilles Henry. Ed: Helene Viard. Pro Des: Yann Arlaud. M: Philippe Eidel. Costumes: Valerie Pozzo Di Borgo. (Les Films Pelleas/Locofilms–Gala.) Rel: 8 July 1994. 97 mins. Cert 15.

Wolf

New York; 1994. Will Randall is facing a mid-life crisis. He has been demoted to East European editor of his publishing house, his marriage is decomposing and he's been bitten by a wolf in

A law unto himself: Kevin Costner brings some weight to the legend of Wyatt Earp, *with Dennis Quaid as Doc Holliday (from Warner)*

Codgers in paradise: Robert Duvall and Richard Harris busy acting in Randa Haines' sentimental Wrestling Ernest Hemingway *(from Warner)*

Vermont. However, the last-named incident would seem to have its advantages as Randall finds his senses enhanced, while the wolf in him is transforming him into a more ruthless adversary for his enemies ... It's hard to imagine Mike Nichols directing a werewolf movie, but the filmmaker has brought an enormous class and human texture to his subject, and elicits first-rate performances from his stars. Michelle Pfeiffer, who turned her part down several times before accepting it, is particularly alluring.

Cast: Jack Nicholson (Will Randall), Michelle Pfeiffer (Laura Alden), James Spader (Stewart Swinton), Kate Nelligan (Charlotte Randall), Richard Jenkins (Det. Bridger), Christopher Plummer (Raymond Alden), Eileen Atkins (Mary), Om Puri (Dr Vijay Alezias), David Hyde Pierce, Ron Rifkin, Prunella Scales, Brian Markinson, Peter Gerety, Madhur Jaffrey.

Dir: Mike Nichols. Pro: Douglas Wick. Ex Pro: Neil Machlis and Robert Greenhut. Screenplay: Jim Harrison and Wesley Strick. Ph: Giuseppe Rotunno. Ed: Sam O'Steen. Pro Des: Bo Welch. M: Ennio Morricone. Costumes: Ann Roth. Make-Up FX: Rick Baker. (Columbia TriStar.) Rel: 26 August 1994. 125 mins. Cert 15.

Wrestling Ernest Hemingway

The Florida coast; 1993. Profoundly sentimental character study of two old codgers who forge a tenuous relationship in spite of their differences. Neither Richard Harris nor Robert Duvall look as old as their characters, and consequently appear to be acting when they should be speaking their lines. Duvall, as a retired Cuban barber, manages to retain some dignity, although scenes of him urinating into the sea and flashing his rear end will be hard to live down. And, while the film appears to be well meaning, it is so engineered to produce sobs that it makes one gag. Ultimately, one's left with the awful feeling of having spent the winter at Bognor Regis.

Cast: Robert Duvall (Walter), Richard Harris (Frank), Shirley MacLaine (Helen), Piper Laurie (Georgia), Sandra Bullock (Elaine), Micole Mercurio (Bernice), Jody Wilson.
   Dir: Randa Haines. Pro: Todd Black and Joe Wizan. Co-Pro: Jim Van Wyck. Screenplay: Steve Conrad. Ph: Lajos Koltai. Ed: Paul Hirsch. Pro Des: Waldemar Kalinowski. M: Michael Convertino; numbers performed by Barbarito Diez, Fred Astaire, Nelson Riddle, Maria Teresa Vera, etc. Costumes: Joe I. Tompkins. (Warner.) Rel: 9 September 1994. 123 mins. Cert 12.

Wyatt Earp

Lawrence Kasdan is an intelligent director with some grown-up meditative films to his credit (*Body Heat, The Big Chill, The Accidental Tourist, Grand Canyon*). And Kevin Costner is an intelligent actor (and filmmaking force) who knows where he's coming from. Together, however, they have failed to find a unison of tone for this highly personal, over-long, $60 million saga covering the violent life of Wyatt Berry Stapp Earp, the coffee-drinking law student, horse thief, buffalo hunter, marshal, outlaw and legend. At times resembling a masterpiece wrestling to break out of a self-indulgent testosterone binge, *Wyatt Earp* is a film full of unforgettable moments superbly photographed by Owen Roizman, whose subtle touches – the reflection of fireworks in Wyatt's first gun, a steaming mug of coffee – bring a wonderful resonance to the film. And Dennis Quaid more than matches Val Kilmer's consumptive Doc Holliday in *Tombstone*, for which he lost 43 pounds to look the part.

Cast: Kevin Costner (Wyatt Earp), Dennis Quaid (Doc Holliday), Gene Hackman (Nicholas Earp), Jeff Fahey (Ike Clanton), Mark Harmon (Johnny Behan), Michael Madsen (Virgil Earp), Catherine O'Hara (Allie Earp), Bill Pullman (Ed Masterson), Isabella Rossellini (Big Nose Kate), Tom Sizemore (Bat Masterson), JoBeth Williams (Bessie Earp), Mare Winningham (Mattie Blaylock), David Andrews (James Earp), Linden Ashby (Morgan Earp), Joanna Going (Josie Marcus), Annabeth Gish (Urilla Sutherland), Ian Bohen (young Wyatt), Alison Elliott (Lou Earp), Tea Leoni (Sally), Scotty Augare (Indian Charlie), John Lawlor (Judge Spicer), James Gammon, Rex Linn, Randle Mell, Adam Baldwin, Lewis Smith, Betty Buckley, Todd Allen, Mackenzie Astin, James Caviezel, Karen Grassle, John Denis Johnston, Martin Kove, Norman Howell, Boots Sutherland, Gabriel Folse, Monty Stuart, Mary Jo Niedzielski, Owen Roizman, John Furlong, Jon Kasdan, Michael Huddleston, John Doe.
   Dir: Lawrence Kasdan. Pro: Kasdan, Jim Wilson and Kevin Costner. Ex Pro: Jon Slan, Dan Gordon, Charles Okun and Michael Grillo. Screenplay: Kasdan and Dan Gordon. Ph: Owen Roizman. Ed: Carol Littleton. Pro Des: Ida Random. M: James Newton Howard. Costumes: Colleen Atwood. (Tig Productions–Warner.) Rel: 9 September 1994. 189 mins. Cert 12.

Zero Patience

Earning full marks for originality, Canadian filmmaker John Greyson uses a full-scale musical format for a fantasy which deals with a wholly serious issue. His model lies in the Brecht-Weill stage collaborations, but his concern is to challenge the authorities and the media which, setting up scapegoats, have treated – and still treat – the theoretical origin and development of AIDS as certainties. There are a few rough edges here (the lead performances are merely passable), but the concept is audacious and successful, genuinely entertaining as well as seriously angry. [*Mansel Stimpson*]

Cast: John Robinson (Sir Richard Francis Burton), Normand Fauteux (Zero), Dianne Heatherington (Mary), Richardo Keens-Douglas (George), Bernard Behrens (Dr Placebo), Michael Callen (Miss HIV), Charlotte Boisjoli, Marla Lukofsky, Brenda Kamino, Louise Garfield.
   Dir and Screenplay: John Greyson. Pro: Louise Garfield and Anna Stratton. Ex Pro: Alexandra Raffe. Ph: Miroslaw Baszak. Ed: Miume Jan. Pro Des: Sandra Kybartas. M: Glenn Schellenberg. Costumes: Joyce Schure. Choreography: Susan McKenzie. (Telefilm Canada/Ontario Film Development Corporation/Channel Four–Blue Dolphin/Dangerous To Know.) Rel: 5 August 1994. 100 mins. Cert 18.

Video Releases

Compiled by James Cameron-Wilson

(from July 1994 through to June 1995)

❐ denotes films released theatrically in the US
* denotes films of special merit

Above Suspicion

Wry thriller in which a disabled, retired detective engineers his own murder so that his unfaithful wife and her lover can reap the financial benefits.

With Christopher Reeve, Joe Mantegna, Kim Cattrall. Dir: Steven Schachter. 18. May 1995 (Columbia TriStar).

Against the Wall *

Tough, hard-hitting dramatisation of the brutal riots at Attica prison in 1971 – as witnessed by a Black Panther and an inexperienced prison guard. Directed with teeth bared by John Frankenheimer.

With Kyle MacLachlan, Samuel L. Jackson, Clarence Williams III, Frederic Forrest, Philip Bosco, Tom Bower, Harry Dean Stanton. 18. (20/20 Vision).

Amelia Earhart: The Final Flight *

Photogenic biography of the first woman to fly the Atlantic, with Diane Keaton a dead ringer as the aviatrix.

Also with Rutger Hauer, Bruce Dern, Paul Guilfoyle, Denis Arndt. Dir: Yves Simoneau. PG. October 1994 (PolyGram).

And Then There Was One *

First-rate TV movie based on the real-life case of Roxy and Vinnie Ventola, two TV sitcom writers who discover that they, and their daughter, have AIDS. Very moving.

With Amy Madigan, Dennis Boutsikaris, Jane Daly. Dir: David Jones. 15. October 1994 (Odyssey).

Arctic Blue

Spirited, picturesque thriller in which a berserk poacher (Rutger Hauer) locks horns with a couple of environmentalists in Alaska.

Also with Dylan Walsh, Rya Kihlstedt. Dir: Peter Masterson. 15. July 1994 (EV).

Being Human ❐

Bizarre but oddly arresting saga in which five men (all played by Robin Williams) search for contentment in their respective time frames – from the Bronze Age to contemporary New York. For very selected tastes only.

Also with John Turturro, Anna Galiena, Vincent D'Onofrio, Hector Elizondo, Lorraine Bracco, Lindsay Crouse, Theresa Russell. Dir and Screenplay: Bill Forsyth. Pro: David Puttnam. 15. June 1995 (Warner).

Bitter Blood

Serpentine, occasionally self-deprecatory and well acted soap about a wife and her lover who plot to kill the former's husband.

With Kelly McGillis, Harry Hamlin, Keith Carradine, Holland Taylor, Elizabeth Wilson, Louise Latham. Dir: Jeff Bleckner. 15. November 1994 (Odyssey).

Black Fox

So-so revisionist Western in which a racially abused black man rescues a group of kidnapped women and children.

With Christopher Reeve, Tony Todd. Dir: Steven H. Stern. 15. September 1994 (Reflective).

Blue Chips ❏

Coach Pete Bell (Nick Nolte) has carved himself an impressive niche in basketball history. A winner of two national championships with the Western University Dolphins, he now finds himself on his first losing season. And he doesn't like to lose. But then Pete Bell doesn't like to cheat, either. A smart, muscular drama detailing the corruption, greed and big money involved in America's tallest university sport – and yet another winner from the dependable pen of Ron Shelton. Nolte, too, is on top form, belting out an intense, bullish performance as the coach wrestling with his conscience, while real-life basketball dynamo Shaquille O'Neal is quite a presence as an unstoppable, not-so-dumb seven-foot dunking machine. Only Mary McDonnell seems ill at ease in the underwritten role of Nolte's ubiquitous ex-wife.

Also with Ed O'Neill, J.T. Walsh, Alfre Woodard. Dir: William Friedkin. 15. March 1995 (Paramount/CIC).

Blue Tiger

Slick, atmospheric and very violent crime thriller in which a mother searches for the killer of her young son and falls in love with a Yakuza mobster. Virginia Madsen is on particularly good form, while first-time director Norberto Barba lifts his B-movie material into a class of its own.

Also with Toru Nakamura, Dean Hallo, Harry Dean Stanton. 18. November 1994 (Medusa).

Body Bags

Better-than-average and frequently amusing trio of unsettling tales from the dark side. John Carpenter, as a wise-cracking cadaver, is your host and directs the first two segments: *The Gas Station* and *Hair*. Tobe Hooper helms the weaker *Eye*.

With Stacy Keach, Mark Hamill, Robert Carradine, David Warner, David Naughton, Alex Datcher, Twiggy, Sheena Easton, Deborah Harry, Roger Corman, Wes Craven. 18. April 1995 (PolyGram).

The Burning Season ✳

In startling contrast to his demonic villain in *Street Fighter*, the late Raul Julia gives arguably the greatest performance of his career as the hero of the Brazilian rain forest, Chico Mendes. Long in pre-production, David Puttnam's poetic, provocative drama addresses the exploitation of the Amazon at the hands of grasping land speculators. A minor classic.

With Sonia Braga, Nigel Havers, Tomas Milian, Esai Morales, Edward James Olmos. Dir: John Frankenheimer. Pro: Puttnam. Screenplay: Michael Tolkin. M: Gary Chang. February 1995 (Warner).

Cabin Boy ❏

Decidedly odd, uneven farce in which a stuck-up snot undergoes his rites of passage when he accidentally boards a Pacific-bound fishing boat. This is the one that spawned all those cod auditions at the 1995 Academy Awards – remember Paul Newman intoning 'wanna buy a monkey?'

With Chris Elliott, Ritch Brinkley, James Gammon, Brian Doyle-Murray, Brion James, Ann Magnuson, Russ Tamblyn, Ricki Lake, David Letterman. Dir: Adam Resnick. 12. May 1995 (Touchstone).

Calendar Girl ❏

Thunderingly tedious morality tale about a trio of jocks from Nevada who move to Hollywood to try and date Marilyn Monroe.

With Jason Priestley, Gabriel Olds, Jerry O'Connell, Joe Pantoliano, Steve Railsback, Stephen Tobolowsky, Chubby Checker. Dir: John Whitesell. 15. December 1994 (Columbia TriStar).

Camp Nowhere ❏

Contrived, juvenile comedy in which a gaggle of young ne'er-do-wells collaborate with a crazy ex-drama professor to establish their own parent-free summer camp.

With Jonathan Jackson, Christopher Lloyd, Andrew Keegan, Ray Baker, Kate Mulgrew, Burgess Meredith. Dir: Jonathan Prince. PG. May 1995 (Touchstone).

Car 54, Where Are You? ❏

Execrable film version of the first TV sitcom (1961-63) set in a police station. Unbelievably awful.

With David Johansen, John C. McGinley, Fran Drescher, Nipsey Russell (who recreates his role from TV), Rosie O'Donnell, Daniel Baldwin. Dir: Bill Fishman. 15. July 1994 (Columbia TriStar).

The Cisco Kid ✳

Lively and funny TV movie exploring the Californian outlaw's early days. Jimmy Smits, as the womaniser introduced in O. Henry's turn-of-the-century short story, is ideal casting, and the backdrops look great.

Also with Cheech Marin, Sadie Frost, Bruce Payne, Ron Perlman. Dir: Luis Valdez. PG. September 1994 (First Independent).

Clean Slate ❏

Maurice L. Pogue is a private detective who suffers from amnesia whenever he falls asleep. But, with the help of a tape recorder, he has pieced together a mystery in which he seems to have the starring role. Apparently he's the sole witness to a mob killing involving a valuable coin (worth $7m) which he's hidden somewhere. Oh yeah, and he's supposedly in love with Beth. Or is it Paula? Or maybe Sarah? An engagingly daft comedy directed with some flair by England's Mick Jackson, *Clean Slate* was originally a vehicle for Robert Redford but was then modified for the goofy, throwaway charm of Dana Carvey. Carvey is no comic genius, but the script does reveal unexpected bursts of wit, and the ubiquitous Barkley (*This Boy's Life*, *Problem Child 2*, *It Runs in the Family*, etc) is a comic original as Pogue's one-eyed Jack Russell.

Also with Valeria Golino, James Earl Jones, Kevin Pollak, Michael Gambon. 12. March 1995 (Warner).

Cold Heaven ❏

Typically entangled Nicolas Roeg saga in which an adulterous wife imagines the return of her late husband. An acid trip for intellectuals.

With Theresa Russell, Mark Harmon, James Russo, Talia Shire, Will Patton, Richard Bradford. 18. June 1995 (Fox/Guild).

The Colour of Love ✳ ❏

Zack is a white, Jewish student at an integrated high school in Detroit. Nikki is an attractive, forthright black girl, fresh from Brooklyn. What subsequently attracts them and divides them is not so much a result of their skin colour as the incompatibility of their sex. A largely unknown cast deliver vivid, telling performances, while the film's snappy rhythm and use of rap and hip-hop constantly engages the attention. Arguably the most distinctive and arresting portrait of urban black America since *Boyz N the Hood*, this is actually the semi-autobiographical work of a white filmmaker: first-time writer-director Anthony Drazen. US title: *Zebrahead*.

With Michael Rapaport, DeShonn Castle, N'Bushe Wright, Ron Johnson, Ray Sharkey, Helen Shaver. 15. August 1994 (20/20 Vision).

Cops & Robbersons ❑

Chevy Chase, a cop show addict, is in seventh heaven when a hardened cop takes his house over for a stakeout. Yet another sitcom vehicle for the comic in search of a hit.

Also with Jack Palance, Dianne Wiest, Robert Davi, Jason James Richter, Fay Masterson. Dir: Michael Ritchie. PG. June 1995 (Columbia TriStar).

Crossing the Bridge ❑

Mildly diverting nostalgia trip about a group of sixties' Detroit teenagers crossing the border into Canada to pick up hashish. Stephen Baldwin is particularly memorable.

Also with Josh Charles, Jason Gedrick, Cheryl Pollak, Jeffrey Tambor, Rita Haggart, Hy Anzell, Richard Edson, David Schwimmer. Dir: Mike Binder. 15. November 1994 (Entertainment).

David's Mother

Thanks to Kirstie Alley's selfless central performance, some neat editing and Ackerman's mobile direction, this uneven drama about a single mother and her autistic son keeps our interst.

Also with Sam Waterston, Stockard Channing, Michael Goorjian, Chris Sarandon. Dir: Robert Allan Ackerman. M: David Mansfield. 15. November 1994 (Odyssey).

Fallen Angels

Intriguing, visually arresting odyssey in which a Mafia hitman undergoes a psychological metamorphosis as he drives to his inevitable death through the Nevada desert.

With James Remar, Michael Wright, Emily Longstreth. Dir: Larry Leahy. 15. June 1995 (Hi-Fliers).

Fatal Instinct ❑

Prostrate, witless, crude and heavy-handed spoof of erotic thrillers, in par-ticular *Basic Instinct*, *Fatal Attraction*, *Body Heat* and *Cape Fear*. Still, Sean Young is good value as the *femme fatale* who constantly gets gum stuck to her high heels.

Also with Armand Assante, Sherilyn Fenn, Kate Nelligan, Christopher McDonald, James Remar, Tony Randall. Dir: Carl Reiner. 15. August 1994 (MGM/UA).

Fatherland ✳

Miranda Richardson won a Golden Globe award for this, a speculative look at Europe in the sixties under Nazi rule. Based on Robert Harris's controversial novel, the film fails to engender much credibility, a crucial ingredient in a piece that expects us to forget that Hitler lost the war. Still, the first hour is pretty intriguing.

Also with Rutger Hauer, Jean Marsh, Peter Vaughan, Michael Kitchen, John Woodvine. Dir: Christopher Menaul. 15. January 1995 (Warner).

Fathers and Sons

A serial killer inadvertently brings an estranged father and son together in this foggy, unconvincing melodrama.

With Jeff Goldblum, Rory Cochrane, Ellen Greene, Rosanna Arquette. Dir & Screenplay: Paul Mones. 18. August 1994 (20/20 Vision).

The Favour ❑

Starry but terribly unfunny fable in which a bored housewife hires her best friend to consummate her high school love affair. Unfortunately, the vicarious nature of the plot also reflects the second-hand laughs.

With Harley Jane Kozak, Elizabeth McGovern, Bill Pullman, Brad Pitt, Ken Wahl, Larry Miller, Holland Taylor. Dir: Donald Petrie. 15. November 1994 (20/20 Vision).

Foreign Student ❑

Sweet, old-fashioned but somewhat limp tale of a French exchange student at a Virginia college in 1955 who falls for an attractive black maid.

With Marco Hofschneider, Robin Givens, Edward Herrmann, Charles S. Dutton. Dir: Eva Sereny. PG. June 1995 (CIC).

Freaked ❑

Heavy-handed black farce in which a crazed big top impresario transforms a movie star and his minions into circus freaks. The make-up is amazing, though.

With Alex Winter, Megan Ward, Randy Quaid, Mr T, Brooke Shields, Keanu Reeves. Dir: Alex Winter and Tom Stern. 15. June 1995 (Fox/Guild).

FTW

Mediocre and hackneyed road movie in which an ex-con rodeo star and petty thief go on the run together.

With Mickey Rourke, Lori Singer, Brion James, Peter Berg, Rodney A. Grant, Aaron Neville, Charlie Sexton. Dir: Michael Karbelnikoff. M: Gary Chang. 18. February 1995 (Columbia TriStar/Medusa).

Geronimo ✳

Intelligent and sensitive biopic of the legendary Apache warrior, shown in his youth to old age. Not to be confused with the theatrical version directed by Walter Hill.

With Joseph Running Fox, Nick Ramus, Tailinh Forest Flower, Jimmy Herman, August Schellenberg. Dir: Roger Young. Ex Pro: Norman Jewison. 15. October 1994 (Reflective).

Getting Gotti ✳

Powerful TV movie about the seven-year investigation of US attorney Diane Giacalone into the dubious deeds of reputed Mafia capo John Gotti. Terrific performances, direction, script and photography paper over the usual clichés of the gangster genre.

With Lorraine Bracco (as Giacalone), Anthony John Denison (as Gotti), August Schellenberg, Kenneth Welsh, Ellen Burstyn. Dir: Roger Young. 15. January 1995 (Odyssey).

Getting Out

Insipid TV movie of Marsha Norman's stageplay about an ex-con facing up to her past. Still, Rebecca De Mornay is on exceptionally good form.

Also with Ellen Burstyn, Robert Knepper, Richard Jenkins, Tandy Cronin. Dir: John Korty. 15. September 1994 .

Golden Gate ❑

Episodic, unconvincing drama which covers the years 1952, 1962 and 1968, in which Matt Dillon plays a cub lawyer forced to invent evidence to implicate a trio ripe for prosecution under

McCarthy's communist witch hunt. Dillon's good and so is everybody else, but nobody can make a silk purse out of fool's gold.

Also with Joan Chen, Bruno Kirby, Teri Polo. Dir: John Madden. 15. November 1994 (20/20 Vision).

Greedy ❑

If the price is right, everybody is susceptible to greed. And the price of old Joseph McTeague's fortune is worth upwards of $20m. And so the old man's crazy brood of relatives come fawning and scheming to his door attempting to ingratiate themselves into his will. Only young Danny, an honourable, likeable lad ranked 63rd best professional bowler in the world, is beyond the reach of his uncle's monetary influence. Until, that is, his cousins invite him to the McTeague mansion and he witnesses the trickery going on … No offence, but as Michael J. Fox's name is above the title you'd be right to expect predictable, formulaic entertainment painted Hollywood lite. But with Babaloo Mandel and Lowell Ganz (*Parenthood*, *City Slickers*) supplying the gags, there are plenty of laughs – and it's a delight to see Kirk Douglas in a big screen leading role after an absence of eight years. Inspired by Charles Dickens' *Martin Chuzzlewitt*.

Also with Nancy Travis, Olivia d'Abo, Ed Begley Jr, Colleen Camp. Dir: Jonathan Lynn. 12. December 1994 (Universal/CIC).

Gunmen ❑

A good cast is criminally wasted in this violent, mechanical scrap of exploitation in which a US agent vows revenge on the drug dictator who killed his father.

With Christopher Lambert, Mario Van Peebles, Denis Leary, Patrick Stewart, Kadeem Hardison, Sally Kirkland, Brenda Bakke, Big Daddy Kane, Dr Dre. Dir: Deran Sarafian. 18. August 1994 (Columbia TriStar).

The Hard Truth

Excessively routine action-thriller in which a suspended cop enlists his girlfriend and a techno freak to steal $3 million from a corrupt businessman. Seen it, done it.

With Eric Roberts, Michael Rooker, Lysette Anthony, Ray Baker. Dir: Kristine Peterson. 18. October 1994 (Hi-Fliers).

Heart and Souls ✳ ❑

San Francisco; 1959-today. Four characters too busy, blind or afraid to live their lives completely die in a bus crash and – by a complete fluke – get trapped in the soul of a new-born baby boy. Stuck to him like molasses and invisible to the outside world, the ghosts are forced to resolve their former lives through the grown-up body of their human anchor. However, the latter (Robert Downey Jr, splendid as usual) is reluctant to lead the lives of a quartet of hallucinations. Shamelessly manipulative and sentimental, *Heart and Souls* comes into its own halfway through and, then, thanks to excellent playing and a strong moral centre, wrings the tear ducts dry. A sugary pill, but one with an addictive side-effect.

Also with Charles Grodin, Kyra Sedgwick, Tom Sizemore, Alfre Woodard, David Paymer, Elisabeth Shue. Dir: Ron Underwood. PG. December 1994 (Universal/ CIC).

Heart of Darkness

Surprisingly pedestrian, small-scale reading of Joseph Conrad's 1902 novella in which a merchant seaman meets innumerable obstacles in the Belgian Congo while tracking down the elusive and enigmatic figure of Kurtz.

With Tim Roth, John Malkovich, Isaach de Bankole, James Fox, Patrick Ryecart, Peter Vaughan, Iman. Dir: Nicolas Roeg. 15. November 1994 (Reflective).

Honour Thy Father and Mother: The True Story of the Menendez Killings ✳

Well made, level-headed and competently acted drama focusing on brothers Erik and Lyle Menendez, who murdered their parents. Amazing that this TV movie was knocked out in a matter of weeks to beat the competition of other films covering the well-documented case.

With James Farentino, Jill Clayburgh, Billy Warlock, David Beron, Susan Blakely, Erin Gray, John Beck. Dir: Paul Schneider. 15. July 1994 (Odyssey).

In the Best of Families: Marriage, Pride and Madness
See *Bitter Blood*.

It Runs in the Family
See *My Summer Story*.

It's Pat ❑

Atrocious, crass addition to the slew of big-screen spin-offs of NBC-TV's *Saturday Night Live*. This one is co-written by and stars comedienne Julia Sweeney, who expands her one-joke act about an androgynous frump who drives everybody crazy.

Also with David Foley, Charles Rocket, Kathy Najimy, Camille Paglia. Dir: Adam Bernstein. 12. May 1995 (Touchstone).

Le Jeune Werther – Young Werther ✳ ❑

Paris; 1992. Director Jacques Doillon must be applauded for his handling of the adolescent cast in this unusual, curiously arresting document, the story of a group of young teenagers who must come to terms with the suicide of a classmate. Devoid of sentimentality and sensationalism, the film is impressive

The kids aren't all right: Ismael Jole, Marie-Isabelle Rousseau and Thomas Bremond in a scene from Jacques Doillon's masterful and uncompromising Le Jeune Werther, *sadly denied a theatrical release in Britain (from Tartan Video)*

for its accurate, totally credible portrait of French youth today, revealing its anxiety for the future, disillusionment with authority and fixation with all things American.

With Ismael Jole, Marie-Isabelle Rousseau, Thomas Bremond, Miren Capello, Faye Anastasia, Pierre Mezerette, Simon Claviere. Screenplay: updated from Goethe's *Les Souffrances du Jeune Werther*. 15. August 1994 (Tartan Video).

Jimmy Hollywood ❏
Following the financial catastrophe of *Toys*, writer-director Barry Levinson has attempted something entirely more modest with this three-character piece set on and around Hollywood Boulevard. Unfortunately, Levinson seems to have lost his touch here with an unfunny story chronicling the desperate attempts of an out-of-work actor to get his name in the papers.

With Joe Pesci, Christian Slater, Victoria Abril, Jason Beghe. 15. January 1995 (Paramount/CIC).

Judgement Night ❏
Competent, suspenseful and well-directed (if far-fetched) thriller in which four young men find themselves in an inner-city nightmare when they take a wrong turning in LA.

With Emilio Estevez, Cuba Gooding Jr, Denis Leary, Stephen Dorff, Jeremy Piven, Peter Greene. Dir: Stephen Hopkins. 18. August 1994 (Universal/CIC).

The Last Outlaw
Downbeat Western with Mickey Rourke on excellent sleazy form as a Confederate colonel who betrays his reprobate soldiers.

Also with Dermot Mulroney, Geoff Murphy, Steve Buscemi, Keith David. Dir: Geoff Murphy. Screenplay: Eric Red. 15. July 1994 (20/20 Vision).

Leave of Absence
Standard drama in which a man is torn between the love of his wife and the love of his life. And to make matters worse, the latter is dying …

With Brian Dennehy, Jacqueline Bisset, Blythe Danner, Polly Bergen, Noelle Parker, Jessica Walter. Dir: Tom McLoughlin. 15. September 1994 (Odyssey).

The Lost Souls
Adequate adaptation of Rudyard Kipling's tale of a father who contacts his dead daughter through an enigmatic blind medium.

With Patrick Bergin, Vanessa Redgrave, Valerie Mahaffey. Dir: John Korty. PG. November 1994 (Columbia TriStar).

Men of War
Decent action-thriller in which the He-Man from Sweden is instructed to seize the mineral rights from the people of a small South Pacific island – but has a change of heart. Suddenly deadly Dolph is all agog at the natural beauty of the place and pitches in to defend the natives from a squad of assassins.

With Dolph Lundgren, Charlotte Lewis, B.D. Wong, Anthony John Denison. Dir: Andrew Pfeffer. Screenplay: John Sayles. 18. February 1995 (Entertainment).

Money for Nothing ❏
Lugubrious, lumpy drama about an out-of-work docker who stumbles across $1.2m in the street and decides to keep it.

With John Cusack, Debi Mazar, Michael Madsen, Michael Rapaport, Maury Chaykin, James Gandolfini. Dir: Ramon Menendez. 15. August 1994 (Hollywood Pictures/Buena Vista).

Monolith
Low-budget horror opus in the *Alien* vein, buoyed by some throwaway humour supplied by Bill Paxton and Lindsay Frost as a couple of cops on the trail of a Creature from Outer Space.

Also with Louis Gossett Jr, John Hurt. Dir: John Eyres. 18. September 1994 (First Independent).

Growing fonder: Brian Dennehy and Jacqueline Bisset supply star power in Tom McLoughlin's Leave of Absence *(from Odyssey)*

My Summer Story ❏
More chuckles at the expense of rural folk, but with Charles Grodin and Mary Steenburgen on board, this holiday hillbilly comedy has some warmth and class. US title: *It Runs in the Family*.

Also with Kieran Culkin. Dir: Bob Clark. PG. June 1995 (Warner).

Next Door
Somewhat disappointing satire in which a college professor and his oafish neighbour come to blows in a battle of cultural sophistication versus raw machismo. A little morally one-sided, this, with an uneven balance of belly laughs and sheer horror.

With James Woods, Randy Quaid, Kate Capshaw, Lucinda Jenney. Dir: Tony Bill. 15. April 1995 (Columbia TriStar).

Night of the Running Man
Adequately performed but routine (and very nasty) thriller in which a ruthless killer sets about torturing a young thief.

With Scott Glenn, Andrew McCarthy, Janet Gunn, John Glover. 18. Dir: Mark L. Lester. April 1995 (Hi-Fliers).

Nobody's Children ✳
Set in 1990, this is the true story of an American woman who travels to Romania to adopt a child but becomes enmeshed in political intrigue. A sobering, well played drama made for cable.

With Ann-Margret, Dominique Sanda, Clive Owen, Jay O. Sanders. Dir: David Wheatley. 12. May 1995 (Odyssey).

Out of Darkness ✳
Episodic but extremely well acted (particularly by Diana Ross in the lead) telefilm about a paranoid schizophrenic getting her life together with the help of family, therapy and a new drug.

Also with Rhonda Stubbins, Beah Richards, Carl Lumbly, Lindsay Crouse. Dir: Larry Elikann. Ex Pro: Diana Ross. 15. August 1994 (Odyssey).

Past Tense
Daft but entertaining and occasionally suspenseful corkscrew thriller in which a cop investigates a possible murder.

With Scott Glenn, Lara Flynn Boyle, Anthony LaPaglia. Dir: Graeme Clifford. 18. March 1995 (PolyGram).

Payback

Neat little genre outing in which an ex-con hunts down a retired prison guard in order to abscond with a small fortune. A sexy, gripping and satisfying wallow.

With C. Thomas Howell, Joan Severance, Marshall Bell. Dir: Anthony Hickox. 18. February 1995 (Hi-Fliers).

Pentathlon

Appallingly acted, monotonous thriller in which an East German athlete confronts his arch enemy after the Berlin Wall comes down.

With Dolph Lundgren, David Soul, Roger E. Mosley. Dir: Bruce Malmuth. 15. September 1994 (First Independent).

A Place for Annie ✳

Intelligent, perceptive TV drama (inspired by a true story) with an exemplary performance from Sissy Spacek as a paediatric nurse who adopts an HIV-positive baby. Knowing that she's destined for a broken heart, Susan Lansing (Spacek) turns her life upside down to care for the abandoned child, only to find that Annie's mother, an ex-drug addict with AIDS, wants her baby back.

Also with Mary-Louise Parker, Joan Plowright, Jack Noseworthy. Dir: John Gray. PG. August 1994 (Odyssey).

The Positively True Adventures of the Alleged Texas Cheerleader-Murdering Mom ✳

The title says it all. A sly, tongue-in-cheek portrait of an obsessed Texan mother who plots the murder of her daughter's main competitor in the cheerleading stakes. Amazing, but true. Holly Hunter, coating her malice with candyfloss, won an Emmy for her performance, although the film itself frequently seems a lot about nothing.

Also with Beau Bridges, Swoozie Kurtz, Matt Frewer, Elizabeth Ruscio, Edie Jones, Gary Grubbs. Dir: Michael Ritchie. 15. November 1994 (First Independent).

Prince of Shadows ❑

Summoned from Scarborough to kill a suspected police informer in Madrid, exiled Communist Captain Darman reflects back on an assignment sixteen years earlier that bears remarkable

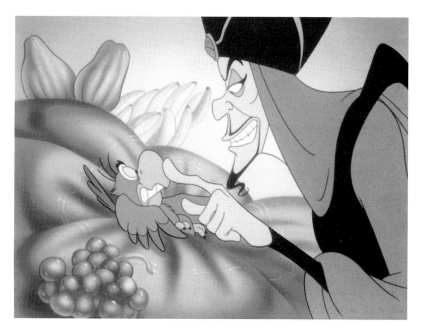

Parrot fashion: Iago and Jafar return for more mischief in Disney's entertaining The Return of Jafar

similarities. Cross-cutting between 1946 and 1962, this murky Spanish thriller strives for originality but is emasculated by unspeakable dialogue, a convoluted narrative and a prevailing lethargy. The most fun is had watching Terence Stamp's hair colour change – from dark grey to light grey and back to dark grey – to establish the film's time frame. Shoot the interpreter.

Also with Patsy Kensit, Geraldine James, Jose Luis Gomez, Bernice Stegers. Dir: Pilar Miro. 18. July 1994 (Tartan).

The Programme ❑

Stodgy look at unethical practices in American college football. This is the film that was temporarily withdrawn from US cinemas when teenagers imitated a scene in which some goons lie in the middle of a street to illustrate their machismo. Apparently, one practitioner of the made-up sport was actually killed. US title: *The Program*.

With James Caan, Craig Sheffer, Halle Berry, Omar Epps, Kristy Swanson. Dir: David S. Ward. 15. June 1995 (Touchstone).

The Return of Jafar ✳

Can it be true? Has the villainous parrot Iago changed his spots? In this top-selling video sequel to *Aladdin*, the grating Iago (voiced by Gilbert Gottfried) is promoted to centre stage, while everybody's favourite genie (Dan Castellanata stepping in for Robin Williams) is somewhat trimmed back.

Still, this is very serviceable children's fare, with all the old characters (Aladdin, Jasmine, Abu, Carpet, etc.) back for more rip-roaring adventures. Not as funny as the original, but very entertaining.

Dir: Toby Shelton, Tad Stones and Alan Zaslove. U. January 1995 (Disney).

Roswell ✳

Fascinating and credible look at the extraordinary cover-up by the American military following the 1947 crash landing of a UFO in New Mexico. Artfully mixing fact and supposition, the film poses many intriguing questions. A must for all UFO fanatics.

With Kyle MacLachlan, Kim Greist, Dwight Yoakam, Martin Sheen, Peter MacNicol, Bob Gunton, Charles Martin Smith. Dir: Jeremy Paul Kagan. 12. April 1995 (PolyGram).

Royce

Enjoyable action-comedy with James Belushi on the trail of a gang of shady agents intent on stealing a hoard of nuclear warheads.

Also with Peter Boyle, Miguel Ferrer, Chelsea Field. 15. August 1994 (ITC).

Scam

Miami/Jamaica; now. A sexy con artist lures randy men back to their hotel

The hustlers: Lorraine Bracco and Christopher Walken walk the thin line in John Flynn's preposterous Scam *(from PolyGram)*

rooms, drugs them and steals their valuables. She then meets her match in a dubious FBI agent who has a few ploys of his own ... John Flynn has directed some good crime thrillers in his time (*The Outfit, Best Seller*), but is defeated here by a preposterous plot and stars well past their sell-by date.

With Christopher Walken, Lorraine Bracco, Miguel Ferrer, Martin Donovan. 15. December 1994 (PolyGram).

Scarlett

Hypothetically a sequel to *Gone With the Wind*, this farcical, six-hour soap opera is more Barbara Cartland than Margaret Mitchell. Still, Joanne Whalley-Kilmer does the most she can with the one-dimensional, under-written role of Scarlett, who has lost all of her complexity and become a goody two-shoes (while her propensity for fainting quickly becomes laughable). Meanwhile, the American South has been replaced by Ireland, where the majority of the action takes place.

Also with Timothy Dalton (as Rhett Butler), Ann-Margret, Sean Bean, Stephen Collins (as Ashley Wilkes), John Gielgud, Annabeth Gish, Julie Harris, Melissa Leo, Colm Meaney, Esther Rolle, Paul Winfield, Sara Crowe, Tina Kellegher, Ronald Pickup, Dorothy Tutin, and 184 other cast members. Dir: John Erman. Screenplay: William Hanley, from the book by Alexandra Ripley. 15. December 1994 (Odyssey).

Secret Sins of the Father

There's trouble in the Nebraska heartland when a cop suspects his father of killing his mother. Thanks to the pairing of real-life father and son Lloyd and Beau Bridges, the film's dramatic intensity is virtually palpable.

Also with Lee Purcell, Frederick Coffin, Ed Lauter, Bert Remsen. Dir: Beau Bridges. 15. August 1994 (Hi-Fliers).

Son of the Pink Panther ❑

Eighth chapter in the Inspector Clouseau series with the Italian comic genius Roberto Benigni jumping into Sellers' shoes as the illegitimate clone of Clouseau. Herbert Lom, Burt Kwouk and Graham Stark return to back up the proceedings, but here, sadly, familiarity breeds contempt. Only Benigni himself extracts some laughs from the vulgar buffoonery.

Also with Claudia Cardinale, Debra Farentino, Jennifer Edwards, Robert Davi, Anton Rodgers. Dir: Blake Edwards. PG. September 1994 (Warner).

The Substitute Wife

Period comedy with a difference, in which a dying woman encourages her husband to strike up a relationship with a whore to keep the domestic status quo after her death. For the most part the laughs seem unintentional.

With Farrah Fawcett, Peter Weller, Lea Thompson. Dir: Peter Werner. 15. November 1994 (PolyGram).

Surviving the Game ❑

Flat, familiar genre thriller in which a vagrant becomes a human pawn in

Still don't give a damn: Joanne Whalley-Kilmer and Timothy Dalton turn Scarlett *(from Odyssey)*

a deadly game of cat-and-mouse. Haven't we seen this before?

With Rutger Hauer, Ice-T, Gary Busey, F. Murray Abraham, Charles Dutton, John C. McGinley, Jeff Corey. Dir: Ernest Dickerson. 15. February 1995 (Entertainment).

Taking the Heat

When a Yuppie corporate raider refuses to appear in court as the sole witness to a mob killing, he is forcibly dragged across New York by a black, beautiful detective – with a gang of ruthless hit men in pursuit. Starring the effortlessly bland Tony Goldwyn, this slick, utterly mindless action-romance is desperately in need of charisma and wit.

A mug's game: George Segal, Peter Boyle and Alan Arkin play it for laughs in Tom Mankiewicz's limp Taking the Heat *(from PolyGram)*

Also with Lynn Whitfield, Alan Arkin, George Segal, Peter Boyle, Joe Grifasi, Will Patton, Rachel York. Dir: Tom Mankiewicz. 18. November 1994 (PolyGram).

There Are No Children Here ∗

Gritty, superbly acted adaptation of Alex Kotlowitz's book which examines the dead-end life of an Afro-American family in inner-city Chicago.

With Oprah Winfrey, Keith David, Mark Lane, Norman D. Golden II, Maya Angelou, Vonte Sweet. Dir: Anita W. Addison. PG. December 1994 (Odyssey).

To Dance With the White Dog ∗

Eccentric, charming story in which an old widower believes the white dog he finds is an incarnation of his late wife. Nominated for seven Emmy awards.

With Hume Cronyn, Jessica Tandy, Christine Baranski, Harley Cross, Esther Rolle, Frank Whaley, Amy Wright. Dir: Glenn Jordan. U. October 1994. (Odyssey).

Twenty Bucks ❏

Gimmicky, trivial diversion which follos the varied human path of a twenty dollar bill.

With Linda Hunt, Brendan Fraser, Elisabeth Shue, Steve Buscemi, Christopher Lloyd, Spalding Gray, Gladys Knight, William H. Macy, Matt Frewer. Dir: Keva Rosenfeld. 15. June 1995 (Columbia Tri-Star).

We're Back: A Dinosaur's Story ❏

Continuing Steven Spielberg's obsession with dinosaurs, this cartoon fantasy, in which four friendly dinos get lost in New York, should appeal to children of all ages. Impressive animation and above-average voice characterisations sweeten the brew.

Voices: John Goodman, Rhea Perlman, Jay Leno, Felicity Kendal, Walter Cronkite, Julia Child, Kenneth Mars, Martin Short. Dir: Dick Zondag, Ralph Zondag, Phil Nibbelink and Simon Wells. Ex Pro: Spielberg. U. December 1994 (Universal/CIC).

When the Bough Breaks

Disturbing, gripping thriller plainly influenced by *The Silence of the Lambs*, in which a female investigator interrogates a mute psychiatric patient in order to expose a child killer.

With Ally Walker, Martin Sheen, Ron Perlman. Dir: Michael Cohn. 18. December 1994 (Medusa).

Where the Day Takes You ❏

Strangely confused designer take on the homeless in LA which attempts to glamorise a decidedly grim subject. It doesn't work, even though some of the performances are praiseworthy.

With Sean Astin, Lara Flynn Boyle, Peter Dobson, Balthazar Getty, Ricki Lake, James Le Gros, Dermot Mulroney, Will Smith, Rachel Ticotin, Laura San Giacomo, Kyle MacLachlan, Christian Slater. Dir: Marc Rocco. 18. October 1994 (20/20 Vision).

Where the Rivers Flow North

Strikingly photographed but simplistically played story of a crusty old logger whose livelihood is threatened by the construction of a new dam.

With Rip Torn, Tantoo Cardinal, Michael J. Fox, Treat Williams. Dir: Jay Craven. 15. July 1994 (Entertainment).

White Mile ∗

Following his turn as the heavy in HBO's *And the Band Played On*, Alan Alda adds another villain to his CV as a ruthless advertising executive in this cuticle-chewing drama. Based on court transcripts, the film explores the nefarious dealings of a manipulative tyrant who drags colleagues along on a disastrous white water rafting trip to shape them up for business dealings. Another HBO triumph.

With Peter Gallagher, Robert Loggia, Bruce Altman, Fionnula Flanagan, Jack Gilpin, Robert Picardo. Dir: Robert Butler. Screenplay: Michael Butler. M: Pray For Rain. 15. January 1995 (Guild).

Witch Hunt ∗

Wickedly stylish, confidently scripted (by Joseph Dougherty) and consummately acted HBO movie in which witchcraft has taken over Hollywood. Private eye H. Phillip Lovecraft (Dennis Hopper) is determined to locate a tycoon's mistress without the use of magic, plunging him into a deadly plot that casts a sly jab at the McCarthy witch hunts of the late forties. Paul Schrader makes his TV directing debut with aplomb.

Also with Penelope Ann Miller, Eric Bogosian, Sheryl Lee Ralph, Julian Sands, Debi Mazar. 18. June 1995 (Guild).

The Wrong Man

With each successive movie John Lithgow attempts to top his previous performance. After *Cliffhanger* it was hard to imagine thicker ham, but in this outrageous cod 'erotic thriller' Lithgow wheezes, coughs, snarls, screams and guffaws his way to new heights of mugging. This would be all right for a Mel Brooks movie, but this is an atmospheric thriller that promises much as a merchant seaman (Kevin Anderson) – on shore leave in Tampico, Mexico – has his wallet stolen, only later to find it in a dead man's apartment. Overcome by panic, he hitches up with two crazy Americans (Lithgow and a frequently undressed Rosanna Arquette) and the film slows down from there. It's like watching James M. Cain rewritten with a marker pen.

Dir: Jim McBride. 18. October 1994 (PolyGram).

Zebrahead

See *The Colour of Love*.

Other Video Releases:

Accidental Meeting. Linda Gray, Linda Purl, Leigh J. McCloskey. 15. August 1994 (Paramount/CIC).

Airborne. Shane McDermott, Seth Green. PG. January 1995 (Entertainment).

Alien Intruder. Maxwell Caulfield, Tracy Scoggins, Billy Dee Williams. 15. August 1994 (Imperial).

Armed and Innocent. Gerald McRaney, Kate Jackson. 15. July 1994 (Odyssey).

Automatic. Olivier Gruner, Daphne Ashbrook. 15. May 1995 (First Independent).

Babewatch. Julie Strain. 18. August 1994 (Columbia TriStar).

Bachelor Party II. Linnea Quigley, Burt Ward. 18. December 1994 (Guild).

Bachelor Party III. 18. July 1994 (Marquee).

Bandit 1: Bandit Goes Country. Brian Bloom, Brian Krause. PG. January 1995 (Universal/CIC).

Bandit 2: Bandit, Bandit. Brian Bloom, Brian Krause. PG. January 1995 (Universal/CIC).

Bandit 3: Beauty and the Bandit. Brian Bloom, Brian Krause, Kathy Ireland, Tony Curtis. PG. January 1995 (Universal/CIC).

Bandit 4: Bandit's Silver Angel. Brian Bloom, Brian Krause, Traci Lords. PG. January 1995 (Universal/CIC).

Barbara Taylor Bradford's Remember. Stephen Collins, Donna Mills, Derek De Lint, Ian Richardson, Claire Bloom, Cathy Tyson. 15. February 1995 (Odyssey).

Beach Babes From Beyond. Jacqualine Stallone, Joey Travolta, Don Swayze, Joe Estevez, Burt Ward. 18. July 1994 (Medusa).

Beanstalk. J.D. Daniels, Amy Stock-Poynton, Margot Kidder. U. May 1995 (CIC).

Betrayal of the Dove. Helen Slater, Kelly LeBrock, Billy Zane. 15. March 1995 (Entertainment).

A Better Tomorrow II. Chow Yun-Fat. 18. October 1994 (Made in Hong Kong).

Beyond Fear. Mimi Lesseos. 18. August 1994 (Hi-Fliers).

Blindfold: Acts of Obsession. Shannen Doherty, Michael Woods, Judd Nelson. 18. September 1994 (Poly Gram).

Blind Justice. Armand Assante, Robert Davi, Elisabeth Shue, Adam Baldwin. 12. February 1995 (Columbia TriStar).

Bloodfist V: Human Target. Don 'The Dragon' Wilson. 18. August 1994 (Universal/CIC).

Bloodlust: Subspecies III. Anders Hove. 18. October 1994 (Paramount/CIC).

Blood of the Hunter. Michael Biehn. 15. June 1995 (Hi-Fliers).

Born to Run. Richard Grieco, Jay Acovone, Joe Cortese. 18. July 1994 (FoxVideo).

Boulevard. Rae Dawn Chong, Kari Wuhrer, Lance Henriksen, Lou Diamond Phillips. 18. February 1995 (20/20 Vision).

The Boxer's Adventure. Tao Liang Tan. 18. November 1994 (Imperial).

Breach of Conduct. Peter Coyote, Courtney Thorne-Smith. 15. June 1995 (CIC).

Broken Pledges. Linda Gray. PG. September 1994 (Hi-Fliers).

Butterbox Babies. Susan Clark, Michael Riley, Nicholas Campbell. 15. June 1995 (Odyssey).

The Cage 2 ... The Arena of Death. Lou Ferrigno, Reb Brown. 18. April 1995 (Guild).

Caged Seduction. Judith Light, Stacy Keach, Kay Lenz. 15. March 1995 (Odyssey).

Caught in the Crossfire. Dennis Franz, Daniel Roebuck. PG. January 1995 (Hi-Fliers).

Chaku Master. Bruce Ly. 18. January 1995 (Imperial Entertainment).

Children of the Corn III: Urban Harvest. Daniel Cerny, Michael Ensign. 18. June 1995 (Hi-Fliers).

Children of the Dark. Peter Horton, Tracy Pollan. PG. September 1994 (Odyssey).

City Hunter. Jackie Chan. 12. May 1995 (20/20 Vision).

The Class of 1999 II – The Substitute. Nick Cassavetes. 18. July 1994 (Reflective).

The Club. Kim Coates. 18. July 1994 (Hi-Fliers).

Cobra. Michael Dudikoff, James Tolkan. 15. August 1994 (First Independent).

The Countess Contessa. Tea Leoni, D. W. Moffet. U. September 1994 (FoxVideo).

Crackerjack. Thomas Ian Griffith, Nastassja Kinski, Christopher Plummer. 18. March 1995 (20/20 Vision).

Cult Rescue. Joan Van Ark, Tom Kurlander, Daniel Hugh-Kelly, Stephen Macht. 12. February 1995 (Hi-Fliers).

Cyborg Cop 2. David Bradley. 18. March 1995 (Columbia TriStar).

Cyborg 3: The Creation. Malcolm McDowell, Richard Lynch, Zach Galligan. 18. June 1995 (20/20 Vision).

The Dangerous. Robert Davi, Michael Pare, John Savage, Cary-Hiroyuki Tagawa, Joel Grey, Elliott Gould. 18. January 1995 (Medusa).

Dangerous Intentions. Donna Mills, Corbin Bernsen. 15. May 1995 (Odyssey).

Danielle Steel's Changes. Cheryl Ladd, Michael Nouri, Charles Frank. PG. February 1995 (Imperial).

Danielle Steel's Fine Things. D.W. Moffet, Tracy Pollan. PG. February 1995 (Imperial).

Danielle Steel's Kaleidoscope. Jaclyn Smith, Perry King. 15. February 1995 (Imperial).

Danielle Steel's Once in a Lifetime. Lindsay Wagner, Barry Bostwick. PG. August 1994 (Imperial).

Danielle Steel's A Perfect Stranger. Robert Urich. 12. December 1994 (Imperial Entertainment).

The Dark. Brion James, Jaimz Woolvett. 18. September 1994 (Hi-Fliers).

Dark Waters. 18. September 1994 (Tartan).

Dazzle. Lisa Hartman Black, Cliff Robertson, Linda Evans, James Farentino. 15. July 1994 (Odyssey).

Deadly Deception. Andrew Stevens. 18. October 1994 (Hi-Fliers).

Deadly Reunion. Chuck Norris, Noble Willingham. June 1995 (Warner).

Deadly Vows. Gerald McRaney, Josie Bissett, Peggy Lipton. 15. February 1995 (Odyssey).

Deadly Whispers. Tony Danza, Pamela Reed, Ving Rhames. 15. June 1995 (Odyssey).

Dead Man's Revenge. Bruce Dern, Michael Ironside, Randy Travis. PG. September 1994 (Universal/CIC).

Dead On. Matt McCoy, Tracy Scoggins. 18. September 1994 (Odyssey).

Deep Red. Michael Biehn, Joanna Pacula. 15. August 1994 (Universal/CIC).

Digital Man. Mathias Hues, Ed Lauter, Adam Baldwin. 15. June 1995 (Columbia TriStar).

Don't Talk to Strangers. Pierce Brosnan, Shanna Reed, Terry O'Quinn. 12. April 1995 (CIC).

Doomsday Gun. Frank Langella, Alan Arkin, Kevin Spacey. 15. February 1995 (Guild).

Double Cross. Patrick Bergin, Jennifer Tilly, Kelly Preston, Kevin Tighe. 18. January 1995 (Guild).

Double Exposure. Dede Pfeiffer. 18. July 1994 (New Age Entertainment/20/20 Vision).

The Double O Kid. Corey Haim, Brigitte Nielsen, Wallace Shawn, John Rhys-Davies. 15. May 1995 (Hi-Fliers).

Dragonworld. Brittany Powell, Lila Kaye, John Woodvine. U. November 1994 (CIC/Paramount).

Drunken Master. Jackie Chan. 18. October 1994 (Made in Hong Kong).

Ernest Rides Again. Jim Varney. PG. June 1995 (First Independent).

Escape From Terror: The Teresa Stamper Story. Adam Storke, Maria Pitillo, Brad Dourif. 15. May 1995 (Odyssey).

Evolver. Ethan Randall, Cindy Pickett, Paul Dooley. 15. April 1995 (Medusa).

Fast Getaway II. Corey Haim, Cynthia Rothrock, Leo Rossi. 12. December 1994 (First Independent).

Fatal Vows. John Stamos, Cynthia Gibb, Ben Gazzara. 15. April 1995 (Odyssey).

Five Venoms. Chiang Sheng. 18. October 1994 (Made in Hong Kong).

The Force. Jason Gedrick, Kim Delaney. 15. October 1994 (Reflective).

Forced to Kill. Corey Michael Eubanks, Michael Ironside, Don Swayze. 18. July 1994 (Imperial Entertainment).

For Love Alone. Sanna Vraa, Madeline Kahn, Trevor Eve, Stephen Collins. PG. January 1995 (FoxVideo).

For the Love of Nancy. Tracey Gold, Jill Clayburgh, William Devane. PG. April 1995 (Odyssey).

Fortunes of War. Matt Salinger, Michael Ironside, Haing S. Ngor, Michael Nouri, Martin Sheen. 15. August 1994 (20/20 Vision).

Full Eclipse. Patsy Kensit, Mario Van Peebles, Bruce Payne. 18. January 1995 (20/20 Vision).

Ghoulies IV. Pete Liapis. 18. August 1994 (Warner).

Guardian Angel. Cynthia Rothrock. 18. July 1994 (Guild).

Guns of Honour: Rebel Rousers. Jurgen Prochnow, Martin Sheen, Corbin Bernsen, Christopher Atkins. 15. July 1994 (Reflective).

Guns of Honour: Trigger Fast. Jurgen Prochnow, Martin Sheen, Corbin Bernsen, Christopher Atkins. 15. July 1994 (Reflective).

Guyver: Dark Hero. David Hayter. 15. August 1994 (20/20 Vision).

Gypsy Eyes. Jim Metzler. 18. November 1994 (Hi-Fliers).

Hard Drive. Edward Albert, Christina Fulton, Matt McCoy. 18. March 1995 (First Independent).

Hard Evidence. Kate Jackson, John Shea, Dean Stockwell. 15. June 1995 (Odyssey).

Harmful Intent. Tim Matheson, Emma Samms, Alex Rocco, Robert Pastorelli. 15. December 1994 (Odyssey).

The Haunting of Seacliff Inn. Ally Sheedy, William R. Moses. 15. May 1995 (CIC).

Heart of a Child. Ann Jillian, Michelle Greene, Rip Torn, Terry O'Quinn. PG. September 1994 (Odyssey).

Hellbound. Chuck Norris, Calvin Levels, Sheree J. Wilson, Christopher Neame. 18. July 1994 (Cannon).

High Boot Henny. Marc O'Shea, Frances Tomelty, Alan Devlin. 15. November 1994 (Imagine).

The High Crusade. Rick Overton, John Rhys-Davies, Michael Des Barres. 15. May 1995 (Medusa).

High Lonesome. Louis Gossett Jr,

Joseph Mazzello, Don Swayze. 12. December 1994 (Odyssey).

Hollywood Madam. Michael Nouri, William Devane, Meg Foster. 18. March 1995 (Odyssey).

Hong Kong '97. Robert Patrick, Brion James, Tim Thomerson. 18. March 1995 (Hi-Fliers).

House Call. Renee Soutendjik. 18. May 1995 (PolyGram).

House Party 3. 15. July 1994 (EV).

Ice. Traci Lords, Zach Galligan. 18. September 1994 (Imperial).

The Ice Runner. Edward Albert, Victor Wong. May 1995 (Guild).

Incident at Deception Ridge. Michael O'Keefe, Ed Begley Jr, Linda Purl, Michelle Johnson, Miguel Ferrer. 15. May 1995 (CIC).

Indecent Behaviour II. Shannon Tweed, James Brolin, Chad McQueen. 18. March 1995 (Hi-Fliers).

In the Line of Duty: Kidnapped. Dabney Coleman, Timothy Busfield, Lauren Tom, Tracey Walter, Barbara Williams. 15. February 1995 (Odyssey).

Invisible: The Chronicles of Benjamin Knight. Brian Cousins. 18. July 1994 (Paramount/CIC).

Irresistible Force. Stacy Keach, Cynthia Rothrock, Paul Winfield. 15. July 1994 (FoxVideo).

Island City. Kevin Conroy. 18. August 1994 (Warner).

Jack Reed: A Search for Justice. Brian Dennehy, Charles S. Dutton, Susan Ruttan, Joe Grifasi, Miguel Ferrer. 15. April 1995 (Odyssey).

Knights. Kris Kristofferson, Lance Henriksen, Kathy Long. 15. July 1994 (FoxVideo).

The Legend of Emmanuelle. Sylvia Kristel, Marcella Walerstein, George Lazenby. 18. March 1995 (New Age).

Legends of the North. George Corraface, Sandrine Holt, Randy Quaid. March 1995 (Hi-Fliers).

The Man From Left Field. Burt Reynolds, Reba McEntire. PG. July 1994 (20/20 Vision).

M.A.N.T.I.S. Carl Lumbly, Steve James. PG. September 1994 (Universal/CIC).

Metal Beast. Barry Bostwick, Kim Delaney. 18. April 1995 (New Age).

The Mirror. Roddy McDowall, Sally

Kellerman. 15. August 1994 (New Age Entertainment).

Mirror Images II. 18. July 1994 (Columbia TriStar).

Murder of Innocence. Valerie Bertinelli, Stephen Caffrey, Graham Beckel, Jerry Hardin, Millie Perkins. 18. August 1994 (Odyssey).

My Boyfriend's Back. Andrew Lowery, Traci Lind, Danny Zorn. PG. July 1994 (Touchstone/Buena Vista).

My Breast. Meredith Baxter, Jamey Sheridan, Sara Botsford, R.H. Thomson, Barbara Barrie. PG. January 1995 (Odyssey).

Natural Causes. Linda Purl, Ali MacGraw, Will Patton. 15. May 1995 (First Independent).

Night Caller. Gary Busey, Peter Fonda, Fred Williamson. 18. December 1994 (Hi-Fliers).

No Ordinary Summer. Larenz Tate, Jada Pinkett. 15. May 1995 (Touchstone).

Not Our Son. Neil Patrick Harris, Gerald McRaney, Cindy Pickett. 15. June 1995 (Odyssey).

Official Denial. Parker Stevenson, Dirk Benedict. PG. September 1994 (Paramount/CIC).

The O.J. Simpson Story. Jessica Tuck, Bobby Hosea. March 1995 (FoxVideo).

One of Her Own. Lori Loughlin, Martin Sheen. 15. October 1994 (Odyssey).

One Wedding and Lots of Funerals. Warwick Davis. 18. January 1995 (Columbia TriStar).

Open Fire. Jeff Wincott, Mimi Craven. 18. August 1994 (Reflective).

The Paperboy. Alexandra Paul, William Katt. 18. January 1995 (First Independent).

Party Animals. Jeremy Piven, Chris Young, David Spade, Megan Ward, Sarah Trigger, Jessica Walter. 15. February 1995 (FoxVideo).

Perfect Alibi. Hector Elizondo, Teri Garr, Kathleen Quinlan. 15. May 1995 (Hi-Fliers).

Pet Shop. Leigh Ann Orsi. U. December 1994 (Paramount/CIC).

Pointman. Jack Scalia, Bruce A. Young. 15. July 1994 (Warner).

Police Story 3: Supercop. Jackie Chan, Maggie Cheung. 15. September 1994 (Imperial).

Precious Victims. Richard Thomas, Robby Benson, Park Overall, Frederic Forrest, Eileen Brennan. PG. November 1994 (Odyssey).

Project Shadowchaser: Night Siege. 18. September 1994 (Medusa).

Public Access. Ron Marquette. 18. January 1995 (Imagine).

Quest For Justice. Jane Seymour, Richard Kiley, D.W. Moffet. 15. March 1995 (Odyssey).

Red Scorpion 2. Matt McColm, John Savage, Jennifer Rubin, Michael Ironside. 18. November 1994 (First Independent).

Red Sun Rising. Don 'The Dragon' Wilson, Terry Farrell, Mako, Michael Ironside. 18. August 1994 (Guild).

The Refrigerator. 18. July 1994 (Hi-Fliers).

Relative Fear. Darlanne Fluegel, Martin Neufeld, James Brolin, Denise Crosby, M. Emmet Walsh. 15. April 1995 (Columbia TriStar).

Relentless – The Redeemer. Leo Rossi, Famke Janssen. 18. February 1995 (Warner).

Renegade: Murderer's Row. Lorenzo Lamas, Kathleen Kinmont. 15. June 1995 (Warner).

Return to Two Moon Junction. 18. September 1994 (Hi-Fliers).

The Revenge of Pumpkin Head: Blood Wings. Amy Dolenz, Andrew Robinson, Steve Kanaly. 18. January 1995 (Hi-Fliers).

Revenge of the Nerds IV: Nerds in Love. Curtis Armstrong, Robert Carradine. PG. October 1994 (FoxVideo).

Ring of Steel. Joe Don Baker, Carol Alt. 18. September 1994 (20/20 Vision).

Rise and Walk. Peter Berg, Kathy Morris. August 1994 (FoxVideo).

Roadflower. Christopher Lambert, Craig Sheffer, Christopher McDonald, David Arquette, Adrienne Shelly. 18. August 1994 (EV).

Search For Grace. Lisa Hartman Black, Suzanne Douglas, Ken Wahl, Richard Masur. 15. March 1995 (FoxVideo).

The Secret World of Emmanuelle. Sylvia Kristel, Marcella Walerstein, George Lazenby. 18. March 1995 (New Age).

The Sect. Kelly Leigh Curtis, Herbert Lom. 18. April 1995 (Guild).

Seeds of Deception. Melissa Gilbert, Shanna Reed, R. H. Thomson, George Dzundza. 15. January 1995 (Odyssey).

Sensation. Eric Roberts, Ron Perlman. 18. January 1995 (New Age).

Shadow Force. Dirk Benedict, Lise Cutter. 18. August 1994 (Hi-Fliers).

Shattered Trust. Melissa Gilbert, Kate Nelligan. 15. July 1994 (Odyssey).

She Led Two Lives. Connie Selleca, Perry King, A. Martinez. PG. May 1995 (Odyssey).

Showdown. Ken Scott, Brion James. 18. August 1994 (Columbia TriStar).

Silent Hunter. Miles O'Keefe. 18. December 1994 (Reflective).

Silhouette. JoBeth Williams, Corbin Bernsen, Stephanie Zimbalist. 15. March 1995 (Odyssey).

Skeeter. Tracy Griffiths, Jim Youngs, Michael J. Pollard, Charles Napier. 15. September 1994 (Reflective).

Ski School 2. Dean Cameron, Heather Campbell. 18. February 1995 (First Independent).

Snakeeater III … His Law. Lorenzo Lamas. 18. July 1994 (Paramount/CIC).

Snake in the Eagle's Shadow. Jackie Chan. 18. October 1994 (Made in Hong Kong).

South Beach. Yancy Butler, John Glover. PG. August 1994 (Universal/CIC).

Spitfire. Tim Thomerson, Lance Henriksen. 15. May 1995 (Hi-Fliers).

Stalked. Maryam d'Abo, Jay Underwood, Lisa Blount. April 1995 (First Independent).

Sudden Fury. Neil Patrick Harris. 18. July 1994 (Guild).

Target Witness. Marc Singer, Deborah Shelton, Charles Napier, Mark Hamill. 18. October 1994 (Columbia TriStar).

T-Force. Jack Scalia, Erin Gray, Vernon Wells. 18. May 1995 (Guild).

Thunder in Paradise 3. Hulk Hogan, Chris Lemmon, Carol Alt. PG. January 1995 (Imperial).

To Save the Children. Richard Thomas, Wendy Crewson, Robert Urich. 15. January 1995 (Odyssey).

Touch of Truth. Melissa Gilbert, Patty Duke, Lisa Banes. 12. February 1995 (Odyssey).

To Walk Again. Blair Brown, Ken Howard. PG. July 1994 (Hi-Fliers).

Trancers 5: Sudden Death. Tim Thomerson. 15. April 1995 (CIC).

Trapped in Space. Jack Wagner, Jack Coleman, Kay Lenz. 15. March 1995 (CIC).

The Ultimate Betrayal. Marlo Thomas, Mel Harris, Ally Sheedy. 15. October 1994 (Odyssey).

Undercover Angel. Darlene Vogel, Roddy McDowall. 18. April 1995 (Hi-Fliers).

Under Lock and Key. Wendi Westbrook. 18. November 1994 (New Age Entertainment).

Unlawful Vengeance. George Hamilton, Robert Conrad. 15. July 1994 (Guild).

Untamed Love. Cathy Lee Crosby, John Getz, Gary Frank. 12. February 1995 (Odyssey).

Victim of Rage. Jaclyn Smith, Brad Johnson. 15. August 1994 (Odyssey).

Viper. Lorenzo Lamas. 18. January 1995 (New Age).

Virgin Hunters. Ian Abercrombie, Morgan Fairchild. 18. August 1994 (Medusa).

Warriors. Gary Busey, Michael Pare. 15. February 1995 (Columbia TriStar).

Warrior Spirit. Lukas Haas. PG. April 1995 (Hi-Fliers).

A Woman Scorned. Shannon Tweed, Andrew Stevens. 18. April 1995 (Columbia TriStar).

X-Tra Private Lessons. Mariana Morgan. 18. March 1995 (Medusa).

Zero Tolerance. Robert Patrick. 18. October 1994 (New Age Entertainment).

TV Feature Films of the Year

F. Maurice Speed

In this section you will find listed made-for-television movies shown for the first time in the UK during the year 1 July 1994 to 30 June 1995. In the interests of space, however, the films included are restricted to features made within the last five years. None the less, many TV films broadcast in the period covered have been reviewed in previous editions of this annual.

The date given in brackets after each title is the year when the movie was made or originally shown (often in the US).

In a few cases, despite being first shown on television, these films may have been made originally for the cinema.

When a film made for American TV receives its first UK showing in a cinema, it is of course reviewed in the 'Releases of the Year' section.

Absolute Strangers (1991). Topical, truth-based drama about a man having to face up to a choice of having to let his wife or unborn child die. Dignified and moving. With Henry Winkler, Jennifer Hetrick. Dir: Gilbert Gates. BBC2, 1 June 1995.

Against Her Will – Incident in Baltimore (1992). Walter Matthau is a tower of strength as a small-time lawyer fighting to get his client freed from the institution which is holding her. A less but still very good follow-up to TV's *The Incident*. With Harry Morgan. Dir: Delbert Mann. BBC2, 13 December 1994.

Always Remember I Love You (1990). Above-average weepie about a teenager trying to track down his real parents. With Stephen Dorff. Dir: Michael Miller. ITV, 23 December 1994.

Babylon 5 (1993). Excellent pilot feature introducing the popular SF series. With Michael O'Hara, Tamlyn Tomita. Dir: Richard Compton. Channel 4, 9 October 1994.

Bare Essentials (1990). Lightly amusing story of two New Yorkers marooned on a tropical island. Nice to look at. Dir: Martha Coolidge. BBC2, 15 February 1995.

Backfield in Motion (1991). Roseanne Arnold in slim but likeable family comedy-drama. With Tom Arnold. Dir: Richard Michaels. Channel 4, 12 July 1994.

Bed of Lies (1991). Good thriller – and true story about a passionate waitress's love which leads to murder. With Susan Dey. Dir: William A. Graham. Channel 4, 17 January 1995.

Blind Hate (1990). Racial drama about one man's struggle to bring the Klu Klux Klan to justice. Based on fact. With Corbin Bernsen. Dir: John Korty. BBC2, 25 January 1995.

Blind Judgement (1991). Happy and successful lawyer Peter Coyote finds his life changes when he agrees to defend Lesley Ann Warren on a murder charge. Dir: George Kaczender. BBC2, 11 May 1995.

Brothers of the Gun (1992). More or less routine Western, set in New Mexico. Dir: Vern Gillum. ITV, 14 April 1995.

Carolina Skeletons (1991). Tightly scripted story of racial prejudice in the American Deep South circa 1960s. Slow but deep. With Bruce Dern, Louis Gossett Jr. Dir: John Erman. BBC1, 3 August 1994.

The Crucifer of Blood (1991). Fraser C. Heston directs his dad Charlton in a Sherlock Holmes adventure about an ancient Indian curse. Richard Johnson is Dr Watson and though all far from authentic Conan Doyle, it is good entertainment. BBC1, 20 November 1994.

Dagger Island (1992). Richard Beymer offering a nice, amusing plate of ham in this routine thriller. Dir: Tommy Lee Wallace. ITV, 10 May 1995.

Danielle Steel's Once in a Lifetime (1994). Soap opera stuff about Lindsay Wagner's love and tragedy and then her chance to rebuild her life. Smiles through the tears! Dir: Michael Miller. ITV, 31 December 1994.

Darkness Before Dawn (1992). Grim, true story about drug addiction. With Stephen Lang, Meredith Baxter. Dir: John Patterson. Channel 4, 13 April 1995.

Dead on the Money (1991). Mixture of moods and themes in poorly-acted story about an actress who meets the man of her dreams. With Amanda Pays, Corbin Bernsen. Dir: Mark Cullingham. BBC2, 2 June 1995.

Death Dreams (1991). Routine TV thriller with Christopher Reeve as a man whose wife hears mysterious voices. With Marg Helenberger. Dir: Martin Donovan. BBC1, 24 April 1995.

Decoration Day (1990). Beautifully played (especially by James Garner) and directed story of a retired judge trying to persuade his black friend to accept his rightful war medal. A very superior TV movie. Dir: Robert Markowitz. ITV, 25 August 1994.

Desperate Rescue (1993). Headline-hitting news story about an American mother (Mariel Hemingway) trying to recover her daughter who was stolen and taken to the Middle East by her Arab husband. All very slickly done. Dir: Richard Colla. ITV, 9 December 1994.

Double Edge (1992). Fast-moving murder mystery. Totally improbable but watchable. With Susan Lucci. Dir: Stephen Stafford. ITV, 9 September 1994.

El Diablo (1990). Pleasantly amusing Western. Anthony Edwards is the schoolmaster who finds the thrills of his dreams when one of his pupils is kidnapped by a Mexican bandit. Dir: Peter Markle. Channel 4, 20 April 1995.

Elvis and the Colonel: The Untold Story (1993). As it all might have been! But wasn't. With Beau Bridges. Dir: William Graham. Channel 4, 2 January 1995.

Exclusive (1992). Rather dreary story of newscaster who turns investigative reporter and wades into plenty of trouble. With Suzanne Somers, Ed Begley Jr. Dir: Alan Metzger. Channel 4, 2 August 1994.

The Good Fight (1992). Christine Lahti stars as the small-time lawyer opposing the corporate giant and giving a very good account of herself. Holding courtroom drama. Dir: John David Coles. Channel 4, 31 January 1995.

Heat Wave (1990). A searing relating of the 1965 Los Angeles race riots with director Kevin Hooks making no bones about where he thinks the responsibility lies. With James Earl Jones, Cicely Tyson. BBC2, 15 November 1994.

In a Stranger's Hand (1991). Well directed and gripping chiller involving kidnapping and murder. Robert Urich is the witness to a crime and doesn't want to become involved – but soon is! Dir: David Greene. BBC1, 9 May 1995.

In Defence of a Married Man (1990). Ludicrous courtroom drama about a female criminal lawyer defending her husband on a charge of murdering his mistress! With Judith Light, Michael Ontkean. Dir: Joel Oliansky. BBC2, 22 June 1995.

In My Daughter's Name (1992). Real life thriller about a vengeful mom who takes the law into her own gun and fills her daughter's killer with lead. With Donna Mills, Lee Grant. Dir: Jud Taylor. BBC1, 18 November 1994.

In the Best Interest of the Children (1992). Moving and truth-based TV story of a mother's fight to regain her in-care children, taking them away from their happy foster home. A moving dilemma. With Sarah Jessica Parker. Dir: Michael Ray Rhodes. Channel 4, 4 May 1995.

In the Eyes of a Stranger (1992). Pacy, stylish and gripping new slant on the old story about a girl who comes across a dangerous secret about the crooks' hoard. With Justine Bateman, Richard Dean Anderson. Dir: Michael Toshiyuki Uno. Channel 4, 7 February and 3 March 1995.

Journey into Darkness (The Bruce Curtis Story) (1991). Real life Canadian courtroom drama about the trial of two teenagers, one of whom is accused of murdering his father and mother. Dir: Graeme Clifford. BBC2, 6 December 1994.

The Last Best Year (1990). Tissues obligatory for this sobbie about the last days of cancer patient Bernadette Peters. The doctor is Mary Tyler Moore. Two good performances. Dir: John Erman. BBC2, 27 November 1994.

The Legend of Grizzly Adams (1990). Fascinating backgrounds add to this story of mountain man Adams – a spin-off from the popular TV series of the seventies. With Gene Edwards. Dir: Ken Kennedy. BBC1, 5 January 1995.

Lethal Charm (1991). The shadow of *All About Eve* hovers over this sketchy press drama. But Barbara Eden rises above it. With Heather Locklear. Dir: Richard Michaels. BBC2, 25 July 1994.

Liar, Liar (1993). High standard Canadian TV feature about child abuse. Serious and absorbing. With Art Hindle, Rosemary Dunsmore. Dir: Jorge Montesi. Channel 4, 19 July 1994.

Lies Before Kisses (1991). Polished, fast-moving, ably directed routine story about a wife who finds a lot of dirt under her husband's carpet. With Jaclyn Smith, Ben Gazzara. Dir: Lou Antonio. ITV, 3 February 1995.

The Little Kidnappers (1990). Surprisingly good Canadian remake of the British children's classic *The Kidnappers*. A real treat for all the family. With Charlton Heston. Dir: Donald Shebib. ITV, 27 December 1994.

Married for Murder (1991). Good, truth-based murder thriller about the insurance business. With Treat Williams. Dir: Yves Simoneau. BBC1, 1 May 1995.

A Mind to Kill (1992). There's been a horrid murder in a small Welsh town. Can the cops arrest the killer before he strikes again? Neat little psychological thriller. With Hywel Bennett, Philip Madoc. Dir: Peter Edwards. ITV, 21 October 1994.

Mission of the Shark (1991). Above-average TV film: the true account of the sinking of the USS *Indianapolis* by the Japs during World War Two in shark-infested waters. Gripping stuff, well crafted. With Stacy Keach. Dir: Robert Iscove. BBC1, 23 September 1994.

The Mousehole Cat (1994). British animated film for toddlers. Mousehole refers to the delightful little Cornish village. Channel 4, 27 December 1994.

Murder on Sycamore Street (1991). Welcome back Dick Van Dyke – who has all his old charm as the medical amateur sleuth. Highly entertaining. Dir: Christian Nyby. BBC1, 27 August 1994.

Murder in Mississippi (1990). The true story of the murder of three Civil Rights members by the Klu Klux Klan. With Tom Hulce, Blair Underwood. Dir: Roger Young. Channel 4, 30 March 1995.

Murder 101 (1991). Routine thriller which rattles along at a very fair pace. With Pierce Brosnan. Dir: Bill Condon. ITV, 10 February 1995.

Nightmare (1991). A mother fights back when a killer abducts her daughter. With Victoria Principal. Dir: John Pasquin. ITV, 17 February 1995.

Night of the Hunter (1991). Surprisingly effective remake of the classic film starring Robert Mitchum, now with Richard Chamberlain as the suspect preacher. A tense tale. Dir: David Greene. ITV, 7 October 1994.

Notorious (1992). Tedious, uninspired remake of the classic Hitchcock thriller. With John Shea, Jenny Robertson. Dir: Colin Bucksey. ITV, 14 December 1994.

The Other Side of Murder (1991). Said to be a true story of the victim of a bungled burglary. With Richard Chamberlain. Dir: Glenn Jordan. BBC1, 9 September 1994.

Our Sons (1991). Two worried mums, Julie Andrews and Ann Margret, having come to terms with the fact that their sons are homosexuals are tested further when one of them develops AIDS. Good performances show up a less acceptable script. With Hugh Grant. Dir: John Erman. ITV, 26 November 1994.

A Pair of Aces (1990). Pleasantly loose-reined Western featuring thief Willie Nelson and lawman Kris Kristofferson. Dir: Michael Pressman. ITV, 11 November 1994.

Perry Mason: The Case of the Glass Coffin (1991). Perry solves the mysterious death of the magician's assistant. With Raymond Burr. BBC1, 4 June 1995.

Presumed Guilty (1991). A New York teenager arrested for a drugs murder is stoutly defended by his devoted daddy. All pretty effective. With Brendan Fraser, Martin Sheen. ITV, 2 September 1994.

The Rape of Dr Willis (1991). Non-credible story of a doctor raped on the first day of her hospital duties, who then finds the raper a patient – who dies. Rumours abound! A good unintended chuckle. With Jaclyn Smith. Dir: Lou Antonio. BBC2, 8 June 1995.

The Return of Eliot Ness (1991). Robert Stack comes out of retirement to solve a buddy's murder. Shadow of the classic *The Untouchables* series in which Robert Stack played Ness. Dir: James Contner. BBC1, 14 October 1994.

Runaway Heart (1990). Jill Eikenberry is the willing victim of inept bank robber Michael Tucker in this unlikely romantic comedy. Dir: James Frawley. BBC2, 20 September 1994.

Running Out (1993). After a twelve year absence, a wife and mother walks back into the family. And thanks to fine playing and tight direction this soap-suds story becomes moving and even absorbing. With Deborah Raffin, Tony Bill. Dir: Robert Day. ITV, 4 December 1994.

The Secret (1992). Kirk Douglas strengthens the appeal of this story about dyslexia. Dir: Karen Arthur. BBC2, 19 June 1995.

She'll Take Romance (1990). Good old-fashioned romantic comedy. Familiar stuff but well presented and tolerably amusing. With Linda Evans. Dir: Piers Haggard. BBC1, 2 December 1994.

Silent Motive (1991). Missable. Thriller writer who finds a real killer following her plots in real life with all the expected ramifications. With Patricia Wettig. Dir: Lee Philips. BBC1, 22 May 1995.

A Son's Promise (1990). Tear-jerker (a true story) about the dutiful son who promises his dying mother that he will take care of her considerable brood. Sincere but soapy. With Ricky Schroder. Dir: John Korty. ITV, 28 July 1994.

The Take (1990). Expertly presented familiar story of cops v. drug dealers. With Ray Sharkey. Dir: Leon Ichaso. ITV, 2 December 1994.

Tanya and Nancy – The Inside Story (1994). Fictional story based on the ice-skating feud between the two girls which made headlines. Very watchable with expert skating. Alexandra Powers, Heather Langenkamp. Dir: Larry Shaw. BBC1, 16 September 1994.

A Town Torn Apart (1992). Sincere if somewhat stodgy story of a teacher who takes over a run-down and 'difficult' school and slowly works wonders with it. With Michael Tucker, Carole Galloway, Jill Eikenberry. Dir: Daniel Petrie. ITV, 14 July 1994.

Vestige of Honour (1990). Story of the Vietnam war aftermath and the shabby treatment accorded some of the natives who supported the US. Sincere. With Don Scott, Michael Gross. Dir: Jerry London. ITV, 18 November 1994.

Victim of Love (1991). Dismayingly routine human triangle story about psychologist JoBeth Williams, oversexed professor Pierce Brosnan and pretty patient Virginia Madsen struggling in their own spun web of deceit. Dir: Jerry London. BBC1, 30 September 1994.

Violence – The Last Resort (1993). Outstanding German telefilm set in a high school where passions flare and racism is rampant. A political thriller of stature. Dir: Rainer Kaufmann. BBC2, 23 October 1994.

When You Remember Me (1990). Muscular dystrophy victim Fred Savage struggles against fate (nurse Ellen Burstyn in particular) to live as normal a life as possible. Tear-stained story lifted high by the acting. With Kevin Spacey. Dir: Harry Winer. Channel 4, 6 April 1995.

Wild Texas Wind (1991). A Dolly Parton showcase. Dir: Joan Tewkesbury. BBC2, 13 April 1995.

Wildflower (1991). Moving story, directed by actress Diane Keaton, of an epileptic girl (Patricia Arquette) kept imprisoned by her cruel stepfather who is convinced Satan is inside her. Set against a background of rural Georgia of the thirties. With Reese Witherspoon, William McNamara. BBC2, 15 June 1995.

Without Her Consent (1990). Routine story about a man vowing vengeance on the character who has raped his girlfriend. Dir: Sandor Stern. ITV, 16 September 1994.

Letter From Hollywood

Anthony Slide

The loudest and longest standing ovation President Bill Clinton received when he delivered his State of the Union address before Congress on 24 January 1995 was in response to an attack on the film and television industry for its depiction of violence. Blaming the media for the problems in American society was even more popular than condemning unwed teenage mothers or illegal aliens. Nobody likes Hollywood, least of all the politicians.

The political pendulum has swung to the right, and the first victims of the new purge are the National Endowment for the Arts and the Corporation for Public Broadcasting. The latter acquires and funds programming for the public television network, and while a cutback in Federal funds will not mean the end of public broadcasting – both radio and television – it will mean fewer quality shows. In that public television relies in large part on programming from the BBC, this may eventually lead to retrenchment in London.

Unlike Europe, where filmmakers receive subsidies from the governments of individual countries and the European Commission, there is no subsidised government filmmaking in the United States. The only area in which the US government supports films is through a limited number of grants, given by the National Endowment for the Arts, to the producers of documentaries and art-orientated film. The National Endowment for the Arts has come in for increased criticism from the right wing in recent years for its funding of controversial performance artists, whose acts involve nudity and obscene language, and exhibits and programmes that criticise religion or advocate alternate lifestyles; notably the photographs of Robert Mapplethorpe.

Freedom of speech, which is taken for granted in Western Europe, is under attack in the United States, where, supposedly, it is protected by the Constitution. The Catholic Church has mounted a concerted attack on the British feature, *Priest*, starring Linus Roache, and was able to force the US distributor, Miramax, to hold back the film's release at least until after Easter.

Aside from support from the Federal government, public television relies on sponsors, enabling it to present programming without commercials. Threats of consumer boycotts against companies that sponsor controversial shows have resulted in a timidity by many major American companies. For example, the BBC drama, *The Lost Language of Cranes*, was aired by public television in a series sponsored by Texaco, but because of threats by the religious right, the company decided to end its sponsorship of the series the day the gay-orientated film was scheduled to be broadcast. The BBC recognises that what British viewers routinely see may not be acceptable to Americans; in the UK the actors in *The Lost Language of Cranes* were nude in some scenes, but in the US they were always shown in their underwear.

One programme the BBC was unable to 'sell' either to public or network television in the United States was

Tom Hanks receives the award for Best Actor from the Screen Actors' Guild

Absolutely Fabulous, the behaviour of whose principal characters was deemed inappropriate. Smoking pot, sniffing cocaine, boozing and enjoying sex, Patsy and Edina were considered bad role models for Americans. The fact that that was the whole point was lost on American television executives. Eventually, the series was acquired by a cable network, Comedy Central (which also airs *Whose Line is it Anyway?*), and *Absolutely Fabulous* is now repeated ad nauseum with the 'naughty words' bleeped and commercials every five minutes. The current presentation on Comedy Central hardly does the show much good, but, presumably, the BBC's interest lies only in money rather than artistic presentation.

The American political scene is no laughing matter, but Hollywood can always be relied upon to cheer our spirits, if not our intellect. A number of comedy legends were in the news in the past year. On 5 November 1994, a plaque was unveiled at 923 Vendome Street, just off Sunset Boulevard as it heads for downtown Los Angeles. Why a plaque here? Because at this site are the steps up which Stan Laurel and Oliver Hardy pushed the piano in their 1932 classic, *The Music Box*. (The steps were also utilised in the 1927 Laurel and Hardy film, *Hats Off.*) The neighbourhood is not quite as elegant as it was in Laurel and Hardy's day. It is now home to immigrants from South and Central America, many of them illegal, and would-be sightseers are warned to watch out for muggers, rapists, murderers and other undesirables who represent a growing number of the population of Los Angeles.

All too often in the British press, one reads comments from producers and directors who denounce Thatcherism and Britain today and find so much to praise in President Clinton and American society. I often wonder how many of those British filmmakers see anything of America outside of the protected affluence of Bel Air, Beverly Hills and other multi-million dollar communities.

A legal battle between descendants of the Three Stooges took on all the elements of one of the comedy group's films, when, in December 1994, Larry Fine's and Curly Joe DeRita's families won a $4 million judgement against the grandson and daughter of Moe Howard. The law suit involved merchandising profits, and the defence claimed the major issue was which of the Stooges was the most popular. The lead attorney for the plaintiffs was none other than Bela Lugosi Jr, a 56-year-old lawyer who bears a remarkable resemblance to his late father, and who was responsible for pushing through a law in California establishing that the name and likeness of a deceased celebrity belongs to, and can be promoted by, his or her heirs.

And talking of comedy, what has Zsa Zsa Gabor been up to lately? Not too much it would appear, because, according to the American tabloid press, she is in a bad way financially as a result of last year's judgement against her in favour of Elke Sommer. The only other publicity Zsa Zsa managed to garner in the past year was in January 1995, when she was hit on the head by a descending parking lot pole at the Thrifty Drugstore in Beverly Hills. It was, presumably, not the first time that a Hungarian had been hit by a pole.

A Comedy Arts Festival was held in March 1995 – not in Los Angeles, but in Aspen, Colorado. As part of the event, the American Film Institute sponsored a retrospective of the work of Albert Brooks, and also presented him with a career achievement award. A large contingent of the Hollywood crowd were present at Aspen, but totally absent from the Razzie Awards, held on 26 March, the day after the Comedy Arts Festival closed. Now in its fifteenth year, the Razzies are presented by the Golden Raspberry Foundation, in answer to the Oscars, to the worst performers of the year. The worst actor award went to Kevin Costner for *Wyatt Earp*, the worst actress award to Sharon Stone for *The Specialist* and *Intersection*. Rosie O'Donnell was named worst supporting actress of the year for her work in *Car 54, Where Are You?*, and O.J. Simpson worst supporting actor of the year for *Naked Gun 33¹/₃*. (The Comedy Central cable network suggested Simpson should be named best actor of the year for the performance in his double-murder trial.) Steven Seagal won the award for worst director for *On Deadly Ground*, and there was a tie in the worst couples category, with Razzies going to Sylvester Stallone and Sharon Stone for *The Specialist*, and Tom Cruise and Brad Pitt for *Interview With the Vampire*. The 375 members of the Golden Raspberry Foundation named *The Color of Night* the worst picture of 1994.

George Burns celebrated his 99th birthday with a quiet dinner with a couple of friends at the Hillcrest Country Club on 20 January 1995. He admitted to still drinking three Martinis a day, but was down from a dozen cigars to a mere three. The day before his birthday, Burns dedicated Gracie Allen Drive, a one-block street that intersects George Burns Road at the Cedars-Sinai hospital complex on the border between the cities of Beverly Hills and West Hollywood. At the inaugural Screen Actors' Guild Awards on 25 February 1995, George Burns received the Life Achievement Award. He stood at his table to accept the honour from Ann-Margret, and announced, 'Now I'm going to do something that's not easy to do. I'm going to sit down.'

The Screen Actors' Guild Awards honoured outstanding performances in theatrical motion pictures and television, and the event was broadcast live by NBC. As expected, Tom Hanks won the award for Best Actor for his performance in *Forrest Gump*, Martin Landau was named Best Supporting Actor for

Ed Wood, Best Actress award went to Jodie Foster for *Nell*, and Dianne Wiest was named Best Supporting Actress for *Bullets Over Broadway*. The Screen Actors' Guild has named its award, appropriately enough, The Actor; the 10¼ pound, fifteen inches high sculpture is cast in bronze. If the 1994 winners are anything to go by, the Screen Actors' Guild Awards may well serve to indicate who the winners will be in the acting categories at the Oscars.

Almost as old as George Burns – he was born in Sussex in 1899 – Charles Bennett received the Screen Laurel Award at the 47th annual Writers' Guild of America awards ceremony on 19 March 1995 from actress Angela Lansbury. Still active, Bennett's first involvement in film was as the author of the play on which Alfred Hitchcock's *Blackmail* is based. He scripted many of Hitchcock's greatest films, including *The Thirty-Nine Steps*, *Secret Agent*, *Sabotage*, *Young and Innocent* and *Foreign Correspondent*, and has lived and worked in the United States since 1938.

Charles Bennett is a fascinating raconteur, as attendees at the 30th annual Cinecon convention discovered. Held at the Hollywood Roosevelt Hotel over the Labor Day weekend (1-5 September 1994), the Cinecon brings together film buff members of the Society for Cinephiles, and is one of the best organised events of its type, with a host of celebrities introducing their films and talking to the audience. Luise Rainer flew in from Europe for the Sunday evening banquet, and other honourees included Burgess Meredith, Jane Greer, Anita Page, Toby Wing and Joan Leslie. Harry Carey Jr, John Agar and Ruth Clifford participated in a fascinating panel discussion on the work of John Ford. From behind the camera, Rudy Fehr, William Tuttle and Sydney Guilaroff discussed the work of the editor, the make-up artist and the hair stylist, respectively. Turhan Bey was another visitor from Europe, asking the audience – hopefully tongue-in-cheek – to appreciate the nuances of his performances in *Arabian Nights* and *Ali Baba and the Forty Thieves*. Character actress Mary Wickes was a delightfully dry and sarcastic commentator, accidentally(?) pouring a glass of water into the bag of her interviewer.

She may be long dead, but Gloria Swanson dominated the Hollywood scene as Glenn Close gave a triumphant

performance as her character Norma Desmond in *Sunset Boulevard* on stage both in Los Angeles and New York. As a result of the success of the Andrew Lloyd Webber musical, in December 1994, Dickson Hughes presented the musical play, *Swanson on Sunset*, also at the Hollywood Roosevelt Hotel. The show told the story of Dickson and his lover-collaborator Richard Stapley's work with Swanson in trying to stage a musical version of *Sunset Boulevard* back in 1955, and utilised songs from the abortive effort. In an example of life imitating art, the project foundered when Swanson developed a sexual interest in collaborator Stapley.

On a more serious level, the animal rights organisation, the Ark Trust, Inc., presented its Genesis Awards on 12 March 1995 at the Beverly Hilton Hotel. Among the winners were the

Jane Greer receives her Cinecon Award from veteran Paramount producer A.C. Lyles

producers of *The Simpsons*, for the episode in which Bart wins an elephant and sells it to an animal sanctuary. The Doris Day Music Award went to the group Consolidated, and the Brigitte Bardot International Genesis Award to the BBC's *On the Line*.

Faye Dunaway did not get to play Norma Desmond on Broadway, but she did receive the Lifetime Achievement Award from the National Association of Theatre Owners (NATO) on 9 March 1995. Other awards went to Tom Hanks, director Robert Zemeckis,

The John Ford panel at the annual Cinecon Convention. From left to right: Harry Carey Jr, Ruth Clifford, Kathleen O'Malley (leading lady in Wagonmaster*), and John Agar*

*Margaret O'Brien reunited with her 1944
Oscar*

producer James Cameron and Demi
Moore. It is apropos that the theatre
owners of America should honour
Moore as female star of the year, for she
and her husband, Bruce Willis, are currently renovating a cinema in Hailey,
Idaho.

Another Life Achievement Award
went to Steven Spielberg – this time
from the American Film Institute on 2
March 1995. At age 47, Spielberg was

the youngest of the 23 recipients to
date, and obviously selected with an eye
to the commercial potential resulting
from his appearance, particularly the
edited television presentation of the
event on NBC on 27 May. Tom Hanks
(who is in danger of overexposure) host-
ed the event, which included appearances by Whoopi Goldberg, Ben
Kingsley, Dan Aykroyd, Jim Carrey
and Dustin Hoffman. MCA/Universal
president Sid Sheinberg hailed Spielberg as 'the première filmmaker of the
twentieth century', ignoring the work of

such talented individuals as D.W.
Griffith and Jean Renoir. The long
evening ended at 11:30 with Bernadette
Peters singing, 'When You Wish Upon
A Star', accompanied on the piano by
John Williams.

Absolut Vodka paid for the dinner
and also, much to its credit, donated
$100,000 to film preservation. Here, as
at the Academy Awards, the emphasis
was on saving the National Endowment
for the Arts and the government subsidies that go to film preservation.
While the film community urges the
American taxpayer to save its heritage,
no one seems willing to suggest that if
the wealthy members of the industry –
those whose yearly income is in excess
of one million dollars – were to donate,
say, ten per cent of their earnings to film
preservation, every American film currently in danger of deterioration could
be saved. Actress Jane Alexander, who
heads the NEA, is known to have
expressed such thoughts in private, but
at two receptions in Hollywood honouring her and the National Endowment for the Arts on 26 February 1995,
she kept her silence.

Meanwhile, film preservation in Los
Angeles is the bailiwick on the UCLA
Film and Television Archive, whose
preservation staff is headed by Robert
Gitt. UCLA's efforts were on display
at the seventh annual Festival of
Preservation, held from 6 April through
to 4 May. Two films with an English
bent were the highlights of the pro-
gramme: *A Man for All Seasons*, starring
Paul Scofield, and the 1926 version of
Bruce Bairnsfather's *The Better 'Ole*,
starring Syd Chaplin. The Festival of
Preservation coincided with the annu-
al meeting in Los Angeles of the
International Federation of Film
Archives, sponsored by UCLA, the
American Film Institute and the
Academy of Motion Picture Arts and
Sciences.

While filmmakers such as Steven
Spielberg are willing to lend their
names to promoting film preservation,
they are remarkably shy in delivering
funds. Spielberg's charitable activities,
such as they are, may not have garnered
him much attention, but the director
has certainly been in the news in the last
year. With Jeffrey Katzenberg and
David Geffen, he founded the multi-
million dollar production company,
DreamWorks. Also with Katzenberg,
Spielberg opened a deli restaurant,

Dive!, in Century City in May 1994. The Century City eatery is the first of what is planned to be a series of submarine-themed restaurants, all, of course, offering submarine sandwiches.

Steven Spielberg was also on hand at the Center for Motion Picture Study of the Academy of Motion Picture Arts and Sciences, when, in April 1994, the Academy and the International Documentary Association announced the creation of a documentary film archive. Spielberg presented Academy president Arthur Hiller with a copy of the BBC documentary, *Schindler*, which he used in preparation for his feature, *Schindler's List*.

The Academy has been expanding its film archival and preservation activities, under the guidance of Michael Friend. Working in collaboration with the Merchant and Ivory Foundation, it was able to preserve and restore a number of the films of Satyajit Ray, including *Pather Panchali*, the newly-restored version of which was screened at the Academy on 10 April 1995.

The Oscars were in the news in March when Margaret O'Brien was reunited with the miniature Academy Award she had won as Outstanding Child Actress of 1944. The Oscar was taken by a maid when the actress was seventeen years old, and resurfaced at a flea market at Pasadena City College in December 1994, when it was purchased for $500. The two men who acquired the Oscar had never heard of Margaret O'Brien, and confusedly thought she was the little girl in *Miracle on 34th Street* – in reality, Natalie Wood. The couple generously returned the Oscar to O'Brien, and the Academy, in return, gave them tickets to this year's Awards presentation. Margaret O'Brien was delighted to have her Oscar back, despite having been given a replacement Award several years ago. 'It means a lot more now than when it was lost,' she commented.

Oscar night on 27 March 1995 was pretty much a dull affair, with David Letterman – a popular comedian on late-night television – proving a poor host who found his humour far more entertaining than did his audience. It was a foregone conclusion as to the big winners, but it was good to see the Academy membership spreading the Oscars around a little more, honouring the underrated *Ed Wood* with two, and naming *Speed* and *The Adventures of Priscilla, Queen of the Desert* as surprise Oscar recipients. The most touching moment of the evening came with Jack Nicholson's presentation of an Honorary Oscar to stroke victim Michelangelo Antonioni, whose wife gave a brilliant acceptance speech, noting, 'Michelangelo always went beyond words to meet silence, the mystery and the power of the silence.' The big winner was *Forrest Gump* with six Oscars, followed by *Ed Wood*, *The Lion King* and *Speed* with two each.

The big question facing the Academy Awards audience is always where to eat after the show, which begins at 6.00 p.m. The Academy always hosts a Governors' Ball after the ceremony, but most nominees and winners put in only a perfunctory appearance there before going on elsewhere. This year, in an effort to encourage guests to stay, the Academy hired Wolfgang Puck, who is a bigger name than many of the stars, to be the chef. The National Council on Alcoholism and Drug Dependency organised its first Oscar party – alcohol free – at the Bel Age Hotel in West Hollywood, and guests there included Alec Baldwin, Martin Landau and Michael Douglas. The big party was probably Elton John's at the Four Seasons Hotel in Beverly Hills, benefiting his Aids Foundation, and with guests including Hugh Grant, Tom Hanks, Liam Neeson and Natasha Richardson.

The Oscar parties were a reminder that Hollywood lost one of its best-known restaurants in the last year. In April, Chasen's closed its doors for the last time, with the building to be demolished and replaced by a shopping mall. Opened on 13 December 1936, Chasen's was once the most popular eating place for Hollywood's élite, primarily noted for its chilli, but in recent years, the old-fashioned establishment had gone out of vogue, and has now gone the way of such other classic dining places as Perino's (which closed in 1985) and the Coconut Grove (closed in 1988).

The transitory nature of Hollywood fame is exemplified by the closing of Chasen's. Loretta Young, 'Buddy' Rogers and others had a taste of ignomy in April 1994, when their stars were removed from the Hollywood Walk of Fame, to prevent them from being damaged during construction of a subway line under Hollywood Boulevard. The movie *Speed* made use of the projected Los Angeles subway system, depicting its path past Grauman's Chinese Theatre, but, in reality, the subway will turn north several blocks prior to the theatre.

With so much of the past constantly being lost, it was good to welcome back the Beverly Hills Hotel, which re-opened after a $100 million facelift, paid for by its new owner, the Sultan of Brunei. The hotel came back to life on 3 June 1994 with a $1,000 a plate opening gala in benefit of the Center for Motion Picture Study of the Academy of Motion Picture Arts and Sciences. No better recipient could be found than the latter, which has done so much to preserve Hollywood history at least in paper form, and which makes its holdings available to all, in or out of the industry, without charge. British Film Institute take note!

Movie Quotations of the Year

'There are two things I hate about you, Felicia. Your face. So shut both of them.'

    Hugo Weaving to drag queen Guy Pearce in *The Adventures of Priscilla, Queen of the Desert*

Drag queen to yokel with dog: 'What a nice dog. What's its name?' Yokel: 'Herpes. If she's good, she'll heel.'

    Terence Stamp and yokel in *The Adventures of Priscilla, Queen of the Desert*

Terence Stamp, in The Adventures of Priscilla, Queen of the Desert

'Your hand is on my shoulder. That's third base.'

    Marcia Brady (Christine Taylor) defending her honour in *The Brady Bunch Movie*

'She's harder to get into than a Pearl Jam concert.'

    Lustful student ogling Marcia Brady in *The Brady Bunch Movie*

'As a wise man once said, "Wherever you go, there you are."'

    Gary Cole as Mike Brady in *The Brady Bunch Movie*

'For me, love is very deep. Sex need only go a few inches.'

    Observer in *Bullets Over Broadway*

'I wish I smoked. Then at times like these I could smoke.'

    An exasperated Maury Chaykin in *Camilla*

'If this is dying, I don't think much of it.'

    Jonathan Pryce as the biographer Lytton Strachey, on his deathbed, in *Carrington*

Wife, talking about her husband and his brother: 'I can't believe you two are from the same gene pool.' Husband: 'He's from the shallow end.'

    Patricia Wettig and Billy Crystal in *City Slickers II: 'The Legend of Curly's Gold'*

'This job would be great if it weren't for the fucking customers.'

    Shopkeeper Jeff Anderson in *Clerks*

'The course of action I'd suggest is not a course of action I can suggest.'

    Donald Moffat as the President of the United States – pushed to deal with the drug cartels in Columbia – in *Clear and Present Danger*

'Don't climb up too close to God. He might shake the tree.'

    Caroline Goodall warning husband Michael Douglas of the perils of ambition in *Disclosure*

'Give a man $400m and you create a frustrated billionaire.'

    Rosemary Forsythe in *Disclosure*

'Catherine Alvarez would change her name to TV Listings to get in the paper.'

    Donald Sutherland on the ambitious lawyer played by Roma Maffia in *Disclosure*

'Going down?'

    Demi Moore's veiled invitation to Michael Douglas in the elevator in *Disclosure.*

Donald Sutherland, in Disclosure

Kathy Bates, in Dolores Claiborne

'If you deny me my wedding night, I'll be with you on yours.'

> Robert De Niro as The Creature in *Mary Shelley's Frankenstein*

Reporter to cop at scene of urban chaos: 'Do you know what happened here?' Cop: 'No. You can quote me on that.'

> Amy Yasbeck and Peter Riegert in *The Mask*

'Most men in this town think monogamy is a type of wood.'

> Amy Yasbeck in *The Mask*

'At my age you sometimes need a volcano to light a match.'

> Paul Mazursky on the decline of his sexual desire in *Miami Rhapsody*

'You ooze you lose.'

> A flip aside from *Mighty Morphin Power Rangers: The Movie*

Melanie Griffith, in Milk Money

'In my experience men always listen better with their pants off.'

> Melanie Griffith in *Milk Money*

'Sometimes, being a bitch is all a woman has to hold on to.'

> Kathy Bates, Jennifer Jason Leigh and Judy Parfitt in *Dolores Claiborne*

'Anything lost can be found again. Except time.'

> Samuel L. Jackson teaching his son (Sean Nelson) the value of time in *Fresh*

'Show me the man who's perfectly content and I'll show you the lobotomy scar.'

> Sean Connery in *A Good Man in Africa*

'It's your coffin, my love. Enjoy it.'

> Tom Cruise pushing a prospective victim (Indra Ové) into a coffin in *Interview With the Vampire*

Tim Robbins, on falling in love at first sight: 'It was like death – except in a good way.'

> From *I.Q.*

'It's like we're on two different channels now. I'm CNN, she's the Home Shopping Network.'

> Nicolas Cage on the estrangement from his wife (Rosie Perez) after their win of $2m in the New York lottery. From *It Could Happen to You*

'I'm pregnant!'

> Arnold Schwarzenegger in *Junior*

'My body! My choice!'

> A pregnant Arnold Schwarzenegger in *Junior*

'Do I have a soul? Or did you leave that bit out?'

> Robert De Niro as The Creature in *Mary Shelley's Frankenstein*

'Now my life is as good as an Abba song; as good as "Dancing Queen".'

> Toni Collette in *Muriel's Wedding*

'Why are you wearing a neck tie? You're not in trouble with the police again?'

> Jessica Tandy to Paul Newman in *Nobody's Fool*

'Look at me, Faith. I married a liar. Why? Because I married a man.'

> Bonnie Hunt in *Only You*

'Oh, I'm sorry. Did I break your concentration?'

> Samuel L. Jackson to Frank Whaley after blowing his friend Roger to kingdom come in *Pulp Fiction*

Arnold Schwarzenegger, in Junior

'Butch? Will you give me oral pleasure?'

> Maria de Medeiros to Bruce Willis in *Pulp Fiction*

'Pretty please, with sugar on top – clean the fucking car.'

> Harvey Keitel cordially barking orders to John Travolta in *Pulp Fiction*

Female gunslinger: 'I'm gonna kill you if I have to ride all the way to hell to do it.' Male gunslinger: 'Do you have a problem with me?'

> Sharon Stone and Gene Hackman in *The Quick and the Dead*

'My own stools, sir, are gigantic, and have no more odour than a hot biscuit.'

> Anthony Hopkins as vegetarian fanatic Dr John Harvey Kellogg in *The Road to Wellville*

'It's the living who have to resurrect themselves, not the dead.'

> Recent widower Albert Finney in *The Run of the Country*

'Pack your bags, we're going on a guilt trip.'

> Charlie Sheen in *Terminal Velocity*

'Harvard doesn't have any standards left. They let in anybody who's bright.'

> Harvard student Patrick Dempsey in *With Honors*

Patrick Dempsey, owner of a broken-down van, to Joe Pesci: 'You a mechanic?' Pesci: 'No, I'm a Zen Buddhist. But that's close enough.'

> From *With Honors*

The transforming kiss: Brendan Fraser and Moira Kelly in With Honors

Moira Kelly, as she is kissed by room-mate Brendan Fraser: 'What are you doing?' Fraser: 'I'm ending our friendship.'

From *With Honors*

'Perfection is my speciality.'

Ian Williams in Peter Mackenzie Litten's *To Die For*

'Never apologise for speaking the truth.'

Ian Williams in Peter Mackenzie Litten's *To Die For*

'For me, life was a series of illusions that only science could strip away.'

Hugh O'Conor, mild-mannered serial killer, in *The Young Poisoner's Handbook*

The gospel according to *Forrest Gump* (courtesy of Tom Hanks):

'I'm not a smart man. But I know what love is.'

'That's all I have to say about that.'

'Stupid is as stupid does.'

'Life is like a box of chocolates. You never know what you're gonna get.'

Say that again:

Victoria Hass in *Attack of the 50 Foot Woman*: 'I'd like to buy a vowel.'

Billy Crystal in *City Slickers II: The Legend of Curly's Gold*: 'Can I buy a vowel?'

Danny DeVito in *Renaissance Man*: 'Can I buy a vowel?'

Scenes from Whit Stillman's *Barcelona*:

Ted: 'Spanish girls tend to be really promiscuous.' Fred: 'You're such a prig.' Ted: 'I wasn't using the word "promiscuous" pejoratively. It's just a fact.' Fred: 'I wasn't using "prig" pejoratively.'

Taylor Nichols and Chris Eigeman in Whit Stillman's *Barcelona*

Ted to date: 'You know how at parties everyone ends up talking about marketing ..?' Date confused): 'No ...'

Taylor Nichols in *Barcelona*

Challenged that America is more violent than other nations, Fred defends his country: 'Shooting doesn't mean Americans are more violent than other people. We're just better shots.'

Chris Eigeman in *Barcelona*

Fred to Ted: 'Maybe you can clarify something for me ... This thing about sub-text. Plays, novels, songs. They all have a sub-text, which I take to mean a hidden message or import of some kind. So sub-text we know. But what do you call the message or meaning that's right there on the surface, completely open and obvious? They never talk about that. What do you call what's *above* the sub-text?' Ted, patronisingly: 'The text.'

From *Barcelona*

Marta, comforting a self-deprecatory Fred: 'You seem very intelligent for an American.'

Mira Sorvino in *Barcelona*

Unintentional bon mots: *Taylor Nichols, Tushka Bergen, Chris Eigeman and Mira Sorvino promoting the sub-text in Whit Stillman's* Barcelona

Say that again (continued):

'I told you you been watching too much of that Oprah shit.'

Wesley Snipes to Malcolm-Jamal Warner in *Drop Zone*

William Hootkins: 'What is this? Fucking Oprah Winfrey?' Brad Dourif: 'No. This is top quality. Geraldo.'

From *Death Machine*

Scene from a Hal Hartley movie:

Girl: 'Will you make love to me?'
Man: 'When?'
Girl: 'After your bath.'
Man: 'Have you ever had sex before?'
Girl: 'No.'
Man: 'How can you be a nympho-maniac if you've never had sex?'
Girl: 'I'm choosy.'
Man: 'I need a shave.'

Isabelle Huppert and Martin Donovan in Hal Hartley's *Amateur*

The Ten Most Promising Faces of 1995

James Cameron-Wilson

Tim Allen

While displaying a certain arrogance as the man about the toolshed in ABC TV's *Home Improvement*, Tim Allen's character pinpoints the vanity of Everyman. Boastful he may be, but he's also vulnerable, embarrassed and, well, just lovable. The sitcom's phenomenal success in the States is not just due to its emotional accessibility, but to the warm glow of recognition it casts. With it, we can laugh at ourselves. Aw shucks, aren't we ridiculous?

TV stars come and go, yet when Allen made his film debut in Disney's modest Christmas comedy *The Santa Clause*, it was the surprise hit of the season. Actually, it was *the* hit of the season. With a domestic gross of $144.8m, the movie knocked *Interview With the Vampire*, *Dumb and Dumber*, *Pulp Fiction*, *Star Trek: Generations* and *Junior* into a cocked hat. Now Allen has been offered $7 million to star in Island Pictures' comedy *Friend of the Family*.

Born on 13 June 1953 in Denver, Allen spent two and a half years in prison on a charge of selling cocaine. Inside, he dreamed of a better life and shortly after his release was doing voice-overs on commercials. This led to work in comedy clubs, TV specials and then *Home Improvement*.

As Tim Taylor, the strutting father of three sons who hosts his own cable show, *Tool Time*, Allen became a household name in America. He also penned a bestselling autobiography, *Don't Stand Too Close to a Naked Man*, and then played Scott Calvin, the reluctant Father Christmas in *The Santa Clause*.

He also teamed up with Tom Hanks to supply the vocal talents for Disney's digitally animated *Toy Story*.

Ellen DeGeneres

Exuding a goofy and irresistible charm, Ellen DeGeneres has become the most successful female comic on American TV since Roseanne. So successful, in fact, that she's had to move address three times and admits to changing her telephone number every four weeks. Now Hollywood is after her wacky, fresh-faced talent, with Touchstone Pictures reportedly paying her $2.2 million to star in *Mr Wrong*.

Tim Allen in his TV incarnation of Tim Taylor

Ellen DeGeneres

Born on 1 January 1958 in New Orleans, Ellen was raised a Christian Scientist and taught to respect other people's feelings. She still feels that way and goes to great lengths to temper her comedy with altruism – not an easy trick at the best of times. But that is her appeal: to shed light on life's absurdities without putting the boot in. Hers is the ultimate feel-good humour.

Graduating from stand-up comedy in New Orleans to winner of Showtime's 'Funniest Person in America' award of 1982, Ellen has paid her debt on the comedy circuit. But it was her sitcom on ABC TV, *These Friends of Mine*, that made her a national star. Virtually playing an extension of herself, she was a girl called Ellen who worked in a book shop – Buy The Book – while jockeying life's hiccups. When, in its second season, the show's title was changed to just plain *Ellen*, the ratings soared and its heroine became the It Girl of American TV.

Film-wise, DeGeneres made a memorable appearance in the compilation movie *Wisecracks* (1992), alongside Whoopi Goldberg, and had a small role in the ill-fated *Coneheads* (1993). Since *Ellen* she has been inundated with movie offers, opting for the lucrative overture from Touchstone. In *Mr Wrong* she plays a TV talk-show producer who's pressurised into a relationship with the boyfriend from hell, played by Bill Pullman. The comedienne notes, 'I didn't want to push too far. I don't think too many people would run out to see me play a nun.' She's also lined up for Disney's *Ball and Chain* and has written a book for Bantam, comprising a selection of comic musings.

Cameron Diaz

It was the entrance that would-be screen sirens dream of. Right up there with Rebecca De Mornay sauntering into Tom Cruise's living room in *Risky Business* and Bo Derek slinking out of the ocean in *10*. And, luckily for Cameron Diaz, her arrival was ogled by millions.

Strolling out of the rain and into Jim Carrey's libido, she was the personification of lust on legs. Sporting a dress the size of a handkerchief and a stare that could melt steel, Diaz dazzled – and then some. To paraphrase Katharine Hepburn's remark about Astaire and Rogers, she gave Carrey sex appeal and he gave her the giggles.

The film was *The Mask* and its worldwide gross of over $300 million cemented the actress's celebrity. Born 22 years ago in Long Beach, California, Cameron started modelling at sixteen and commuted between Paris and Los Angeles, appearing in commercials and on the cover of such magazines as *Seventeen* and *Spanish Vogue*.

Flirting with the idea of acting, she was offered the role of Brandon Lee's squeeze in *The Crow*, but changed her mind when she looked at the script. She liked what she read in *The Mask*, but had no idea she was up for the lead or that the film was an A-feature. 'The studio wanted a woman with a name that would sell overseas,' she insists. 'I went

Cameron Diaz

Reece Dinsdale

back to read with Carrey every day for twelve days. I was getting an ulcer.'

She also got the part, took emergency acting lessons and proved she could hold the screen. Refusing to take the next bimbo that came along, she tried for a role in *Mortal Kombat,* but lost it when she broke her hand on the trainer's head at the audition. She will, however, be seen in *Feeling Minnesota,* opposite Keanu Reeves, and in *Head Above Water,* with Harvey Keitel.

Reece Dinsdale

While cited as a newcomer by the British cinema press, Reece Dinsdale has actually been around for fifteen years. He was even the star of one of the most controversial British TV films ever made, *Threads,* which received a theatrical release in the States in 1984. Dinsdale himself noted, 'I'd been waiting fifteen years to break into films and I wasn't going to let this part get away.'

The part he's referring to is John, an undercover cop who infiltrates an organised gang of football hooligans. The film is *i.d.,* a BBC co-production that tackles the subject of lager culture with uncompromising brutality. Although superbly realised by the actor-turned-director Philip Davis, and insightfully scripted by Vincent O'Connell, *i.d.* largely owes its gripping intensity to Dinsdale's performance. Subtly shifting from committed law enforcer into the animal he's impersonating,

Dinsdale left no hair on the neck unpricked. Not a pretty sight.

'I believe we are all capable of this type of violence, and if we taste it we can get to like it,' he said. 'We all have anger inside us and to play John I had to go to those places and dig deep. It was upsetting; at times, very, very upsetting.'

For now Dinsdale will have to cope with the inevitable identification that the role of the demented copper will bring. Yet he took the part to break the stranglehold of typecasting.

'A lot of other people wanted the part,' he noted, 'but I was in danger of being typecast as an actor who specialised in light roles. So when I auditioned I went a bit mad.'

The 'light' roles included regular spots on the TV sitcoms *Home to Roost* and *Haggard,* as well as leading parts in the series *Full Stretch* and *Take Me Home.*

The son of a West Yorkshire miner, Reece was born 35 years ago and studied acting at the Guildhall. Although there have been stretches of unemployment, he has an impressive body of stage work behind him (the West Yorkshire Playhouse, the Royal Court, the National), had a supporting role in the Alan Bennett film *A Private Function* and secured good parts in the TV movie *Winter Flight* and the Anglo-Canadian-Russian mini-series *Young Catherine.*

Joanne Going

By now we should be sick and tired of Joanne Going. But the film that should've launched this stunningly beautiful actress into the Hollywood stratosphere sank – not without trace, but with its bows severely waterlogged.

A veteran of the daytime soaps *Search for Tomorrow* and *Another World,* Going made her feature film debut as Josie, the strong-willed, progressive woman who stole the heart of Wyatt Earp. In Lawrence Kasdan's film of the same

Joanne Going as Josie Marcus in Wyatt Earp

Ian Hart

name, budgeted at a colossal $60 million, Going was in strong company for a first-timer. Kevin Costner, Dennis Quaid, Gene Hackman, Mark Harmon, Michael Madsen and Isabella Rossellini are not your customary colleagues for a debut outing.

The film itself – part folly, part masterpiece – came up against the knives of too many critics to break the box-office stranglehold of its thematic competitor, *Tombstone*. And Costner, once everybody's darling, was finding the top rungs of the Hollywood ladder becoming ever more slippery. *Wyatt Earp* was not a bad film; it just rode into town at the wrong time.

Masterfully photographed by Owen Roizman and played with conviction by a legendary cast, the Western was too long for most backsides and Costner's blank canvas acting had lost its allure. Furthermore, the latter had become a victim of his own success and was taking up too many column inches in

the tabloids to retain his credibility. Nevertheless, *Wyatt Earp* deserved more attention than it received and will undoubtedly look better after the years have passed it by. Joanne Going, as the pioneering woman who stuck by Wyatt's side, was one of its better points. Displaying a classical beauty and the talent to match, Going held her own in among the grit and testosterone.

Born in Washington DC and raised in Newport, Rhode Island, Going contracted the acting bug in high school and enrolled at the American Academy of Dramatic Art. Besides her daytime TV service, she starred opposite Ben Cross in NBC's gruesome series *Dark Shadows*, as the governess Victoria Winters. Equally at home on stage, she has appeared in *Suddenly, Last Summer* and, on Broadway, in *Flowering Peach*.

Most recently she starred in the critically-acclaimed Western mini-series *Children of the Dust*, playing a white girl in love with a Cheyenne Indian.

Next, she joined the all-star cast of Oliver Stone's *Nixon*.

Ian Hart

Having stolen the notices for his sly impersonation of John Lennon in *Backbeat*, Ian Hart went on to create a totally different character in his next film, *Clockwork Mice*. A gently engaging dramatic comedy, the latter blended elements of *To Sir With Love* with an Ealingesque tint and sported an array of priceless supporting performances. Hart was Steve Drake, a young teacher at a loss as to how to control the troubled souls under his tutelage. Shyly courted by a female colleague, he was further torn between the mandates of duty and romance.

Hart, who previously played John Lennon in the low-budget *The Hours and Times* in 1992, is fast emerging as one of the most in-demand of British actors. Born on 8 October 1964 in Liverpool, he was a regular face at the Liverpool Playhouse, appeared in the films *Zip* and *No Surrender* and popped up in such TV fare as *The Monocled Mutineer*, *Medics* and the TV movie *Chain*. More recently he played Dave Carr, the Liverpudlian fighting fascism in the Spanish Civil War in Ken Loach's ambitious, critically-acclaimed *Land and Freedom*. Again drawing on his skill for detailed, subtle characterisation, Hart reaped ecstatic reviews.

Next he played a shell-shocked Welsh native in Chris Monger's eccentric comedy *The Englishman Who Went Up a Hill, but Came Down a Mountain*, journeyed to Dublin to star in Thaddeus O'Sullivan's *All Our Fault*, joined Martin Donovan and Joely Richardson in Angela Pope's *The Hollow Reed* and co-starred alongside Liam Neeson and Julia Roberts in Neil Jordan's *Michael Collins*. That's busy.

Tina Majorina

Suddenly they seemed to be everywhere. There was Fairuza Balk, Thora Birch, Anna Chlumsky, Kirsten Dunst, Eliza Dushku, Gaby Hoffman, Christina Ricci, Mara Wilson ... Some were cute, others funny, all precocious. But of the sum total of mushrooming Shirley Temple wannabes, only Tina Majorino displayed a talent that looked set to last. There was something effortless, natural, even – dare I say it – intelligent about her relationship with the camera. In the space of six months little Miss Majorino popped up in three major motion pictures and distinguished herself against some fierce competition.

In *When a Man Loves a Woman* she played the older daughter of Meg Ryan and Andy Garcia, struggling to comprehend her parents' deteriorating marriage. Combining a wisdom beyond her years, Majorino, at the age of nine, gave the most natural, multifold performance of a child actress since Jodie Foster started stealing notices in 1972.

In *Corrina, Corrina* she was the linchpin in the romantic liaison of Ray Liotta and Whoopi Goldberg, a widower and his black maid. Struck dumb by the trauma of her mother's death, Majorino's Molly Singer was required to evolve through a series of emotional tangents as the love and understanding of Corrina (Goldberg) coaxed her out of her shell. Again, Majorino gave a performance of remarkable complexity and spontaneity.

She had less to do in *Andre*, and was frequently upstaged by the clowning seal of the title, but she did have the (human) lead and made the most of her opportunities. Furthermore, she was a good deal more convincing than some of the stereotypical supporting characters.

Born in 1985 in Westlake, California, Tina Majorino started out performing in commercials before landing the regular role of Sophie in ABC TV's *Camp Wilder* – at the age of seven. Making her film debut in *When a Man Loves a Woman*, she quickly established her staying power. More recently, she has starred opposite Kevin Costner and Jeanne Tripplehorn in *Waterworld* which, at a reported budget of $200m, has the distinction of being the most expensive film ever made.

Julia Ormond

In 1993 Julia Ormond made her big screen debut in Peter Greenaway's *The Baby of Macon*. A brave, intelligent and deeply disturbing drama, the film worked on a multitude of levels, caressing the eye, provoking the mind and punishing the emotions. Ormond, top-billed as an eighteenth-century virgin who claims to have experienced an immaculate conception, gave a display of surprising intensity and sexuality. Romping naked with her unknown co-star Ralph Fiennes, the actress made it

abundantly clear that she was cut from star material. However, the critics reacted badly to the film and Ormond was put on hold.

Two years later she was to be found

Moppet of the year: Tina Majorino as she looked in Andre

Julia Ormond as Guinevere with Richard Gere as Lancelot in First Knight

in the embrace of such American icons as Brad Pitt, Richard Gere and Harrison Ford – Hollywood was all over her. As I write, the box-office performance of *First Knight* and *Sabrina* has yet to be recorded, but *Legends of the Fall*, in which she played the innocent downfall of three hormonally-enhanced brothers, was a certified hit. Steven Spielberg pronounced her 'the new Audrey Hepburn' and the way things are going she is shaping up as our hottest female export since Emma Thompson.

Born in 1965, Julia Ormond studied at the Webber Douglas Academy of Dramatic Art and was soon making a name for herself on the British stage. In 1989 she was voted most promising newcomer by London's theatre critics,

Linus Roache in Priest, *a film that ruffled feathers in the States*

and she quickly moved on to the small screen. She was a junkie in Channel Four's multi-award-winning *Traffik*, was nominated for a Canadian Gemini for the title role in *Young Catherine* (supported by Vanessa Redgrave, Christopher Plummer and Maximilian Schell) and won much praise as Stalin's anguished wife in the Emmy- and Golden Globe-winning *Stalin*, with Robert Duvall.

Following her starring role in *The Baby of Macon*, she made a token appearance in a Europudding – as the wife of *Nostradamus* – and then headed west. TriStar, the production company financing *Legends of the Fall*, was not thrilled with the idea of an unknown leading lady for such an epic, but director Edward Zwick persevered. It helped that the film's star, Brad Pitt, was impressed, and rumours of an on-set romance quickly circulated. Refusing

to comment, Pitt did allow that, 'Julia has this kind of timeless class I haven't seen anywhere else.'

Back in London, Julia found herself in the arms of Tim Roth, an actor who – if not as hot as Pitt or Gere – was earning his own reams of media coverage. The occasion was *Captives*, a well-meaning drama which begged us to believe that a woman as attractive as Julia Ormond would risk her life and career for a man like Roth, a convict she hardly knew. Still, the auspicious timing of the film's release – the same day as *Legends* in London – helped fuel the interest surrounding our new Audrey.

Next, she played Guinevere to Richard Gere's Lancelot and Sean Connery's King Arthur in *First Knight*, a $45 million epic from Jerry Zucker, director of *Ghost*. Then, to complete the Hollywood hat-trick, she landed the sought-after title role in *Sabrina*. A high-profile remake of Billy Wilder's 1954 romantic comedy – which starred Humphrey Bogart, William Holden and, yes, Audrey Hepburn – *Sabrina* will rise or fall on the calibre of its stars' charisma. While Harrison Ford, a consummate thinking woman's action man, proved his comedy smarts in *Working Girl*, Ormond is untried territory. Sexy, yes. Talented, definitely. But funny? By the time you read this the truth will be out.

Linus Roache

Thirty years ago, a role like the haunted, righteous, homosexual Father Greg in *Priest* would have made Linus Roache an overnight star. Today, things are rather more tenuous. Nevertheless, the 31-year-old Mancunian actor has shown that he's got what it takes and, as the star of one of the best British films of the year, he ought to be heading in an upward direction, professionally speaking.

Articulate, challenging and incredibly moving, *Priest*, by rights, should have become *The Crying Game* of 1995. Yet devoid of a feel-good patina, pretty costumes or an American co-star (or any star, for that matter), the film was hardly box-office candy. Then again, it was released – coincidentally – at a time when homosexuality in the clergy was big news. Such God-given publicity cannot be bought, so one can only presume that the film's lacklustre performance in the UK was due to dire mismanagement on the part of the distributor. The critics, at least, gave *Priest* a hearty welcome.

The son of the actors Anna Cropper and William Roache – the latter best known as Ken Barlow in *Coronation Street* – Linus debuted as the son of Barlow at the age of eleven. He was also a kid with the bubonic plague on the BBC's *The Onedin Line* and had fleeting roles in the films *Link* and *No Surrender* (alongside fellow newcomer Ian Hart).

On stage, Roache acted at the Manchester Royal Exchange, the Royal National Theatre and RSC, and secured the title role in the BBC's Omnibus feature *Vincent Van Gogh*. Also for the Beeb he played Tom in *Keeping Tom Nice* and starred as the vicious bent cop in the controversial police drama *Black and Blue*. He then played Bob Longman in the BBC's ambitious ten-part drama series *Seaforth*.

As Father Greg, the Catholic priest confronting his own sexual demons, Roache summoned up a turmoil and intensity that made the man's plight virtually unbearable. Indeed, Father Greg was all of a hypocrite, angel, warrior, victim and sexual being, and Roache conveyed him as a man we could believe in and feel for.

Next, he landed the starring role in Channel 4 Film's adaptation of Thomas Hardy's title, *The Woodlanders*.

Will Smith

Will Smith got the best of both worlds. In *Six Degrees of Separation*, he showed he could act the socks off his co-stars (Stockard Channing, Donald Sutherland, Sir Ian McKellen, no less). And in *Bad Boys* he exhibited the cool and confidence of a movie star. The first film, while soundly praised by the critics, was little seen in farming communities round Iowa. The second, however, boasted the biggest opening dollar gross of the first five months of 1995.

Smith, who made his name as the streetwise kid in NBC TV's sitcom *The Fresh Prince of Bel Air*, should soon be huge. Not only is he a very fine actor with a great physique, he's handsome and charismatic to boot. He's got *star* power. And that's just not fair in one body. He's also got the critics on his side

The versatile Will Smith

and *Bad Boys* is bound to reap a sequel, if not a series. If his luck holds out, Will Smith will be the next Denzel Washington.

Unlike Denzel, though, Smith was born in 1969, fifteen years later than his idol and mentor. That means he's got time to flourish – and then some.

A native of West Philadelphia, Smith entered showbusiness early, performing rap at parties at the age of twelve. At seventeen he formed the hip-hop act DJ Jazzy Jeff & The Fresh Prince – with Jeff Townes – and was an instant success. To date, Will and Jeff have produced five rap albums, all of which have gone either gold or platinum. Furthermore, their 1988 hit single 'Parents Just Don't Understand' won the Grammy for best rap performance, as did their 1989 single 'Summertime'.

Smith recreated his rap persona on the sitcom *The Fresh Prince of Bel Air*, then made his film debut in *Where the Day Takes You*, about a group of homeless teenagers. He then played the boyfriend of Whoopi Goldberg's daughter (Nia Long) in the hit comedy *Made in America*. However, securing the central role in *Six Degrees of Separation* was not so easy.

The part, that of a con artist who convinces a wealthy Manhattan couple that he is the son of Sidney Poitier, demanded grace and charisma. Smith, a rap and sitcom star, seemed totally wrong.

'They didn't think I could do it,' he allows. 'They thought I was the *worst* choice you could have for the role. But that gave me the strength and energy to win the part.' As one watches him seduce Stockard Channing and Donald Sutherland with his radical theories on *Catcher on the Rye*, it's hard to imagine any other actor who could've been as perfect.

Then, to illustrate his versatility, he took the role of the rich, womanising and heroic cop in *Bad Boys*. The ease with which he slipped into the part belied his talent. This guy looked as if he'd been playing fearless law enforcers all his life. But rewind to *Six Degrees of Separation* to witness the confused mix of vulnerability and intellectual conceit that he brought to the role and one begins to realise what a skilful actor Will Smith really is.

Next, he will star in the big-budget *Independence Day* with Bill Pullman.

Film World Diary

James Cameron-Wilson

July 1994

Liam Neeson and **Natasha Richardson** tie the knot in New York. **Steven Spielberg**, **Vanessa Redgrave**, **Mia Farrow** and **Emma Thompson** look on ★ **Gary Oldman** turns down the role of the British heavy in *Under Siege II*, so Warner Brothers are now talking to **Julian Sands** and **Jeff Goldblum**. Oldman is also being sought for the villain in *Waterworld* ★ **Hugh Grant** signs a two-year, first-look agreement with Castle Rock Entertainment, the company that produced *City Slickers* and *A Few Good Men*. Per the contract, the English actor will develop films in which he will star and/or produce ★ Following DNA tests, **Sylvester Stallone** discovers that he is not the father of Savannah Rodin, daughter of his new girlfriend Janice Dickinson. Convinced of his paternity, the actor had set up a $1 million trust fund for the five-month-old ★ **Jeremy Irons** agrees to play the villain in *Die Hard With a Vengeance* – after **David Thewlis** turns the part down ★ **James Caan** is sued by his ex-girlfriend Leesa Roland for assault ★ *The Lion King* passes the $150m mark in the US – in under five weeks ★ **Michael Douglas** jumps ship on the $70m pirate epic *Cutthroat Island*, leaving co-star **Geena Davis** high and dry ★ Following **Michael Keaton**'s defection as the Caped Crusader in *Batman Forever*, **Rene Russo** opts out of the female lead to star opposite **Dustin Hoffman** in *Outbreak* ★ **Jodie Foster** drops out of **Ridley Scott**'s *Crisis in the Hot Zone*, leaving **Robert Redford** without a leading lady. **Robin Wright** is approached ★ **Gary Oldman** turns down the heavy in *Waterworld* and is replaced by **Dennis Hopper** ★ **Oliver Stone** opts out of directing *Noriega*, in which **Al Pacino** was due to play the pizza-faced dictator – and then ditches *Evita* (for a second time) ★ **Eddie Murphy** leaves the giant ICM agency ★ **Liam Neeson** is approached by Carolco to play the male lead in *Cutthroat Island*. He says 'no' ★ **Gene Kelly**, 81, is hospitalised following a mild stroke ★ New Line pays scriptwriter **Shane Black** (*Lethal Weapon*, *Last Action Hero*) a record $4 million for his screenplay *The Long Kiss Good Night* ★ **James Caan** voluntarily admits himself into a secret clinic for drug addiction ★ **Robin Wright** turns down the female lead in *Batman Forever*, putting **Nicole Kidman** in the line of fire ★ **Robin Wright** also turns down the female lead in *Crisis in the Hot Zone*. Twentieth Century-Fox is now talking to **Holly Hunter** and **Susan Sarandon** ★ Both **Daniel Day-Lewis** and **Ralph Fiennes** turn down the offer of replacing **Michael Douglas** in *Cutthroat Island*, so **Jeff Bridges** is approached ★ **Nicole Kidman** accepts the female lead in *Batman Forever* ★ *Speed* grosses $100m in the US – in seven weeks ★ *Forrest Gump* grosses $100m Stateside – in eighteen days ★ *The Lion King* grosses $207,155,000 in the US – in just 30 days.

August 1994

Forrest Gump passes the $150m mark in the US ★ **Sharon Stone** passes on

Crisis in the Hot Zone and signs on to star opposite **Robert De Niro** in *Casino* ★ **Michelle Pfeiffer** is the proud mama of a bouncing baby boy – John Henry Kelley ★ **Gary Oldman**, 36, and **Isabella Rossellini**, 42, announce their engagement ★ **Mickey Rourke** is arraigned in a Los Angeles court for 'manhandling' his wife, **Carre Otis**. According to a prosecutor, the star 'slapped her, knocked her down and kicked her' ★ **Daryl Hannah** and **John F. Kennedy Jr** finally split up after persistent rumours of imminent marriage ★ **Meryl Streep** passes on *Crisis in the Hot Zone* and signs on to star opposite **Clint Eastwood** in *The Bridges of Madison County* ★ **Susan Sarandon**, 47, and **Tim Robbins**, 35, announce plans to marry at Christmas – much to the delight of their three children ★ **Peter Cushing**, 81, dies of cancer in Canterbury ★ *True Lies* grosses $100m in the US. **Arnie** is back ★ **Robert Redford** leaves the cast of *Crisis in the Hot Zone* ★ After **Jeff Bridges** turns down the male lead in Carolco's *Cutthroat Island*, **Gabriel Byrne** is pursued ★ **Jack Nicholson**, 56, is the proud father of a baby girl, courtesy of former waitress Jennine Gourin, 21 ★ *Forrest Gump* grosses $200m in the US – in 46 days ★ Top restaurants in London impose a ban on **Michael Winner** following a series of contemptuous restaurant reviews by the filmmaker in *The Sunday Times* ★ After **Robin Wright** turns down the lead in *Congo*, Paramount approaches **Julianne Moore**. However, Ms Moore appears more interested in starring opposite **Hugh Grant** in *Nine Months*. Now Paramount is talking to **Penelope Ann Miller** ★ **Luke Perry** and his wife Minnie are expecting ★ **Warren Beatty** and **Annette Bening** announce the birth of a baby boy ★ **Jeffrey Katzenberg**, chairman of Walt Disney Studios, hands in his notice. **Joe Roth** takes over his desk ★ **Arnold Schwarzenegger** receives death threats thanks to the anti-Arabic content of *True Lies* ★ **Lindsay Anderson**, 71, dies of a heart attack in the south of France.

September 1994

Kim Basinger, who bought the Georgia town of Braselton back in 1989, auctions the local bank to help pay her debts ★ **O.J. Simpson** is found innocent of the murder of his ex-wife Nicole and her companion Ronald Goldman in two 'test trials'. A third mock jury, assembled by the Los Angeles District Attorney's office, said they would not convict the star if he faced the death penalty ★ In under ten weeks, *The Lion King* grosses $260m in the US, making it the sixth biggest money-making film of all time ★ At the eleventh hour **Matthew Modine** agrees to play the male lead – opposite **Geena Davis** – in Carolco's $70 million pirate epic *Cutthroat Island* – after **Michael Douglas**, **Liam Neeson**, **Daniel Day-Lewis**, **Ralph Fiennes**, **Jeff Bridges** and **Gabriel Byrne** turned it down ★ After **Robin Wright**, **Julianne Moore** and **Penelope Ann Miller** decline the female lead in *Congo* – based on Michael Crichton's

Kim Basinger: out to auction and expecting an investment

mega-selling novel – the role lands in the lap of TV actress **Laura Linney** ★ **Terence Young**, 79, director of *Dr No*, *From Russia With Love*, *Goldfinger* and *Thunderball*, dies of a heart attack in Cannes, France ★ *The Mask* passes the $100m mark in the US ★ **Johnny Depp** is in court – for trashing his room at New York's Mark Hotel. The actor vandalised a table and chair, a glass-topped coffee table and seventeenth-century picture frames holding valuable prints ★ The debonair character actor **Patrick O'Neal**, 66, dies from respiratory failure in Los Angeles ★ **Jessica Tandy**, 85, dies of ovarian cancer at her Connecticut home ★ **Doug McHenry**, director and producer of *Jason's Lyric*, buys advertising slots on

Sharon Stone: choosing Scorsese, dropping Diabolique, *changing her mind*

a number of black radio stations to protest the cuts inflicted on his film's love scenes. 'In this country,' he complained, 'there seems to be greater licence for violence than for lovemaking – particularly when it comes to African-Americans' ★ **Mickey Rourke** pleads not guilty to assaulting his wife **Carre Otis** ★ According to reports in the Hong Kong press, production on **Zhang Yimou**'s latest film, *Shanghai Triad*, a big-budget Franco-Chinese co-production, has been suspended by China's Ministry of Radio, Film and Television. Furthermore, Zhang has been temporarily forbidden to work on any other international co-productions and has been banned from visiting foreign film festivals – as has his lover and leading lady **Gong Li** ★ Bodyguard Pierre DeJean, aka Patrick Doe, claims he was forced to have sex with actress-model **Anna Nicole Smith**, and was fired when he refused to continue physical relations. Ms Smith alleges that DeJean assaulted her ★ **Johnny Depp** agrees to pay $9,767 for the damage he caused in his New York hotel room. The judge, presiding at the Manhattan Criminal Court, said he would consider dropping charges of 'felony criminal mischief' if Depp kept out of trouble for six months ★ A Los Angeles judge orders the Samuel Goldwyn Co. to cough up $3.3 million plus legal costs to Virgin Vision. Apparently, Samuel Goldwyn

forgot to credit the British video company on foreign copies of *sex, lies and videotape* ★ *Forrest Gump* clocks up $250m in the US, making it Paramount's highest-grossing domestic film of all time ★ *The Lion King* grosses $350m worldwide ★ After **Julia Roberts**, **Winona Ryder** and **Robin Wright** turn down the female lead in *Sabrina* – opposite **Harrison Ford** – Paramount zeros in on **Juliette Binoche** and the British actress **Julia Ormond**. The original 1954 film starred **Humphrey Bogart** and **Audrey Hepburn** ★ *Maverick* grosses $100m Stateside ★ *The Flintstones* grosses $300m worldwide.

October 1994

Steven Seagal and **Kelly LeBrock** split after seven years of marriage ★ An investment group led by filmmaking siblings **Ridley** and **Tony Scott** forks out over $10m to buy Shepperton Studios ★ **Whoopi Goldberg** marries union organiser Lyle Trachtenberg ★ **Robert Redford**, following his departure from **Ridley Scott**'s *Crisis in the Hot Zone*, drops out of **Rob Reiner**'s *The American President*. Apparently, Redford objected to the political edge that Reiner intended to give the film. Leading lady **Emma Thompson** is left high and dry ★ The widow of the actor **Roy Kinnear**, who died while performing a horse stunt on *The Return of the Musketeers* six years ago, receives damages of £650,000 plus costs estimated at £350,000 ★ **Sharon Stone** ducks out of *Diabolique* after Warner Brothers refuses to pay her her $5 million fee. They would only go so far as $4m ★ In a Hollywood first, **John Travolta** is promised $750,000 if he gets an Oscar nomination for *Pulp Fiction* and $1.5m if he wins. And this from MGM, the company making his next film *Get Shorty* ★ Following his affair with a Hawaiian hula dancer while filming *Waterworld*, **Kevin Costner** separates from his wife Cindy. Like *Waterworld* needed any more negative publicity ★ **Melissa Gilbert** calls off her marriage to **Bruce Boxleitner** – for the second time ★ **Michael Douglas** replaces **Robert Redford** as Warner's *The American President*. The company is now talking to **Annette Bening** to substitute **Emma Thompson** ★ *Four*

Weddings and a Funeral grosses $200m worldwide ★ The Russian filmmaker and actor **Sergei Bondarchuk**, 74, dies in Moscow. As a director, he will be best remembered for his *War and Peace* and *Waterloo* ★ **Sharon Stone** seems to have had a change of heart about *not* starring in *Diabolique* for Warner. Will she now accept their paltry offer of $4m for the film? ★ **Burt Lancaster**, 80, dies of a heart attack in Century City ★ *Philadelphia* grosses $200m worldwide ★ **Raul Julia**, 54, dies of a stroke on Long Island ★ **Mildred Natwick**, 89, dies in Manhattan ★ **Burt Reynolds** announces that he's $11.8 million in debt and can no longer afford the $11,000-a-month alimony fees for ex-wife **Loni Anderson**. Besides, he argues, Loni is making a small fortune from her TV work ★ *Natural Born Killers* is banned in Britain.

November 1994

Two months after the halt of production, **Zhang Yimou**'s *Shanghai Triad* resumes filming, now that the picture has been classified as a solely Chinese feature. However, Zhang is still prohibited from making foreign-financed pictures ★ *The Lion King* grosses $450m worldwide ★ **Mickey Rourke** is thrown out of **Donald Trump**'s Plaza Hotel in New York after causing $20,000 worth of damage to his room ★ **Sidney Poitier**, 67, is appointed to the board of the Walt Disney Company, replacing the president Frank G. Wells, who died in April ★ *The Specialist* grosses $110m worldwide ★ **Richard Gere**, 45, and **Cindy Crawford**, 28, announce their separation after three years of marriage and endless negative speculation in the press ★ **Lionel Stander**, 86, the cigar-chomping, gravel-voiced character actor, dies of lung cancer in Brentwood, California. He was probably best known as the chauffeur Max in TV's *Hart to Hart* ★ **Roseanne** and **Tom Arnold** are officially divorced ★ In South Kensington, London, four girls threaten **Elizabeth Hurley** with a knife and steal £10 from her ★ **Prince Charles** negotiates with **Michael Eisner**, chairman of Walt Disney, to turn a story he wrote as a young man – *The Legend of Lochnagar* – into an animated video ★ **Sharon Stone** *will* star in *Diabolique* after all – and will get $6 million for her trouble. Warner Brothers originally refused to pay the actress more than $4m, but then Morgan Creek took over the project and reached into their pockets ★ English director **Tony Scott**, 50, and actress **Donna Wilson**, 29, say 'I do' ★ **Holly Hunter** is engaged to the Oscar-winning cinematographer **Janusz Kaminsky** ★ **Sylvester Stallone** bails out of **Joel Silver**'s big-budget actioner *Dead Reckoning*, which was previously deserted by **Jodie Foster**, **Geena Davis** and **Steven Seagal**. This is a shame, as Warner paid scenarist **Christine Roum** $1 million for her script which originally featured a female protagonist ★ *True Lies* grosses over $115m outside of the US.

December 1994

When a Man Loves a Woman grosses $100m worldwide ★ **Dudley Moore** and his fourth wife, **Nicole Rothschild**, are expecting ★ **Jean-Claude Van Damme** leaves his fourth wife, Darcy, after nine months of marriage. He moves back in with his third wife, Gladys ★ After twelve years together, **Ryan O'Neal** and **Farrah Fawcett** call it a day – reportedly ★ **Winona Ryder** allegedly says 'yes' to the marriage proposal of Soul Asylum lead singer **Dave Pirner** ★ Following the success of his first film *The Santa Clause*, **Tim Allen** is offered $7m by Island to star in their comedy *Friend of the Family* ★ **Spike Lee** is the proud father of a bouncing baby girl ★ **Gian Maria Volonte**, 61, dies of a heart attack in northern Greece. The Italian actor was best known for his roles in *A Fistful of Dollars*, *Investigation of a Citizen Above Suspicion*, *The Mattei Affair*, *Lucky Luciano*, *Christ Stopped at Eboli* and *Chronicle of a Death Foretold* ★ A Los Angeles judge clears **Mickey Rourke** of charges of beating his wife **Carre Otis** after she refuses to testify at the trial ★ **Alan Parker** is signed up to direct *Evita* – with **Michelle Pfeiffer** still pencilled in for the title role ★ **Winona Ryder** hotly denies rumours that she is engaged to her boyfriend, rock star **David Pirner**, relaying, 'I'm not engaged, and I'm very happy. Happily unengaged' ★ The British Board of Film Classification decides to pass *Natural Born Killers* uncut ★ Savoy Pictures, the producers of *Shadowlands*, offers **Sylvester Stallone** an unprece-

dented $20m to star in an as-yet-unnamed action-thriller ★ **Mara Wilson**, seven, is signed to a $1.5m contract by Twentieth Century-Fox. Previously seen in *Mrs Doubtfire* and *Miracle on 34th Street*, the young actress will have two films specially tailored for her ★ **Gary Oldman** calls off his wedding to **Isabella Rossellini** and checks into a clinic for alcoholics ★ An LA judge issues a restraining order against the bodyguard who reputedly assaulted the actress/model **Anna Nicole Smith** back in September ★ **Rossano Brazzi**, 78, dies in Rome ★ Croatian cover girl **Sylva Koscina**, 61, also dies in Rome – of heart complications. Her numerous credits include such sixties films as *Hot Enough for June*, *Deadlier Than the Male* and *The Secret War of Harry Frigg*, the latter opposite Paul Newman ★ **Laura Dern** says 'yes' to **Jeff Goldblum**'s Christmas Day marriage proposal ★ **Christian Slater** is arrested at John F. Kennedy airport in New York for attempting to board a plane with a .32-calibre Beretta ★ *The Santa Clause* grosses over $100 million in the US ★ *Forrest Gump* claims the crown of box-office hit of the year – beating *The Lion King* by $2m ★ **Woody Strode**, 80, the muscular, 6'5" character actor, dies of cancer in Los Angeles.

January 1995

Actor **Robert Stephens** and producer **David Puttnam** are both bestowed with knighthoods in the New Year's Honours ★ *The Lion King* grosses over $600m worldwide ★ *Interview With the*

Sylvester Stallone: denied paternity, bailing ship, pocketing $20m

Vampire grosses $100m in the US ★ **Jim Carrey** and his leading lady from *Dumb and Dumber*, **Lauren Holly**, are reportedly talking marriage ★ **Peter Cook**, 57, dies from a gastrointestinal haemorrhage in Hampstead, London ★ *The Lion King* grosses $300m in the US ★ **Martin Lawrence** marries Patricia Southall, former Miss Virginia ★ **Richard Dreyfuss** is hospitalised after crashing his Lexus coupé

Jim Carrey (with Lauren Holly, his bride-to-be): ex-wife trouble, wedding bells and the ring of box-office tills

into a lamp-post in Los Angeles. In 1982 he wrapped his Mercedes 450SL convertible around a palm tree – in LA – and was charged with driving under the influence of drink and for possession of cocaine ★ A Los Angeles Superior Court judge refuses to set up a preliminary injunction against the Academy of Motion Picture Arts and Sciences as sought by ITC Entertainment and October Films. ITC and October went to court when their film, *The Last Seduction*, was denied eligibility for the Academy Awards. The AMPAS barred *Seduction* from Oscar competition after it was aired on cable TV ★ Word has it that **Kyle MacLachlan** and **Linda Evangelista** are expecting ... and, according to *The New York Post*, so are **William Baldwin** and fiancée **Chynna Phillips** ★ *The Specialist* grosses $150m worldwide ★ **Margot Hemingway** is committed to a psychiatric clinic against her will. The actress, formerly known as **Margaux Hemingway**, is considered to be a danger to herself and her family after hearing voices and claiming that she could exorcise the devil out of people ★ **Chevy Chase** is booked for drunken driving ★ *Forrest Gump* grosses $300m in the US ★ **Roger Moore** and his wife of 27 years, Luisa, part their ways ★ **Hugh Grant**'s hilarious acceptance speech for his Golden Globe (as Best Comedy Actor) becomes as famous as his girlfriend **Elizabeth Hurley**'s Versace dress ★ **O.J. Simpson** finally goes on trial ★ **Michelle Pfeiffer** pulls out of playing *Evita*, joining the ranks of such ex-Mrs Peróns as **Meryl Streep**, **Barbra Streisand**, **Bette Midler** and **Gloria Estefan**. Could **Madonna** play the role yet? ★ *Dumb and Dumber* grosses $100m in the US – in seven weeks.

February 1995

Donald Pleasence, 75, dies of heart complications in France. The actor, who was awarded an OBE in 1993, was in the middle of filming *Halloween VI* ★ The rumour mill is grinding: **Brad Pitt** and **Uma Thurman** are reportedly 'making couple' ★ **Michael J. Fox** and **Tracy Pollan** are the proud parents of twin girls ★ **Philip Borsos**, 41, the Canadian director of *The Grey Fox*, *The Mean Season*, *Bethune: The Making of a Hero*, *One Magic Christmas* and *Far From Home: The Adventures of Yellow*

Julia Roberts: ignoring Sabrina *and leaving* Lovett

Dog, dies of leukaemia in Vancouver ★ **Zhang Yimou**, the Chinese filmmaker, and **Gong Li**, his leading lady of seven films, announce their separation ★ **Jim Carrey**'s estranged wife Melissa activates court proceedings to snare a chunk of the $7 million Carrey was paid for *The Mask* ★ **Mickey Rourke** and **Carre Otis** get engaged – again – on St Valentine's Day ★ A pregnant **Roseanne** marries her former bodyguard, Ben Thomas, also on St Valentine's Day – in Nevada ★ **Will Smith** and his wife of two-and-a-half years, Sheree, call the whole thing off ★ **Ted Danson** and **Mary Steenburgen** announce their engagement ★ **Doug McClure**, 59, dies of cancer at his home in Sherman Oaks, California. He will be best remembered for his role as Trampas in the 1962-70 TV series *The Virginian* and for starring in such British pictures as *The Land That Time Forgot*, *At the Earth's Core* and *Warlords of Atlantis* ★ *Timecop* grosses $100m worldwide ★ But is it true? The French press reports that **Daniel Day-Lewis** has left his girlfriend **Isabelle Adjani**, even though she is pregnant with his child ★ After an attack of stage fright, **Stephen Fry** goes missing ★ *Speed* grosses $200m worldwide ★ **Pamela Anderson** marries Motley Crue drummer **Tommy Lee** in Mexico. According to the officiating judge, Ms Anderson wore 'a very tiny – an extremely tiny – white bikini' for the occasion ★ **Tom Cruise** and **Nicole Kidman** adopt an Afro-American son,

Connor Antony Kidman Cruise. The couple previously adopted a girl in 1993 ★ **Stephen Fry** contacts his agent from Belgium to say he's safe and thinking his life over ★ **Demi Moore** accepts $12.5m to play a stripper in her next film, *Striptease* ★ Actor **Michael V. Gazzo**, an Oscar nominee for *The Godfather Part II*, dies from a stroke at the age of 71 ★ **Jack Clayton**, 73, director of *Room at the Top* and *The Great Gatsby*, dies from heart and liver complications.

March 1995

Junior grosses $100m worldwide ★ Iolanda Quinn files for separation from her husband of 33 years, **Anthony Quinn**, who has openly been conducting an affair with his personal secretary, Kathy Bevin ★ **Mick Jagger** and film producer **Steve Tisch** (*Forrest Gump*, *Risky Business*) set up their own production company, Lip Service ★ **Elizabeth Hurley** signs a £2.5m contract to promote the products of Estée Lauder, replacing **Paulina Porizkova** ★ The word is so hot on the upcoming *Nine Months* that **Hugh Grant**'s asking price has soared to $7m a movie ★ *Disclosure* grosses $200m worldwide ★ **Marilu Henner** and her husband, film producer **Rob Lieberman**, are expecting their second child later this year ★ **Kim Basinger**, 41, and **Alec Baldwin**, 37, are also expecting ★ After announcing her intention to marry tennis star **Andre Agassi**, **Brooke Shields** fires her lifelong manager – her mother, Teri ★ **Mike White**'s documentary *Who Do You Think You're Fooling?* causes a stir at the New York Underground Film Festival for accusing **Quentin Tarantino** of stealing the plot of *Reservoir Dogs* from the 1987 Hong Kong film *City on Fire* ★ In just two weeks, *The Lion King* grosses $450m in US video sales ★ **Christian Slater** is sentenced to three days' community work with homeless children for attempting to carry a gun on to a plane last December ★ One week before its release in Germany, **Robert Altman**'s *Prêt-à-Porter* is withdrawn following an official complaint from fashion guru **Karl Lagerfeld**, who is referred to as a plagiarist by **Forest Whitaker** in the film ★ **Julia Roberts** and **Lyle Lovett** separate after 21 months of marriage. Recently Ms Roberts was seen in the company of **Ethan Hawke** and **Richard Gere** ★ **Tom Hanks** becomes the fifth actor in history to win two consecutive Oscars – for *Philadelphia* and *Forrest Gump*. Previous sequential winners were **Luise Rainer**, **Spencer Tracy**, **Katharine Hepburn** and **Jason Robards**.

April 1995

In the US, *Forrest Gump* overtakes *Star Wars* to become the third highest-grossing film in history ★ Universal Pictures signs **Sylvester Stallone** to star in *Daylight* – at a cost of $17.5m ★ **Michael Keaton**, 43, pops the question to actress **Courteney Cox**, 30. She says 'yes' ★ **Priscilla Lane**, 76, leading lady of the 1930s and 40s, dies in a nursing home in Massachusetts. Her films included *The Roaring Twenties* and *Arsenic and Old Lace* ★ **Cy Enfield**, 80, writer and director of *Zulu* and *The Sands of Kalahari*, dies of cerebral vascular disease in Warwickshire ★ In an historical divorce settlement, **Kevin Costner** is expected to cough up $80m for former wife Cindy ★ **Nicolas Cage**, 31, and **Patricia Arquette**, 27, tie the knot ★ **Christian Slater** is sued for palimony by girlfriend of five years, Nina Huang ★ After 26 weeks of release, *Pulp Fiction* grosses $100m in the US ★ **Jean-Claude Van Damme**, having left his fourth wife, Darcy, for his third wife, Gladys, has had third thoughts. He's now left Gladys for Darcy a second time and the couple are expecting a little one in October ★ *The Mask* grosses $300m worldwide ★ After a ban of two years in Britain, *Reservoir Dogs* is finally released on video – uncut ★ **Marlon Brando**'s daughter, Cheyenne, 25, hangs herself after being refused custody of her four-year-old son, Tuki ★ **Burl Ives**, 85, dies in Washington State. He was suffering from mouth cancer ★ The legendary **Ginger Rogers**, 83, dies in California.

May 1995

Sir Michael Hordern, 83, dies in Oxford ★ **Alexander Godunov**, 45, former ballet star and occasional film actor (*Witness*, *Die Hard*) dies in New York of 'natural causes' ★ **Elizabeth Montgomery**, 62, star of ABC-TV's

Bewitched (1964-72) dies in Los Angeles ★ £10m, siphoned from the profits of the British lottery, is to be invested into British film production annually. However, only the producers of certified box-office hits will be eligible for the subsidy ★ **Gary Busey** is charged with possession of cocaine, hallucinogenic mushrooms, marijuana and for being under the influence of cocaine ★ **Stefanie Powers**, 52, is ordered by the Los Angeles Superior Court to stay away from a former employee, 29, following his claims of sexual harassment ★ **Elisha Cook Jr**, 92, pre-eminent character actor (*Shane*, *The Big Sleep*, etc), dies in California ★ *Mary Shelley's Frankenstein* grosses $106m worldwide ★ *Pulp Fiction* grosses $200m worldwide ★ Not one Caucasian American male is top-billed in a film in the US box-office Top Ten. The line-up of stars currently on offer include four Afro-Americans (**Denzel Washington**, **Ice Cube**, **Martin Lawrence** and **Mario Van Peebles**), two actresses (**Meg Ryan** and **Sandra Bullock**), one Englishman (**Hugh Grant**), a Hispanic (**Edward James Olmos**), an Irishman (**Liam Neeson**) and one piglet (**Gordy**) ★ Nothing is sacred in Hollywood. *InStyle* magazine, having taken an exhaustive poll of fitness trainers and casting directors, has come up with a register of the best body parts in Tinseltown. Apparently, the best abdominal muscles belong to **Brad Pitt** and **Nicolette Sheridan**, while the gluteus

Hugh Grant: into production, making speeches, getting expensive and meeting the law

maximus award goes to **Mel Gibson** and **Madonna**. Now you know ★ **Goldie Hawn** and **Kurt Russell** are reportedly talking about tying the knot. This will be a big leap as they have only been living together for twelve years ★ **Christopher Reeve**, 42, breaks his neck and is paralysed after a fall from his horse in a competitive jumping event ★ **Louis Gossett Jr** seeks a restraining order against a woman, Mary Kay Nelson, who has been bombarding him with racist hate mail.

June 1995

Right-wing senator **Robert Dole** publicly condemns Walt Disney Productions for distributing the British picture *Priest* through their Miramax subsidiary. Great news for *Priest*, which should now reach a much wider audience ★ **Jim Carrey** is to be paid $20 million by Columbia Pictures to star in *Cable Guy*, making him – in a tie with **Sylvester Stallone** – the highest-paid star of all time ★ **Alan Parker** and **Alan Bates** are made Commanders of the British Empire in the Queen's birthday honours ★ *Batman Forever* shatters box-office records by grossing a phenomenal $53.3 million in its opening weekend ★ **Pamela Anderson** and her husband, Motley Crue drummer **Tommy Lee**, are expecting. 'I can't wait,' says Pam ★ **Hugh Grant** is arrested in Hollywood with a black prostitute – Divine Brown (aka Stella Marie Thompson) – for 'lewd conduct' (enjoying fellatio) in a public place (his white BMW convertible) ★ **Macaulay Culkin** and five of his six siblings are returned to their parents' joint custody – just three days after Patricia Brentrup had won custody of her kids ★ **Elizabeth Taylor** undergoes hip replacement surgery ★ **Lana Turner**, 75, dies of throat cancer ★ **Elizabeth Hurley** and **Hugh Grant** part their ways to think things over. Ms Hurley meanwhile dons a blonde wig to elude photographers – much to the amusement of the mass media ★ According to newspaper reports **Melanie Griffith** is playing house with **Antonio Banderas** ★ The wife of **Michael Douglas**, Diandra, files for separation. The couple have been married for eighteen years ★ *Batman Forever*, in two weeks, becomes the first 1995 release to surpass the $100m mark at the US box office.

Film Soundtracks

James Cameron-Wilson

It was not a fantastic year for soundtracks. At least, artistically speaking. Of course, the previous year was pretty hard to beat. Not only did we have the chart-prevailing likes of *Sleepless in Seattle*, *Philadelphia* and *Four Weddings and a Funeral* but also such outstanding scores as **Michael Nyman**'s *The Piano*, **Kitaro**'s *Heaven & Earth* and, best of all, **John Williams**' *Schindler's List*.

Glancing at the film music nominated for Oscars in 1995, I am not so impressed. While **Hans Zimmer**'s sweeping, magical – and Oscar-winning – score for *The Lion King* would have received my vote out of the five films shortlisted, the residual quartet seemed wanting.

To me, **Thomas Newman**'s composition for *The Shawshank Redemption* was remarkably undistinctive. Yet because the film (a masterpiece) held together so well, Newman's contribution must have worked. However, his lush orchestrals accompanying the destitution and travails of the March children in *Little Women* seemed entirely misplaced. I'm not disputing Newman's craftsmanship, I just feel that he abetted in transforming what should have been a delicate, austere call for female unity into a soapy, gushing 'woman's picture'.

On the other hand, **Eliot Goldenthal** seemed much more in tune with the mood of Neil Jordan's *Interview With the Vampire* – although, isolated on CD, the music is surprisingly undistinguished. This leaves **Alan Silvestri**'s *Forrest Gump*, a competent work that would have vanished into the subconscious had the film not been so ridiculously successful.

Of course, the whole scenario of the film soundtrack is an intriguing predicament. If music is to serve a film, it should be invisible to the ear: that is, subliminal. Indeed, the very term 'film music' is largely oxymoronic. Once the soundtrack has been noted by the audience, the movie will have lost a good deal of its credibility. But if the music is to sell in shops, there has to be a semblance of melody – and enough variety – to make the CD a commercially viable option.

Ignoring the caution that less is more, too many film composers today overcompensate for their handsome pay cheques. This then creates the ludicrous situation of musicians drowning their films in sound so as to meet the marketing demands of the album. And to confound matters more, soundtracks really *can* sell films. Just look at the crossover successes of *The Bodyguard* and *Four Weddings*.

Mark Isham, who must write in his sleep to meet his punishing schedule, has recently scored *Made in America*, *Short Cuts*, *Romeo is Bleeding*, *The Getaway*, *Mrs Parker and the Vicious Circle*, *The Browning Version*, *Quiz Show*, *Timecop*, *Nell*, *Safe Passage*, *Miami Rhapsody* and *Losing Isaiah*. But, if I were a filmmaker, I wouldn't let him within a tone's throw of my product.

And Isham is just one of a legion of composers who commits the sin of writing music over an actor's lines. Lines are to be spoken, not propped up by a covert orchestra squeezed into a cupboard on the set. To my ear, Isham's most intrusive score was for *The Browning Version*. In one scene he underlines a particularly dramatic reading from Albert Finney with a welling of strings that completely distracts from the content of the actor's speech. Thank you, Mr Isham.

I shall go further. Film music today has become like a disease, eating its way through the narrative and permeating every precious milli-second of screen time. Ultimately, the music begins to act like a blanket, wrapping the film in a symphonic cocoon that separates the actors from their audience. Sure, music has its place. In thrillers it can be used most effectively, and in action films it is virtually essential. However, in pictures in which human interaction takes centre screen, the treacly introduction of an orchestra pit of violins instantly demolishes the illusion of reality.

Yet, to be fair, how much is this the fault of the composer? The final look and sound of a film must rest with the director. John Carpenter, who scores his own work, saturated *In the Mouth of Madness* so thoroughly that the effect was like watching an Aerosmith concert. Peter Weir, on the other hand, knows how to sculpt silence to enormous dramatic effect. But when was Weir last responsible for a top-selling soundtrack? It doesn't matter – he makes great movies.

Having said all that, I now present my favourite *CDs* of the period covered by this annual. The list is, naturally, highly subjective.

Top Ten Albums of the Year:

Boys on the Side
Nothing to do with film music *per se*, but a wonderful collection of songs from some top female vocalists: Joan Armatrading, The Cranberries, Sheryl Crow, Indigo Girls, Annie Lennox, Stevie Nicks and the sublime Sarah McLachlan.

Dear Diary
Blissful, subtle score from **Nicola Piovani** which perfectly captures the mood of Nanni Moretti's eccentric film.

Dumb and Dumber
A smart mix of class acts from new bands, including The Crash Test Dummies, Deadeye Dick, Echobelly, Butthole Surfers, The Primitives, etc.

Forrest Gump
Hit-infested media event, with 32 golden oldies charting the musical wallpaper of recent American history from the mid-fifties to the seventies, from Elvis's 'Hound Dog' to Bob Seger and the Silver Bullet Band's 'Against The Wind'. Irresistible.

Gettysburg
A surprisingly addictive symphonic work from **Randy Edelman** that gets better with each listening. Quite inspiring.

The Lion King
Boasting the double attraction of **Hans Zimmer**'s Oscar-winning composition and Elton John and Tim Rice's Oscar-winning song 'Can You Feel The Love Tonight', this was the soundtrack of the year – until you heard it once too often at McDonald's.

Nobody's Fool
A delightful, uplifting score from **Howard Shore**, which sounds much better on CD than on celluloid.

Prêt-à-Porter
Terrific collection of numbers kicked off by Ini Kamoze's No.1 hit 'Here Comes The Hostepper', and including Janet Jackson, The Rolling Stones, The Cranberries and much, much more.

Pulp Fiction
A real dog's feast that plunges the listener into the dark humour of Quentin Tarantino's universe. Snatches of dialogue, blasts of surf guitar, old classics (including Dusty Springfield's 'Son Of A Preacher Man', no less) and vibrating new sounds all help to stoke the magic.

Rob Roy
A rousing, moving and diverse work from the estimable **Carter Burwell**, punctuated by stirring reels from the Celtic group Capercaillie and haunting ballads from the latter's soloist Karen Matheson.

More music than sense? Mark Isham with his instrument of choice

Bookshelf

A selection of the year's notable film titles, compiled by Ivan Butler

Actor's Director – Richard Attenborough Behind the Camera, Andy Dougan; Mainstream.

Alec Guinness – Master of Disguise, Garry O'Connor; Hodder.

American Film Comedy, Scott & Barbara Siegel; Simon & Shuster.

American Silent Film Comedies – An Illustrated Encyclopedia of Persons, Studios and Terminology, Blair Miller; McFarland/Shelwing.

Anthony Perkins – A Haunted Life, Ronald Bergen; Little, Brown.

Approaches to Popular Film, ed. Joanna Hollows & Mark Jancovich; Manchester University Press.

Arnold Schwarzenegger, Greg Miller; Orion.

Are They Really So Awful? – Cameraman's Chronicles, Christopher Challis; Janus Publishing.

Attack of the Monster Movie Makers – Interviews With 20 Genre Giants, Tom Weaver; McFarland/Shelwing.

Audrey – The Real Story, Alexander Walker; Weidenfeld & Nicholson.

Audrey Hepburn – A Biobibliography, David Hofstede; Greenwood Press, London.

Audrey Hepburn – A Biography, Warren G. Harris; Simon & Schuster.

Auteur/Provocateur – Films of Denys Arcand, ed. Andre Loiselle & Brian McIlroy; Flicks Books.

Bad Movies We Love, Edward Margulies & Stephen Rebello; M. Boyars.

Barbra Streisand – The Untold Story, Nellie Bly; Pinnacle Books.

Bardot, Sean French; Pavilion.

Barry Norman's Video Guide, Barry Norman & Emma Norman; Mandarin.

Beyond Hollywood's Grasp – American Filmmakers Abroad, 1914-1945, Harry Waldman; Scarecrow/Shelwing.

Bing Crosby – A Biobibliography, J. Roger Osterholm; Greenwood Press.

Branded to Thrill – Delirious Cinema of Yvonne Rainer, Shelley Green; Scarecrow Press/Shelwing.

Brando – The Biography, Peter Manso; Weidenfeld & Nicolson.

Buñuel – A Biography, John Baxter; Fourth Estate.

Burning Passions – Introduction to the Study of Silent Cinema, Paolo Cherchi; BFI Publications.

Burt Lancaster – The Terrible-Tempered Charmer, Michael Munn; Robson Books.

Burton on Burton, Tim Burton & Mark Salisbury; Faber.

Buster Keaton – A Biobibliography, Joanna E. Rapf & Gary L. Green; Greenwood Press.

Cecil B. DeMille and American Culture – The Silent Era, Sumiko Higashi; University of California.

Celluloid Ivy – Higher Education in the Movies 1960-90, David B. Hinton; Scarecrow/Shelwing.

Censored! – History of British Film Censorship, Tom Dewe Matthews; Chatto.

Cheap Tricks and Class Acts – Special Effects, Make-up and Stunts from the Fantastic 50s, John J. J. Johnson; McFarland/Shelwing.

Chien Andalou, Luis Buñuel; Faber.

Christmas in July – Life and Art of

Preston Sturges, Diana Jacobs; University of California.

Chronicle of the Cinema, Karney and Robyn; Chronicle Communications.

Chronicle of the Cinema; Dorling Kindersley.

Cine Goes to Town – French Cinema 1896-1914, Richard Abel; University of California.

Cinema Design, Catherine A. Surowiec; BFI Publications.

Cinema is 100 Years Old, Emmanuelle Toulet; Thames & Hudson.

Cinema of Max Ophuls – Magisterial Vision and the Future of Women, Susan White; California University Press.

Classical Hollywood Comedy, ed. Jenkins, Henry & Karnick, Kristine Brun-ovska; Routledge.

Classical TV Westerns – A Pictorial History, Ronald Jackson; Virgin Film Library.

Clint Eastwood, Minty Clinch; New English Library.

Early Classics of the Foreign Film, Parker Tyler; Virgin.

Eleanor Powell – A Biobibliography, Margie Shultz; Greenwood Press.

Encyclopedia of Indian Cinema, Ashish Rajadhyaksha & Paul Willemann, BFI Publications.

Engaging Characters – Fiction, Emotion and the Cinema, Murray Smith; Oxford University Press.

Fearing the Dark – Val Lewton's Career, Edmund G. Bansak; McFarland/ Shelwing.

Figures of Light – Actors and Directors Illuminate the Art of Film Acting, Carole Zucker; Plexus.

Film Factory – Russian and Soviet Cinema in Documents, ed. Richard Taylor and Ian Christie; Routledge.

Film History – An Introduction, T. Kristin and D. Bordwell; McGraw.

Film Noir, Michael I. Stephens; McFarland/Shelwing.

Films of Alfred Hitchcock, Neil Sinyard; Prion, London.

Films of Andrei Tarkovsky – A Visual Fugue, Vida T. Johnson & Graham Petrie; Indiana University Press.

Films of Frank Capra, Leland Pogue; Cambridge University Press.

Films of Luis Buñuel – Subjectivity and Desire, Peter William Evans; Oxford University Press.

Films of Steven Spielberg, Douglas Brode; Virgin.

Frank Sinatra at the Movies, Roy Pickard; Robert Hale.

French Films 1945-93, Melissa E. Biggs; McFarland/Shelwing.

Gangster Films – Movies, Terms and Persons, Michael L. Stephens; McFarland/Shelwing.

Garbo – I Wanted to be Alone, Barry Paris; Sidgwick & Jackson.

Gaumont – British Cinema, Allen Eyles; BFI Publications.

George Sidney – A Biobibliography, ed. Eric Monder; Greenwood Press.

The Ghost and Mrs Muir, Frieda Grafe; BFI Film Classics.

Ghosts and Angels in Hollywood Films, James Robert Parish; McFarland/ Shelwing.

Gracie Fields – The Authorised Biography, David Bret; Robson Books.

Great Italian Films – From the Thirties to the Present, Jerry Vermilye; Virgin.

Great War Films – From 'The Birth of a Nation' to Today, Lawrence J. Quirk; Virgin.

Guide to the 'Star Wars' Universe, Bill Slavicsek; Boxtree.

Harold Lloyd – A Biobibliography, Annette M. D'Agostino; Greenwood Press.

Hollywood Censored, Gregory D. Black; Cambridge University Press.

Hollywood Cinema – An Introduction, ed. Richard Maltby & Ian Craven.

Hollywood in Berlin – American Cinema and Weimar Germany, Thomas J. Saunders; University of California.

Hollywood Lesbians, Boze Hadleigh; Barricade Books US.

Hollywood Movie Stills – The Golden Age, Joel W. Finler; Batsford.

Hollywood Song – The Complete Film Musical Companion, Ken Bloom; Facts on File.

Hollywood – Weird and Wonderful Trivia about Hollywood's Heroes, Andrew Malone; M. O'Hara Books.

Horror in Silent Films – A Filmography 1896-1929, Roy Kinnard; McFarland/Shelwing.

Illustrated Frankenstein Movie Guide, Stephen Jones; Titan Books.

Immortal and Invisible – Lesbians and the Moving Image, ed. Tamsin Wilton; Routledge.

Inside the Film Factory – New Approaches to Russian and Soviet Cinema; Routledge.

Italian Film – A Who's Who, John Stewart; McFarland/Shelwing.

James Dean – Boulevard of Broken Dreams, Paul Alexander; Little, Brown.

Jayne Mansfield – A Biobibliography, ed. Jocelyn Faris; Greenwood Press.

Jerry Lewis Films, James I. Neibaur & Ted Okuda; McFarland/Shelwing.

Jimmy Durante – His Show Business Career, David Bakish; McFarland/Shelwing.

Joan Crawford – The Last Word, Fred Lawrence Guiles; Pavilion.

Joan Fontaine – A Biobibliography, Marsha Lynn Beeman; Greenwood Press.

Jodie Foster – The Most Powerful Woman in Hollywood, Philippa Kennedy; Macmillan.

Katharine Hepburn, Barbara Leaming; Weidenfeld & Nicolson.

Ken and Em – Biography of Kenneth Branagh and Emma Thompson, Ian Shuttleworth; Headline.

La Moreau – Biography of Jeanne Moreau, Marianne Gray; Little, Brown.

Last Machine – Early Cinema and the Birth of the Modern World, Ian Christie; BBC Education.

The Laurel and Hardy Encyclopedia, Glenn Mitchell; Batsford.

Leonard Maltin's Movie and Video Guide, Leonard Maltin; Signet.

Life and Loves of Lana Turner, Jane Ellen Wayne; Robson Books.

Life of Python, George Perry; Pavilion.

Liza Minnelli, Peter Carrick; Ulverscroft Large Print Books.

Lost Angels – Psychoanalysis and Cinema, Vicky Lebeau; Routledge.

Making of Mary Shelley's 'Frankenstein', Kenneth Branagh; Pan Books.

Married in the Movies, ed. Roderick Kyle; HarperCollins.

'Meet Me in St Louis' – BFI Film Classics, Gerald Kaufman; BFI Publishing.

Memoirs of the Monster Fighters – Interviews With 21 Classic Horror, Science Fiction and Serial Stars, Tom Weaver; McFarland/ Shelwing.

Merchant Ivory's English Landscape, John Pym; Pavilion.

Movie Book of Film Noir, ed. Ian Cameron; Studio Vista.

My Life, Burt Reynolds; Hodder.

My Sister Marilyn – Personal Memories of Marilyn Monroe, Berniece Baker and Mona Rae Miracle; Weidenfeld & Nicolson.

'Napoleon', Nelly Kaplan; BFI Film Classics.

New Hollywood, Jim Hillier; Studio Vista.

Notes – Making of 'Apocalypse Now', Eleanor Coppola; Faber.

Opening Shots – First Roles of 70 Hollywood Stars, Damien Bona; Workman.

Orson Welles – The Road to Xanadu, Simon Callow; Cape.

Peter Cushing's Monster Movies, Peter Haining; Robert Hale.

Picturing the Past – The Rise and Fall of the British Costume Film, Sue Harper; BFI Publishing.

Pirates and Seafaring Swash-bucklers on the Hollywood Screen, James Robert Parish; McFarland/Shelwing.

'Planet of the Apes' as Allegory, Eric Green; McFarland/Shelwing.

Post-Franco, Postmodern – Films of Pedro Almodovar, ed. Kathleen Vernon & Barbara Morris; Greenwood Press.

Preston Sturges and His Work – Critical Analyses of 14 Films, Jay Rozgonyl; McFarland/Shelwing.

Projecting Illusion – Film, Film Theory and the Impression of Reality, Richard Allen; Cambridge University Press.

Projections – Film Makers on Film Making, No.4, ed. John Boorman, etc.; Faber.

Psychological Reflections on Cinematic Terror – Jungian Archetypes in Horror Film, James F. Iaccino; Prager.

Radical Juxtaposition – Films of Yvonne Rainer, Shelley Green; Scarecrow Press/Shelwing.

Radical Visions – American Film Renaissance 1967-76, Glenn Mann; Greenwood Press.

Raymond Burr – Biography and Career History on Film, Radio and Television, Ona L. Hill; McFarland/Shelwing.

Robert Altman, Daniel O'Brien; Batsford.

Robert Wise – A Biobibliography, Frank T. Thompson; Greenwood Press.

Rock Hudson – A Biobibliography, Brenda Scott Royce; Greenwood Press.

Rosco 'Fatty' Arbuckle – A Biobibliography, Robert Young; Greenwood Press.

Roscoe 'Fatty' Arbuckle – Biography of the Silent Film Comedian 1887-1933, Stuart Oderman; McFarland/Shelwing.

Roy Rogers, Roger W. Phillips; McFarland/Shelwing.

Russian Critics on the Cinema of Glasnost, ed. Michael Brashinsky & Andrew Horton; Cambridge University Press.

Sam Fuller – A Critical Study; McFarland/Shelwing.

Science Fiction, Horror and Fantasy Film and Television Credits – Supplement 2, through 1993, Harris M. Lentz; McFarland/Shelwing.

Script Girls – Women Writers in Hollywood, Lizzie Francke; BFI Publications.

Sean Connery – A Biography, Michael Freedland; Weidenfeld & Nicolson.

Secret Language of Film, Jean-Claude Carriere; Faber.

Serials-ly Speaking Essays on Cliffhangers, William C. Cline; McFarland/Shelwing.

Shakespeare and the Moving Image – The Plays on Film and Television, ed. Anthony Davies & Stanley Wells; Cambridge University Press.

Sherlock Holmes – Screen and Sound Guide, Gordon E. Kelly; Scarecrow/Shelwing.

Songs My Mother Taught Me – Autobiography of Marlon Brando, Marlon Brando and Robert Lindsey; Century.

Southern Mountaineers in Silent Films, J.W. Williamson; McFarland/Shelwing.

Spencer Tracy – A Biobibliography, J. Roger Osterholme; Greenwood Press.

Stanley Kubrick – A Narrative and Stylistic Analysis, Mario Falsetto; Greenwood Press.

Starlog – 'Star Wars' Technical Journal, Shane Johnson; Boxtree.

Stars at War, Michael Munn; Robson Books.

'Star Wars' – A New Hope; Boxtree.

Star Wars – The Genesis of a Legend, Dean Conrad; Valis Books.

Strangers in Hollywood – History of Scandinavian Actors in American Films from 1910 to World War Two, Hans J. Wollstein; Scarecrow Press/Shelwing.

Television Cartoon Shows – An Illustrated Encyclopedia 1949 Through 1993, Hal Erickson; McFarland/Shelwing.

Terror on Tape – Complete Guide to Over 2,000 Horror Movies on Video; James O'Neill.

Tony Curtis – The Autobiography, Tony Curtis & Barry Paris; Mandarin.

Tom Hanks – Journey to Stardom, Roy Trakin; Virgin.

Tom Mix – A Biography and Filmography, Paul E. Mix; McFarland/Shelwing.

2001 – Filming the Future, Piers Bizony; Aurum.

Two Lives of Brigitte Bardot, Jeffrey Robinson; Simon & Schuster.

Typically British – A Short History of the Cinema in Britain, Charles Barr & Stephen Frears; BFI Publishing.

The Ultimate Directory of Silent Screen Performers – A Necrology of Births and Deaths and Essays on 50 Lost Players, ed. Anthony Slide; Scarecrow/Shelwing.

Variety International Film Guide, ed. Peter Cowie; Hamlyn.

Variety Movie Guide 1995, ed. Derek Elley; Hamlyn.

Variety Who's Who in the Movies; Hamlyn.

Walt Disney – Hollywood's Dark Prince, Marc Eliot; Andre Deutsch.

Walter Wanger – Hollywood Independent, Matthew Bernstein; University of California.

Wheeler and Woolsey – The Vaudeville Comics and Their Films, Edward Watz; McFarland/Shelwing.

Whom God Wishes to Destroy – Francis Coppola and the New Hollywood, John Lewis; Athlone Press.

'Wild Strawberries', Philip French; BFI Film Classics.

Women's Pictures – Feminism and Cinema, Annette Kuhn; Verso.

Woody Allen on Woody Allen, ed. Stig Bjorkman; Faber.

Woody and Mia – The Nanny's Tale, Kristi Groteke & Marjorie Rosen; Coronet Books.

Wyatt Earp – The Film and the Filmmakers, Lawrence Kasdan and Jake Kasdan; Plexus.

Young Hollywood, James Cameron-Wilson; Batsford.

Young Marilyn – With Unpublished Photographs of Marilyn Monroe in Her Prime, James Haspiel; Smith Gryphon.

In Memoriam

F. Maurice Speed

Lindsay Anderson, the gifted iconoclastic British stage and film director – and sometimes writer and actor – died aged 71 on 30 August 1994 while on holiday in the South of France. Educated at Oxford, after graduation he and Gavin Lambert founded the influential film magazine *Sequence*. During the Second World War he served initially with the British Army Rifles and then the Intelligence Corps. He started making documentary films in 1948 and made a considerable number of non-fictional shorts including *Thursday's Children* which won him an Oscar in 1954. His output of fictional features remained small, though largely memorable, starting with *This Sporting Life* in 1963. Five years later he made his angry film about the English public school system *If...*, which won the Palme d'Or at the 1969 Cannes Film Festival. This was followed by *O Lucky Man!* (1973), *In Celebration* (1974), *Britannia Hospital* (1982), and *The Whales of August* (1989) in which Anderson obtained marvellous performances from the two veteran stars, Lillian Gish and Bette Davis. Anderson was considerably influenced by John Ford, to whom he paid a cinematic tribute in 1981 with the doumentary *About John Ford*. Anderson's final film was the autobiographical feature *Is That All There Is?* in 1993, which was televised by the BBC the following year. Before his death he was full of plans including a 25-years-on follow-up to *If ...* Also, when he wasn't directing, Anderson was kept busy with stage direction and acting – among other roles, he had a part in *Chariots of Fire*. He also directed a number of TV commercials. In contrast to the majority of his films, Anderson was a mild-mannered, quiet man leading a very unpretentious non-Hollywood life, as was revealed in *Is That All There Is?*

Lina Basquette, the silent film star who died in late October 1994 at the age of 87, had a life as exciting and bizarre as any of the characters she played on the screen. To begin with she had so many husbands it is impossible to ascertain their number but it has been estimated at somewhere between six and nine. As a child she was trained by her money-grabbing mother for a career as a dancer, and by the age of eight was known as the Baby Ballerina. When she was sixteen she became the *première danseuse* at the *Folies Bergère*. She made her screen debut as the star of Cecil B. DeMille's *The Godless Girl* in 1929. Meanwhile, her personal life became front-page news. One of her husbands was Sam Warner of Warner Bros, and when he died she embarked on a long and bitter court case with his family for his money. She always maintained that it was she who persuaded Sam to experiment with talking pictures and was also responsible for signing Al Jolson in the first of them. During the legal struggle she was reputed to have twice tried to commit suicide. She was Hitler's favourite American film star and she had a fan letter from him to prove it. When he became all-powerful he invited her to Berchtesgarden, and accord-

Noah Beery

ing to Basquette started to chase her round the table so persistently that she had to kick him in the groin to lessen his ardour. She also had an affair with a Japanese businessman and there was a suggestion that she became a spy and knew in advance about the attack on Pearl Harbour. But as time passed her film roles became less frequent and more minor, and in 1943 she made her last film, *A Night for Crime*. She retired to the country and began a new career as a dog breeder, raising, not unsurprisingly, Great Danes. Films include *Morals for Women* (1931), *The Midnight Lady* (1932), *The Final Hour* (1936), *Ebb Tide* (1937), and *Four Men and a Prayer* (1938). She also appeared in a number of Buck Jones and Hoot Gibson Westerns. Her autobiography *Lina: DeMille's Godless Girl* was published in 1991.

Noah Beery Jr, who died on 1 November 1994 at the age of 81, was the nephew of Wallace Beery and one of a family of actors which included his father, the screen villain Noah Beery. Noah Jr began his film career as a child actor starring with his father in the 1920 silent *The Mark of Zorro*. Never a star, he was always a reliable supporting actor and he played side-kick to such famous Western stars as Tom Mix, Johnny Mack Brown and Buck Jones. More recently he played James Garner's father in the popular TV series *The Rockford Files*, a role which earned him two Emmy Awards. His films include *Of Mice and Men* (1940), *Sergeant York* (1941), *Red River* (1948), *Davy Crockett* (1950), *The Texas Rangers* (1951), *The Cimarron Kid* (1952), *Spirit of St Louis* (1957) and *Inherit the Wind* (1960).

Rossano Brazzi, the perfect, suave Latin lover type of the movies (he was once thought of as Valentino's successor) died on Christmas Eve 1994 at the age of 78. Born in Bologna, Brazzi started out as a fairly successful professional lightweight boxer but soon turned to acting and occasionally directing. After making some films in Italy, Brazzi moved to Hollywood, making his debut there with *Little Women* in 1949. But it was five years later that he really achieved stardom with his performance in *The Barefoot Contessa*. The following year, 1955, he gave a memorable performance alongside Katharine Hepburn in David Lean's sensitive movie *Summertime*. He lived up to his reputation both on and off the screen, bedding several of his co-stars, and was said to have had some 200 affairs. Adoring female fans were reported on one occasion to have ripped the clothes off his back as they mobbed him. And his wives always forgave him – his second wife is reported to have excused him his constant infidelities because 'Rossano is timid and does not like having to say "No" to a woman.' Certainly, he was not timid in other ways and during the German Occupation of his country, he used his position as a distinguished actor to hide and save hundreds of Jews. In the late sixties Brazzi returned to his own country, though continued to appear in American movies and television even though his former huge popularity had waned. Among more than 200 films he made were *Volcano* (1953), *Three Coins in the Fountain* (1954), *Interlude* (1957), *A Certain Smile* (1958), *South Pacific* (1958), *Count Your Blessings* (1959), *Rome Adventure* (1962), *Women Times Seven* (1967), *The Battle of the Villa Fiorita* (1968), *Krakatoa, East of Java* (1968), *The Italian Job* (1969), *The Great Waltz* (1972), *The Final Conflict* (1981), *La Voce* (1982), *Formula for Murder* (1986), and *Russicum* (1989).

To most moviegoers the name of director-producer **Jack Clayton**, who died on 26 February 1995 at the age of 74, will always be associated with the superior kitchen sink drama *Room at the Top*, his feature film debut, although he made a number of other memorable movies including the outstanding *The Innocents*, which was based on the classic story, *The Turn of the Screw*. Clayton entered the film industry as tea boy at the age of fourteen. He worked his way up from third director's assistant to editor and then assistant director with Alexander Korda's London Films. After working with the Woolf Brothers he was given the chance to direct the short film *The Bespoke Overcoat* which won the Short Film Oscar and a prize at the Venice Film Festival. *Room at the Top* (1959) followed, but although he received much critical acclaim he only went on to make eight more films, although he was producer of many more. Films directed include *The Pumpkin Eater* (1964), *The Great Gatsby* (1974), *Something Wicked This Way Comes* (1983) and *The Lonely Passion of Judith Hearne* (1987).

Once described as a lightweight heavy, **Elisha Cook Jr** died on 18 May, 1995 at the age of 91, with more than 100

Rossano Brazzi

movies to his credit. On the stage from the age of fourteen, Cook made his first movie, *Her Unborn Child*, in 1929 but did not make another film until 1936's *Two in a Crowd*. Only seldom did Cook play anything but villainous characters – one of those rare occasions being his performance in *Shane*. His favourite role was the oily aide to Greenstreet in *The Maltese Falcon* (1941). Other films included *Dillinger* (1945), *The Big Sleep* (1946), *The Great Gatsby* (1949), *Shane* (1953), *One-Eyed Jacks* (1961), *The Great Bank Robbery* (1975), *The Black Bird* (1975), *The Champ* (1979) and what was to be his final screen appearance in *Hammett* (1982).

One of the most liked and popular of screen villains and mainstay of so many of the old 'Hammer Horrors', **Peter Cushing** died, aged 81, on 11 August 1994. Born in Surrey (with his impeccable English accent nobody could have mistaken his origin), he started out in a surveyor's office, but soon after winning a scholarship to the Guildhall School of Music and Drama his future was assured, and in 1935 he made his professional stage debut, appearing as leading man in Laurence Olivier's Old Vic Theatre Company. And it was in Olivier's *Hamlet* that he made his initial film impact. That was in 1948 and thereafter Cushing spent little time away from film studios, making almost 100 films in his lifetime including Laurel and Hardy's *A Chump at Oxford* (1940), *Hamlet* (1948), *Moulin Rouge* (1952), *The Abominable Snowman* (1957), *The Hound of the Baskervilles* (1959), *The Mummy* (1959), *Dr Terror's House of Horrors* (1964), *The Gorgon* (1964), *Dr Who and the Daleks* (1966), *Blood Beast Terror* (1968), *Dracula A.D.* (1972), *Tales from the Crypt* (1972), *The Beast Must Die* (1974), *Dracula and the 7 Golden Vampires* (1975), *The Ghoul* (1975), *Monster Island* (1981), *Top Secret!* (1984) and *Biggles* (1986).

Virginia Dale, who died on 3 October 1994 at the age of 77, was a popular leading lady in the romantic films of the forties. First trained as a dancer, she was persuaded to make films by Darryl F. Zanuck. She played opposite many of the leading male stars of the period including Clark Gable (*Idiot's*

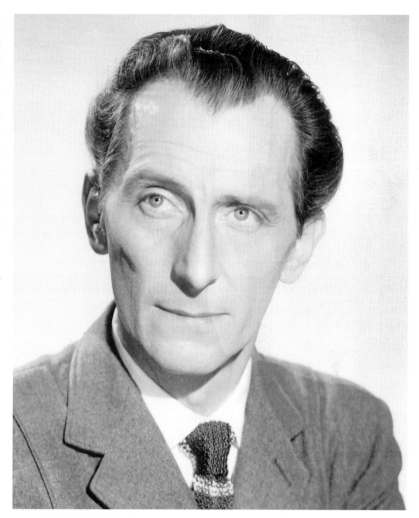

Peter Cushing

Virginia Dale

Delight, 1939), Jack Benny (*Buck Benny Rides Again*, 1940), Jimmy Durante (*Start Cheering*, 1938), Bing Crosby (*Holiday Inn*, 1942), and Fred Astaire (*Love Thy Neighbour*, 1940), etc. She also played Annie Oakley in *The Kid From Texas* (1950). In the 1950s she spent most of her time acting in TV.

Tom Ewell (real name Yewell Tompkins), the dependably good character actor who co-starred with Marilyn Monroe in *The Seven Year Itch*, died on 17 September 1994 at the age of 85. Ewell's speciality was the amorous character who never quite seduces the pretty woman, the role he played to perfection opposite Monroe. He began his career taking dramatic studies at the

Tom Ewell

University of Winconsin and made his professional stage debut in 1928, but his first success was in a production of *The Apple of His Eye* in 1940. In the interim he washed dishes and worked in the New York department store Macy's. He made his screen debut in 1940 but it was *Adam's Rib* in 1949 in which he first received critical acclaim. His many films included *Mr Music* (1950), *Finders Keepers* (1951), *The Lieutenant Wore Skirts* (1955), *State Fair* (1962), *Suppose They Gave a War and Nobody Came?* (1970), *They Only Kill Their Masters* (1972), *The Great Gatsby* (1974) and *Easy Money* (1983). He also claimed a Broadway record of appearing in 28 flops in fourteen years!

Never a 'star', **Robert Flemyng**, who died in May 1995 at the age of 83, outshone many of them. With his clipped, perfect English and his natural aristocratic bearing, he was the perfect upper-class Englishman. He was also something of a real-life wartime hero, having won a Military Cross, a mention in dispatches and an OBE, rising from private to become one of the youngest colonels in the British Army. Trained as a doctor, he switched to the theatre when he was twenty. Flemying made his screen debut in 1937 in the Jessie Matthew musical *Head Over Heels*. Other film appearances were in *The Guinea Pig* (1948), *The Blue Lamp* (1950), *Blind Date* (1959), *The Horrible Dr Hitchcock* (1962), *The Man Who Never Was* (1955), *The Quiller Memorandum* (1966), *The Battle of Britain* (1966), *Young Winston* and *Travels With My Aunt* (1972).

John Halas was one half of Halas and Batchelor, who made British film history by producing the first British full-length animated cartoon, *Animal Farm* (1954), based on the Orwell story. The Batchelor half of the firm was Halas's wife and partner (who died aged 77 in 1991 – see *Film Review 1991-2*). The duo's output was vast and diverse, embracing advertising and information films, documentaries, military instructional and fictional films. They employed a staff of some 70 artists who turned out a total of more than 2000 shorts and 7 features. Although even at their peak Halas and Batchelor were little known compared with Disney, they were as important as the Hollywood studios in the sense that they were both experimental and innovative.

With some 80 stage appearances, 100 films and as many TV shows to his credit, **Michael Hordern** – who died on 2 May 1995 at the age of 83 – must have had little spare time during his 50-year career. Starting out as a teacher, Hordern soon switched to an acting career, making his theatrical debut in 1937, and his first film, *The Girl in the News*, in 1940. After war service he resumed his career with *A Girl in a Million* and *School for Secrets* in 1946. His range was enormous, from the comedy *A Funny Thing Happened on the Way to the Forum* (1966) to the drama *The Bed Sitting Room* (1969) and from *Macbeth* (1960) to *The Wildcats of St Trinians* (1966). He was knighted in 1983. Other films include *Passport to Pimlico* (1949), *The Magic Box* (1951), *The Man Who Never Was* (1955), *Sink the Bismarck!* (1960), *The Spy Who*

Michael Hordern

Alexander Knox

Came in From the Cold (1965), *Futtock's End* (1969), *Theatre of Blood* (1973), *The Slipper and the Rose* (1976), *Lady Jane* (1986) and *The Fool* (1990).

A distinguished actor and a talented writer, **Alexander Knox** – who died on 1 May 1995 at the age of 88 – once complained that the only way he could get to play comedy roles was to write his own scripts, which he successfully did in the film *The Judge Steps Out* (1947). But he was at his best in solid, serious roles such as doctors, lawyers, and US presidents: his performance in the title role of *Wilson* brought him worldwide acclaim and an Oscar nomination. Born in Ontario, Canada, Knox began his working life as a journalist but soon turned to acting, making his debut in Boston in 1929. The following year he crossed the Atlantic and for several years graced the British stage with some splendid performances. He made his film debut in 1938 as *The Gaunt Stranger*, followed by *The Four Feathers* a year later. At the outbreak of the Second World War Knox returned to America, where he soon became a busy character actor. Back in England in the late 1940s he continued his stage and screen career, the latter including *The*

Night My Number Came Up (1955), *The Two-Headed Spy* (1958), *Oscar Wilde* (1960), *The Longest Day* (1962), *Woman of Straw* (1964), *Modesty Blaise* (1966), *Accident* (1964), *Nicholas and Alexandra* (1961), *The Damned* (1961) and his last film appearance, in *Gorky Park* in 1983. His literary output included whodunnits, plays, film scripts and serious studies of Eskimos and American Indians. His marriage – to actress Doris Nolan – remained stable throughout his life.

To many moviegoers the name of **Burt Lancaster**, who died at the age of 80 after a long illness on 20 October 1994, will recall a tough, physical actor – and indeed he was that. But he was also a highly accomplished actor – versatile and subtle – although he never had a drama lesson in his life. One has only to think of him in *Elmer Gantry* (a role which brought him the Best Actor Oscar of 1960), *The Leopard*, *Judgement at Nuremberg*, *Sweet Smell of Success*, *Birdman of Alcatraz*, *The Swimmer*, *Atlantic City* and several other intelligent and in-depth performances, three of which (*From Here to Eternity*, *Birdman of Alcatraz* and *Atlantic City*) earned him Best Actor Oscar nominations. Burton Stephen Lancaster was born in Harlem, a tough New York neighbourhood from which he escaped thanks to his athletic powers, which earned him a place at New York University. He gave up his education when he was offered the chance of appearing as an acrobat in a circus – a career which came to an abrupt end when he badly injured his hand. After several jobs he went into the US Army, serving three years. Back in civilian life he secured a part in the Broadway play *A Sound of Hunting* which, although it ran for only a few weeks, established Lancaster as an actor. His first film was *Desert Fury* (1947), although it was released after the more impressive, but later made *The Killers* (1946). It was not long before Lancaster formed his own production company with his agent and they produced a number of movies, some of

Burt Lancaster

which he acted in – such as *The Kentuckian* (1955), which he also directed, and some, including the Oscar-winning *Marty* (1955), which he only produced. His 40-year-old career produced nearly 100 films, his final performance being in the 1991 TV film *Separate But Equal*. Some of his best-known films included *The Killers* (1946), *Brutal Force* (1947), *Sorry, Wrong Number* (1948), *The Flame and the Arrow* (1950), *Come Back Little Sheba* (1953), *The Crimson Pirate* (1952), *From Here to Eternity* (1953), *The Kentuckian* (1955), *Gunfight at the O.K. Corral* (1957), *Sweet Smell of Success* (1957), *Elmer Gantry* (1960), *Judgement at Nuremberg* (1961), *Birdman of Alcatraz* (1962), *The Professionals* (1966), *The Swimmer* (1968), *1900* (1976), *The Cassandra Crossing* (1977), *Atlantic City* (1980), *Local Hero* (1983) and *Field of Dreams* (1989).

Best known for his TV appearances in such long-running series as *High Chaparral*, **Cameron Mitchell,** who died aged 75 in July 1994, made a large number of films in America, Italy, Spain, France, Germany and Eastern Europe and was also the first American actor to make movies in Russia. The son of a Scottish minister and a German mother, Mitchell (real name Mizell) seemed destined for the ministry but ran away to New York to take on vari-

Cameron Mitchell

ous jobs, including that of an usher at Radio City. Fascinated by the theatre, he secured a job with the famous Lunts (Alfred Lunt and his wife Lynn Fontaine), who cast him in small parts during their 1939-40 season. He made his debut in *The Taming of the Shrew*. Joining the American Air Force as a bombadier, he served until he was demobbed in 1944. He made his film debut the following year in *They Were Expendable* and had a considerable success in both the play and the film adaptation of Miller's *Death of a Salesman*. Always fascinated by the Old West (the first thing he did when he made enough money was to buy a ranch) he made the first of many Westerns, *Man in the Saddle*, in 1951, followed the next year by *Outcasts of Poker Flat* and *Powder River*. In 1973 he formed his own production company with the intention of making a Western but the adventure proved a disaster, and a year later he went bankrupt owing a reputed sum of \$2.5 million. To pay off his debt he accepted almost anything he was offered and made a number of unsuccessful films like *Low Blow* (1986) and *The Messenger* (1987). His other films included *Cass Timerlane* (1947), *Okinawa* (1952), *Desirée* (1954), *Strange Lady in Town* (1955), *Carousel* (1954), *Hombre* (1967) and the first American films after several years in Europe, *Buck and the Preacher* (1972) and *The Swarm* (1978). But Mitchell will always be best remembered as the hard-drinking, pistol-packing cowboy 'Buck' Cannon in TV's *High Chaparral*.

Donald Pleasence, who died on 2 February 1995, was born in Worksop in 1919. He first found fame on the London stage, making his debut in 1939. In 1942 he joined the RAF and became a prisoner of war, and it wasn't until the mid-1950s that he began appearing in films. He soon became an impressive character actor, his roles in Harold Pinter's *The Caretaker* in 1963 and in Roman Polanski's *Cul-De-Sac* in 1966 being particularly memorable. Undoubtedly at his best when he played the evil villain, this was exploited to the full, and in the eighties he appeared in numerous low-budget horror thrillers. His many films included *The Beachcomber* (1954), *Look Back in Anger* (1959), *The Great Escape* (1963), *You Only Live Twice* (1967), *Henry VIII and*

Donald Pleasence

His Six Wives (1973), *The Eagle Has Landed* (1976), *Oh God* (1977), *Dracula* (1979), *Halloween II* (1981), *Phantom of Death* (1988), *Buried Alive* (1990) and *Shadows and Fog* (1992).

Martha Raye, a singer and comic of screen, stage, TV and cabaret, who died aged 78 on 19 October 1994 after a long illness, was a great entertainer who had a unique, musical, foghorn voice, a rubber face and a letter-box mouth. She will, perhaps, be best remembered as one of the most durable of the wives in Charlie Chaplin's *Monsieur Verdoux*. Margaret Teresa Yvonne Reed, to give her real name, was born of vaudeville parents in the charity ward of a Montana hospital, began appearing in her parents' act by the age of three, and by her teens had her own act in cabaret and revues. In 1936, director Norman Taurog picked her out to star with Bing Crosby in *Rhythm on the Range*, where she scored a triumph with the number 'Mr Paganini'. The result was a rapid succession of roles in films like *Artists and Models* (1937), *Waikiki Wedding* (1937) and *Hellzapoppin'* (1941). After *Monsieur Verdoux* it was fifteen years before she made another movie, although she was kept frantically busy in the interim in cabaret, on TV and on stage where she starred in *Hello Dolly!*, *No, No, Nanette* and *Annie Get Your Gun*. Martha Raye was also a great charity worker and during World War Two and the Vietnam and Korean wars she worked tirelessly entertaining the troops. She made a return to the screen

Martha Raye

in *Jumbo* in 1962 but thereafter was plagued with illness and she made her final screen appearance in *Concorde: Airport 79*. No one who ever saw Miss Raye could forget her vivacity and attacking sense of humour; she was indeed a great entertainer in all mediums. She received a special Academy Award in 1969. Her other films include *Rhythm on the Range* (1936), *The Big Broadcast of 1937* (1937), *College Swing* (1938), *Never Say Die* (1939), *The Farmer's Daughter* (1940), *Navy Blues* (1941) and *Four Girls in a Jeep* (1944).

To many, the name **Ginger Rogers** – who died on 2 May 1995 at the age of 83 – will bring memories of a bygone era of the cinema; one in which the aim was to *entertain*; a happy escapist period before the advent of kitchen sink dramas and blood-and-guts adventures. The ten musicals which Rogers (real name Virginia Katherine McMath) made with Fred Astaire were all classics of the musical movie, not always strong in story but always rich in glamour, colour, vivacity and romance. Rogers started early, pushed on by the archetypal ambitious momma. She made her professional debut as a dancer when she was fourteen and at seventeen was already married for the first time. She made her Broadway debut in the 1929 musical *Top Speed*. In her earlier movies she was usually cast as the tough, wise-cracking self-sufficient young lady and the transformation to glamorous star really began when she

appeared with Astaire in *Flying Down to Rio* (1933). Though not the stars of the movie, they stole the show and ensured their future fame. Rogers had met Astaire when he was engaged to teach her to dance for the stage musical *Girl Crazy*. Rogers' remuneration rose as rapidly as her fame and it wasn't long before she became the highest-paid star in Hollywood. In spite of all her musical success however, Rogers always wanted to play straight, dramatic parts and she won an Oscar for the straight role she played in *Kitty Foyle* (1940). Her last film was in 1965 although she did subsequently perform in a highly successful cabaret act. Her films include *Follow the Leader* (1930), *Hat Check Girl* (1932), *42nd Street*, *Flying Down to Rio* and *Gold Diggers of 1933* (1933), *The Gay Divorce* (1934), *In Person*, *Roberta* and *Top Hat* (1935), *Follow the Fleet* and *Swing Time* (1936), *Shall We Dance* and *Stage Door* (1937), *Vivacious Lady* (1938), *Kitty Foyle* (1940), *Tom, Dick and Harry* (1941), *The Major and the Minor* and *Roxie Hart* (1942), *Lady in the Dark* (1944), *The Barkleys of Broadway* (1949), *Monkey Business* (1952) and *Harlow* (1965).

Craggy-faced, gravel-voiced **Lionel Stander**, who died on 30 November 1994 at the age of 86, was a dependably good feature player whose popularity waxed during the thirties and forties with producers and public alike. He is probably best known today for his role as Max in TV's *Hart to Hart*. Stander started acting when he was in his teens, and by the time he reached 30 he had some 25 Broadway appearances to his credit. He turned to films in 1932. A staunch supporter of the political left,

Ginger Rogers

Lionel Stander

he soon fell foul of the infamous House of Un-American Activities Committee and was blacklisted so that he was not allowed to work in Hollywood. He promptly returned to the stage and, somewhat surprisingly, became a broker on the New York Stock Exchange. He lived in Rome for a short time and made several spaghetti Westerns, Italy being unaffected by the ban. He returned to Hollywood in 1965, where he won a minor role in *The Loved One*. This was followed by an impressive performance in Roman Polanski's *Cul-De-Sac*, and parts in Steven Spielberg's *1941* and Martin Scorsese's *New York, New York*. His final performance in *The Last Good Time* has yet to be seen, at the time of writing. His films included *The Last Gangster* and *A Star is Born* (1937), *The Crowd Roars* (1938), *The Bride Wore Crutches* (1941), *Hangmen Also Die* (1943), *Gentleman Joe Palooka* (1946), *Call Northside 777* (1948), *The Moving Finger* (1963), *The Loved One* (1966), *Once Upon a Time in the West* (1969), *Treasure Island* (1972) and *The Cassandra Crossing* (1977).

Jessica Tandy, who died at the age of 85 on 11 September 1994, was a British actress as highly acclaimed in America as in her native Britain. In a career that spanned some 60 years she won many theatrical and film honours, including an Oscar when she was 80 for *Driving Miss Daisy* (1989). Essentially a stage actress, she gave a number of distinguished film performances in the 25 or

so movies in which she starred. Born in London, she studied law at the University of Ontario, and then spent three years at the Ben Greet Academy of Acting. She made her professional debut at the age of eighteen in *The Manderson Girls*, after which she joined the Birmingham Repertory Company, where she performed Shakespeare and the classics. She made her West End debut in *The Rumour* in 1929, and enjoyed success in *Children in Uniform*. After her divorce from Jack Hawkins in 1940 she moved to America. Her career was at a low ebb when she met and married actor Hume Cronyn with whom she moved to Hollywood. Co-starring with her husband she established herself in Hollywood with *The Seventh Cross* (1944). Her films included *Dragonwyck* (1946), *Forever Amber* (1947), *The Desert Fox* (1951), Alfred Hitchcock's *The Birds* (1963), *The World According to Garp* (1982), *The Bostonians* (1984), *Cocoon* (1985), *batteries not included* (1987), *Cocoon:*

The Return (1988), *Driving Miss Daisy* (1989) and *Fried Green Tomatoes* (1991) – a role which brought Tandy another Oscar nomination. Her final screen appearance was in *Nobody's Fool* with Paul Newman.

Known as 'The Sweater Girl' (due to her tight jumpers) **Lana Turner,** who died on 29 June 1995, was discovered, according to Hollywood legend, at Schwab's drugstore when she should have been at school. After appearing in a number of films, she eventually found her niche in melodrama. Within this genre, she put in some good performances and was nominated for an Oscar for her part in *Peyton Place* in 1957. Her first really notable role was as the murdering adulteress in *The Postman Always Rings Twice* (1946). Her professional career was long and highly successful although she was perhaps better known for her glamour

Jessica Tandy

rather than her acting skills (she was one of the nation's top pin-up girls during the Second World War).

Married many times, Miss Turner always managed to cling to her clean image despite the fact that her private life was a stormy one which received much media attention. Most dramatic was the murder of Johnny Stompanato, Turner's lover, who was killed by her daughter Cheryl in 1958. However, the huge amount of publicity which went hand in hand with the murder trial did not prevent her from continuing her career and she starred in films until the mid-seventies. By 1992, when she was diagnosed as having cancer, she had become a virtual recluse although she did attend the première of *Sunset Boulevard* in 1993. She was 75 when she died.

Her numerous films included *The Great Garrick* (1937), *Ziegfeld Girl* (1942), *Johnny Eager* (1942), *The Bad*

Lana Turner

and the Beautiful (1952), *Betrayed* (1954), *Imitation of Life* (1959), *Madam X* (1966) and *Bittersweet Love* (1976).

Terence Young, the British director, who died aged 79 on 10 September 1994, directed the first and arguably the best James Bond film, *Dr No*, and two later Bond epics, *From Russia With Love* (1963) and *Thunderball* (1965). He began his career by working at Elstree studios during long vacations from Cambridge, and went on to serve as assistant to such famous names as Rene Clair, Korda, Vidor and Feyder. After the war (he served with the Guards Armoured Division) he wrote a number of scripts. His first film as director was *One Night With You* (1948), followed by *Corridor of Mirrors* (1948). His variable output included *Valley of the Eagles* (1951), *The Red Beret* (1953), *Action of the Tiger* (1957), *Too Hot to Handle* (1960), *The Amorous Adventures of Moll Flanders* (1965), *Triple Cross* (1966), *Wait Until Dark* (with Audrey

Hepburn as the blind victim), *Mayerling* (re-make 1968), *The Klansman* (1974), the disastrous *Inchon* (1982) and *The Jigsaw Man* (1984).

Others who died during the year:

Iris Adrian (real name Hostetter) made her professional debut as a dancer with the Ziegfeld Follies after winning a beauty contest in 1929. She played numerous supporting and leading roles in over 100 films, often in the dumb blonde or gangster's moll role. She died in October 1994, aged 81.

Benny Baker, a former truck driver who made more than 100 films, died in October 1994, aged 67. His career also included work in vaudeville and repertory theatres.

Harold Berens, who died during the first week of May 1995 at the age of 92, was a vaudeville and television comedian who made many films

including *Hotel Sahara* (1951), *Surprise Package* (1960), *Hear My Song* and *Carry On Columbus* (1992). His biggest success, however, was in the radio show *Ignorance is Bliss* which ran from 1946 to 1953 and attracted millions of fans.

Sergei Bondarchuk, the Russian actor and director who died at the end of October at the age of 74, will always be remembered for his gargantuan film of Tolstoy's *War and Peace*. One of the most costly and spectacular epics in the history of the cinema, it ran for almost eight and a half hours and was more than five years in production, finishing in 1967. The film had a budget of $100 million. An actor turned director, Bondarchuk also made the impressive *Waterloo* in 1970. His several awards included a Best Foreign Film Oscar for *War and Peace* and a Lifetime Achievement Award at the Venice Film Festival in 1983.

Janis Carter, who died in September 1994 at the age of 80, was trained for the opera and appeared in a number of Broadway musicals before making here film debut in *Cadet Girl* in 1941. Her wide range of films included *I Married an Angel* (1942), *Lady of Burlesque* (1943), *Night Editor* (1946), *A Woman of Distinction* (1950), *Santa Fe* (1951) and her final movie, *The Half Breed*, in 1952.

Ernest Clark, who died in mid-November 1994 at the age of 82, was a familiar face in British films, plays and television. He was famous for his upper-class characters, and he made more than 40 films including *Billy Liar*, *Sink the Bismarck!*, *Doctor in the House*, *The Dam Busters*, *Beau Brummel*, *Gandhi* and *A Tale of Two Cities*.

To many **Peter Cook**, who died on 9 January 1995 at the age of 57, was one of Britain's sharpest and funniest satirists. Actor, writer, satirist and publisher of the satirical magazine *Private Eye*, he was best known for his cabaret/ television act with long-time partner Dudley Moore. He also wrote the scripts for several films, produced one, and was the star of others. He appeared in *The Wrong Box* (his debut, 1966), *Bedazzled* (actor and scriptwriter, 1967), *Monte Carlo or Bust* (1969), *The Hound of the Baskervilles* (1978), *The Secret Policeman's Ball* (also scripted,

1979), *Derek and Clive Get the Horn* (actor and executive producer), *Yellowbeard* (actor and screenplay, 1983), *Without a Clue* (1988), *Great Balls of Fire!* (1989), *Kokada Crescent* (script only, 1989).

John Doucette, who died on 10 August 1994 at the age of 73, was a veteran of the screen, making 150 films over 40 years starting with 1943's *Two Tickets to London*. Other films included *Julius Caesar*, *True Grit* and *Patton*. He was also a popular TV Western star.

Anita Garvin, who died in July 1994 at the age of 88, was a former Mack Sennett Bathing Beauty and Ziegfeld stage star who was 'discovered' by Hal Roach, for whom she made more than 150 comedy shorts. A popular Laurel and Hardy leading lady, she appeared in their feature *Swiss Miss*. She retired with the advent of the sound film in the 1940s.

Nadia Gray (real name Nadia Kujnin Herescu), died at the age of 70 in late June 1994. She was the leading lady in a number of British and American films including *The Spider and the Fly* (1949), *Night Without Stars* (1949) and *Top Secret* (1952).

Nadia Gray

James Hill, the British documentary-trained director who was best known for directing *Born Free* (1966) and who won an Oscar for his short film *Giuseppina*, died in October 1994 at the age of 75. As an airman photographing the bombing of Germany he was shot down and taken prisoner. After the war he did a lot of TV directing and made occasional feature films including *The Dock Brief* (1962), *A Study in Terror* (1965), *An Elephant Called Slowly*, *Black Beauty* (1971) and *The Belstone Fox* (1976).

Robert Hutton, star of many of the forties and fifties movies – mostly 'B' productions – died on 7 August 1994 at the age of 73. His first film was *Destination Tokyo* in 1943, but he will probably be best remembered for his role in 1944's *Hollywood Canteen*.

Big, burly **Burl Ives**, real name Burle Icle Ivanhoe, who died at the age of 85 on 15 April 1995, was equally popular as a folk singer ('Blue Tailed Fly', 'The Foggy, Foggy Dew' and 'Rock Candy Mountain'), actor and film star (some 30 films including a Supporting Actor Oscar for *The Big Country* in 1958, although his performance in *Cat on a Hot Tin Roof* the same year was more memorable). Other films of this ex-professional football player included *East of Eden* (1955), *Desire Under the Elms* (1958), *Our Man in Havana* (1939), *Ensign Pulver* (1944) and *Heidi* (1939).

Raul Julia, the Puerto Rican actor who died in October 1994 at the age of 54, had a full career on stage, in cabaret and in films before gaining world-wide recognition for his performance in the two *Addams Family* films and *Kiss of the Spider Woman* (1985).

Nancy Kelly, who died on 2 January 1995 at the age of 73, was a major Oscar nominated (for *The Bad Seed*) star of her day. Her films include *Jesse James* (1939), *Stanley and Livingstone* (1939), *To the Shores of Tripoli* (1942), *Murder in the Music Hall* (1940) and *The Bad Seed* (1950). She once received a congratulatory telegram from Greta Garbo for one of her performances.

Sylvia Koscina, who died in Rome at the end of 1994, aged 61, was born in Zagreb and successfully survived the devastation of World War One despite having been buried in the rubble of the city three times. Winning a beauty contest in Italy, she

Sylvia Koscina

was seen by a film producer for whom she made numerous films. In order to keep up her high style of living, she made films all over Europe and America. She made two British movies – *Hot Enough for June* (1964) and *Deadlier Than the Male* (1966) – in between which she appeared in Fellini's *Juliet of the Spirits*. Her Hollywood films included *Three Bites of the Apple* (1967) and *Hornet's Nest* (1970).

Priscilla Lane (real name Mullican), who died on 4 April 1995, began as a child performer but got her first real chance singing with her sister with Fred Waring's Band and she made her Hollywood debut with them in the 1937 musical *Varsity Show*. She subsequently appeared with sisters Lola and Rosemary in a popular series: *Four Daughters* (1938), *Four Wives* (1939) and *Four Mothers* (1940). In 1940 she married and retired to raise a family, though she did return to make the occasional movie. Films include *Yes, My Darling Daughter* (1939), *The Meanest Man in the World* (1943) and *Bodyguard* (1948).

Arthur Lubin, who died on 11 May 1995 at the age of 96, was a prolific director who started out as an actor. As well as directing some of the *Abbott and Costello* and *Francis the Mule* series he made *Rhubarb* (1951), *Star of India* (1956) and *Thief of Baghdad* (1961). His most ambitious movie was *The Phantom of the Opera* (starring Claude Rains) in 1943.

Doug McClure, an actor known both on television and in film, died on 5 February 1995 at the age of 59. At the age of eight, he began riding horses and in his teens took part in rodeos. He made his TV debut in *Men of Anapolis* but his first big success was in the long running TV series *The Virginian*. His occasional film appearances included *The Enemy Below* (1957), *The Unforgiven* (1960) and *The Land That Time Forgot* (1974).

Actor/producer **William Marshall** died in Paris in 1994 at the age of 75. He appeared in *Blackmail* in 1947, and also starred in *Santa Fe Trail* in 1940 and *Belle of the Yukon* in 1944. Among his four wives were Ginger Rogers and Michele Morgan.

Ralph Michael, who died in November 1994 at the age of 87, was one of those efficient and reliable actors of which Britain has had so many. His record of 60 years in plays, films and television is impressive; and he never gave anything but a flawless performance. His real name was Ralph Champion Shotter and he made his professional debut at the Chelsea Palace in 1930 in Henry Irving's famous melodrama *The Bells*. His films included *John Halifax, Gentleman* (1938), *Dead of Night* (1945), in which he gave an outstanding performance, *The Hasty Heart* (1949), *The Heroes of Telemark* (1965), *Khartoum* (1966) and *House of Cards* (1968).

Elizabeth Montgomery, who died at the age of 62 in May 1995, was best known as the witch in the long running TV series *Bewitched*. She made only a few films including *The Court Martial of Billy Michell* (1955) and *Johnny Cool* (1963).

Dennis Morgan (real name Stanley Morner), the debonair singing-dancing star of the forties and fifties, died at the age of 85 on 19 September 1994. A former radio announcer and repertory player, he made his film

debut in the 1930s. His films include *The Great Ziegfeld* (1936), *Kitty Foyle* (1939), *Wings of the Eagle* (1942), *Desert Song* (1943), *Shine On Harvest Moon* (1944), *Pretty Baby* (1950), *Cattle Town* (1952), *The Gun That Won the West* (1955) and *Uranium Boom* (1956). He retired in 1960 to manage his ranch.

Mildred Natwick, who died on 25 October 1994 at the age of 89, was a distinguished actress of stage and screen who made her Broadway debut in 1932 and became known for playing characters older than herself. In 1967 she was nominated for a Supporting Actress Oscar for her performance in *Barefoot in the Park*. Other films included *The Long Voyage Home* (1940), *The Enchanted Cottage* (1945), *The Late George Apley* (1947), *3 Godfathers* and *She Wore a Yellow Ribbon* (1949), *The Quiet Man* (1952), *The Trouble With Harry* (1955) and *At Long Last Love* (1975). Her final screen appearance was in *Dangerous Liaisons* in 1981.

Dependable Old Vic veteran **John Phillips** made a number of films including *Richard III* (1954), *The Village of the Damned* (1959) and *Quadrophenia* (1978). He died, aged 80, on 18 May 1995.

Eric Porter, the distinguished stage actor who died on 15 May 1995 at the age of 67, will be best recalled for his masterly performance as the central character Soames in the worldwide

Dennis Morgan

TV success *The Forsyte Saga*. A performer on the stage since 1945, he turned to films in the sixties. They included *The Pumpkin Eater* (1964), *Heroes of Telemark* (1965), *Nicholas and Alexandra* (1971), *Antony and Cleopatra* (1972), *The Belstone Fox* (1973) and the re-make of *The Thirty-Nine Steps* (1979).

Yuli Raizman, who died on 13 December 1994 at the age of 90, was one of the great masters of Russian cinema. He directed his first silent film, *The Circle*, in 1927 and had his first major success in 1930 with *The Early Thirsts*. He won a number of the Soviet's highest awards and became one of the most decorated of Soviet cultural figures.

Dany Robin, the popular and pretty French actress, died on 25 May 1995 at the age of 68. She made few films outside her own country but they included the British production *The Best House in London* and Hitchcock's American thriller *Topaz* (1969) which was to be her last screen appearance.

Canadian born, American and French educated **Harry Saltzman**, who died in early September at the age of 78, is best recalled as the producer of the Bond films *To Russia With Love*, *Dr No*, *Goldfinger* and *Thunderball*, but he also promoted Woodfall Films (*Look Back in Anger*), and was at one time chief executive of Technicolor and also owned a London Thames-side night club. He produced a number of West End plays and became chairman of the H.M. Tennant theatrical agency.

Terry Scott, the popular TV comedian, who appeared in several of the *Carry On* films, died on 26 July 1994 at the age of 67.

Sebastian Shaw died at the age of 89 at the beginning of 1995. He was primarily a stage actor, but in the thirties played the hero in several British films, later turning to character roles. Among his films were *Four Masked Men* (1934), *Men Are Not Gods* (1936), *The Squeaker* (1939), *The Glass Mountain* (1948) and *A Midsummer Night's Dream* (1968).

Vienna-born **Lilia Skala**, who died on 18 December 1994 in her 90th year,

William Sylvester

was the Oscar-nominated, Golden Globe-winning actress who received both honours for her unforgettable performance in *Lilies of the Field* (1963). She also appeared in *Call Me Madam* (1953), *Ship of Fools* (1965), *Roseland* (1977) and *Men of Respect* (1991).

John Smith, the character actor who died on 21 January 1995, at the age of 63, changed his name from Robert Earl Van Orden because he would be the 'only John Smith in the business'.

Woody Strode, an actor who featured in several John Ford films, died on 31 December 1994 at the age of 80. A former professional footballer and wrestler of impressive physique, he made his screen debut in *Sundown* in 1941, but his career didn't fully take off until the 1950s. He played the title role in Ford's *Sergeant Rutledge* (1960), and appeared in other Ford films - *Two Rode Together* (1961), *The Man Who Shot Liberty Valance* (1962), and *Seven Women* (1966). He was the gladiator who fought Kirk Douglas to the death in *Spartacus* (1960), and was one of the stars in *The Professionals* (1966). His final appearance was in 1994's *The Quick and the Dead* which he completed just prior to his death.

William Sylvester, the Californian-born actor who died at the beginning of 1995 at the age of 72, came to Brit-

ain after the war, studied at RADA and was kept busy playing 'Yanks' in British films. He will probably be best remembered for his moving performance as the betrayed P.O.W. in *Albert R.N.* Other titles include *The Yellow Balloon* (1952), *Portrait of Alison* (1955), *Devils of Darkness* (1964) and *2001: A Space Odyssey* (1968).

Rachel Thomas, who died aged 82 in February 1995, is best remembered for her outstanding performance as the supporter of black ship's stoker Paul Robeson in *The Proud Valley* (1953). Her other films included *The Valley of Song* (1953), *Tiger Bay* (1959), *The Half-Way House* (1944) and *Under Milk Wood* (1971).

Robert Urquhart, the Scottish actor who died in April 1995, was equally at home in the theatre, films, TV and radio. Although critically acclaimed, he never became a star. His final triumph was to convert the house in which he was born into a popular restaurant – where he was also the chef. Serving in the Merchant Navy during the war, he was one of only three survivors when torpedoed. After the war he went to RADA and started his career in repertory theatre in Glasgow, Edinburgh and Stratford-upon-Avon. His films included *Restless Natives* (1985) and *The Kitchen Toto* (1987).

Sydney Walker died on 30 September 1994 at the age of 73, following an acting career spanning almost 50 years. He made his feature film debut in *Love Story* in 1970. His most recent films were *Mrs Doubtfire* and *Getting Even With Dad*.

David Wayne (real name Wayne James McMeekan), the prolific and versatile character actor, died on 9 February 1995 at the age of 81. He worked on stage, screen and TV after his professional stage debut in Shakespeare's *As You Like It* in 1936. He made his movie debut in *Portrait of Jenny* and *Adam's Rib* in 1949. His films include *As Young As You Feel* (1951), *O'Henry's Full House* (1952), *How to Marry a Millionaire* (1953), *The Tender Trap* (1955), *The Three Faces of Eve* (1957), *The Andromeda Strain* (1971) and *The Front Page* (1974).

Awards and Festivals

We have always concentrated principally on the major established festivals and award ceremonies around the world. There are of course several hundred others which space does not allow us to include here; some are highly specialised events appealing principally to a small minority, while we have also – some may say unfairly – excluded many Middle and Far East festivals.

Nationality is stated only where films originate from a country other than that in which the award is given – though when this information would be unnecessary or repetitive, we have not included it.

The 67th American Academy of Motion Picture Arts and Sciences Awards ('The Oscars') and Nominations for 1994, March 1994

Best Film: *Forrest Gump*. Nominations: *Four Weddings and a Funeral*; *Pulp Fiction*; *Quiz Show*; *The Shawshank Redemption*.

Best Director: Robert Zemeckis, for *Forrest Gump*. Nominations: Woody Allen for *Bullets Over Broadway*; Krzysztof Kieslowski, for *Three Colours Red*; Robert Redford, for *Quiz Show*; Quentin Tarantino, for *Pulp Fiction*.

Best Actor: Tom Hanks, for *Forrest Gump*. Nominations: Morgan Freeman, for *The Shawshank Redemption*; Nigel Hawthorne, for *The Madness of King George*; Paul Newman, for *Nobody's Fool*; John Travolta, for *Pulp Fiction*.

Best Actress: Jessica Lange, for *Blue Sky*. Nominations: Jodie Foster, for *Nell*; Miranda Richardson, for *Tom & Viv*; Winona Ryder, for *Little Women*; Susan Sarandon, for *The Client*.

Best Supporting Actor: Martin Landau, for *Ed Wood*. Nominations: Samuel L. Jackson, for *Pulp Fiction*; Chazz Palminteri, for *Bullets Over Broadway*; Paul Scofield, for *Quiz Show*; Gary Sinise, for *Forrest Gump*.

Best Supporting Actress: Dianne Wiest, for *Bullets Over Broadway*. Nominations: Rosemary Harris, for *Tom & Viv*; Helen Mirren, for *The Madness of King George*; Uma Thurman, for *Pulp Fiction*; Jennifer Tilly, for *Bullets Over Broadway*.

Best Original Screenplay: Quentin Tarantino and Roger Avary, for *Pulp Fiction*. Nominations: Woody Allen, for *Bullets Over Broadway*; Richard Curtis, for *Four Weddings and a Funeral*; Frances Walsh and Peter Jackson, for *Heavenly Creatures*; Krzysztof Piesiewicz and Krzysztof Kieslowski, for *Three Colours Red*.

Best Screenplay Adaptation: Eric Roth,

Robin Wright and Tom Hanks in Robert Zemeckis's multi-Oscar-winning Forrest Gump, *the film that took America by storm*

for *Forrest Gump*. Nominations: Alan Bennett, for *The Madness of King George*; Robert Benton, for *Nobody's Fool*; Paul Attanasio, for *Quiz Show*; Frank Darabont, for *The Shawshank Redemption*.

Best Cinematography: John Toll, for *Legends of the Fall*. Nominations: Don Burgess for *Forrest Gump*; Piotr Sobocinski, for *Three Colours Red*; Roger Deakins, for *The Shawshank Redemption*; Owen Roizman, for *Wyatt Earp*.

Best Editing: Arthur Schmidt, for *Forrest Gump*. Nominations: Frederick Marx, Steve James and Bill Haugse, for *Hoop Dreams*; Sally Menke, for *Pulp Fiction*; Richard Francis-Bruce, for *The Shawshank Redemption*; John Wright, for *Speed*.

Best Original Score: Hans Zimmer, for *The Lion King*. Nominations: Alan Silvestri, for *Forrest Gump*; Elliot Goldenthal, for *Interview With the Vampire*; Thomas Newman, for *Little Women*; Thomas Newman, for *The Shawshank Redemption*.

Best Original Song: 'Can You Feel The Love Tonight' from *The Lion King*, music by Elton John, lyrics by Tim Rice. Nominations: 'Circle of Life', from *The Lion King*, music by Elton John, lyrics by Tim Rice; 'Hakuna Matata', from *The Lion King*, music by Elton John, lyrics by Tim Rice; 'Look What Love Has Done', from *Junior*, music and lyrics by Carol Bayer Sager, James Newton Howard, James Ingram and Patty Smyth; 'Make Up Your Mind', from *The Paper*, music and lyrics by Randy Newman.

Best Art Direction: Ken Adam (art) and Carolyn Scott (set) for *The Madness of King George*. Nominations: Santo Loquasto (art) and Susan Bode (set) for *Bullets Over Broadway*; Rick Carter (art) and Nancy Haigh (set) for *Forrest Gump*; Dante Ferretti (art) and Francesca Lo Schiavo (set) for *Interview With the Vampire*; Lilly Kilvert (art) and Dorree Cooper (set) for *Legends of the Fall*.

Best Costume Design: Lizzy Gardiner and Tim Chappel, for *The Adventures of Priscilla, Queen of the Desert*. Nominations: Jeffrey Kurland, for *Bullets Over Broadway*; Colleen Atwood, for *Little Women*; April Ferry, for *Maverick*; Moidele Bickel, for *La Reine Margot*.

Best Sound: Gregg Landaker, Steve Maslow, Bob Beemer and David R. B. MacMillan, for *Speed*. Nominations: Donald O. Mitchell, Michael Herbick, Frank A. Montano and Arthur Rochester, for *Clear and Present Danger*; Randy Thom, Tom Johnson, Dennis Sands and William B. Kaplan, for *Forrest Gump*; Paul Massey, David Campbell, Christopher David and Douglas Ganton, for *Legends of the Fall*; Robert J. Litt, Elliot Tyson, Michael Herbick and Willie Burton, for *The Shawshank Redemption*.

Best Sound Effects Editing: Stephen Hunter Flick, for *Speed*. Nominations: Bruce Stambler and John Leveque, for *Clear and Present Danger*; Gloria S. Borders and Randy Thom, for *Forrest Gump*.

Best Make-Up: Rick Baker, Ve Neill and Yolanda Toussieng, for *Ed Wood*. Nominations: Daniel C. Striepeke, Hallie D'Amore and Judith A. Cory, for *Forrest Gump*; Daniel Parker, Paul Engelen and Carol Hemming, for *Mary Shelley's Frankenstein*.

Best Visual Effects: Ken Ralston, George Murphy, Stephen Rosenbaum and Allen Hall, for *Forrest Gump*; Nominations: Scott Squires, Steve Williams, Tom Bertino and John Farhat, for *The Mask*; John Bruno, Thomas L. Fisher, Jacques Stroweis and Patrick McClung, for *True Lies*.

Best Animated Short Film: *Bob's Birthday* (UK/Canada), by Alison Snowden and David Fine. Nominations: *The Big Story*, *The Janitor*, *The Monk and the Fish* and *Triangle*.

Best Live Action Short Film: *Franz Kafka's It's a Wonderful Life* (UK), produced by Peter Capaldi and Ruth Kenley-Letts; and *Trevor*, produced by Peggy Rajski and Randy Stone. Nominations: *Kangaroo Court*; *On Hope*; *Syrup*.

Best Documentary Feature: *Maya Lin: A String Clear Vision* (USA). Nominations: *Complaints of a Dutiful Daughter*; *D-Day Remembered*; *Freedom on My Mind*; *A Great Day in Harlem*.

Best Documentary Short: *A Time For Justice* (USA). Nominations: *Blues Highway*; *89mm Od Europy* (89mm From Europe); *School of the Americas Assassins*; *Straight From the Heart*.

Best Foreign Language Film: *Burnt By the Sun* (Russia). Nominations: *Before the Rain* (Macedonia); *Eat Drink Man Woman* (Taiwan); *Farinelli: Il Castrato* (Belgium); *Strawberry and Chocolate* (Cuba).

The Jean Hersholt Humanitarian Award: Quincy Jones.

Honorary Academy Award: Michelangelo Antonioni.

The Irving G. Thalberg Memorial Award: Clint Eastwood.

The 36th Australian Film Institute Awards, 4 November 1994

Best Film: *Muriel's Wedding*.
Best Actor: Nicholas Hope, for *Bad Boy Bubby*.
Best Actress: Toni Collette, for *Muriel's Wedding*.
Best Supporting Actor: Max Cullen, for *Spider and Rose*.
Best Supporting Actress: Rachel Griffiths, for *Muriel's Wedding*.
Best Director: Rolf de Heer, for *Bad Boy Bubby*.
Best Original Screenplay: Rolf de Heer, for *Bad Boy Bubby*.
Best Screenplay Adaptation: David Stevens, for *The Sum of Us*.
Best Cinematography: Nino Martinetti, for *The Exile*.
Best Editing: Suresh Ayyar, for *Bad Boy Bubby*.
Best Music: Douglas Stephen, for *Traps*.
Best Production Design: Owen Patterson, for *The Adventures of Priscilla, Queen of the Desert*.
Best Costumes: Lizzy Gardiner and Tim Chappel, for *The Adventures of Priscilla, Queen of the Desert*.
Best Sound: *Muriel's Wedding*.
Best Foreign Film: *Four Weddings and a Funeral*, by Mike Newell (UK).
The Byron Kennedy Award: actor John Hargreaves.
The Raymond Longford Award: actor Jack Thompson.

The 45th Berlin International Film Festival, 20 February 1995

Golden Bear for Best Film: *Fresh Bait*, by Bertrand Tavernier (France).
Special Jury Prize: *Smoke*, by Wayne Wang (USA).
Best Director: Richard Linklater, for *Before Sunrise* (USA).
Best Actor: Paul Newman, for *Nobody's Fool* (USA).
Best Actress: Josephone Siao, for *Summer Snow* (Hong Kong).
Outstanding Performance (Special Mention): Harvey Keitel, for *Smoke* (USA).
Blue Angel Prize: *Cross My Heart and Hope to Die*, by Marius Holst (Norway).
Silver Bear: *Blush*, by Li Shaohong

(China–Hong Kong); and *Play For a Passenger* (Russia).
Special Mentions: *Midaq Alley* (Mexico); *Sh'chur* (Israel); and *Moon Shadow* (Italy).
Wolfgang Staudte Prize: *Double Happiness* (Canada).
International Film Critics' Jury:
Best Competing Film: *Smoke*.
Best Panorama Film: *Priest* (UK).
Best Forum Film: *Citizen Langlois* (France).
Children's Film Jury Prize: *The Purse Snatcher* (Holland).
Gay Teddy Bear: *The Last Supper* (Canada).

The 1994 British Academy of Film and Television Arts Awards ('BAFTAs'), 23 April 1995

Best Film: *Four Weddings and a Funeral*, by Mike Newell.
Best Film (public vote): *Four Weddings and a Funeral*.
David Lean Award for Best Direction: Mike Newell, for *Four Weddings and a Funeral*.
Best Original Screenplay: Quentin Tarantino and Roger Avary, for *Pulp Fiction*.
Best Adapted Screenplay: Paul Attanasio, for *Quiz Show*.
Best Actor: Hugh Grant, for *Four Weddings and a Funeral*.
Best Actress: Susan Sarandon, for *The Client*.
Best Supporting Actor: Samuel L. Jackson, for *Pulp Fiction*.
Best Supporting Actress: Kristin Scott Thomas, for *Four Weddings and a Funeral*.
Best Cinematography: Philippe Rousselot, for *Interview With the Vampire*.
Best Editing: John Wright, for *Speed*.
Best Production Design: Dante Ferretti, for *Interview With the Vampire*.
The Anthony Asquith Award for Best Music: Don Was and Bob Last, for *Backbeat*.
Best Costumes: Lizzy Gardiner and Tim Chappel, for *The Adventures of Priscilla, Queen of the Desert*.
Alexander Korda Award for Best British Film: *Shallow Grave* by Danny Boyle.
Best Foreign Film: *To Live*, by Zhang Yimou (China).

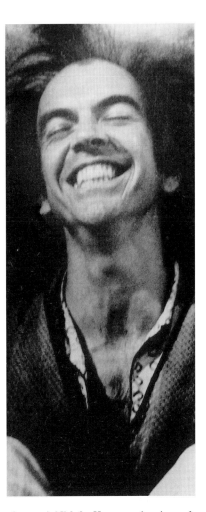

An ecstatic Nicholas Hope, surprise winner of the best actor honour (for his astounding performance in Bad Boy Bubby*) at the 36th Australian Film Institute Awards*

The 1994 Canadian Film Awards ('Genies'), 7 December 1994

Best Film: *Exotica*.
Best Director: Atom Egoyan, for *Exotica*.
Best Actor: Maury Chaykin, for *Whale Music*.
Best Actress: Sandra Oh, for *Double Happiness*.
Best Supporting Actor: Don McKellar for *Exotica*.
Best Supporting Actress: Martha Henry, for *Mustard Bath*.
Best Original Screenplay: Atom Egoyan, for *Exotica*.
Best Screenplay Adaptation: Brad Fraser, for *Love and Human Remains*.
Best Cinematography: Paul Sarossy, for *Exotica*.

Best Editing: Alison Grace, for *Double Happiness*.

Best Art Direction/Production Design: Linda Del Rosario and Richard Paris, for *Exotica*.

Best Music: Mychael Danna, for *Exotica*.

Best Original Song: 'Claire', by Rheostatics, from *Whale Music*.

Best Costumes: Linda Muir, for *Exotica*.

Best Sound Editing: *Whale Music*.

Best Feature-Length Documentary: *In the Gutter and Other Good Places*.

Best Live-Action Short Drama: *Arrowhead*, by Peter Lynch and Emmet Sheil.

Air Canada Award: Rene Malo, chairman of Malofilm Communications, for his outstanding contribution to the business of filmmaking in Canada.

The 48th Cannes Film Festival Awards, 28 May 1995

Palme d'Or for Best Film: *Underground*, by Emir Kusturica (France-Germany-Hungary).

Grand Prix du Jury: *Ulysses' Gaze*, by Theo Angelopoulos (Greece-France-Italy).

Jury Prize: *Don't Forget You're Going to Die*, by Xavier Beauvois (France).

Special Jury Prize: Christopher Hampton, writer-director of *Carrington* (UK-France).

Best Actor: Jonathan Pryce, for *Carrington*.

Best Actress: Helen Mirren, for *The Madness of King George* (UK).

Best Director: Mathieu Kassovitz, for *La Haine* (France).

Best Screenplay: Christopher Hampton, for *Carrington*.

International Critics' Prize: *Ulysses' Gaze*; and *Land and Freedom*, by Ken Loach (UK-Spain-Germany).

Fipresci International Critics' Prize: *The White Balloon*, by Jafar Panahi (Iran).

Palme d'Or for Best Short: *Gagarine*, by Alexei Kharitidi (Russia).

Jury Prize for Best Short: *Swinger*, by Gregor Jordan (Australia).

Camera d'Or: *Denise Calls Up*, by Harold Salwen (USA).

Camera d'Or for First Feature: *The White Balloon*.

Grand Prix Technique: *Shanghai Triad*, by Zhang Yimou (China-France).

Jury: Jeanne Moreau (president), Nadine Gordiner (for South Africa), Norma Heyman (for the UK), Maria Zverva (Russia), Gianni Amelio (Italy), Jean-Claude Brialy (France), Emilio Garcia Riera (Mexico), Gaston Kabore (Burkino Faso), Philippe Rousselot (France), John Waters (US).

The David di Donatello Awards ('Davids'), Rome, 3 June 1995

Best Film: *School*, by Daniele Luchetti.

Best First Feature: *Living It Up*, by Paolo Virzi.

Best Director: Mario Martone, for *L'Amore Molesto*.

Best Actor: Marcello Mastroianni, for *Pereira Declares*.

Best Actress: Anna Bonaiuto, for *L'Amore Molesto*.

Best Supporting Actor: Giancarlo Giannini, for *Like Two Crocodiles*.

Best Supporting Actress: Angela Luce, for *L'Amore Molesto*.

Best Producer: Pietro Valsecchi, for *Ordinary Hero*.

Best Screenplay: Alessandro D'Alatri, for *No Skin*; tied with Luigi Magni and Carla Vistarini, for *Childhood Enemies*.

Best Cinematography: Luca Bigazzi, for *Lamerica*.

Best Editing: Roberto Perpignani, for *The Postman*.

Best Production Design: Andrea Crisanti, for *A Pure Formality*.

Best Music: Franco Piersanti, for *Lamerica*.

Costumes: Olga Berluti, for *Farinelli*.

Sound: Alessandro Zanon, for *Lamerica*.

Best Foreign Film: *Pulp Fiction* (USA).

Best Foreign Actor: John Travolta, for *Pulp Fiction*.

Best Foreign Actress: Jodie Foster, for *Nell*.

Luchino Visconti Career Achievement Award: *Pupi Avati*.

Special David Awards:

Milcho Manchesvski, for *Before the Rain* (Macedonia).

Vittorio Cecchi Gori, for his production activity.

Aurelio De Laurentiis, for his work as a distributor.

Actor-director Michele Placido, for *Ordinary Hero*.

The 'Evening Standard' 1994 Film Awards, London, 30 January 1995

Best Film: *In the Name of the Father*.

Best Actor: Ben Kingsley, for *Schindler's List*.

Best Actress: Kristin Scott Thomas, for *Four Weddings and a Funeral*.

Best Screenplay: Richard Curtis, for *Four Weddings and a Funeral*.

Best Technical Achievement: Richard Hutchinson, producer, and Dave Borthwick, director, for *The Secret Adventures of Tom Thumb*.

Most Promising Newcomer: Ian Hart, for *Backbeat*; and Gurinder Chadha, director and co-writer of *Bhaji On the Beach*.

The Peter Sellers Comedy Award: Hugh Grant, for *Four Weddings and a Funeral*.

Special Award: Alec Guinness.

The 20th French Academy (César) Awards, 25 February 1995

Best Film: *Les Roseaux Sauvages*.

Best Director: André Téchiné, for *Les Roseaux Sauvages*.

Best Actor: Gerard Lanvin, for *Le Fils Préféré*.

Best Actress: Isabelle Adjani, for *La Reine Margot*.

Best Supporting Actor: Jean-Hugues Anglade, for *La Reine Margot*.

Best Supporting Actress: Virna Lisi, for *La Reine Margot*.

Best Young Actor: Mathieu Kassovitz, for *Regarde les Hommes Tomber*.

Best Young Actress: Elodie Bouchez, for *Les Roseaux Sauvages*.

Best First Film: *Regarde les Hommes Tomber*.

Best Original Screenplay: André Téchiné, Gilles Taurand and Olivier Massart, for *Les Roseaux Sauvages*.

Best Photography: Philippe Rousselot, for *La Reine Margot*.

Best Editing: Juliette Welfling, for *Regarde les Hommes Tomber*.

Best Production Design: Gianni Quaranta, for *Farinelli*.

Best Music: Zbigniew Preisner, for *Three Colours Red*.

Best Costumes: Moidele Bickel, for *La Reine Margot*.

Best Sound: Jean-Paul Muguel and Dominique Hennequin, for *Farinelli*.

Best Documentary: *Delits Flagrants*, by Raymond Depardon.

Best Foreign Film: *Four Weddings and a Funeral*, by Mike Newell (UK).

Best Short: *La Vis*, by Didier Flamand.

César d'Honneur: Gregory Peck, Steven Spielberg.

The 52nd Hollywood Foreign Press Association (Golden Globes) Awards, January 1995

Best Film – Drama: *Forrest Gump*.

Best Film – Comedy or Musical: *The Lion King*.

Best Actor – Drama: Tom Hanks, for *Forrest Gump*.

Best Actress – Drama: Jessica Lange, for *Blue Sky*.

Best Actor – Comedy or Musical: Hugh Grant, for *Four Weddings and a Funeral*.

Best Actress – Comedy or Musical: Jamie Lee Curtis, for *True Lies*.

Best Supporting Actor: Martin Landau, for *Ed Wood*.

Best Supporting Actress: Dianne Wiest, for *Bullets Over Broadway*.

Best Director: Robert Zemeckis, for *Forrest Gump*.

Best Screenplay: Quentin Tarantino, for *Pulp Fiction*.

Best Original Score: Hans Zimmer, for *The Lion King*.

Best Original Song: 'Can You Feel The Love Tonight', music by Elton John, lyrics by Tim Rice, from *The Lion King*.

Best Foreign Language Film: *Farinelli* (France-Belgium-Italy).

Best TV Film: *The Burning Season*, by John Frankenheimer.

Cecil B. De Mille Award for Lifetime Achievement: Sophia Loren.

The 10th Independent Spirit Awards, Los Angeles, 25 March 1995

Best Film: *Pulp Fiction*.

Best First Film: *Spanking the Monkey*, by David Russell.

Best Actor: Samuel L. Jackson, for *Pulp Fiction*.

Best Actress: Linda Fiorentino, for *The Last Seduction*.

The 2nd ITV Movie Awards, June 1995

(as voted by British cinemagoers)

Best Film: *Speed*.

Best British Film: *Four Weddings and a Funeral*.

Hero of the Year: Keanu Reeves, in *Speed*.

Heroine of the Year: Sandra Bullock, in *Speed*.

Best Male Body: Keanu Reeves, in *Speed*.

Best Female Body: Jamie Lee Curtis, in *True Lies*.

The Screen's Sexiest Kiss: Hugh Grant and Andie MacDowell, in *Four Weddings and a Funeral*.

Best Action Sequence: *Speed*.

Best Shoot-Out: *True Lies*.

Funniest Movie Moment: *Four Weddings and a Funeral* (featuring Hugh Grant, Simon Kunz and Andie MacDowell).

Best Song: 'Love is All Around' by Wet Wet Wet, from *Four Weddings and a Funeral*.

The 16th London Film Critics' Awards ('The Alfs'), 2 March 1995

Best Film: *Schindler's List*.

Best Actor: John Travolta, for *Pulp Fiction*.

Best Actress: Linda Fiorentino, for *The Last Seduction*.

Best Director: Steven Spielberg, for *Schindler's List*.

Best Screenwriter: Quentin Tarantino, for *Pulp Fiction*.

Non-British Newcomer: Jim Carrey, star of *Ace Ventura: Pet Detective* and *The Mask*.

Best British Film: *Four Weddings and a Funeral*.

Best British Producer: Duncan Kenworthy, for *Four Weddings and a Funeral*.

Best British Director: Mike Newell, for *Four Weddings and a Funeral*.

Best British Screenwriter: Richard Curtis, for *Four Weddings and a Funeral*.

Jean-Hugues Anglade and Isabelle Adjani in their César award-winning roles in La Reine Margot *(which also speared trophies for Virna Lisi, cinematography and costumes)*

Best British Actor: Ralph Fiennes, for *Schindler's List*.

Best British Actress: Crissy Rock, for *Ladybird, Ladybird*.

Best British Newcomer: Iain Softley, writer-director of *Backbeat*.

Best British Technical Achievement: Roger Deakins, cinematographer of *The Hudsucker Proxy*.

Best Foreign Language Film: *Farewell My Concubine* (Hong Kong-China).

Dilys Powell Award: Lord Attenborough.

Special Award: Barry Norman, for services to film reviewing.

Outstanding Comedy Performance of the Year: Hugh Grant, for *Four Weddings and a Funeral*.

Worst Male Performance of the Year: Kenneth Branagh, for *Mary Shelley's Frankenstein*.

Worst Female Performance of the Year: Julia Roberts, for *The Pelican Brief*.

Worst Film of the Year: *The House of the Spirits*.

The Los Angeles Film Critics' Association Awards, 10 December 1994

Best Film: *Pulp Fiction*.

Best Actor: John Travolta, for *Pulp Fiction*.

Best Actress: Jessica Lange, for *Blue Sky*.

Best Supporting Actor: Martin Landau, for *Ed Wood*.

Best Supporting Actress: Dianne Wiest, for *Bullets Over Broadway*.

Best Director: Quentin Tarantino, for *Pulp Fiction*.

Best Screenplay: Quentin Tarantino, for *Pulp Fiction*.

Best Cinematography: Stefan Czapsky, for *Ed Wood*.

Best Production Design: Dennis Gassner, for *The Hudsucker Proxy*.

Best Score: Howard Shore, for *Ed Wood*.

Best Foreign Film: *Three Colours Red*.

Best Documentary: *Hoop Dreams*, by Steve James, Frederick Marx and Peter Gilbert.

Best Animation: *The Lion King*.

New Generation Award: John Dahl, director, for *Red Rock West* and *The Last Seduction*.

Career Achievement Award: Billy Wilder, writer-director.

Special Achievement Award: Pauline Kael, film critic.

Douglas Edwards Award for Independent/Experimental Film & Video: *Remembrance of Things Fast* (UK), John Maybury.

The National Board of Review of Motion Pictures, New York, December 1994

Best Film: *Forrest Gump* and *Pulp Fiction*.

Best Actor: Tom Hanks, for *Forrest Gump*.

Best Actress: Miranda Richardson, for *Tom & Viv*.

Best Supporting Actor: Gary Sinise, for *Forrest Gump*.

Best Supporting Actress: Rosemary Harris, for *Tom & Viv*.

Best Director: Quentin Tarantino, for *Pulp Fiction*.

Best Foreign Film: *Eat Drink Man Woman* (Taiwan).

Best Documentary: *Hoop Dreams*.

Best TV Movie: *The Final Seduction*.

Best TV Series: *Tales of the City*.

Special Awards: *Prêt-à-Porter*, for its ensemble cast; *The Lion King*, for best family film.

The 60th New York Film Critics' Circle Awards, 15 December 1994

Best Film: *Quiz Show*.

Best Actor: Paul Newman, for *Nobody's Fool*.

Best Actress: Linda Fiorentino, for *The Last Seduction*.

Best Supporting Actor: Martin Landau, for *Ed Wood*.

Best Supporting Actress: Dianne Wiest, for *Bullets Over Broadway*.

Best Director: Quentin Tarantino, for *Pulp Fiction*.

Best Screenplay: Quentin Tarantino, for *Pulp Fiction*.

Best Cinematography: Stefan Czapsky, for *Ed Wood*.

Best Foreign Film: *Three Colours Red*.

Best Documentary: *Hoop Dreams*, by Steve James, Frederick Marx and Peter Gilbert.

Best Directorial Debut: Darnell Martin, for *I Like It Like That*.

The 17th Sundance Film Festival, Utah, 29 January 1995

The Grand Jury Prize (best feature): *The Brothers McMullen*.

The Grand Jury Prize (best documentary): *Crumb*.

Audience Award (best feature): *Picture Bride*.

Audience Award (best documentary): *Ballot Measure 9*; and *Unzipped*.

Filmmaker's Trophy (best feature): *Angela*.

Filmmaker's Trophy (best documentary): *Black Is ... Black Ain't*.

Waldo Scott Screenwriting Award: Tom DiCillo, for *Living in Oblivion*.

Freedom of Expression Award: *When Billy Broke His Head ... And Other Tales of Wonder*.

The 51st Venice International Film Festival Awards, September 1994

Golden Lion for Best Film shared by: *Before the Rain*, by Milcho Manchevski (Macedonia-UK-France); and *Aiging Wansui*, by Tsai Mingliang (Taiwan).

Special Jury Prize: *Natural Born Killers*, by Oliver Stone (USA).

Silver Lion shared by: *Heavenly Creatures*, by Peter Jackson (New Zealand); *Little Odessa*, by James Gray (USA); and *The Bull*, by Carlo Mazzacurati (Italy).

Best Actor: Xia Yu, for *In the Heat of the Sun* (Hong Kong-Taiwan-China).

Best Actress: Maria de Medeiros, for *Two Brothers, My Sister* (Portugal/France).

Best Supporting Actor: Roberto Citran, for *The Bull*.

Best Supporting Actress: Vanessa Redgrave, for *Little Odessa*.

Best Director: Gianni Amelio, for *Lamerica* (Italy-France).

Best Screenplay: Juan Jose, Bigas Luna and Cuca Canals, for *The Tit and the Moon* (Spain-France).

Best Cinematography: Wong Kar-wai and Christopher Doyle, for *Ashes of Time* (Hong Kong).

Gold Medal of the Senate: Jiri Menzel, for *The Life and Extraordinary Adventures of Private Ivan Chonkin* (UK-France).

Golden Lion for Career Achievement: Al Pacino, Ken Loach and Italian screenwriter Suso Cecchi D'Amico.

Jury: David Lynch, Uma Thurman, novelist Mario Vargas Llosa and critic David Stratton.

Index